America's Second Century

Topical Readings
1865–Present

Second Edition

Kenneth G. Alfers
Larry Pool
William F. Mugleston
Mountain View College

KENDALL/HUNT PUBLISHING COMPANY
Dubuque, Iowa

Acknowledgments

1. "Andrew Carnegie: Captain of Industry," by Robert L. Heilbroner, *American Heritage,* © 1960. Reprinted by permission of the author.
2. "Hell on Saturday Afternoon," by John F. McCormack, Jr., Copyright © 1976 by *Mankind* Magazine. Feb. 1976; reprinted by permission.
3. "The Causes of the Great Crash," by John Kenneth Galbraith, *American Heritage,* © 1958. Reprinted by permission of the author.
4. "The Poor in the Great Depression," by David J. Rothman, © 1972 by American Heritage Publishing Co., Inc. Reprinted by permission.
5. "Shut the Goddam Plant," by Stephen W. Sears, © 1982 by American Heritage Publishing Co., Inc. Reprinted by permission.
6. "Was Bryan A Reformer?" by John A. Garraty, © 1961 by American Heritage Publishing Co., Inc. Reprinted by permission.
7. "Consumer Protection: The Pure Food and Drugs Act," by Gerald H. Carson, © 1956 by American Heritage Publishing Co., Inc. Reprinted by permission.
8. "FDR: A Practical Magician," by John Kenneth Galbraith, *American Heritage,* © 1983. Reprinted by permission of the author.
9. "How the Media Seduced and Captured American Politics," by Richard C. Wade, *American Heritage,* © 1983. Reprinted by permission of the author.
10. "I Am Not a Crook! Corruption in Presidential Politics," by Kenneth G. Alfers, © 1980. Reprinted by permission of the Dallas County Community College District, from *America: The Second Century Study Guide* by Kenneth G. Alfers.
11. "Whatever Became of Jimmy Carter?" by Tom Wicker, Copyright © 1984 by Tom Wicker. Reprinted by permission of John Hawkins and Associates, Inc.
12. "The Needless War With Spain," by William E. Leuchtenburg, © 1957 by American Heritage Publishing Co., Inc. Reprinted by permission.
13. "Woodrow Wilson and the League of Nations," by Thomas A. Bailey, © 1957 by American Heritage Publishing Co., Inc. Reprinted by permission.
14. "Pearl Harbor: Who Blundered?" by Col. T. N. Dupuy, © 1962 by American Heritage Publishing Co., Inc. Reprinted by permission.
15. "The Cold War," by Charles L. Mee, Jr., © 1977 by American Heritage Publishing Co., Inc. Reprinted by permission.
16. "The U.S. and Castro, 1959–1962," by Hugh Thomas, © 1978 by American Heritage Publishing Co., Inc. Reprinted by permission.
17. "Machismo in the White House: LBJ and Vietnam," by Larry L. King, *American Heritage,* © 1976. Reprinted by permission of the author.
18. "Reluctant Conquerors: American Army Officers and the Plains Indians," by Thomas C. Leonard, © 1976 by American Heritage Publishing Co., Inc. Reprinted by permission.
19. "Ride-In: A Century of Protest Begins," by Alan Westin, © 1962 by American Heritage Publishing Co., Inc. Reprinted by permission.
20. "The Week the World Watched Selma," by Stephen B. Oates, *American Heritage,* © 1982. Reprinted by permission of the author.
21. "The Great Fight: Mr. Jake vs. John L. Sullivan" by James A. Cox, *Smithsonian* Magazine, December 1984. Reprinted by permission of the author.
22. "Jane Addams: Urban Crusader," by Anne Firor Scott, © 1960 by American Heritage Publishing Co., Inc. Reprinted by permission.
23. "Full Speed Ahead and Damn the Tomorrows: Our Frontier Heritage of Waste," by Ray Allen Billington, *American Heritage,* © 1977. Reprinted by permission of Mrs. Ray A. Billington.
24. "What Is Part Is Prologue: An Interview with Professor Henry Steele Commager," by Henry Steele Commager, © 1980. Reprinted by permission of Professor Commager.

Contents

Preface to the Second Edition

We have been gratified by the kind remarks of many users of the first edition of *America's Second Century*. They report that many of the essays are provocative reading and, more important, that they arouse student interest in history.

In the second edition we have shortened the number of selections, rearranged them a bit, and added two new articles: Number 11 on the Carter administration and number 21 on the 1889 Sullivan-Kilrain heavyweight championship bout, the last bare-knuckles contest in American history. We have also retained the chronological guide, which many readers have found helpful.

Kenneth G. Alfers
Larry Pool
William F. Mugleston

Preface

We Americans living in the 1980s have had special reasons to reflect upon our nation's past. Nearly a decade ago we began celebrating the bicentennial of the Declaration of Independence. In the next few years greater attention will be focused on the 200th anniversary of our Constitution.

It is well that those special occasions serve to remind us that we do indeed have a rich and vibrant history. The technological changes occurring in the 1980s sometimes appear to be moving forward so rapidly that we do not have or take the time to gain an historical perspective on events.

A prime purpose of this reader is to help students develop that needed historical perspective. Furthermore, we acknowledge the fact that the U.S. history survey course is perhaps our only chance to reach most students in American colleges and universities. This reader, therefore, is intended to serve as an integral part of a survey of U.S. history since 1865. It can be used to supplement texts, monographs, historical novels, and/or lectures. Although organized topically, the articles can be used selectively along traditional chronological lines (see the accompanying guide).

In choosing articles, we were primarily concerned with readability and sound scholarship. Too often we have heard from our entering students that history has been boring and uninteresting. We want students to enjoy reading history while they are gaining that understanding and developing that habit of critical thinking which we think so important.

One unique feature of this reader is its topical organization. The articles are grouped into four core themes which cut through any study of our past—economic, political, diplomatic, and social. Although many students may be unfamiliar with a topical approach to U.S. history, that is not an impediment to learning. In fact, our experience has shown that a new approach can provide fresh insights to the study of history, especially as it relates to our understanding of present conditions. When that happens, we have the satisfaction of knowing that we have helped students achieve a worthwhile objective.

We wish to thank Raymond W. Smock of the Instructional Resources Corporation for his efficient help in securing photographs.

Kenneth G. Alfers
Larry Pool
William F. Mugleston
Mountain View College
Dallas, Texas

Chronological Guide

	Economic	Political
1865–1898:	—"Andrew Carnegie: Captain of Industry"	—"Was Bryan a Reformer?"
1898–1920:	—"Hell on Saturday Afternoon"	—"Consumer Protection: The Pure Food and Drugs Act"
1920–1945:	—"The Causes of the Great Crash" —"The Poor in the Great Depression" —"Shut the Goddam Plant!"	—"FDR: A Practical Magician"
1945–Present:		—"How the Media Seduced and Captured American Politics: —"I Am Not a Crook! Corruption in Presidential Politics" "Whatever Became of Jimmy Carter?"

Epilogue: "What is Past is Prologue: An Interview with Professor Henry Steele Commager"

	Diplomatic	Social
1865–1898:	—"The Needless War With Spain"	—"Reluctant Conquerors: American Army Officers and the Plains Indians" —"Ride-in: A Century of Protest Begins"
1898–1920:	—"Woodrow Wilson and the League of Nations"	"The Great Fight: Mr. Jake vs. John L. Sullivan" —"Jane Addams: Urban Crusader"
1920–1945:	—"Pearl Harbor: Who Blundered?"	
1945–Present:	—"The Cold War" —"The U.S. and Castro, 1959–1962" —"Machismo in the White House: LBJ and Vietnam"	—"The Week the World Watched Selma" —"Full Speed Ahead and Damn the Tomorrows: Our Frontier Heritage of Waste"

Part I

Economic Developments during America's Second Century

During its second century, the United States underwent an economic transformation which changed the nation from a primarily agricultural nation to a highly industrialized one. As a consequence, the economic system of the United States has become much more complicated than it was one hundred years ago. As the noted economist Dr. Robert Heilbroner has remarked, "Everything is bigger, more massive, more technological. . . . That's the great thrust of American history."

The theme of "bigness" is a recurring one in any discussion of U.S. economic developments. Big Business, Big Labor, and Big Government all came into being during the past century. Even farmers, who lost priority in terms of numbers, status, and influence, engaged in big operations by means of their increased acreage and production.

The Great Depression of the 1930s did much to alter the make-up of business, labor, agriculture, and the federal government and their relationships with each other. It also brought home the issue of poverty to all segments of society. In fact, the effects of the Depression years are so great that the words of historian David Shannon are still applicable: ". . . if one would understand the United States today he must know the Great Depression."

The essays in Part I enhance our understanding of U.S. economic history by providing perspective on industrial leadership, labor-management relations, the Depression and poverty.

1

Andrew Carnegie: Captain of Industry

by Robert L. Heilbroner

One of the major reasons for the rapid industrialization of the United States during the late nineteenth century was the emergence of the entrepreneurs. Ingenuity, managerial expertise, willingness to take risks, and hard work were some of the qualities displayed in large measure by these men. None of them are more appealing than Andrew Carnegie. In him we see the personification of the American Dream. We also see what we hope the real-life Horatio Alger figures did with their money before they died.

Professor Robert Heilbroner, an economist at the New School for Social Research, is noted for his writings on economic history and thought. Among his well-known works are *The Worldly Philosophers, The Future as History, The Limits of American Capitalism,* and *An Inquiry into the Human Prospect.* In this essay he once again demonstrates his ability to enliven the study of our past.

Toward the end of his long life, at the close of World War I, Andrew Carnegie was already something of a national legend. His meteoric rise, the scandals and successes of his industrial generalship—all this was blurred into nostalgic memory. What was left was a small, rather feeble man with a white beard and pale, penetrating eyes, who could occasionally be seen puttering around his mansion on upper Fifth Avenue, a benevolent old gentleman who still rated an annual birthday interview but was even then a venerable relic of a fast-disappearing era. Carnegie himself looked back on his career with a certain savored incredulity. "How much did you say I had given away, Poynton?" he would inquire of his private secretary; "$324,657,399" was the answer. "Good Heaven!" Carnegie would exclaim. "Where did I ever get all that money?"

Where he *had* got all that money was indeed a legendary story, for even in an age known for its acquisitive triumphs, Carnegie's touch had been an extraordinary one. He had begun, in true Horatio Alger fashion, at the bottom; he had ended, in a manner that put the wildest of Alger's novels to shame, at the very pinnacle of success. At the close of his great deal with J. P. Morgan in 1901, when the Carnegie steel empire was sold to form the core of the new United States Steel Company, the banker had extended his hand and delivered the ultimate encomium of the times: "Mr. Carnegie," he said, "I want to congratulate you on being the richest man in the world."

It was certainly as "the richest man in the world" that Carnegie attracted the attention of his contemporaries. Yet this is hardly why we look back on him with interest today. As an enormous moneymaker Carnegie was a flashy, but hardly a profound, hero of the times; and the attitudes of Earnestness and Self-Assurance, so engaging in the young immigrant, become irritating when they are congealed in the millionaire. But what lifts Carnegie's life above the rut of a one-dimensional success story is an aspect of which his contemporaries were relatively unaware.

Going through his papers after his death, Carnegie's executors came across a memorandum that he had written to himself fifty years before, carefully preserved in a little yellow box of keepsakes and mementos. It brings us back to December, 1868, when Carnegie, a young man flushed with the first taste of great success, retired to his suite in the opulent Hotel St. Nicholas in New York, to tot up his profits for the year. It had been a tremendous year and the calculation must have been extremely pleasurable. Yet this is what he wrote as he reflected on the figures:

> Thirty-three and an income of $50,000 per annum! By this time two years I can so arrange all my business as to secure at least $50,000 per annum. Beyond this never earn—make no effort to increase fortune, but spend the surplus each year for benevolent purposes. Cast aside business forever, except for others.
>
> Settle in Oxford and get a thorough education, making the acquaintance of literary men—this will take three years of active work—pay especial attention to speaking in public. Settle then in London and purchase a controlling interest in some newspaper or live review and give the general management of it attention, taking part in public matters, especially those connected with education and improvement of the poorer classes.
>
> Man must have an idol—the amassing of wealth is one of the worst species of idolatry—no idol more debasing than the worship of money. Whatever I engage in I must push inordinately; therefore should I be careful to choose that life which will be the most elevating in its character. To continue much longer overwhelmed by business cares and with most of my thoughts wholly upon the way to make more money in the shortest time, must degrade me beyond hope of permanent recovery. I will resign business at thirty-five, but during the ensuing two years I wish to spend the afternoons in receiving instruction and in reading systematically.

It is a document which in more ways than one is Carnegie to the very life: brash, incredibly self-confident, chockablock with self-conscious virtue—and more than a little hypocritical. For the program so nobly outlined went largely unrealized. Instead of retiring in two years, Carnegie went on for thirty-three more; even then it was with considerable difficulty that he was persuaded to quit. Far from shunning further money-making, he proceeded to roll up his fortune with an uninhibited drive that led one unfriendly biographer to characterize him as "the greediest little gentleman ever created." Certainly he was one of the most aggressive profit seekers of his time. Typically, when an associate jubilantly cabled: "No. 8 furnace broke all records today," Carnegie coldly replied, "What were the other furnaces doing?"

It is this contrast between his hopes and his performance that makes Carnegie interesting. For when we review his life, what we see is more than the career of another nineteenth-century acquisitor. We see the unequal struggle

Andrew Carnegie four years after selling his steel interests to U.S. Steel. (Library of Congress)

between a man who loved money—loved making it, having it, spending it—and a man who, at bottom, was ashamed of himself for his acquisitive desires. All during his lifetime, the money-maker seemed to win. But what lifts Carnegie's story out of the ordinary is that the other Carnegie ultimately triumphed. At his death public speculation placed the size of his estate at about five hundred million dollars. In fact it came to $22,881,575. Carnegie *had* become the richest man in the world—but something had also driven him to give away ninety per cent of his wealth.

Actually, his contemporaries knew of Carnegie's inquietude about money. In 1889, before he was world-famous, he had written an article for the *North American Review* entitled "The Gospel of Wealth"—an article that contained the startling phrase: "The man who dies thus rich dies disgraced." It was hardly surprising, however, if the world took these sentiments at a liberal discount: homiletic millionaires who preached the virtues of austerity were no novelty;

Carnegie himself, returning in 1879 from a trip to the miseries of India, had been able to write with perfect sincerity, "How very little the millionaire has beyond the peasant, and how very often his additions tend not to happiness but to misery."

What the world may well have underestimated, however, was a concern more deeply rooted than these pieties revealed. For, unlike so many of his self-made peers, who also rose from poverty, Carnegie was the product of a *radical* environment. The village of Dunfermline, Scotland, when he was born there in 1835, was renowned as a center of revolutionary ferment, and Carnegie's family was itself caught up in the radical movement of the times. His father was a regular speaker at the Chartist rallies, which were an almost daily occurrence in Dunfermline in the 1840's, and his uncle was an impassioned orator for the rights of the working class to vote and strike. All this made an indelible impression on Carnegie's childhood.

"I remember as if it were yesterday," he wrote seventy years later, "being awakened during the night by a tap at the back window by men who had come to inform my parents that my uncle, Bailie Morrison, had been thrown in jail because he dared to hold a meeting which had been forbidden. . . . It is not to be wondered at that, nursed amid such surroundings, I developed into a violent young Republican whose motto was 'death to privilege.' "

From another uncle, George Lauder, Carnegie absorbed a second passion that was also to reveal itself in his later career. This was his love of poetry, first that of the poet Burns, with its overtones of romantic egalitarianism, and then later, of Shakespeare. Immense quantities of both were not only committed to memory, but made into an integral—indeed, sometimes an embarrassingly evident—part of his life: on first visiting the Doge's palace in Venice he thrust a companion in the ducal throne and held him pinioned there while he orated the appropriate speeches from *Othello*. Once, seeing Vanderbilt walking on Fifth Avenue, Carnegie smugly remarked, "I would not exchange his millions for my knowledge of Shakespeare."

But it was more than just a love of poetry that remained with Carnegie. Virtually alone among his fellow acquisitors, he was driven by a genuine respect for the power of thought to seek answers for questions that never even occurred to them. Later, when he "discovered" Herbert Spencer, the English sociologist, Carnegie wrote to him, addressing him as "Master," and it was as "Master" that Spencer remained, even after Carnegie's lavishness had left Spencer very much in his debt.

But Carnegie's early life was shaped by currents more material than intellectual. The grinding process of industrial change had begun slowly but ineluctably to undermine the cottage weaving that was the traditional means of employment in Dunfermline. The Industrial Revolution, in the shape of new steam mills, was forcing out the hand weavers, and one by one the looms which constituted the entire capital of the Carnegie family had to be sold. Carnegie never forgot the shock of his father returning home to tell him, in despair, "Andra, I can get nae mair work."

A family council of war was held, and it was decided that there was only one possible course—they must try their luck in America, to which two sisters of Carnegie's mother, Margaret, had already emigrated. With the aid of a few friends the money for the crossing was scraped together, and at thirteen Andrew found himself transported to the only country in which his career would have been possible.

It hardly got off to an auspicious start, however. The family made their way to Allegheny, Pennsylvania, a raw and bustling town where Carnegie's father again sought work as an independent weaver. But it was hopeless to compete against the great mills in America as in Scotland, and soon father and son were forced to seek work in the local cotton mills. There Andrew worked from six in the morning until six at night, making $1.20 as a bobbin boy.

After a while his father quit—factory work was impossible for the traditional small enterpriser—and Andrew got a "better" job with a new firm, tending an engine deep in a dungeon cellar and dipping newly made cotton spools in a vat of oil. Even the raise of $3 a week—and desperately conjured visions of Wallace and the Bruce—could not overcome the horrors of that lonely and foul-smelling basement. It was perhaps the only time in Carnegie's life when his self-assurance deserted him: to the end of his days the merest whiff of oil could make him deathly sick.

Yet he was certain, as he wrote home at sixteen, that "anyone could get along in this Country," and the rags-to-riches saga shortly began. The telegraph had just come to Pittsburgh, and one evening over a game of checkers, the manager of the local office informed Andrew's uncle that he was looking for a messenger. Andy got the job and, in true Alger fashion, set out to excel in it. Within a few weeks he had carefully memorized the names and the locations, not only of the main streets in Pittsburgh, but of the main firms, so that he was the quickest of all the messenger boys.

He came early and stayed late, watched the telegraphers at work, and at home at night learned the Morse code. As a result he was soon the head of the growing messenger service, and a skilled telegrapher himself. One day he dazzled the office by taking a message "by ear" instead of by the commonly used tape printer, and since he was then only the third operator in the country able to turn the trick, citizens used to drop into the office to watch Andy take down the words "hot from the wire."

One such citizen who was especially impressed with young Carnegie's determination was Thomas A. Scott, in time to become one of the colorful railway magnates of the West, but then the local superintendent of the Pennsylvania Railroad. Soon thereafter Carnegie became "Scott's Andy"—telegrapher, secretary, and general factotum—at thirty-five dollars a month. In his *Autobiography* Carnegie recalls an instance which enabled him to begin the next stage of his career.

> One morning I reached the office and found that a serious accident on the Eastern Division had delayed the express passenger train westward, and that

the passenger train eastward was proceeding with a flagman in advance at every curve. The freight trains in both directions were standing on the sidings. Mr. Scott was not to be found. Finally I could not resist the temptation to plunge in, take the responsibility, give "train orders" and set matters going. "Death or Westminster Abbey" flashed across my mind. I knew it was dismissal, disgrace, perhaps criminal punishment for me if I erred. On the other hand, I could bring in the wearied freight train men who had lain out all night. I knew I could. I knew just what to do, and so I began.

Signing Scott's name to the orders, Carnegie flashed out the necessary instructions to bring order out of the tangle. The trains moved; there were no mishaps. When Scott reached the office Carnegie told him what he had done. Scott said not a word but looked carefully over all that had taken place. After a little he moved away from Carnegie's desk to his own, and that was the end of it. "But I noticed," Carnegie concluded good-humoredly, "that he came in very regularly and in good time for some mornings after that."

It is hardly to be wondered at that Carnegie became Scott's favorite, his "white-haired Scotch devil." Impetuous but not rash, full of enthusiasm and good-natured charm, the small lad with his blunt, open features and his slight Scottish burr was every executive's dream of an assistant. Soon Scott repaid Andy for his services by introducing him to a new and very different kind of opportunity. He gave Carnegie the chance to subscribe to five hundred dollars' worth of Adams Express stock, a company which Scott assured Andy would prosper mightily.

Carnegie had not fifty dollars saved, much less five hundred, but it was a chance he could ill afford to miss. He reported the offer to his mother, and that pillar of the family unhesitatingly mortgaged their home to raise the necessary money. When the first dividend check came in, with its ornate Spencerian flourishes, Carnegie had something like a revelation. "I shall remember that check as long as I live," he subsequently wrote. "It gave me the first penny of revenue from capital—something that I had not worked for with the sweat of my brow. 'Eureka!' I cried, 'Here's the goose that lays the golden eggs.' " He was right; within a few years his investment in the Adams Express Company was paying annual dividends of $1,400.

It was not long thereafter that an even more propitious chance presented itself. Carnegie was riding on the Pennsylvania line one day when he was approached by a "farmer-looking" man carrying a small green bag in his hand. The other introduced himself as T. T. Woodruff and quite frankly said that he wanted a chance to talk with someone connected with the railroad. Whereupon he opened his bag and took out a small model of the first sleeping car.

Carnegie was immediately impressed with its possibilities, and he quickly arranged for Woodruff to meet Scott. When the latter agreed to give the cars a trial, Woodruff in appreciation offered Carnegie a chance to subscribe to a one-eighth interest in the new company. A local banker agreed to lend Andy the few hundred dollars needed for the initial payment—the rest being financed from dividends. Once again Andy had made a shrewd investment: within two years the Woodruff Palace Car Company was paying him a return of more than $5,000 a year.

Investments now began to play an increasingly important role in Carnegie's career. Through his railroad contacts he came to recognize the possibilities in manufacturing the heavy equipment needed by the rapidly expanding lines, and soon he was instrumental in organizing companies to meet these needs. One of them, the Keystone Bridge Company, was the first successful manufacturer of iron railway bridges. Another, the Pittsburgh Locomotive Works, made engines. And most important of all, an interest in a local iron works run by an irascible German named Andrew Kloman brought Carnegie into actual contact with the manufacture of iron itself.

None of these new ventures required any substantial outlay of cash. His interest in the Keystone Bridge Company, for instance, which was to earn him $15,000 in 1868, came to him "in return for services rendered in its promotion"—services which Carnegie, as a young railroad executive, was then in a highly strategic position to deliver. Similarly the interest in the Kloman works reflected no contribution on Carnegie's part except that of being the human catalyst and buffer between some highly excitable participants.

By 1865 his "side" activities had become so important that he decided to leave the Pennsylvania Railroad. He was by then superintendent, Scott having moved up to a vice presidency, but his salary of $2,400 was already vastly overshadowed by his income from various ventures. One purchase alone—the Storey farm in Pennsylvania oil country, which Carnegie and a few associates picked up for $40,000—was eventually to pay the group a million dollars in dividends in *one* year. About this time a friend dropped in on Carnegie and asked him how he was doing. "Oh, I'm rich, I'm rich!" he exclaimed.

He was indeed embarked on the road to riches, and determined, as he later wrote in his *Autobiography,* that "nothing could be allowed to interfere for a moment with my business career." Hence it comes as a surprise to note that it was at this very point that Carnegie retired to his suite to write his curiously introspective and troubled thoughts about the pursuit of wealth. But the momentum of events was to prove far too strong for these moralistic doubts. Moving his headquarters to New York to promote his various interests, he soon found himself swept along by a succession of irresistible opportunities for money-making.

One of these took place quite by chance. Carnegie was trying to sell the Woodruff sleeping car at the same time that a formidable rival named George Pullman was also seeking to land contracts for his sleeping car, and the railroads were naturally taking advantage of the competitive situation. One summer evening in 1869 Carnegie found himself mounting the resplendent marble stairway of the St. Nicholas Hotel side by side with his competitor.

"Good evening, Mr. Pullman," said Carnegie in his ebullient manner. Pullman was barely cordial.

"How strange we should meet here," Carnegie went on, to which the other replied nothing at all.

"Mr. Pullman," said Carnegie, after an embarrassing pause, "don't you think we are making nice fools of ourselves?" At this Pullman evinced a glimmer of interest: "What do you mean?" he inquired. Carnegie quickly pointed out that competition between the two companies was helping no one but the railroads. "Well," said Pullman, "what do you suggest we do?"

"Unite!" said Carnegie. "Let's make a joint proposition to the Union Pacific, your company and mine. Why not organize a new company to do it?" "What would you call it?" asked Pullman suspiciously. "The Pullman Palace Car Company," said Carnegie and with this shrewd psychological stroke won his point. A new company was formed, and in time Carnegie became it largest stockholder.

Meanwhile, events pushed Carnegie into yet another lucrative field. To finance the proliferating railway systems of America, British capital was badly needed, and with his Scottish ancestry, his verve, and his excellent railroad connections Carnegie was the natural choice for a go-between. His brief case stuffed with bonds and prospectuses, Carnegie became a transatlantic commuter, soon developing initmate relations both with great bankers like Junius Morgan (the father of J. P. Morgan), and with the heads of most of the great American roads. These trips earned him not only large commissions—exceeding on occasion $100,000 for a single turn—but even more important, established connections that were later to be of immense value. He himself later testified candidly on their benefits before a group of respectfully awed senators:

> For instance, I want a great contract for rails. Sidney Dillon of the Union
> Pacific was a personal friend of mine. Huntington was a friend. Dear Butler
> Duncan, that called on me the other day, was a friend. Those and other men
> were presidents of railroads. . . . Take Huntington; you know C. P.
> Huntington. He was hard up very often. He was a great man, but he had a
> great deal of paper out. I knew his things were good. When he wanted credit I
> gave it to him. If you help a man that way, what chance has any paid agent
> going to these men? It was absurd.

But his trips to England brought Carnegie something still more valuable. They gave him steel. It is fair to say that as late as 1872 Carnegie did not see the future that awaited him as the Steel King of the world. The still modest conglomeration of foundries and mills he was gradually assembling in the Allegheny and Monongahela valleys was but one of many business interests, and not one for which he envisioned any extraordinary future. Indeed, to repeated pleas that he lead the way in developing a steel industry for America by substituting steel for iron rails, his reply was succinct: "Pioneering don't pay."

What made him change his mind? The story goes that he was awe-struck by the volcanic, spectacular eruption of a Bessemer converter, which he saw for the first time during a visit to a British mill. It was precisely the sort of display that would have appealed to Carnegie's mind—a wild, demonic, physical process miraculously contained and controlled by the dwarfed figures of the steel men themselves. At any rate, overnight Carnegie became the perfervid prophet of steel. Jumping on the first available steamer, he rushed home with the cry, "The day of iron has passed!" To the consternation of his colleagues, the hitherto reluctant pioneer became an advocate of the most daring technological and business expansion; he joined them enthusiastically in forming Carnegie, McCandless & Company, which was the nucleus of the empire that the next thirty years would bring forth.

The actual process of growth involved every aspect of successful business enterprise of the times: acquisition and merger, pools and commercial piracy, and even, on one occasion, an outright fraud in selling the United States government overpriced and underdone steel armor plate. But it would be as foolish to maintain that the Carnegie empire grew by trickery as to deny that sharp practice had its place. Essentially what lay behind the spectacular expansion were three facts.

The first of these was the sheer economic expansion of the industry in the first days of burgeoning steel use. Everywhere steel replaced iron or found new uses—and not only in railroads but in ships, buildings, bridges, machinery of all sorts. As Henry Frick himself once remarked, if the Carnegie group had not filled the need for steel another would have. But it must be admitted that Carnegie's company did its job superlatively well. In 1885 Great Britain led the world in the production of steel. Fourteen years later her total output was 695,000 tons less than the output of the Carnegie Steel Company alone.

Second was the brilliant assemblage of personal talent with which Carnegie surrounded himself. Among them, three in particular stood out. One was Captain William Jones, a Homeric figure who lumbered through the glowing fires and clanging machinery of the works like a kind of Paul Bunyan of steel, skilled at handling men, inventive in handling equipment, and enough of a natural artist to produce papers for the British Iron and Steel Institute that earned him a literary as well as a technical reputation. Then there was Henry Frick, himself a self-made millionaire, whose coke empire naturally complemented Carnegie's steelworks. When the two were amalgamated, Frick took over the active management of the whole, and under his forceful hand the annual output of the Carnegie works rose tenfold. Yet another was Charles Schwab, who came out of the tiny monastic town of Loretto, Pennsylvania, to take a job as a stake driver. Six months later he had been promoted by Jones into the assistant managership of the Braddock plant.

These men, and a score like them, constituted the vital energy of the Carnegie works. As Carnegie himself said, "Take away all our money, our great works, ore mines and coke ovens, but leave our organization, and in four years I shall have re-established myself."

But the third factor in the growth of the empire was Carnegie himself. A master salesman and a skilled diplomat of business at its highest levels, Carnegie was also a ruthless driver of his men. He pitted his associates and subordinates in competition with one another until a feverish atmosphere pervaded the whole organization. "You cannot imagine the abounding sense of freedom and relief I experience as soon as I get on board a steamer and sail past Sandy Hook," he once said to Captain Jones. "My God!" replied Jones. "Think of the relief to us!"

But Carnegie could win loyalties as well. All his promising young men were given gratis ownership participations—minuscule fractions of one per cent, which were enough, however, to make them millionaires in their own right. Deeply grateful to Jones, Carnegie once offered him a similar participation. Jones hemmed and hawed and finally refused; he would be unable to work effectively with the men, he said, once he was a partner. Carnegie insisted that his contribution be recognized and asked Jones what he wanted. "Well," said the latter, "you might pay me a hell of a big salary." "We'll do it!" said Carnegie. "From this time forth you shall receive the same salary as the President of the United States." "Ah, Andy, that's the kind of talk," said Captain Bill.

Within three decades, on the flood tide of economic expansion, propelled by brilliant executive work and relentless pressure from Carnegie, the company made immense strides. "Such a magnificent aggregation of industrial power has never before been under the domination of a single man," reported a biographer in 1902, describing the Gargantuan structure of steel and coke and ore and transport. Had the writer known of the profits earned by this aggregation he might have been even more impressed: three and a half million dollars in 1889, seven million in 1897, twenty-one million in 1899, and an immense forty million in 1900. "Where is there such a business!" Carnegie had exulted, and no wonder—the majority share of all these earnings, without hindrance of income tax, went directly into his pockets.

Nevertheless, with enormous success came problems. One of these was the restiveness of certain partners, under the "Iron-Clad" agreement, which prevented any of them from selling their shares to anyone but the company itself—an arrangement which meant, of course, that the far higher valuation of an outside purchaser could not be realized. Particularly chagrined was Frick, when, as the culmination of other disagreements between them, Carnegie sought to buy him out "at the value appearing on the books." Another problem was a looming competitive struggle in the steel industry itself that presaged a period of bitter industrial warfare ahead. And last was Carnegie's own growing desire to "get out."

Already he was spending half of each year abroad, first traveling, and then, after his late marriage, in residence in the great Skibo Castle he built for his wife on Dornoch Firth, Scotland. There he ran his business enterprises with one hand while he courted the literary and creative world with the other, entertaining Kipling and Matthew Arnold, Paderewski and Lloyd George, Woodrow Wilson and Theodore Roosevelt, Gladstone, and of course, Herbert

Spencer, the Master. But even his career as "Laird" of Skibo could not remove him from the worries—and triumphs—of his business: a steady flow of cables and correspondence intruded on the "serious" side of life.

It was Schwab who cut the knot. Having risen to the very summit of the Carnegie concern he was invited in December, 1900, to give a speech on the future of the steel industry at the University Club in New York. There, before eighty of the nation's top business leaders he painted a glowing picture of what could be done if a super-company of steel were formed, integrated from top to bottom, self-sufficient with regard to its raw materials, balanced in its array of final products. One of the guests was the imperious J. P. Morgan, and as the speech progressed it was noticed that his concentration grew more and more intense. After dinner Morgan rose and took the young steel man by the elbow and engaged him in private conversation for half an hour while he plied him with rapid and penetrating questions; then a few weeks later he invited him to a private meeting in the great library of his home. They talked from nine o'clock in the evening until dawn. As the sun began to stream in through the library windows, the banker finally rose. "Well," he said to Schwab, "if Andy wants to sell, I'll buy. Go and find his price."

Carnegie at first did not wish to sell. Faced with the actual prospect of a withdrawal from the business he had built into the mightiest single industrial empire in the world, he was frightened and dismayed. He sat silent before Schwab's report, brooding, loath to inquire into details. But soon his enthusiasm returned. No such opportunity was likely to present itself again. In short order a figure of $492,000,000 was agreed on for the entire enterprise, of which Carnegie himself was to receive $300,000,000 in five per cent gold bonds and preferred stock. Carnegie jotted down the terms of the transaction on a slip of paper and told Schwab to bring it to Morgan. The banker glanced only briefly at the paper. "I accept," he said.

After the formalities were in due course completed, Carnegie was in a euphoric mood. "Now, Pierpont, I am the happiest man in the world," he said. Morgan was by no means unhappy himself: his own banking company had made a direct profit of $12,500,000 in the underwriting transaction, and this was but a prelude to a stream of lucrative financings under Morgan's aegis, by which the total capitalization was rapidly raised to $1,400,000,000. A few years later, Morgan and Carnegie found themselves aboard the same steamer en route to Europe. They fell into talk and Carnegie confessed, "I made one mistake, Pierpont, when I sold out to you."

"What was that?" asked the banker.

"I should have asked you for $100,000,000 more than I did." Morgan grinned. "Well," he said, "you would have got it if you had."

Thus was written *finis* to one stage of Carnegie's career. Now it would be seen to what extent his "radical pronouncements" were serious. For in the *Gospel of Wealth*—the famous article combined with others in book form— Carnegie had proclaimed the duty of the millionaire to administer and distribute his wealth *during his lifetime*. Though he might have "proved" his worth by his fortune, his heirs had shown no such evidence of their fitness. Carnegie bluntly concluded: "By taxing estates heavily at his death, the State marks its condemnation of the selfish millionaire's unworthy life."

Coming from the leading millionaire of the day, these had been startling sentiments. So also were his views on the "labor question" which, if patronizing, were nonetheless humane and advanced for their day. The trouble was, of course, that the sentiments were somewhat difficult to credit. As one commentator of the day remarked, "His vision of what might be done with wealth had beauty and breadth and thus serenely overlooked the means by which wealth had been acquired."

For example, the novelist Hamlin Garland visited the steel towns from which the Carnegie millions came and bore away a description of work that was ugly, brutal, and exhausting: he contrasted the lavish care expended on the plants with the callous disregard of the pigsty homes: "the streets were horrible; the buildings poor; the sidewalks sunken and full of holes. . . . Everywhere the yellow mud of the streets lay kneaded into sticky masses through which groups of pale, lean men slouched in faded garments. . . ." When the famous Homestead strike erupted in 1892, with its private army of Pinkerton detectives virtually at war with the workers, the Carnegie benevolence seemed revealed as shabby fakery. At Skibo Carnegie stood firmly behind the company's iron determination to break the strike. As a result, public sentiment swung sharply and suddenly against him; the St. Louis *Post-Dispatch* wrote: "Three months ago Andrew Carnegie was a man to be envied. Today he is an object of mingled pity and contempt. In the estimation of nine-tenths of the thinking people on both sides of the ocean he has . . . confessed himself a moral coward."

In an important sense the newspaper was right. For though Carnegie continued to fight against "privilege," he saw privilege only in its fading aristocratic vestments and not in the new hierarchies of wealth and power to which he himself belonged. In Skibo Castle he now played the role of the benign autocrat, awakening to the skirling of his private bagpiper and proceeding to breakfast to the sonorous accompaniment of the castle organ.

Meanwhile there had also come fame and honors in which Carnegie wallowed unshamedly. He counted the "freedoms" bestowed on him by grateful or hopeful cities and crowed. "I have fifty-two and Gladstone has only seventeen." He entertained the King of England and told him that democracy was better than monarchy, and met the German Kaiser: "Oh, yes, yes," said the latter worthy on being introduced. "I have read your books. You do not like kings." But Mark Twain, on hearing of this, was not fooled. "He says he is a scorner of kings and emperors and dukes," he wrote, "whereas he is like the rest of the human race: a slight attention from one of these can make him drunk for a week. . . ."

And yet it is not enough to conclude that Carnegie was in fact a smaller man than he conceived himself. For this judgment overlooks one immense and irrefutable fact. He did, in the end, abide by his self-imposed duty. He did give nearly all of his gigantic fortune away.

As one would suspect, the quality of the philanthropy reflected the man himself. There was, for example, a huge and sentimentally administered private pension fund to which access was to be had on the most trivial as well as the most worthy ground: if it included a number of writers, statesmen, scientists, it also made room for two maiden ladies with whom Carnegie had once danced as a young man, a boyhood acquaintance who had once held Carnegie's books while he ran a race, a merchant to whom he had once delivered a telegram and who had subsequently fallen on hard times. And then, as one would expect, there was a benevolent autocracy in the administration of the larger philanthropies as well. "Now everybody vote Aye," was the way Carnegie typically determined the policies of the philanthropic "foundations" he established.

Yet if these flaws bore the stamp of one side of Carnegie's personality, there was also the other side—the side that, however crudely, asked important questions and however piously, concerned itself with great ideals. Of this the range and purpose of the main philanthropies gave unimpeachable testimony. There were the famous libraries—three thousand of them costing nearly sixty million dollars; there were the Carnegie institutes in Pittsburgh and Washington, Carnegie Hall in New York, the Hague Peace Palace, the Carnegie Endowment for International Peace, and the precedent-making Carnegie Corporation of New York, with its original enormous endowment of $125,000,000. In his instructions to the trustees of this first great modern foundation, couched in the simplified spelling of which he was an ardent advocate, we see Carnegie at his very best:

> Conditions on erth [sic] inevitably change; hence, no wise man will bind
> Trustees forever to certain paths, causes, or institutions. I disclaim any intention
> of doing so. . . . My chief happiness, as I write these lines lies in the thot [sic]
> that, even after I pass away, the welth [sic] that came to me to administer as a
> sacred trust for the good of my fellow men is to continue to benefit
> humanity. . . .

If these sentiments move us—if Carnegie himself in retrospect moves us at last to grudging respect—it is not because his was the triumph of a saint or a philosopher. It is because it was the much more difficult triumph of a very human and fallible man struggling to retain his convictions in an age, and in the face of a career, which subjected them to impossible temptations. Carnegie is something of America writ large; his is the story of the Horatio Alger hero *after* he has made his million dollars. In the failures of Andrew Carnegie we see many of the failures of America itself. In his curious triumph, we see what we hope is our own steadfast core of integrity.

2

Hell on Saturday Afternoon

by John F. McCormack, Jr.

Although they were far removed geographically from Idaho miners, workers at the Triangle Shirtwaist Company in New York City had much in common with their western brethren. Hours were long, wages were low, and working conditions were poor. Employer resistance to unionism was equally bitter. Tragically, working at the factory proved to be as dangerous as mining.

John F. McCormack, Jr., graphically describes the conditions of the shirtwaist workers, the factors which contributed to the disaster, and the short- and long-term effects of the fire. His commentary also provides us with insights regarding the status of women in the work force in the early twentieth century and illustrates the connection between industrialization, immigration, and urbanization. Lastly, it is interesting to note how many prominent political careers were touched and how much legislation was formulated by the investigations surrounding "the worst factory fire in history."

It was payday for the girls working at the Triangle Shirtwaist Company. A gentle early spring breeze wafted in the open windows of the ten-story Asch Building, situated on the northwest corner of Greene Street and Washington Place, New York City. The machines hummed along as they stitched the lace, lawn and silk into shirtwaists. At 4:30 p.m. they were shut down and the garment workers prepared to leave. Suddenly, flames burst forth from a cluttered rag bin. Efforts to extinguish the fire failed and hell on Saturday afternoon, March 25, 1911 was less than minutes away for over 500 factory employees.

As the eighth story fire began to spread, a bookkeeper alerted the New York City Fire Department at approximately 4:45 p.m. She also tried to warn those on the two floors above to evacuate the building. At first some of the girls thought the message was a prank. After all, the building was fire-proof. However, flames drawn in the open windows from the eighth floor below soon brought panic to the disbelievers. A babble of foreign languages added to the confusion since a large proportion of the workers were Jewish and Italian immigrants. There were 146 lives lost in what National Fire Protection Association figures show to be the worst factory fire in history.

Life was difficult for all blue collar workers at the beginning of the twentieth century. Organized labor had made few gains and these concerned skilled laborers. Semi-skilled garment workers spent their lives living in tenements

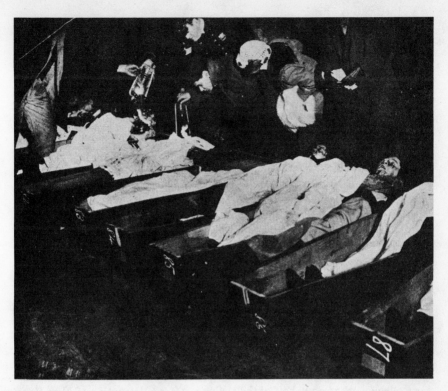

Bodies of victims from the Triangle Shirt Waist Fire.
(Brown Brothers)

and working in sweatshops. One of these girls who worked in Brownsville (Brooklyn) described her work:

> The machines go like mad all day, because the faster you work the more money you get. Sometimes in my haste I get my finger caught and the needle goes right through it. It goes so quick though, that it does not hurt much. I bind the finger up with a piece of cotton and go on working. We all have accidents like that. Where the needle goes through the nail it makes for a sore finger, or where it splinters a bone it does much harm. Sometimes a finger has to come off. . . .

This same woman earned $4.50 per week, paying out $2.00 of that for room and board near the factory.

The shirtwaist industry at the time of the Triangle fire employed over 40,000 workers in about 450 New York City factories. About eighty percent of these were single women between the ages of eighteen and twenty-five. These girls worked between fifty-six and fifty-nine hours a week and as high as seventy during the busy season. Wages ranged from $4.00 to as high as $10.00 per week. Idle periods, however, could last as long as three months.

Moreover, substantial reductions were made in the workers' wages for use of electric power, needles and thread. If an operator was a few minutes late to work, she was docked a half-day's pay. Frequently, factory managers would actually lock employees in to force them to work overtime. Very few ill workers were permitted to leave before the day's work was finished. Lunch hours were habitually cut short and known union members were summarily dismissed.

It was the latter action which led to an unexpected and spectacular strike against Triangle Shirtwaist Company and another firm in 1909. The Shirtwaist Makers Union ordered the strike when some of its members were fired because of their union affiliation. The strike spread to the whole industry. The Triangle Company then decided to physically break the union by hiring toughs with criminal records as "special police" to "protect" its property. The *Jewish Daily Forward* printed some photos of the brutalized strikers and public opinion forced Triangle to find a new solution. It did. The company now came up with one of the most unique solutions ever employed to settle a strike. The toughs were replaced outside the factory by prostitutes!

Meanwhile, the shirtwaist makers managed to secure some powerful allies of their own: Mary Dreier, President of the Women's Trade Union League, Mrs. Alva E. Belmont, Mrs. Mary Beard, Anne Morgan, Inez Milholland, Lenora O'Reilly, Victoria Pike, John Mitchell of the United Mine Workers, Rabbi Stephen S. Wise and lawyer Samuel Untermeyer. Rallies and benefits were held under the guidance of these persons and others. The girls from Vassar College worked on behalf of the strikers. After a delegation of New Yorkers visited Philadelphia, the shirtwaist makers there walked off the job. The Philadelphians were visited by Helen Taft, the U.S. President's daughter, a student at nearby Bryn Mawr College. She felt sorry for them and would "speak to papa about the terrible conditions" there. She then left for the opera.

The strike ended with the employees gaining much of what they had asked: better working conditions, a fifty-two hour week with no more than two hours per day overtime and time and a half for that with a fixed wage scale. Unfortunately, the issue of union recognition was never accepted by the manufacturers and there were no guarantees that the employers would not revert to form when they felt they could get away with it.

Among the most obstinate of the employers were Isaac Harris and Max Blanck, owners of the Triangle Shirtwaist Co. The firing of union members by their firm had precipitated the great strike of 1909. As the largest shirtwaist manufacturers, they intended to maintain their leadership in the field by any means possible. For instance, during the strike they hired strike breakers, thugs and prostitutes to cow the strikers. They also set up a phonograph on the ninth floor of the Asch Building so that their workers could dance during lunch time. Blanck even gave out prizes to the best dancers. When the strike ended, so did the dancing.

The owners were constantly concerned that their employees were trying to steal yard goods. In 1907 an incident occurred which indicated the great lengths to which the management would go to safeguard the company from such thefts. Two sisters were accused of taking materials by Samuel Bernstein, superintendent. They were returned to the building and forced to disrobe before two female employees. The sisters further charged that three men watched the proceedings through a transom. No stolen items were found. Nevertheless, this obsession that employees were stealing was to cost many lives in the fire. As a matter of course, the eighth and ninth floor doors on the Washington Place side of the building were locked. This forced the girls to go through a narrow passageway to the freight elevators on the Greene Street side. It also afforded an opportunity for the management to make certain no one was pilfering yard goods.

Other factors contributed to the disaster. There were large bins filled with scraps of cloth waiting for the rag man to come for them. He had last appeared in January. Wicker baskets filled with finished goods lined the aisles. Finished garments hung on racks. Cardboard and wooden boxes were stacked on the tenth floor. Gasoline, used to heat the pressing irons, was stored on the eighth floor. The ninth floor tables had wooden wells where oil drippings from the machines collected just above the knees of the operators. In addition, a large barrel of oil was stored by a door. Stairwells were not illuminated. A small fire escape led to a back courtyard. Fire officials later estimated that it would have taken three hours for the five hundred people on the top three floors to go down this way. Water valves were corroded shut with their attached hoses rotting in the folds. The Asch Building was fire proof, yet events showed it to be as fire proof as any furnace is, consuming all combustibles within it.

When the bookkeeper tried to alarm the two floors above her, the workday had just ended. The unbelieving girl who answered on the tenth floor finally comprehended and reported the fire to Mr. Blanck. On the ninth floor Max Hochfield was the first one to learn of the fire. He worked near the forelady. As she reached out to ring the quitting bell, he dashed past her into the stairwell and down the stairs. He saw the flames as he passed the eighth floor. He turned to go back for his sister when a hand grabbed him and pushed him downward. The first fireman had penetrated the burning building.

Flames had lapped in the open windows of the two floors above and panic gripped those frantically trying to escape. Girls tried in vain to leave by the locked doors. Others bunched up against the doors to the elevator shafts. Still others horrified the crowds now gathering on the street below by appearing on window ledges. "Don't jump!" "Don't jump!" they screamed. The horses of Hook and Ladder Company 20 soon appeared pulling their apparatus behind them. Quickly the firemen raised their ladders, the tallest in New York City. The crowds gasped! The ladders, when fully extended, could only reach the sixth story. Other firemen and citizen volunteers grasped life nets. Garment workers jumped for them. The men were simply bowled over by the impact of the plummeting figures, some of them already aflame. It was of little use since the distance was too great for the life nets to perform their purpose.

Bodies had to be removed from atop fire hoses as these were stretched into the building.

At one point a man emerged at a ninth floor window. He helped a young woman to the window then lifted her outwards and let go. He performed this act three times before the horrified onlookers below. A fourth girl came to the window. The two figures embraced and kissed. He then held her out and dropped her. Thereupon, he climbed upon the window sill and leaped to the pavement. It was an act of love never to be forgotten by the witnesses to the Triangle holocaust.

There were others amidst the panic that Saturday afternoon who kept their wits about them. Among these no praise too high could be extended to the elevator operators. In grave danger, themselves, they continued to operate their life-saving machinery until no longer able to raise the elevators. Joseph Zito guessed he had personally brought over a hundred people to safety. Gaspar Mortillalo had his elevator jam when too many forced their way into it and atop it. Men and women slid down the cables to safety while others jumped down the shafts to serious injury and death. One, Herman Meshel, had slid down the cables under an elevator. He was found almost four hours later in water up to his neck still in the shaft, dazed, bleeding and whimpering pathetically.

Those trapped on the tenth floor owed their lives to a quick thinking college professor and his students. Professor Frank Sommer, former Essex County, N.J., sheriff, was lecturing to a class of fifty New York University Law School students on the tenth floor of the New York University-American Bank Company building next door to the Triangle concern. The fire gongs disrupted the class and Sommer rushed to the faculty room which looked across an areaway at the Asch Building. What he saw he described as a "building that was fast becoming a roaring furnace." He swiftly led his students to the roof of the N.Y.U. structure, which was about fifteen feet higher than its neighbor. They found two ladders left around by painters who were redecorating the building. These were lowered to the roof of the Asch Building. Some fifty persons, including Harris and Blanck and the latter's two children, who were visiting their father, were saved by the college students. Several rooms in the college building were scorched and firemen had to be directed there. Hundreds of valuable books were carried to safety by the students before the firemen put out the smoldering college rooms.

By this time all who could get out of the Asch Building had left. Only the doomed remained to be found by shaken fire fighters.

The Edison Company of New York strung lights along Greene Street and Washington Place and throughout the burned-out floors of the Asch Building. Firemen slowly lowered the wrapped bundles which had once been human beings. Bodies were removed to the Twenty-sixth Street pier where the city's morgue attendants and a number of derelicts were pressed into service. Soon grieving families came to identify, if possible, their loved ones. The police were hard-pressed to keep back the grief-stricken. When the latter were let in, the officers had to watch out for suicides and the hysterical. Seven victims would remain unidentified. Meanwhile, the ghouls were at work near the Asch Building. Among other sounds on Monday morning were those of young street hawkers selling alleged "dead girls' earrings" and "finger rings from the fire."

However, most Americans were stunned by the disaster. Officials sought to place the blame—somewhere, anywhere. Charitable organizations appealed for aid for families of the victims. Mayor William J. Gaynor issued a call for public contributions. The respondents ranged from the great of the land to the insignificant. Andrew Carnegie immediately gave $5,000. A little boy and his cousin donated $10, the proceeds of their "savings bank . . . to use it for somebody whose littel (sic) girl jumped out of a window. . . ." The Red Cross was the official agency designated by the mayor to receive funds through its well-known treasurer, investment banker Jacob H. Schiff. As frequently happens, the theatrical community in New York City was quick to respond. Marcus Loew, Guilio Gatti-Casazza, the Shuberts, the Hammersteins, Sam Harris, Al Jolson and George M. Cohan among others responded at once. Their benefit performances raised $15,000. In all, the gigantic sum (for those days) of $120,000 was raised. The major difficulty was getting the people to accept the money. The Red Cross found even the most destitute to be maddeningly independent.

Several protest meetings were held during the days following the tragedy. These ranged from threats of withholding tuition from frightened N.Y.U. students to calls for violent action from leftist orators. Perhaps the most poignant of all protests was the funeral parade called for April 5, after the city decided to bury the seven remaining unidentified victims in Evergreen Cemetery, East New York (Brooklyn).

Mayor Gaynor decided to bury these unfortunates because he feared that the release of their remains would lead to violence. Nevertheless, the Women's Trade Union League called for a public memorial parade on the same day. Rain drenched the marchers, as if the elements, themselves, mourned the victims. The parade consisted of two processions, one beginning uptown on Fourth Avenue between 19th and 22nd Streets; the other started at Seward Park where East Broadway and Canal Street meet. They joined at Washington Square Park and when the Asch Building was sighted a bone chilling wail was emitted by the marchers. Little Rose Schneiderman, the outspoken enemy of the exploiters, felt queasy in her stomach.

A reporter asked if she was ill. She was, for good reason. "As we marched up Fifth Avenue, there they were. Girls right at the top of hundreds of buildings, looking down on us. The structures were no different from the Asch Building . . . many were . . . worse. . . . There they were, leaning out of the upper windows, watching us. This, not the rain, is making me sick."

On April 11 the grand jury investigating the fire handed up indictments for first and second degree manslaughter against Messrs. Harris and Blanck.

Judge O'Sullivan released them on $25,000 bail each. The main evidence against them was a bolted lock attached to a charred piece of wood. It came from the ninth floor of the Asch Building. The owners were charged with the deaths of a girl aged sixteen and a woman of twenty-two whose bodies were found among fifty jammed up at the locked door.

The "Shirtwaist Kings," as they were known in the trade, had made a fortune manufacturing the tops made famous by the illustrator, Charles Dana Gibson. The "Gibson Girl" was the epitome of American womanhood of the time, with her upswept hair, slender figure, long skirt and trim shirtwaist. Harris and Blanck catered to the demands of the American woman through their New York and Philadelphia factories. Now all that they had built up was threatened.

Their trial did not begin until December, 1911. When they entered the New York Criminal Court Building on December 5, a crowd of 300 women surged at them, waving photographs of lost loved ones and crying, "Murderers, murderers! Kill the murderers!" Max D. Steuer, their attorney and some court officers managed to get them to the courtroom. Police cleared the corridors. The next day both men were again mobbed as they entered and left a nearby restaurant at lunch time. The trial dragged on with much contradictory testimony until the embattled owners received a belated holiday gift on December 27. After an hour and three-quarters, the jury found them innocent of the charges. Both the acquitted and the jurors were smuggled out of the courtroom for fear for their lives. Incomprehensibly, the next day's *New York Times* printed the names and addresses of the jurymen!

Nonetheless, reform elements in New York continued to press for measures which would protect factory workers. They were following the admonition pronounced by Rabbi Wise: "The lesson of the hour is that while property is good, life is better, that while possessions are valuable, life is priceless."

New York State authorized a Factory Investigating Commission of nine members during the early summer of 1911. The chairman was Robert F. Wagner, Sr., later U.S. Senator from New York, who sponsored much labor and safety legislation. Vice-Chairman was Alfred E. Smith, later governor of the state and 1928 Democratic candidate for President. Sam Gompers, A.F.L. President, and Mary Dreier were other members. Among the commission's inspectors were Rose Schneiderman and Frances Perkins, who became Franklin D. Roosevelt's Secretary of Labor. Henry Morgenthau provided free top legal counsel in Abram Elkus and Bernard Shientag because the state had not appropriated enough money for legal fees. Within three years, thirty-six new pieces of legislation bolstered the state's labor laws. All were the result of findings by the commission. The sacrifices of the 146 had not been in vain, after all.

Frances Perkins stated later that much of the philosophy and legislation of the New Deal rose, like a phoenix, from the ashes of that hell on a Saturday afternoon almost three quarters of a century ago, the "Great Triangle Fire."

3

The Causes of the Great Crash

by John Kenneth Galbraith

As illustrated by the difficulties of western miners and by the conditions in the sweatshops of New York City, industrialization had its human as well as material costs. Yet many Americans living in the mid-1920s might well have looked back over the previous half-century and have been quite satisfied. The nation had emerged as an industrial power and prosperity seemed firmly entrenched. Certainly there had been occasional slumps in the economy, but each time a strong recovery pushed the nation forward.

When the great stock market crash of October, 1929, rocked the country, most people expected the acompanying economic stagnation to be only a temporary downslide in the inexorable march of progress. However, this crash was different, for it was followed by the most serious economic depression in American history. This Great Depression was not just an *economic* turning point in American history, but served as a catalyst for numerous social and political changes as well. Thus, understanding the reasons for the Great Crash and the Great Depression helps make our modern society more comprehensible.

No one does a better job of describing the causes of the crash and the subsequent depression than John Kenneth Galbraith, Professor Emeritus of Economics at Harvard University. Among Galbraith's numerous publications are *American Capitalism, The Affluent Society, The New Industrial State, Economics and the Public Purpose,* and *The Age of Uncertainty.* In all of his writings, the lucid narrative is punctuated with wit and humor. The following essay stands as a classic example of how to present a complex subject in a clear and interesting manner.

The decade of the twenties, or more exactly the eight years between the post-war depression of 1920–21 and the sudden collapse of the stock market in October, 1929, were prosperous ones in the United States. The total output of the economy increased by more than 50 per cent. The preceding decades had brought the automobile; now came many more and also roads on which they could be driven with reasonable reliability and comfort. There was much building. The downtown section of the mid-continent city—Des Moines, Omaha, Minneapolis—dates from these years. It was then, more likely than not, that what is still the leading hotel, the tallest office building, and the biggest department store went up. Radio arrived, as of course did gin and jazz.

These years were also remarkable in another respect, for as time passed it became increasingly evident that the prosperity could not last. Contained within it were the seeds of its own destruction. The country was heading into the gravest kind of trouble. Herein lies the peculiar fascination of the period for a study in the problem of leadership. For almost no steps were taken during these years to arrest the tendencies which were obviously leading, and did lead, to disaster.

At least four things were seriously wrong, and they worsened as the decade passed. And knowledge of them does not depend on the always brilliant assistance of hindsight. At least three of these flaws were highly visible and widely discussed. In ascending order, not of importance but of visibility, they were as follows:

First, income in these prosperous years was being distributed with marked inequality. Although output per worker rose steadily during the period, wages were fairly stable, as also were prices. As a result, business profits increased rapidly and so did incomes of the wealthy and the well-to-do. This tendency was nurtured by assiduous and successful efforts of Secretary of the Treasury Andrew W. Mellon to reduce income taxes with special attention to the higher brackets. In 1929 the 5 per cent of the people with the highest incomes received perhaps a quarter of all personal income. Between 1919 and 1929 the share of the one per cent who received the highest incomes increased by approximately one seventh. This meant that the economy was heavily and increasingly dependent on the luxury consumption of the well-to-do and on their willingness to reinvest what they did not or could not spend on themselves. Anything that shocked the confidence of the rich either in their personal or in their business future would have a bad effect on total spending and hence on the behavior of the economy.

This was the least visible flaw. To be sure, farmers, who were not participating in the general advance, were making themselves heard; and twice during the period the Congress passed far-reaching relief legislation which was vetoed by Coolidge. But other groups were much less vocal. Income distribution in the United States had long been unequal. The inequality of these years did not seem exceptional. The trade-union movement was also far from strong. In the early twenties the steel industry was still working a twelve-hour day and, in some jobs, a seven-day week. (Every two weeks when the shift changed a man worked twice around the clock.) Workers lacked the organization or the power to deal with conditions like this; the twelve-hour day was, in fact, ended as the result of personal pressure by President Harding on the steel companies, particularly on Judge Elbert H. Gary, head of the United States Steel Corporation. Judge Gary's personal acquaintance with these working conditions was thought to be slight, and this gave rise to Benjamin Stolberg's now classic observation that the Judge "never saw a blast furnace until his death." In all these circumstances the increasingly lopsided income distribution did not excite much comment or alarm. Perhaps it would have been surprising if it had.

But the other three flaws in the economy were far less subtle. During World War I the United States ceased to be the world's greatest debtor country and became its greatest creditor. The consequences of this change have so often been described that they have the standing of a cliché. A debtor country could export a greater value of goods than it imported and use the difference for interest and debt repayment. This was what we did before the war. But a creditor must import a greater value than it exports if those who owe it money are to have the wherewithal to pay interest and principal. Otherwise the creditor must either forgive the debts or make new loans to pay off the old.

During the twenties the balance was maintained by making new foreign loans. Their promotion was profitable to domestic investment houses. And when the supply of honest and competent foreign borrowers ran out, dishonest, incompetent, or fanciful borrowers were invited to borrow and, on occasion, bribed to do so. In 1927 Juan Leguia, the son of the then dictator of Peru, was paid $450,000 by the National City Company and J. & W. Seligman for his services in promoting a $50,000,000 loan to Peru which these houses marketed. Americans lost and the Peruvians didn't gain appreciably. Other Latin American republics got equally dubious loans by equally dubious devices. And, for reasons that now tax the imagination, so did a large number of German cities and municipalities. Obviously, once investors awoke to the character of these loans or there was any other shock to confidence, they would no longer be made. There would be nothing with which to pay the old loans. Given this arithmetic, there would be either a sharp reduction in exports or a wholesale default on the outstanding loans, or more likely both. Wheat and cotton farmers and others who depended on exports would suffer. So would those who owned the bonds. The buying power of both would be reduced. These consequences were freely predicted at the time.

The second weakness of the economy was the large-scale corporate thimblerigging that was going on. This took a variety of forms, of which by far the most common was the organization of corporations to hold stock in yet other corporations, which in turn held stock in yet other corporations. In the case of the railroads and the utilities, the purpose of this pyramid of holding companies was to obtain control of a very large number of operating companies with a very small investment in the ultimate holding company. A $100,000,000 electric utility, of which the capitalization was represented half by bonds and half by common stock, could be controlled with an investment of a little over $25,000,000—the value of just over half the common stock. Were a company then formed with the same capital structure to hold *this* $25,000,000 worth of common stock, it could be controlled with an investment of $6,250,000. On the next round the amount required would be less than $2,000,000. That $2,000,000 would still control the entire $100,000,000 edifice. By the end of the twenties, holding-company structures six or eight tiers high were a commonplace. Some of them—the utility pyramids of Insull and Associated Gas & Electric, and the railroad pyramid of the Van Sweringens—were marvelously complex. It is unlikely that anyone fully understood them or could.

In other cases companies were organized to hold securities in other companies in order to manufacture more securities to sell to the public. This was true of the great investment trusts. During 1929 one investment house, Goldman, Sachs & Company, organized and sold nearly a billion dollars' worth of securities in three interconnected investment trusts—Goldman Sachs Trading Corporation; Shenandoah Corporation; and Blue Ridge Corporation. All eventually depreciated virtually to nothing.

This corporate insanity was also highly visible. So was the damage. The pyramids would last only so long as earnings of the company at the bottom were secure. If anything happened to the dividends of the underlying company, there would be trouble, for upstream companies had issued bonds (or in practice sometimes preferred stock) against the dividends on the stock of the downstream companies. Once the earnings stopped, the bonds would go into default or the preferred stock would take over and the pyramid would collapse. Such a collapse would have a bad effect not only on the orderly prosecution of business and investment by the operating companies but also on confidence, investment, and spending by the community at large. The likelihood was increased because in any number of cities—Cleveland, Detroit, and Chicago were notable examples—the banks were deeply committed to these pyramids or had fallen under the control of the pyramiders.

Finally, and most evident of all, there was the stock market boom. Month after month and year after year the great bull market of the twenties roared on. Sometimes there were setbacks, but more often there were fantastic forward surges. In May of 1924 the New York *Times* industrials stood at 106; by the end of the year they were 134; by the end of 1925 they were up to 181. In 1927 the advance began in earnest—to 245 by the end of that year and on to 331 by the end of 1928. There were some setbacks in early 1929, but then came the fantastic summer explosion when in a matter of three months the averages went up another 110 points. This was the most frantic summer in our financial history. By its end, stock prices had nearly quadrupled as compared with four years earlier. Transactions on the New York Stock Exchange regularly ran to 5,000,000 or more shares a day. Radio Corporation of America went to 573¾ (adjusted) without ever having paid a dividend. Only the hopelessly eccentric, so it seemed, held securities for their income. What counted was the increase in capital values.

And since capital gains were what counted, one could vastly increase his opportunities by extending his holdings with borrowed funds—by buying on margin. Margin accounts expanded enormously, and from all over the country—indeed from all over the world—money poured into New York to finance these transactions. During the summer, brokers' loans increased at the rate of $400,000,000 a month. By September they totaled more than $7,000,000,000. The rate of interest on these loans varied from 7 to 12 per cent and went as high as 15.

This boom was also inherently self-liquidating. It could last only so long as new people, or at least new money, were swarming into the market in pursuit of the capital gains. This new demand bid up the stocks and made the capital gains. Once the supply of new customers began to falter, the market would cease to rise. Once the market stopped rising, some, and perhaps a good many, would start to cash in. If you are concerned with capital gains, you must get them while the getting is good. But the getting may start the market down, and this will one day be the signal for much more selling—both by those who are trying to get out and those who are being forced to sell securities that are no longer safely margined. Thus it was certain that the market would one day go down, and far more rapidly than it went up. Down it went with a thunderous crash in October of 1929. In a series of terrible days, of which Thursday, October 24, and Tuesday, October 29, were the most terrifying, billions in values were lost, and thousands of speculators—they had been called investors—were utterly and totally ruined.

This too had far-reaching effects. Economists have always deprecated the tendency to attribute too much to the great stock market collapse of 1929: this was the drama; the causes of the subsequent depression really lay deeper. In fact, the stock market crash was very important. It exposed the other weakness of the economy. The overseas loans on which the payments balance depended came to an end. The jerry-built holding-company structures came tumbling down. The investment-trust stocks collapsed. The crash put a marked crimp on borrowing for investment and therewith on business spending. It also removed from the economy some billions of consumer spending that was either based on, sanctioned by, or encouraged by the fact that the spenders had stock market gains. The crash was an intensely damaging thing.

And this damage, too, was not only foreseeable but foreseen. For months the speculative frenzy had all but dominated American life. Many times before in history—the South Sea Bubble, John Law's speculations, the recurrent real-estate booms of the last century, the great Florida land boom earlier in the same decade—there had been similar frenzy. And the end had always come, not with a whimper but a bang. Many men, including in 1929 the President of the United States, knew it would again be so.

The increasingly perilous trade balance, the corporate buccaneering, and the Wall Street boom—along with the less visible tendencies in income distribution—were all allowed to proceed to the ultimate disaster without effective hindrance. How much blame attaches to the men who occupied the presidency?

President Herbert Hoover. (Bureau of Printing and Engraving)

Warren G. Harding died on August 2, 1923. This, as only death can do, exonerates him. The disorders that led eventually to such trouble had only started when the fatal blood clot destroyed this now sad and deeply disillusioned man. Some would argue that his legacy was bad. Harding had but a vague perception of the economic processes over which he presided. He died owing his broker $180,000 in a blind account—he had been speculating disastrously while he was President, and no one so inclined would have been a good bet to curb the coming boom. Two of Harding's Cabinet officers, his secretary of the interior and his attorney general, were to plead the Fifth Amendment when faced with questions concerning their official acts, and the first of these went to jail. Harding brought his fellow townsman Daniel R. Crissinger to be his comptroller of the currency, although he was qualified for this task, as Samuel Hopkins Adams has suggested, only by the fact that he and the young Harding had stolen watermelons together. When Crissinger had had an ample opportunity to demonstrate his incompetence in his first post, he was made head of the Federal Reserve System. Here he had the central responsibility for action on the ensuing boom. Jack Dempsey, Paul Whiteman, or F. Scott Fitzgerald would have been at least equally qualified.

Yet it remains that Harding was dead before the real trouble started. And while he left in office some very poor men, he also left some very competent ones. Charles Evans Hughes, his secretary of state; Herbert Hoover, his sec-

28

retary of commerce; and Henry C. Wallace, his secretary of agriculture, were public servants of vigor and judgment.

The problem of Herbert Hoover's responsibility is more complicated. He became President on March 4, 1929. At first glance this seems far too late for effective action. By then the damage had been done, and while the crash might come a little sooner or a little later, it was now inevitable. Yet Hoover's involvement was deeper than this—and certainly much deeper than Harding's. This he tacitly concedes in his memoirs, for he is at great pains to explain and, in some degree, to excuse himself.

For one thing, Hoover was no newcomer to Washington. He had been secretary of commerce under Harding and Coolidge. He had also been the strongest figure (not entirely excluding the President) in both Administration and party for almost eight years. He had a clear view of what was going on. As early as 1922, in a letter to Hughes, he expressed grave concern over the quality of the foreign loans that were being floated in New York. He returned several times to the subject. He knew about the corporate excesses. In the latter twenties he wrote to his colleagues and fellow officials (including Crissinger) expressing his grave concern over the Wall Street orgy. Yet he was content to express himself—to write letters and memoranda, or at most, as in the case of the foreign loans, to make an occasional speech. He could with propriety have presented his views of the stock market more strongly to the Congress and the public. He could also have maintained a more vigorous and persistent agitation within the Administration. He did neither. His views of the market were so little known that it celebrated his election and inauguration with a great upsurge. Hoover was in the boat and, as he himself tells, he knew where it was headed. But, having warned the man at the tiller, he rode along into the reef.

And even though trouble was inevitable, by March, 1929, a truly committed leader would still have wanted to do something. Nothing else was so important. The resources of the Executive, one might expect, would have been mobilized in a search for some formula to mitigate the current frenzy and to temper the coming crash. The assistance of the bankers, congressional leaders, and the Exchange authorities would have been sought. Nothing of the sort was done. As secretary of commerce, as he subsequently explained, he had thought himself frustrated by Mellon. But he continued Mellon in office. Henry M. Robinson, a sympathetic Los Angeles banker, was commissioned to go to New York to see his colleagues there and report. He returned to say that the New York bankers regarded things as sound. Richard Whitney, the vice-president of the Stock Exchange, was summoned to the White House for a conference on how to curb speculation. Nothing came of this either. Whitney also thought things were sound.

Both Mr. Hoover and his official biographers carefully explained that the primary responsibility for the goings on in New York City rested not with Washington but with the governor of New York State. That was Franklin D. Roosevelt. It was he who failed to rise to his responsibilities. The explanation is far too formal. The future of the whole country was involved. Mr. Hoover was the President of the whole country. If he lacked authority commensurate with this responsibility, he could have requested it. This, at a later date, President Roosevelt did not hesitate to do.

Finally, while by March of 1929 the stock market collapse was inevitable, something could still be done about the other accumulating disorders. The balance of payments is an obvious case. In 1931 Mr. Hoover did request a one-year moratorium on the inter-Allied (war) debts.This was a courageous and constructive step which came directly to grips with the problem. But the year before, Mr. Hoover, though not without reluctance, had signed the Hawley-Smoot tariff. "I shall approve the Tariff Bill. . . . It was undertaken as the result of pledges given by the Republican Party at Kansas City. . . . Platform promises must not be empty gestures." Hundreds of people—from Albert H. Wiggin, the head of the Chase National Bank, to Oswald Garrison Villard, the editor of the *Nation*—felt that no step could have been more directly designed to make things worse. Countries would have even more trouble earning the dollars of which they were so desperately short. But Mr. Hoover signed the bill.

Anyone familiar with this particular race of men knows that a dour, flinty, inscrutable visage such as that of Calvin Coolidge can be the mask for a calm and acutely perceptive intellect. And he knows equally that it can conceal a mind of singular aridity. The difficulty, given the inscrutability, is in knowing which. However, in the case of Coolidge the evidence is in favor of the second. In some sense, he certainly knew what what going on. He would not have been unaware of what was called the Coolidge market. But he connected developments neither with the well-being of the country nor with his own responsibilities. In his memoirs Hoover goes to great lengths to show how closely he was in touch with events and how clearly he foresaw their consequences. In his *Autobiography,* a notably barren document, Coolidge did not refer to the accumulating troubles. He confines himself to such unequivocal truths as "Every day of Presidential life is crowded with activities" (which in his case, indeed, was not true); and "The Congress makes the laws, but it is the President who causes them to be executed."

At various times during his years in office, men called on Coolidge to warn him of the impending trouble. And in 1927, at the instigation of a former White House aide, he sent for William Z. Ripley of Harvard, the most articulate critic of the corporate machinations of the period. The President became so interested that he invited him to stay for lunch, and listened carefully while his guest outlined (as Ripley later related) the "prestidigitation, double-shuffling, honey-fugling, hornswoggling, and skulduggery" that characterized the current Wall Street scene. But Ripley made the mistake of telling Coolidge that regulation was the responsibility of the states (as was then the case). At this intelligence Coolidge's face lit up and he dismissed the entire matter from his mind. Others who warned of the impending disaster got even less far.

And on some occasions Coolidge added fuel to the fire. If the market seemed to be faltering, a timely statement from the White House—or possibly from Secretary Mellon—would often brace it up. William Allen White, by no means an unfriendly observer, noted that after one such comment the market staged a 26-point rise. He went on to say that a careful search "during these halcyon years . . . discloses this fact: Whenever the stock market showed signs of weakness, the President or the Secretary of the Treasury or some important dignitary of the administration . . . issued a statement. The statement invariably declared that business was 'fundamentally sound,' that continued prosperity had arrived, and that the slump of the moment was 'seasonal.' "

Such was the Coolidge role. Coolidge was fond of observing that "if you see ten troubles coming down the road, you can be sure that nine will run into the ditch before they reach you and you have to battle with only one of them." A critic noted that "the trouble with this philosophy was that when the tenth trouble reached him he was wholly unprepared. . . . The outstanding instance was the rising boom and orgy of mad speculation which began in 1927." The critic was Herbert Hoover.

Plainly, in these years, leadership failed. Events whose tragic culmination could be foreseen—and was foreseen—were allowed to work themselves out to the final disaster. The country and the world paid. For a time, indeed, the very reputation of capitalism itself was in the balance. It survived in the years following perhaps less because of its own power or the esteem in which it was held, than because of the absence of an organized and plausible alternative. Yet one important question remains. Would it have been possible even for a strong President to arrest the plunge? Were not the opposing forces too strong? Isn't one asking the impossible?

No one can say for sure. But the answer depends at least partly on the political context in which the Presidency was cast. That of Coolidge and Hoover may well have made decisive leadership impossible. These were conservative Administrations in which, in addition, the influence of the businessman was strong. At the core of the business faith was an intuitive belief in *laissez faire*—the benign tendency of things that are left alone. The man who wanted to intervene was a meddler. Perhaps, indeed, he was a planner. In any case, he was to be regarded with mistrust. And, on the businessman's side, it must be borne in mind that high government office often nurtures a spurious sense of urgency. There is no more important public function than the suppression of proposals for unneeded action. But these should have been distinguished from action necessary to economic survival.

A bitterly criticized figure of the Harding-Coolidge-Hoover era was Secretary of the Treasury Andrew W. Mellon. He opposed all action to curb the boom, although once in 1929 he was persuaded to say that bonds (as distinct from stocks) were a good buy. And when the depression came, he was against doing anything about that. Even Mr. Hoover was shocked by his insistence that the only remedy was (as Mr. Hoover characterized it) to "liquidate labor, liquidate stocks, liquidate the farmers, liquidate real estate." Yet Mellon reflected only in extreme form the conviction that things would work out, that the real enemies were those who interfered.

Outside of Washington in the twenties, the business and banking community, or at least the articulate part of it, was overwhelmingly opposed to any public intervention. The tentative and ineffective steps which the Federal Reserve did take were strongly criticized. In the spring of 1929 when the Reserve system seemed to be on the verge of taking more decisive action, there was an anticipatory tightening of money rates and a sharp drop in the market. On his own initiative Charles E. Mitchell, the head of the National City Bank, poured in new funds. He had an obligation, he said, that was "paramount to any Federal Reserve warning, or anything else" to avert a crisis in the money market. In brief, he was determined, whatever the government thought, to keep the boom going. In that same spring Paul M. Warburg, a distinguished and respected Wall Street leader, warned of the dangers of the boom and called for action to restrain it. He was deluged with criticism and even abuse and later said that the subsequent days were the most difficult of his life. There were some businessmen and bankers—like Mitchell and Albert Wiggin of the Chase National Bank—who may have vaguely sensed that the end of the boom would mean their own business demise. Many more had persuaded themselves that the dream would last. But we should not complicate things. Many others were making money and took a short-run view—or no view—either of their own survival or of the system of which they were a part. They merely wanted to be left alone to get a few more dollars.

And the opposition to government intervention would have been nonpartisan. In 1929 one of the very largest of the Wall Street operators was John J. Raskob. Raskob was also chairman of the Democratic National Committee. So far from calling for preventive measures, Raskob in 1929 was explaining how, through stock market speculation, literally anyone could be a millionaire. Nor would the press have been enthusiastic about, say, legislation to control holding companies and investment trusts or to give authority to regulate margin trading. The financial pages of many of the papers were riding the boom. And even from the speculating public, which was dreaming dreams of riches and had yet to learn that it had been fleeced, there would have been no thanks. Perhaps a President of phenomenal power and determination might have overcome the Coolidge-Hoover environment. But it is easier to argue that this context made inaction inevitable for almost any President. There were too many people who, given a choice between disaster and the measures that would have prevented it, opted for disaster without either a second or even a first thought.

On the other hand, in a different context a strong President might have taken effective preventive action. Congress in these years was becoming increasingly critical of the Wall Street speculation and corporate piggery-pokery. The liberal Republicans—the men whom Senator George H. Moses called the Sons of the Wild Jackass—were especially vehement. But conservatives like Carter Glass were also critical. These men correctly sensed that things were going wrong. A President such as Wilson or either of the Roosevelts (the case of Theodore is perhaps less certain than that of Franklin) who was surrounded in his Cabinet by such men would have been sensitive to this criticism. As a leader he could both have reinforced and drawn strength from the contemporary criticism. Thus he might have been able to arrest the destructive madness as it became recognizable. The American government works far better—perhaps it only works—when the Executive, the business power, and the press are in some degree at odds. Only then can we be sure that abuse or neglect, either private or public, will be given the notoriety that is needed.

Perhaps it is too much to hope that by effective and timely criticism and action the Great Depression might have been avoided. A lot was required in those days to make the United States in any degree depression-proof. But perhaps by preventive action the ensuing depression might have been made less severe. And certainly in the ensuing years the travail of bankers and businessmen before congressional committees, in the courts, and before the bar of public opinion would have been less severe. Here is the paradox. In the full perspective of history, American businessmen never had enemies as damaging as the men who grouped themselves around Calvin Coolidge and supported and applauded him in what William Allen White called "that masterly inactivity for which he was so splendidly equipped."

4

The Poor in the Great Depression

by David J. Rothman

As Professor David J. Rothman of Columbia University so aptly phrases it in the following article, "the poor had more than enough company" during the Great Depression. Poverty was obviously not new to the United States in the 1930s. Despite the fancied "streets paved with gold" and the popularization of the Horatio Alger myth, poverty had always existed in America. With the coming of industrialization and urbanization, it became much more noticeable. When the unemployment rate hit twenty-five percent in 1932, the issue of poverty could no longer be ignored.

Progressive politicians of the early twentieth century had made some gains in attacking the problem in that era, but the widespread misery of the 1930s called for new initiatives. The framework for our modern governmental poverty programs, including work relief, social security, and the minimum wage, was established during those crisis times. Yet, as we know, poverty remains with us—and will likely continue to do so until the nation makes a moral commitment to eliminate it.

The years of the progressive era marked a major shift in public attitudes and policies toward the poor. Beginning in the 1890's and culminating in the administrations of Theodore Roosevelt and Woodrow Wilson, a new and more complex understanding of the origins of dependency spread through the nation, together with a host of fresh alternatives to institutionalization. The innovations were the work of clergymen like Washington Gladden and Walter Rauschenbusch, who preached a new social gospel; of social workers like Robert Hunter, Jane Addams, and Robert Woods, who practiced community work in their settlement houses; of sociologists like Margaret Byington and Crystal Eastman, who provided the first sophisticated and detailed studies of the causes and conditions of poverty; and of popularizers like Jacob Riis, who wrote newspaper articles and books to arouse the American conscience. Taken together, these groups influenced the thinking and responses of ordinary citizens and political leaders.

The new view toward poverty rested first on an understanding of the shortcomings of the economy—the periodic unemployment that forced many laborers below the subsistence line, the prevalent low wages that did not allow even the thrifty among them to accumulate savings. ("Many, many thousand families," wrote Robert Hunter in *Poverty* [1904], "receive wages so inadequate that no care in spending, however wise it may be, will make them suffice for the family needs.") It also was sensitive to the debilitating effects of slums, the crowded and unsanitary tenements through which disease rapidly spread, particularly tuberculosis, robbing households of their main providers. ("Penury and poverty," declared Jacob Riis in *How the Other Half Lives* [1890], "are wedded everywhere to dirt and disease.") It emphasized the dangers inherent in work itself—the inevitable accidents that occurred when managers neglected to install safety devices; when employees were crowded into sweatshops that were firetraps; when laborers, after ten or twelve hours on the job, grew fatigued and careless. (We must do something, pleaded Crystal Eastman in *Work Accidents and the Law* [1910], to insure that modern industry is conducted "without the present wholesale destruction of the workers.") Critics recognized, too, the general misery of life for those at the bottom of society, a misery that drove them to the tavern to gain a temporary respite from their troubles. And they understood how generation after generation would remain trapped in poverty: families, hard pressed to make ends meet, would put young children out to work, depriving them of the education necessary to take skilled jobs. In brief, these reformers taught Americans to think of the needy as the laboring poor who, as Robert Hunter put it, "live miserably . . . [and] know not why. They work sore, and yet gain nothing."

To some degree these conclusions almost forced themselves upon social observers. Forays into the urban slums, whether to bring the gospel to the unchurched or to ameliorate their need, taught ministers and charity workers that the poor were victims not of immorality but of forces beyond their control. The deeper sociologists probed, the more apparent it became that the moralism traditionally characterizing American attitudes toward poverty explained only a fraction of the problem. Ten million Americans, it was reliably estimated in 1904—an eighth of the population—earned less than subsistence incomes, and clearly the great majority of them were feeling the effects of social and economic dislocations. When newly graduated college students went into the ghettos to learn about the poor and to offer their help, whether at Chicago's Hull House or New York's Henry Street Settlement, they too immediately recognized the many disadvantages that the poor could not escape. To all these commentators it was obvious that America had become, once and for all, an urban and industrial nation, with a frontier that was not practically settled and, given successive waves of immigrants, a surplus of labor. The emphasis of earlier reformers on personal reformation and rehabilitation now seemed largely irrelevant, and the isolation of the poor in an almshouse an inadequate response.

The new outlook on poverty also reflected special fears and hopes for American society. The majority of the urban poor (and it was the city's needs that monopolized attention) were also immigrants. To reformers, the newcomers represented both a major threat to the national well-being and an unusual opportunity to do good. Two intimately related problems demanded resolution: the immigrant had to be assimilated into American life, and his standard of living had to be improved. The prospect of failure was haunting, for progressives were deeply suspicious of the aliens, disturbed by many of their idio-syncratic customs (from their strange modes of dress to worshipping in Roman Catholic churches), and frightened that they might act on foreign principles (be it a slavish obedience to Rome or a dedicated allegiance to European so-cialism). And yet, these critics were also confident that American society had the resources to counter these threats. They pinned their hopes on the oppor-tunities for all men to climb the ladder of success and for all families to enjoy an unprecedented material well-being. Once the several barriers that penned the immigrant into his ghetto poverty were removed, once ambitious and en-ergetic foreigners enjoyed the full chance to succeed, then the nation's sta-bility and security would be assured.

Still, the reformers themselves, and many more of their countrymen, could not completely escape a moralistic view of poverty. The equation of the im-migrant with the poor kept alive the conviction that vice helped generate de-pendency. After all, one had only to walk through an ethnic ghetto to discover the omnipresence of taverns, beer halls, dance halls, and houses of prostitu-tion. Even Robert Hunter, as sympthetic an observer as one can find in this period, maintained the older distinction between the worthy and the unworthy poor. "There is unquestionably," he conceded, "a poverty which men deserve, and by such poverty men are perhaps taught needful lessons. It would be un-wise to legislate out of existence . . . that poverty which penalizes the vol-untarily idle and vicious." And progressives, like others before and after them, could not altogether reconcile the presence of poverty with their deep sense of the munificence of American life. A tone of condescension entered their rhetoric, reflecting a certain disdain not only for the "wretched refuse" of Eu-ropean shores but also for those who had not been clever or ambitious enough to profit in the land of opportunity.

Despite such doubts, reformers did put an end to the almshouse monopoly, establishing new procedures that kept at least some of the poor within the community. The persons who benefited immediately were widows with small children—the group least suspect among the needy. In 1909 President Roo-sevelt convened the White House Conference on the Care of Dependent Chil-dren and happily publicized its major findings. "Poverty alone should not disrupt the home," he announced. "Parents of good character, suffering from temporary misfortune, and above all deserving mothers . . . deprived of the support of the normal breadwinner, should be given such aid as may be nec-essary to enable them to maintain suitable homes for the rearing of their chil-dren." To this end, Illinois in 1911 passed a widow's pension bill, and by the close of World War I nearly every industrial state had followed its example. The worthy widow and her children would no longer suffer separation and incarceration in almshouses and orphan asylums.

Reformers also moved to protect the lower classes both on the job and in their communities, to enable them to enjoy more of the advantages of indus-trialism. They enacted accident insurance to compensate injured laborers and

Line of unemployed workers seeking inexpensive meals.
(Library of Congress)

regulated the number of hours women and children could work. They passed stringent building and fire codes to offset the most glaring dangers of slum living. They also tried to rescue the children of the poor from their parents' fate, enacting compulsory school laws and establishing a minimum age (ranging from twelve to sixteen) for factory work.

There was an enormous amount progressives did not do. They paid little attention to the plight of the black, his economic or social disabilities, and they almost completely ignored the rural poverty of tenant farmers, sharecroppers, and migrant laborers. They neither enacted health-care programs nor extended government pension provisions to the general work force. Although proposals for unemployment compensation and retirement benefits were heard between 1890 and 1914 (and indeed, several European countries were already administering them), no such advances were made here. Even the innovations that did occur were carefully circumscribed. Widow's pensions were limited to only the most deserving, so that mothers whose husbands had deserted them were not eligible, nor those with illegitimate children. As a result the majority of the poor still had to rely upon the limited funds of private charities, or turn to public relief for some coal or wood, or suffer a stint in the almshouse. Nevertheless, the progressives did signal a new departure. In attitude and practice, it was they who first broke with tradition.

Few advances in policy or thought occurred during the 1920's. In fact, given the severe tensions that pervaded the nation, it is noteworthy that the moderate advances of the progressives were not eradicated. This was the decade when the K.K.K. and the temperance movement and immigration restriction reached the zenith of their power and appeal, and antialien, antiurban sentiments also led to a resurgence of harsh and critical judgments on the poor, especially those who were first- or second-generation immigrants. If only they would stop drinking, gambling, and paying obeisance to Rome, the argument went, if only they would become full-fledged Americans, then poverty would disappear. To be sure, a few social critics who did not embrace these prejudices continued to circulate among themselves analytic studies of the poor in the best reformist tradition. Some explored the most efficient methods for organizing a national old-age assistance and pension program; others undertook the first investigations of conditions in black ghettos and among tenant farmers. And an occasional state legislature did manage to widen the eligibility requirements for widows' pensions. But in all, the 1920's was not an auspicious time to innovate, and the public achievement against poverty was not impressive.

The one significant change in this period affecting the poor was the organization and professionalization of social work. The good-hearted but casual home visitor to the needy, who dispensed a little cash and a lot of homilies, gave way to the college- and university-trained full-time social worker. The founding ideology of the discipline looked both to helping the poor adjust to society and to encouraging society to offer more help. But not surprisingly, in the 1920's it was the poor who had to do all the accommodating. Casework lost sight of social reform, focussing instead on teaching the lower classes to cope with their situation, to budget more carefully, to be more industrious, to emulate those above them. Part of the severity of this vision reflected the inhospitable climate of public opinion. But it also reflected the impact of Freudian theory and the eagerness of social workers to become professionals. Using psychological therapy as a way to establish and exert their expertise, social workers insisted that many of the difficulties confronting the poor resulted from their emotional problems. The needy were not the victims of vice but of maladjustment, and careful and sympathetic counselling would teach them to achieve. But the net result of this new doctrine was to couch in modern terminology some very traditional ideas. The poor remained essentially responsible for their difficulties. Reformation and rehabilitation returned to the center of the stage, now rationalized in updated language. The "unworthy" poor had become the "emotionally deprived" poor. Hence, by the close of this decade, public programs and attitudes had rigidified. The nation was not well equipped to confront the phenomenon of the Great Depression.

Suddenly, the poor had more than enough company. The crash of 1929 sparked the most massive economic dislocation in our history, at its peak leaving 25 per cent of the work force unemployed. Poverty was no longer the exclusive fate of the ghetto immigrant or the migrant farmer but of blue-collar workers laid off the assembly line and white-collar workers dismissed from brokerage houses. The problem had unexpectedly become national.

At first, both powerful and ordinary Americans denied the magnitude of the crisis, insisting that recovery was imminent. Herbert Hoover, wedded to an older American credo and fearful of undermining the country's moral fiber, refused to involve the federal government in relief. "I am opposed," he declared in 1931, "to any direct or indirect government dole. . . . Our people are providing against distress from unemployment in true American fashion." But true American fashion meant that local governments and private charities had to carry all of the burden, and by 1932 they were without the resources. Cities lacked funds and the taxing power to raise them. The Red Cross distributed bags of flour and the community chest armfuls of coal. Distress was everywhere apparent: migrants pitched camps at one water spot and then another, their life's possessions piled on the back of a broken-down truck. The urban poor pasted together shacks in shantytowns in the parks and along the river banks. Those with some savings cut corners, awaiting a bank's foreclosure or a landlord's eviction. Often unable to clothe their families decently, they kept their children out of school and shunned their neighbors.

New Deal legislation alleviated some of this misery. Less bound by tradition, Franklin D. Roosevelt plunged the national government into the business of relief. By 1936, with the passage of the Social Security Act and the establishment of the Works Progress Administration, Washington was providing the states with relief funds and the unemployed with jobs. New Deal legislation did alter permanently the character of public programs. To meet immediate problems, the unemployable (the aged, blind, and very young) received, after passing a means test, direct relief at home; at the same time, federally sponsored projects made jobs available for destitute but able-bodied workers. Unemployment compensation, funded by a tax on employers, provided incomes for the temporarily unemployed; and retirement pensions, paid for by employee contributions, gave the aged a new measure of security. The almshouse became a thing of the past, abolished through the effects of these innovations.

Still, the New Deal investment in relief fell considerably short of the nation's need. Afraid to violate the sanctity of the balanced budget or the prerogatives of the states, and committed first and foremost to work relief, President Roosevelt insisted on funding relief through the states but would not set national standards. (Thus, the poor in Mississippi received about one third the support of those in Massachusetts.) The sums allotted to the aged were far below subsistence—nineteen dollars a month when forty dollars would barely do. WPA regulations required men to leave the rolls after eighteen months, no matter how grim their economic condition. Social security was not to take effect until 1942—and even then the pension sums were too small to support recipients. The states were no more generous. California, for example, packed migrant workers and the young unmarried unemployed off to work camps that bordered on penal colonies. The states also tried to seal their borders by reviving stringent residence laws.

Despite the magnitude of the problem and the unprecedented government response, a very traditional attitude toward poverty persisted through the Depression. The new leadership continued to preach many ancient axioms, and the average citizen retained older beliefs. F.D.R. himself denigrated direct relief, keeping alive the term "dole." To some degree this was a conscious strategy to swell public support for the millions expended on W.P.A. But it also reflected his inner conviction that relief corrupted and weakened the recipient. Those on relief, or who tottered on the brink, felt an acute sense of dread and guilt, a painful reluctance to take what they still defined as charity. Hence, just when one might have anticipated a public furor over real suffering, when widespread turmoil and vicious riots might have broken out, the nation remained remarkably quiescent. Most Americans remained silent, suffering alone.

In essence, poverty demoralized rather than activated the country. The unemployed insisted on blaming themselves for their misery, defining their problems as internal, not external. If only they looked harder or put up a better front, they would find a job. Instead of joining with others in faulting the system, they became immobilized and isolated. One after another they passionately and honestly told the interviewers that before taking relief they would "rather be dead and buried." Years later, when good times returned, they still vividly recalled these feelings. "I didn't want to go on relief," one small businessman remembered. "Believe me, when I was forced to go to the office of relief, the tears were running out of my eyes. I couldn't bear myself to take money from anybody for nothing." Their actions did not belie their words. Of nearly one thousand unemployed in New Haven, Connecticut, less than one quarter had asked for relief after being without a job for over a year.

Desperation also took more comic or pathetic turns in the Depression. The board game called Monopoly swept the country. If one could not eke out a living in the real world, one could accumulate a paper fortune in a fantasy one. Dale Carnegie's *How to Win Friends and Influence People* became a best seller with an overt message of doubtful relevance: confidence, grace, personal style, and sensitive shrewdness would bring success. Its latent message was also obvious: failures had only their own personalities to blame. Soap operas, which fastened themselves on the radio public in the 1930's, provided a catalogue of troubles for the listener to compare with his own. But the serials usually blamed failure on personal and emotional inadequacy, rarely on external and social events.

Public-opinion polls during the Depression accurately gauged the degree of persistence and change in American attitudes toward poverty and the poor. There can be no doubt of the popularity of the federal involvement in relief among all the sectors of society. In March, 1939, a Roper poll indicated that three-quarters of the American public affirmed the government's obligation to relieve all persons who had no other means of subsistence. Yet, at the same time, a majority of the public continued to think of the poor in hostile and pejorative terms. Reliefers could get jobs, they believed, if only they tried. The New Deal did institute new and important and widely supported relief programs, but the welfare recipient remained a target of suspicion, disparaged by himself and others. Even the Great Depression could not wipe away the stigma of poverty. . . .

5

Shut the Goddam Plant!

by Stephen W. Sears

One of the ironies of American history is that the hard times of the 1930s provided the impetus for the most significant progress yet made by the American laborer. The widespread unemployment forced workers, managers, and the government to reassess old ways and explore new initiatives.

Even though national unions had existed in the United States since the 1860s, the most successful organization, the American Federation of Labor (AFL), was conservative in philosophy and narrow in scope. The breakthrough for unionism came when New Deal legislation guaranteed the workers the right to collective bargaining. Legislation can mean little, however, unless it is enforced. Perhaps the most dramatic testing ground for New Deal labor legislation was in the automobile plants.

The Big Three auto makers—GM, Chrysler, and Ford—had refused to recognize the United Auto Workers (UAW) as the bargaining agent for the workers, no matter what the law said. That position set the stage for the great sit-down strike during the winter of 1936–37. Stephen W. Sears, a former editor with *American Heritage* and author of *The Automobile in America,* calls the incident "the most momentous confrontation between labor and management in this century". Sears takes us to the battle lines and lets us sense the emergence of union strength. "Solidarity"—a word heard in other nations in the 1980s— had made them strong.

At General Motors' Flint, Michigan, Fisher Body Number One, the largest auto-body factory in the world, it was early evening of a chill winter day. Suddenly a bright red light began flashing in the window of the United Automobile Workers union hall across the street from the plant's main gate. It was the signal for an emergency union meeting.

When the swing shift took its dinner break at 8:00 P.M., excited workers crowded into the hall. UAW organizer Robert C. Travis confirmed the rumor crackling through the huge plant: dies for the presses that stamped out car body panels were being loaded into freight cars on a Fisher One spur track. Two days ealier, he reminded the men, fellow unionists had struck the Fisher Body plant in Cleveland; now, fearing Flint would be next, General Motors was trying to transfer the vital stamping dies to its other plants. "Well, what are we going to do about it?" Travis asked.

"Well, them's our jobs," a man said. "We want them left right here in Flint." There was a chorus of agreement. "What do you want to do?" Travis asked.

"Shut her down! Shut the goddam plant!" In a moment the hall was a bedlam of cheering.

As the dinner break ended, the men streamed back into Fisher One. Travis was watching anxiously in front of the union hall when the starting whistle blew. Instead of the usual answering pound of machinery, there was only silence. For long minutes nothing seemed to be happening. Then a third-floor window swung open and a worker leaned out, waving exultantly to Travis. "She's ours!" he shouted.

Thus began, on December 30, 1936, the great Flint sit-down strike, the most momentous confrontation between American labor and management in this century. For the next six weeks Flint would be a lead story in newspapers, newsreels, and radio newscasts. Events there dramatized the new militancy of the American worker, a mass movement that was to produce basic changes in the relationship of capital and labor. To those in sympathy with labor's goal of unionizing the auto industry, the rambunctious young United Automobile Workers union was David challenging the General Motors Goliath. To those dedicated to the sanctity of property, the UAW and its methods posed a radical, revolutionary threat to industrial capitalism. Few observers were neutral about the Flint sit-down.

There was no disputing the fact that the UAW faced a giant. Auto making was America's number-one industry, and General Motors was the number-one auto maker. Indeed, it was the largest manufacturing concern in the world. GM's 1936 sales of 1,500,000 Chevrolets, Pontiacs, Buicks, Oldsmobiles, La Salles, and Cadillacs represented better than 43 per cent of the domestic passenger-car market. It had sixty-nine auto plants in thirty-five cities. Business analysts regarded GM President Alfred P. Sloan, Jr., as a genius and his company as the best managed in America. It was unquestionably the most profitable—$284,000,000 in 1936 pretax profits on $1,400,000,000 in sales. This was a matter of great satisfaction to its 342,384 stockholders, and to one in particular. E. I. Du Pont de Nemours & Company owned nearly one-quarter of GM's common stock, good that year for nearly $45,000,000 in dividends. In short, General Motors was the paragon of industrial capitalism, and there was heavy pressure, both from within and without, to maintain the *status quo* that produced so many golden eggs.

One fundamental tenet of the *status quo* was a fiercely anti-union stance. In this General Motors acted in perfect unanimity with its competitors. Nineteen thirty-six marked the fortieth anniversary of the American automobile industry, and never in those four decades had the open shop seriously been threatened. The very notion of unionism was anathema to captains of the auto industry. "As a businessman, I was unaccustomed to the whole idea," Alfred Sloan wrote blandly in his memoirs.

Before the Great Depression, unionism was in truth not much of an issue in Detroit. The vast labor army recruited during the auto boom of the twenties—white dirt farmers, poor city dwellers, southern blacks, recent immigrants—was docile and innocent of trade-union experience. Any labor grievances were defused by pay scales higher than those in most other industries and by a system of "welfare capitalism" (group insurance, savings programs, housing subsidies, recreational facilities, and the like) in which General Motors was a pioneer. Open-shop Detroit had little to fear from the nation's largest union, the American Federation of Labor. The craft-minded AFL devoted itself to horizontal unionism—organizing all the machinists, for example, regardless of industry. It studiously ignored industrial unionism, the vertical organization of the unskilled or semiskilled workers within a particular industry such as autos, steel, or rubber.

Then the Depression knocked everything haywire. In the early 1930's Detroit auto workers found themselves powerless as the industry collapsed like a punctured balloon. Welfare capitalism was silent on job security. Wages and work time were slashed. As layoffs mounted, workers with ten or twenty years' experience discovered that their seniority counted for nothing; it counted for nothing, either, in the call-backs that marked an upturn in auto sales beginning in 1933. Assembly lines were speeded up mercilessly to raise productivity and restore profit levels. Bitter men protested. "You might call yourself a man if you was on the street," a Fisher Body worker recalled, "but as soon as you went through the door and punched your card, you was nothing more or less than a robot." "It takes your guts out, that line. The speed-up, that's the trouble," another said. "You should see him come home at night, him and the rest of the men. . . ," a Flint auto worker's wife testified. "So tired like they was dead. . . . And then at night in bed, he shakes, his whole body, he shakes. . . ."

More and more auto workers began to see unionism as their only hope to redress the balance. In this they detected an ally in the New Deal. The National Industrial Recovery Act (1933) recognized labor's right to organize and bargain collectively. The NIRA, however, was too weak a reed to support labor's aspirations, for it was largely unenforceable and easily evaded by management; and in any event, the Supreme Court knocked it down in 1935. But labor's hopes were raised anew by the passage of the National Labor Relations Act—the so-called Wagner Act, named for its chief sponsor, New York Senator Robert F. Wagner. The act established a National Labor Relations Board and gave it teeth to enforce collective bargaining and permit unionization efforts without interference by management.

The auto companies ignored the Wagner Act, confidently expecting the Supreme Court to do its duty. While they waited, they turned increasingly to labor spies to quash unionizing efforts. The most notorious spy system flourished at Ford, where goon squads instituted a bloody reign of terror in the massive River Rouge complex in Dearborn, outside Detroit. The General Motors espionage network was nonviolent but no less widespread. Evidence gathered by a Senate investigating committee chaired by Wisconsin's Robert M. La Follette, Jr., revealed that from 1934 to mid-1936 GM hired no fewer than fourteen private detective and security agencies, at a cost of $994,000, to ferret out and fire employees with union sympathies. This "most colossal super-system of spies yet devised in any American corporation," the La Follette committee charged, enveloped the worker in a web of fear. "Fear harries his every footstep, caution muffles his words. He is in no sense any longer a free American."

Launching an effective union in such turbulent waters would be difficult enough, and it was made no easier by an upheaval in labor's ranks. In 1933, prodded into action by the collective bargaining section of the NIRA, the American Federation of Labor had made a cautious stab at organizing Detroit's work force by chartering the United Automobile Workers union. However, leadership in the AFL-affiliated UAW was far too conservative to suit the rank and file. Three years' work produced a few toeholds among independent auto makers but barely a dent in the Big Three. In GM's Flint factories, for example, there was a grand total of 150 paid-up UAW members in June, 1936, just six months before the great sit-down.

This stumbling effort to organize the auto workers reflected the fratricidal conflict within the AFL. Advocates of industrial unionism, led by John L. Lewis of the United Mine Workers, David Dubinsky of the International Ladies' Garment Workers, and Sidney Hillman of the Amalgamated Clothing Workers, formed a rump group, the Committee (later Congress) of Industrial Organization. In the summer of 1936 the CIO seceded from the AFL ranks, taking with it the United Automobile Workers locals. Marching under the new CIO banner, the UAW prepared to do battle with the auto industry. It would be the first modern test of the theory of industrial unionism.

The revitalized UAW settled on General Motors as its first target. Chrysler's Walter Chrysler, who had climbed Horatio Alger—like up through the ranks, was considered the auto magnate most sympathetic to labor; if number-one GM could be conquered, number-two Chrysler might follow along. Ford was simply too tough a nut to crack yet. In addition, General Motors was particularly vulnerable. All bodies for the low-priced Chevrolet and the medium-priced Pontiac, Buick, and Oldsmobile were built by its Fisher Body division. If it came down to a strike—and no labor leader doubted that it would—the closing of only a few selected Fisher Body plants would immediately cripple the company.

And when the strike came, there was no doubt it would focus on Flint, the General Motors citadel. William C. Durant founded the company there in 1908, and it had remained the center of GM auto production. The Flint of 1936 was a drab gray industrial city of 160,000, some sixty miles northwest of Detroit, ringed by GM installations. Fisher Body One was to the south, a huge Buick assembly plant to the north, Fisher Body Two and a Chevrolet complex to the west, AC Spark Plug to the east. Two out of three of the city's breadwinners—more than 47,000 of them—worked for GM. Four out of five families, directly or indirectly, lived off the company payroll. Virtually every aspect of economic, social, and cultural life revolved around GM. Flint was very much a company town.

The union's first job was what a later generation would call consciousness raising. Wyndham Mortimer, a veteran trade unionist, began this task even before the UAW defected to the CIO, combining the five weak Flint locals into one, Local 156, and planting the seeds of unionism. In October, 1936, however, the quiet, hard-working Mortimer was replaced by twenty-seven-year-old Bob Travis, a more personable and energetic organizer. At Travis' side was Roy Reuther, who, with his brothers Victor and Walter, would become a dominant force in the UAW. The sons of a German immigrant, the Reuthers were, in Victor's words, "born into the labor movement." Eloquent, ambitious, and like his brothers deeply committed to trade unionism, Roy Reuther formed a strong partnership with Travis.

Facing a hostile management with a fearful company town infested with labor spies (the only safe topics of conversation in Flint, according to Mortimer, were "sports, women, dirty stories, and the weather"), UAW organizers did the bulk of their recruiting in workers' homes and at clandestine meetings. The labor journalist Henry Kraus was brought in to edit the *Flint Auto Worker,* an important vehicle for airing worker grievances and spreading the UAW gospel. Much effort was devoted to involving workers' wives in the movement. And rather than spreading themselves thin proselytizing the entire Flint GM work force, Travis and Reuther focused on the men in the city's two key Fisher Body plants. Their efforts were made easier by Franklin D. Roosevelt's overwhelming victory in the November elections, which labor took as a good omen for support from Washington.

By late December, Flint Local 156 had signed up 10 per cent of the city's GM workers, largely in secret to foil the spies and mostly in Fisher One and Fisher Two. On December 22, GM Executive Vice-President William S. Knudsen, meeting with UAW President Homer Martin, denied that issues such as union recognition, job security, pay rates, seniority rights, and the speed-up were "national in scope." Corporate headquarters had no say in such matters, he piously declared: they must be settled on the local level with individual plant managers. Martin recognized this account of the workings of the General Motors Corporation for what it was—pure fiction. It was clear that the company had no intention of obeying the Wagner Act and seriously bargaining with any independent union. The stage was set for a strike.

But what kind of strike? Veteran Flint workers remembered an attempt to close Fisher One in 1930 that had been smashed by local lawmen abetted by the Michigan state police. Pickets were scattered and ridden down by mounted officers, and strike leaders were arrested and subsequently fired. Few UAW officials in Flint had any illusions that their forty-five hundred or so members could long sustain a conventional picket-line strike in the heart of General Motors country. The solution might lie in an entirely different kind of strike—a sit-down.

The tactic was ingeniously simple. Instead of walking off the job, strikers stopped work but stayed at their machines, holding valuable company property hostage to enforce their demands. A sit-down was far less vulnerable to police action than outside picketing, and it neutralized a primary weapon in management's arsenal, the use of strikebreakers to resume production. Even more than a conventional striker, the sit-downer was taking his fight directly to management.

The sit-down was not new—some claimed to have traced its origins back to stone masons in ancient Egypt—but its baptism by fire took place in Europe in the twenties and thirties. Italian metal workers, Welsh coal miners, Spanish copper miners, and Greek rubber workers sat down at their jobs, and in the spring of 1936 mass sit-downs in France took on the proportions of a nation-wide general strike. In the United States in 1936 the Bureau of Labor Statistics reported forty-eight sit-down strikes. The ones most closely watched by auto workers took place at Bendix Products (owned in part by GM) in South Bend, Indiana, and at two Detroit parts makers, Midland Steel Products and Kelsey-Hayes Wheel. All three won limited worker gains and deeply impressed UAW militants. Thus far, however, no American sit-down had been played for truly high stakes.

In the midst of the feverish unionizing efforts in Flint's Fisher One, a shop stewart named Bud Simons was asked if his men were ready to strike. "Ready?" Simons exclaimed. "They're like a pregnant woman in her tenth month!" Flint's militants, however, were upstaged by militants in the Fisher Body plant in Cleveland. On December 28, 1936, Fisher Cleveland was shut tight by a sit-down. In Flint Bob Travis and his UAW organizers cast about desperately for some excuse to initiate a strike.

The report on December 30 that the company was moving the stamping dies out of Fisher One was the *casus belli* Travis needed. "Okay!" he said happily, "they're asking for it!" By midnight that day the swing shift's capture of the huge plant was complete. Two miles away the smaller Fisher Two was also taken over by sit-downers. As the new year began, production of Chevrolets and Buicks, General Motors' bread-and-butter cars, ground to a halt. Soon other GM marques were effected, for the occupation of the two Fisher Body plants in Flint and the one in Cleveland had the potential for halting fully 75 per cent of the company's passenger-car production. The sit-down gave David the weapon to use against Goliath.

Over the next few weeks, strikes would shut down more than a dozen other GM plants. Parts shortages forced many additional plant closings. The total number of idled men would reach 136,000. Yet from first to last, the spotlight remained on Flint. The strike's success or failure—and to the strikers, success meant nothing less than management's recognition of the UAW as exclusive bargaining agent—would be decided at the center of the General Motors empire.

The sit-downers began to organize themselves with military precision. Once all nonstrikers (and all female employees) left, the two plants were barricaded and patrolled. "It was like we were soldiers holding the fort," one of them said.

"It was like war. The guys with me became my buddies." Everyone served a regular daily shift on a committee to manage such functions as defense, food supply, sanitation, and recreation. Discipline was strict: the strike leaders were determined to show the public that this was no rabble-in-arms take-over. News reporters and other observers who toured the seized factories remarked on the organization and on the absence of wild-eyed fanatics. "We're just here protecting our jobs," a Fisher Two striker told *The New York Times*. "We don't aim to keep the plants or try to run them, but we want to see that nobody takes our jobs. . . ." Petty violations of strike committee rules meant extra cleanup or K.P. duty, serious offenses (possession of guns or liquor, the sabotaging of company property) meant expulsion. Round-the-clock dining halls were established in the plant cafeterias, and sleeping quarters were improvised from car seats and bodies.

Keeping the men occupied during their new six-hour "work shifts" was not difficult, but it required more ingenuity to fill the off-duty periods and keep morale high. Defense committees set up production lines for the making of blackjacks and billy clubs. Many hours were devoted to cards, checkers, and dominoes, and there was a steady flow of newspapers and magazines into the plants. UAW lecturers spoke on parliamentary procedures, collective bargaining, and labor history. There were improvised games of volleyball and Ping-pong, and here and there men could be seen roller skating between the long rows of idle machinery. Amateur theatricals, in which enthusiasm and raucous humor were more evident than acting skill, played to cheering, jeering audiences. A showing of Charlie Chaplin's satire on assembly-line mass production, *Modern Times,* was greeted enthusiastically. Those who played banjos, mandolins, or harmonicas put on impromptu concerts and almost everyone took up community singing, sometimes writing their own lyrics; to the tune of "Gallagher and Shean," for example, they belted out:

> Oh! Mr. Sloan! Oh! Mr. Sloan!
> Everyone knows your heart was made of stone.
> But the Union is so strong
> That we'll always carry on.
> Absolutely, Mr. Travis!
> Positively, Mr. Sloan!

The population in Fisher One and Fisher Two varied widely during the six-week-strike. Local 156 set up outside picket lines as an aid to maintaining traffic into and out of the plants, which enabled sit-downers to take leave and visit friends and families. The number of men in Fisher One varied from a high of something over one thousand to a low of ninety, in Fisher Two from upwards of four hundred and fifty to as few as seventeen. The problem for the Fisher Two strike leaders was the large number of married men in their ranks; concern for the welfare of families eroded their staying power as the strike dragged on. Fisher One had a higher percentage of single men of the "hard, reckless type" (in the words of a *New York Times* reporter) and who were better able to endure the strike's pressures. Population fluctuated as hopes for a settlement waxed and waned, and when the number of sit-downers fell dangerously low, the UAW called on militant locals from Detroit and Toledo for reinforcements. The arrival of one such group moved Bud Simons to remark, "I have never seen a bunch of guys that were so ready for blood in my life."

On the whole, however, the sit-downers maintained a remarkably strong sense of community. In a letter to his wife, one of them wrote, "I could of came out wen they went on strike But hunny I just thought I join the union and I look pretty yellow if I dident stick with them. . . ." A growing self-esteem strengthened the workers' commitment. As labor historian Sidney Fine writes, they were "transformed from badge numbers and easily replaceable cogs in an impersonal industrial machine into heroes of American labor." A striker remembered that "it started out kinda ugly because the guys were afraid they put their foot in it and all they was gonna do is lose their jobs. But as time went on, they begin to realize they could win this darn thing, 'cause we had a lot of outside people comin' in showin' their sympathy."

Meanwhile, on the outside, Bob Travis and Roy Reuther set up strike headquarters in the Pengelly Building, a down-at-the heels firetrap in downtown Flint. The place was a beehive, with strikers and volunteer helpers cranking out publicity releases, raising money, mobilizing support, planning strategy. The most immediate problem was food. Dorothy Kraus, wife of the *Flint Auto Worker* editor Henry Kraus, directed a strike kitchen set up in a restaurant near Fisher One that was turned over to the union by its owner. Meals were prepared there three times a day and delivered to the plants in large kettles under heavy union guard. (The menus were the work of Max Gazan, former chef of the Detroit Athletic Club, a favorite haunt of the GM Establishment.) Food stocks were purchased or donated by sympathizers or by Flint merchants pressured to do so by the threat of boycott. As many as two hundred people took part in running the strike kitchen, many of them sitdowners' wives. Wives also formed a Women's Auxiliary and a Women's Emergency Brigade. Kraus's newspaper and the mimeographed *Punch Press*, put out by student volunteers from the University of Michigan, kept the men informed. Cars equipped with loudspeakers allowed instant communication with the sit-downers, and outside picket lines lent moral support.

Despite its espionage network, General Motors was caught flat-footed by the sit-down tactic. At first management tried harassment by sporadically cutting back heat and light to the two plants, but it was feared that any serious attempt to starve out or freeze out the strikers would result in violence—and they were right. Groping for a policy to deal with the crisis, the company discovered that nothing in the Michigan statute books forbade the peaceful occupation of a company's property by its employees. Nor were the trespass laws much help: since the workers had entered the plants at management's "invitation," trespass presented a legal thicket. Nevertheless, GM quickly turned to the courts, petitioning on January 2, 1937, for an injunction to "restrain" the strikers from occupying Fisher One and Fisher Two. County Circuit Court Judge Edward D. Black, an eighty-three-year-old lifelong resident of Flint, granted it the same day.

To its subsequent great embarrassment, the corporation in its haste had failed to do its homework on Judge Black. On January 5 the UAW called a press conference to charge that in issuing the injunction Black was guilty of "unethical conduct," for he owned 3,665 shares of GM stock with a market value of almost $220,000. In the ensuing uproar, the Black injunction became a dead letter.

Round One to the UAW.

Round Two, if General Motors had its way, would find the sit-downers under irresistible pressure from the community. On January 5, GM President Alfred Sloan published an open letter to all employees. "Will a labor organization run the plants of General Motors . . . or will the Management continue to do so?" he asked. "You are being forced out of your jobs by sit-down strikes, by widespread intimidation. . . . You are being told that to bargain collectively you must be a member of a labor organization. . . . Do not be misled. Have no fear that any union or any labor dictator will dominate the plants of General Motors Corporation. No General Motors worker need join any organization to get a job or to keep a job. . . ." A campaign of mass meetings, balloting, and petitions—"I Love My Boss" petitions as strikers derisively tagged them—indicated that by company count four out of five Flint workers wanted to return to their jobs. (Only AC Spark Plug among GM's Flint plants was still operating at full capacity.) The UAW charged that coercion and intimidation produced this outpouring of company loyalty. The truth lay somewhere in between. As Sidney Fine points out, there was in Flint "a large middle group of workers, who, although preferring work to idleness, were uncommitted to either side in the dispute and were awaiting its outcome to determine where their best interests lay."

Two days after Sloan's open letter, a local businessman and former mayor named George E. Boysen announced the formation of the Flint Alliance "for the Security of Our Jobs, Our Homes, and Our Community." Membership was open to all Flint citizens, and within a week Boysen claimed that almost twenty-six thousand had signed up. Evidence that GM sponsored the alliance is sketchy, but it clearly had the company's blessing. The UAW viewed the alliance with concern, seeing it as a possible umbrella group for organizing strikebreakers or triggering violence against the occupied plants.

Several main themes marked this campaign to turn public opinion against the strikers—the oppression of the majority by a militant minority; the presence of "outside agitators" disrupting the General Motors family; and the insistence that the sit-down was a "Red Plot" threatening the capitalist system. This last was one of the most persistent charges. It was pointed out that the seizure of private property was a favorite communist tactic, and that the auto workers' union was honeycombed with Red radicals.

Hindsight has magnified this communist conspiracy theory, for such prominent UAW leaders as Wyndham Mortimer, Bob Travis, and Bud Simons, head of the strike committee in Fisher One, were in fact later involved in various communist or communist front activities. Indeed, the UAW itself, for a decade after 1937, was in constant fratricidal turmoil over the issue of communists within its ranks. It is clear, however, that the Flint sit-down strike was a grass-roots revolt owing no allegiance to communist ideology or conspiracy. The sit-downers were men driven to desperation by oppressive working conditions, men convinced that management's attitude toward labor held no hope for improvement. "So I'm a Red?" a worker summed it up for a reporter. "I suppose it makes me a Red because I don't like making time so hard on these goddamned machines. When I get home I'm so tired I can't sleep with my wife."

Tension continued to build in Flint. On January 11, 1937, the thirteenth day of the strike, it exploded into violence. The incident that triggered it was carefully staged. About noon that day General Motors abruptly cut off heat to the Fisher Two plant, where about one hundred sit-downers were holding the second floor. (Unlike more strongly fortified Fisher One two miles away, Fisher Two's first floor and main gate were controlled by company security men.) It was a cold, raw day, with temperatures around sixteen degrees. During the afternoon an unusual number of police cars was seen in the neighborhood. At 6:00 P.M., when the strikers' evening meal was delivered to the Fisher Two main gate, guards refused to let it through. By 8:30, when Victor Reuther drove up in a union sound car to investigate, he found the cold and hungry strikers "in no pleasant mood." It was decided to take over the main gate to link the sit-downers with the pickets outside.

A squad of strikers, armed with homemade billy clubs, marched up to the company guards blocking the gate and demanded the key. When they were refused, a striker yelled, "Get the hell out of there!" and the guards fled to the plant ladies' room, locking themselves in. The head of the security detail telephoned Flint police headquarters to report that his men had been threatened and "captured." Right on cue, squad cars arrived, carrying some thirty riot-equipped city policemen. The police stormed the plant entrance, smashing windows and firing tear gas into the interior. The strikers fought back with a drumfire of bottles, rocks, nuts and bolts, heavy steel car-door hinges, and cascades of water from the plant's fire hoses. Under this barrage, the attackers withdrew to rearm and await reinforcements. The sit-downers put the lull to good use, tossing door hinges and other stocks of "popular ammunition" to pickets outside and rushing a squad to vantage points on the roof.

Soon the police charged a second time, firing their gas guns and hurling gas grenades through the plant windows and among the pickets outside. But now the defensive firepower was doubled as the pickets joined the battle. Fire hoses sent policemen sprawling. Others were felled by hinges, milk bottles, bricks, and pieces of roof coping. The county sheriff's car was tipped over; as

Workers during the sit-down strike against General Motors. (Library of Congress)

he crawled out, a hinge struck him on the head. Tear gas took a toll among the defenders, who were left choking and vomiting and half-blinded. Finally, drenched and bloodied, sliding on pavement icing over from the fire-hose torrents, the attack force fled once more. Watching the "bulls" scramble away, someone gave the struggle a derisive name that stuck—the Battle of the Running Bulls.

Frustrated and humiliated, the police suddenly stopped, turned on a band of strikers pursuing them, and opened fire with pistols and riot guns loaded with buckshot. Then it was the strikers' turn to retreat, dragging their casualties with them. Thirteen suffered gunshot wounds, a dozen struck by buckshot and one hit seriously in the stomach by a pistol bullet. Eleven of the attackers also were hurt, most suffering from gashed heads but one having been hit in the leg by an errant police bullet. Retreating up a hill out of missile range, the police began sniping at the strikers in the plant, their bullets splattering against the walls and shattering windows. Clouds of acrid tear gas drifted across the icy battlefield, and above the shouting and the shooting could be heard the thundering amplified voice of Victor Reuther in the union sound car, directing the defenses and exhorting the men to stand fast. At last it was clear that the recapture effort had failed. Ambulances arrived to carry off the wounded and the injured. About midnight the sniping ceased.

But the battle had turned the sit-down onto a new course.

Hurrying to Flint from the state capital in Lansing, Michigan Governor Frank Murphy ordered in the National Guard troops and the state police. "It won't happen again," Murphy vowed. "Peace and order will prevail. The people of Flint are not going to be terrorized." By January 13 there were almost thirteen hundred Guardsmen in the city; before the strike ended, the number would rise by another two thousand. Whether General Motors had orchestrated every detail of the attempted recapture of Fisher Two, as the UAW charged, remained a matter of heated debate, but Murphy's action ensured that police violence would not "settle" the sit-down.

Organized labor had reason to fear National Guard and state police forces, which in the past had often been used to break strikes. In this instance, however, the union cheered their arrival, for it trusted the man who sent them. Indeed, the timing of the sit-down had been pegged to Democrat Murphy's taking office on January 1, 1937. He had run for governor with strong labor support. "I am heart and soul in the labor movement," he had declared during the campaign. As Wyndham Mortimer later said, "We felt that while he may or may not have been on our side, he at least would not be against us."

It was an accurate assessment. While Murphy disapproved of the sit-down tactic as an invasion of property rights, he strongly approved of the right to organize. Above all, he was determined to defuse the explosive atmosphere in Flint and get the two parties to the bargaining table. At first it appeared he would be quickly and brilliantly successful. On January 15, just four days after the Battle of the Running Bulls, Murphy announced a truce; the union agreed to evacuate Fisher One and Fisher Two, and GM agreed not to resume production while bargaining "in good faith." Then a report leaked out that GM had invited the Flint Alliance, which claimed to speak for the "greatest majority" of the city's idled workers, to attend the talks as a third party. Strike leaders saw this as fatal to their goal of winning exclusive UAW recognition; crying double-cross, they renounced the truce.

As the stalemate continued and positions hardened, new figures joined Frank Murphy in the limelight. On the GM side, Executive Vice President William Knudsen, a bluff, rough-and-ready production genius less concerned with how the strike was settled than when, was joined by two tougher-minded negotiators, Du Pont—trained financial expert Donaldson Brown and company attorney John T. Smith. On the union side, UAW President Homer Martin, an evangelical speaker but a poor negotiator, was eclipsed when the best-known figure in American labor strode onto the scene. John L. Lewis, head of the CIO, was determined to make the Flint sit-down the opening wedge in his crusade for industrial unionism. Supreme orator ("The economic royalists of General Motors—the Du Ponts and Sloans and others—" he thundered, ". . . have their fangs in labor") and a master press agent ("Seeing John Lewis," said journalist Heywood Broun, "is about as easy as seeing the Washington Monument"), Lewis was a figure to reckon with.

Just how potent a publicist he could be was evident when the spotlight shifted from Flint to Washington. The Roosevelt administration, led by Secretary of Labor Frances Perkins, tried to get the strike off dead center by bringing together Lewis and Alfred Sloan, whom Miss Perkins described as "the real principals." For all his brilliance as an administrator, the GM president was saddled with a colorless personality and did not relish taking on the theatrical Lewis. Furthermore, the intense loathing he felt for the New Deal made any dealings with the administration difficult for him. In the end he called off the talks, angering both the President and Miss Perkins. For Sloan the sticking point was bargaining with "a group that holds our plants for ransom without regard to law or justice." Lewis announced to the nation that the GM high command had "run away" to New York "to consult with their allies [a barb at the GM—Du Pont connection] to determine how far they can go in their organized defiance of labor and the law." GM gained no friends in the exchange.

General Motors, in fact, was not doing as well mustering support as might have been expected of the world's largest corporation. Its disdain for the Wagner Act, the fiasco of the Black injunction, and the violence of the Battle of the Running Bulls did little for its corporate image. Despite strong and widespread public concern over the sit-down's threat to cherished property rights, the company's position won only a fifty-three to forty-seven edge in a Gallup poll published on January 31; apparently there was considerable sympathy for the union's stated—and lawful—goal of organizing and bargaining collectively without management interference. *Business Week* analyzed the public's view as "it's 'not right' for the strikers to stay in or for the company to throw them out."

There is little doubt that the union would have done less well on any poll taken in Flint. The city's blue-collar workers were suffering intensely now. By January 20, a full 88 per cent of the city's GM work force was unemployed. The percentage on the relief rolls was greater than it had been during the depths of the Depression. General Motors also was suffering: its January output was just 60,000 cars, instead of a projected figure of 224,000. Yet neither side would budge. Tension began again to build, fueled by violent incidents at GM plants in Anderson, Indiana, on January 25 and in Saginaw, Michigan, two days later. Then two events occurred that would push the sit-down to its climax.

On January 28 General Motors turned once more to the courts, applying for a second injunction to compel the strikers to leave. This time the company first checked out the circuit court judge, Paul V. Gadola, to be sure he was clean. Flint's strike leaders, meanwhile, planned a move of their own, one considerably more dramatic.

To regain the initiative and to demonstrate to General Motors that none of its properties was safe from seizure by sit-down, Travis, Roy Reuther, and other UAW strategists plotted the capture of Chevrolet Four, the Flint factory that produced all Chevrolet engines. Their plan had to be a daring one, for the engine plant was heavily guarded by GM police. Within hearing of auto workers whom their counterintelligence had identified as company spies, the strike leaders "secretly" revealed their next target to be a bearings plant, Chevrolet Nine. Company security snapped up the bait. On February 1, when the diversionary attempt was made on Chevrolet Nine, it was met by every Chevrolet guard the company could muster. After tear gas and wild, club-swinging melees, the unionists were driven out in apparent defeat. While the battle was raging inside Chevrolet Nine, however, three hundred yards away other strikers had swept through unguarded Chevrolet Four and secured the huge plant. "We have the key plant of the GM. . . ," one of the sit-downers would write to his wife. "We shure done a thing that GM said never could be done. . . ." He was right; the brilliantly executed capture of Chevrolet Four was the turning point.

Events now swiftly combined to bring the United Automobile Workers and General Motors to the negotiating table. On February 2 Judge Gadola issued a sweeping injunction that called for evacuation of the Flint Fisher Body plants within twenty-four hours, and the imposition of a $15,000,000 fine if the UAW did not comply. Although there was nothing like that sum to collect from the union treasury—"If the judge can get fifteen million bucks from us, he's welcome to it," a striker scoffed—the injunction did pressure the UAW to bargain. It also pressured Governor Murphy to find a quick strike-ending formula; as chief executive of the state of Michigan, he was obliged to decide how and when to enforce the injunction and uphold the law. As for GM, a massive demonstration of support by unionists outside Fisher One on February 3 seemed proof enough that any attempt to drive out the sit-downers would produce certain bloodshed and probable destruction of three of its most important plants. Reluctantly, like "a skittish virgin" in *Fortune's* irreverent phrase, the company surrendered to collective bargaining.

The talks were held in Detroit. On the GM side were Knudsen, Donaldson Brown, and John T. Smith. John L. Lewis headed the union delegation, seconded by CIO counsel Lee Pressman and UAW President Homer Martin. (The bumbling Martin was soon dispatched on a tour of faraway union locals to get him out of the way.) Murphy acted as chief negotiator, jumping back and forth between the parties "like a jack rabbit," seeking leverage for a settlement. Machinery was agreed to for later bargaining on such specific issues as wages and working conditions, and the union agreed to give up the plants and return to work while those issues were hammered out. GM agreed to take the sit-downers back without penalty or prejudice. The stiffest battle was fought over GM's recognition of the UAW as exclusive bargaining agent.

Hanging threateningly over the talks was the Gadola injunction. The very mention of using the National Guard to enforce the injunction provoked Lewis to one of his characteristic oratorical flights. According to his later recollection (perhaps embellished), he announced to Murphy: "Tomorrow morning, I shall personally enter General Motors plant Chevrolet Number Four. I shall order the men to disregard your order, to stand fast. I shall then walk up to the largest window in the plant, open it, divest myself of my outer raiment, remove my shirt, and bare my bosom. Then when you order your troops to fire, mine will be the first breast those bullets will strike!" In fact, the governor never had any notion of carrying out Judge Gadola's ruling with National Guard arms: "I'm not going down in history as 'Bloody Murphy'!" He did hint, however, at sealing off the captured plants with Guardsmen to prevent food deliveries unless the union made concessions. GM was pushed into concessions of its own by a painful economic fact. In the first ten days of February, the nation's largest auto maker produced exactly 151 cars.

Finally, at 2:35 on the morning of February 11, after sixteen grueling hours of final negotiating, the forty-four-day Flint sit-down strike came to an end. The agreement applied only to the seventeen plants that had gone out on strike, but they were GM's most important plants. As a face-saving gesture, the company did not have to state categorically that it was recognizing the union. But in fact it was: the UAW had six months to sign up auto workers before a representational election, during which time management could not interfere or deal with any other workers' body. "Well, Mr. Lewis, "GM negotiator Smith said, "you beat us, but I'm not going to forget it." Production man Knudsen was not one to hold grudges. "Let us have peace and make automobiles," he proclaimed.

Late on the afternoon of February 11 the sit-downers came out. Carrying American flags, surrounded by throngs of cheering, horn-tooting supporters, the men of Fisher One marched the two miles across town to collect their compatriots in Fisher Two and Chevrolet Four. Then, thousands strong, they held a spectacular torchlight parade through downtown Flint. As they tramped along, they sang what had become their anthem:

Solidarity forever!
Solidarity forever!
Solidarity forever!
For the Union makes us strong!

They had every reason to sing and celebrate; they had won a major victory. UAW locals throughout the auto industry were promptly flooded with workers clamoring to sign up; just eight months after the sit-down settlement, the UAW could count nearly four hundred thousand dues-paying members, a five-fold increase. It easily won the representational elections in plants throughout the GM empire. Independents—Packard, Studebaker, Hudson— soon recognized the union, as did leading parts makers. In April, 1937, after a sit-down, Chrysler also succumbed. Ford held out the longest, but in 1941 it too acknowledged the UAW as exclusive bargaining agent. An important factor in all this was the Supreme Court decision, in April, 1937, upholding the Wagner Act. Unionization without interference by management was confirmed as the law of the land.

The United Automobile Workers failed to handle its success gracefully, however. From the moment of its birth, the union's high command had been rent with problems; its most decisive leaders, like those of Flint Local 156, came from the bottom. Rifts at the top were papered over during the sit-down by the overriding need for a united front, but with victory came chaos. Not until after World War II would the UAW, under the strong hand of Walter Reuther, finally put its house in order, purge itself of communists, and reach stable maturity. As for the CIO, the Flint victory, as John L. Lewis predicted, was industrial unionism's foot in the door. Beginning with Big Steel in March, 1937, the CIO successfully organized one basic industry after another. Union membership in the United States spurted 156 per cent between 1936 and 1941, most of it CIO gains.

The Flint sit-down inspired a rash of imitators. In the early months of 1937 workers of every stripe, from garbage men and dogcatchers to rug weavers and pie bakers, tried the tactic. Public irritation mounted swiftly. Many Americans had accepted the UAW's argument that the sit-down was the sole weapon it possessed to force intransigent General Motors to obey the law and permit union organizing and collective bargaining. Such an argument lost force after the Supreme Court upheld the Wagner Act; now, with both government and law behind it, organized labor was seen as achieving parity with management. Increasingly, the sit-down was condemned as an irresponsible act, and by 1939, when the Supreme Court outlawed the practice as a violation of property rights, it had long since gone out of vogue.

Victory in the Flint sit-down by no means ended the discontents of the auto worker. Yet now, for the first time, he could envision himself as something more than simply an insignificant part of a great impersonal machine; as "Solidarity" phrased it, the union had made him strong. "Even if we got not one damn thing out of it other than that," a Fisher Body worker said, "we at least had a right to open our mouths without fear."

Part II

Politics during America's Second Century

As we enter the latter stages of the twentieth century, one of the major issues confronting us is the role of government in our lives. At almost every turn, whether it be law enforcement, educational services, or income tax returns, we seem to encounter some form of governmental involvement. To understand how and why this has happened, it is necessary to discuss and interpret the political forces which have shaped and are shaping the United States.

Of course, the basic political foundations of the nation were laid during the pre-Civil War era. However, the movement toward Big Government is largely a product of the last century. Big Government is neither the result of some well-designed conspiracy nor an accident. Rather, it is the result of a series of responses to pressing political issues. That these responses became more and more national in scope only reflects the increasing centralization of modern society. Almost every identifiable interest group from businessmen to minority groups has turned to the federal government for help, often as protection against actions by other elements in society.

How and why politicians, political parties, and the government as an institution respond, or fail to respond, to the varied political pressures brought to bear on the issues is the common theme which cuts across the articles included in this section. When discussing political developments, whether it be Populists, Progressives, New Dealers and their opponents, the influence of the media, political corruption, or the presidency of Jimmy Carter, placing the people, events, and issues in proper perspective is essential. The following essays help us to accomplish that task.

6

Was Bryan a Reformer?

by John A. Garraty

Once the Reconstruction era ended, national politics entered twenty years of relative calm. Issues such as civil service, currency reform, and tariff rates were serious matters, but the average citizen likely had trouble distinguishing party positions on them. Republicans and Democrats each could boast of victories during the period, but it seemed to make little difference which party was in power. The heroes of that era were people like Andrew Carnegie, John D. Rockefeller, *et. al.,* who found their fame (and fortune, to be sure) in the business world. Presidents seemed obscure by comparison—and remain so today!

However, the late nineteenth century was not devoid of political excitement, even if it did come from an unusual place. For out on America's plains, farmers had begun to organize and press for political responses to their very real grievances. That they were deserving of being heard is beyond question, for at that time most Americans still lived in rural areas.

John A. Garraty, Professor of History at Columbia University, has written extensively about U.S. history, including a popular survey text as well as such monographs as *Unemployment in History* and *The New Commonwealth.* In the following essay, he describes the growing agrarian protest movement and analyzes the character of its champion in 1896, William Jennings Bryan.

"The President of the United States may be an ass," wrote H. L. Mencken during the reign of Calvin Coolidge, "but he at least doesn't believe that the earth is square, and that witches should be put to death, and that Jonah swallowed the whale." The man to whom the vitriolic Mencken was comparing President Coolidge was William Jennings Bryan of Nebraska, one of the dominant figures in the Progressive movement. According to Mencken, Bryan was a "peasant," a "zany without sense or dignity," a "poor clod," and, in addition, an utter fraud. "If the fellow was sincere, then so was P. T. Barnum," he sneered.

It was certainly easy enough, and tempting, for sophisticates to come to the conclusion that Bryan was a buffoon and a fake. His undignified association in his declining years with the promotion of Florida real estate and his naïve and bigoted religious views, so pitilessly exposed by Clarence Darrow during the famous "Monkey Trial" in Dayton, Tennessee, lent substance to the Mencken view of his character. So did Bryan's smug refusal, while Secretary of State under Woodrow Wilson, to serve alcoholic beverages at Department receptions and dinners because of his personal disapproval of drinking, and his objection to the appointment of ex-President Charles W.

Eliot of Harvard as Ambassador to China on the ground that Eliot was a Unitarian, and therefore not a real Christian. "The new Chinese civilization," said Bryan, "was founded upon the Christian movement." Eliot's appointment might undermine the work of generations of pious missionaries, he implied. Bryan's unabashed partisanship—he talked frankly after Wilson's election of filling government positions with "deserving Democrats"—did not seem to jibe with his pretensions as a reformer. And his oratorical style, magnificent but generally more emotional than logical, was disappointing to thinking people. John Hay called him a "Baby Demosthenes" and David Houston, one of his colleagues in Wilson's Cabinet, stated that "one could drive a prairie schooner through any part of his argument and never scrape against a fact." Being largely a creature of impulse, Bryan was, Houston added, "constantly on the alert to get something which has been represented to him as a fact to support or sustain his impulses."

But these flaws and blind spots were not fundamental weaknesses; they should never be allowed to overshadow Bryan's long years of devoted service to the cause of reform. If there were large areas about which he knew almost nothing, there were others where he was alert, sensible, and well-informed; certainly he was not a stupid man, nor was he easily duped or misled. Although a professional politician, as his remark about "deserving Democrats" makes clear, he was utterly honest personally and devoted to the cause of the people, as he understood it.

He was perfectly attuned to the needs and aspirations of rural America. In the early nineties he was in the forefront of the fight against high tariffs on manufactured goods. Later in the decade he battled for currency reform. At the turn of the century he was leading the assault against imperialism. During Theodore Roosevelt's primacy he was often far ahead of the intrepid Teddy, advocating a federal income tax, the eight-hour day, the control of monopoly and the strict regulation of public utilities, woman suffrage, and a large number of other startling innovations. Under Wilson he played a major part in marshaling support in Congress for the Federal Reserve Act and other New Freedom measures. Whatever his limitations, his faults, or his motives, few public men of his era left records as consistently "progressive" as Bryan's.

For years he led the Democratic party without the advantage of holding office. Three times he was a presidential candidate; although never elected, he commanded the unswerving loyalty of millions of his fellow citizens for nearly thirty years. He depended more on his intuition than on careful analysis in forming his opinions, but his intuition was usually sound; he was more a man of heart than of brain, but his heart was great.

Bryan was known as the Great Commoner, and the title was apt. He was a man of the people in origin and by instinct. He was typical of his age in rendering great respect to public opinion, whether it was informed or not. To Bryan the voice of the people was truly the voice of God. "I don't know anything about free silver," he announced while running for Congress early in the nineties. "The people of Nebraska are for free silver and I am for free silver. I will look up the arguments later." (It should be added that he did indeed "look up the arguments later." Less than a year after making this promise he arose in the House to deliver without notes a brilliant three-hour speech on the money question, a speech of great emotional power, but also fact-laden, sensible, and full of shrewd political arguments. When he sat down, the cheers rang out from both sides of the aisle.)

Bryan was born in Salem, Illinois, in 1860, a child of the great Middle West. Growing up in the heart of the valley of democracy, he absorbed its spirit and its sense of protest from his earliest years. After being graduated from Illinois College in 1881, he studied law in Chicago and for a time practiced his profession in Jacksonville, Illinois. But in 1887, stimulated by a talk with a law-school classmate from that city, he moved west to Lincoln, Nebraska. He quickly made his way in this new locale. Within a year he was active in the local Democratic organization, and in 1890, a month before his thirtieth birthday, he won his party's nomination for congressman.

Nebraska was traditionally a Republican state, its loyalty to the party of Lincoln forged in the heat of the Civil War. But by 1890 tradition was rapidly losing its hold on voters all over the Middle West. For the farmers of the American heartland were in deep trouble, and the Republican party seemed unwilling to do much to help them.

Tumultuous social and economic changes shaped the nation in the years after Appomattox. Within a single generation the United States was transformed from what was essentially a land of farmers into a modern industrial society, and in the process the Middle West was caught in a relentless economic vise. During the flush times of the sixties, when the Union Army was buying enormous amounts of food and fodder, and foreign demand was unusually high, the farmers of the region had gone into debt in order to buy more land and machinery. In the seventies and eighties, however, agricultural prices, especially those of such major staple crops as wheat and cotton, fell steeply. Wheat, which had sold as high as $2.50 a bushel in wartime, was down to fifty cents by the early nineties.

The impact of this economic decline was intensified by the changing social status of the farmer. Agriculture was losing its predominant place in American life. In the days of the Founding Fathers, about ninety per cent of the population was engaged in working the soil, and the farmer was everywhere portrayed as the symbol of American self-reliance and civic virtue. "Those who labor in the earth," Jefferson said, "are the chosen people of God." But as the factory began to outstrip the farm, the farmer lost much of his standing. While the old symbol remained—it was especially in evidence around election time—a new and disturbing image of the farmer as a hick, a rube, a hayseed— a comic mixture of cocky ignorance, shrewd self-interest, and monumental provincialism—began to challenge it.

Naturally the farmers resented their loss of both income and prestige, but there was little they could do about either. Price declines were largely a response to worldwide overproduction, resulting from improvements in transportation and the opening up of new farmlands in Australia, Argentina, Canada, Russia, and elsewhere. Nor did the farmers, who desired manufactured goods as much as everyone else, really want to reverse the trend that was making them a minority group in a great industrial nation. But as they cast about for some way out of their plight, they were profoundly disturbed by certain results of the new development which did seem amenable to reform.

Industrial growth meant the mushrooming of great cities. These gave birth to noxious slums where every kind of vice flourished, where corrupt political organizations like the venal Tweed Ring in New York were forged, and where radical political concepts like socialism and anarchism sought to undermine "the American way of life." In the words of Jefferson, the farmers' hero, cities were "ulcers on the body politic."

Giant industries also attracted hordes of immigrants; these seemed to threaten the Middle West both by their mere numbers and by their "un-American" customs and points of view. Could the American melting pot absorb such strange ingredients without losing much of its own character?

Furthermore, to the citizens of Nebraska and other agricultural states, the new industrial barons appeared bent on making vassals of every farmer in America. The evidence seemed overwhelming: Huge impersonal corporations had neither souls nor consciences; profit was their god, materialism their only creed. The "interests," a tiny group of powerful tycoons in great eastern centers like Boston, New York, and Philadelphia, were out to enslave the rest of the country. Farmers worked and sweated only to see the "interests" make off with most of the fruit of their toil. Too many useless middlemen grew fat off the mere "handling" of wheat and cotton. Monopolistic railroads overcharged for carrying crops to market, unscrupulous operators of grain elevators falsely downgraded prime crops and charged exorbitant fees. Cynical speculators drove the price of staples up and down, sometimes making and losing millions in a matter of minutes, without the slightest regard for the effect of their operations on the producers whose sweat made their deadly game possible.

Conspiring with bankers and mortgage holders, all these groups combined to dictate the federal government's money policy. Population and production were surging forward; more money was needed simply to keep up with economic growth. Yet the government was deliberately cutting down on the amount of money in circulation by retiring Civil War greenbacks. On debt-ridden farmers plagued by overproduction, the effect of this deflation was catastrophic. Or so it seemed from the perspective of rural America.

While undoubtedly exaggerated, this indictment of the "interests" was taken as gospel throughout large sectors of the South and West. As a result, demands for "reform" quickly arose. The leading reformers were for the most part sincere, but few of them were entirely altruistic and many were decidedly eccentric. Participating in the movement for a variety of motives but without coming to grips with the main problem of American agriculture—overproduction—were coarse demagogues like Senator "Pitchford Ben" Tillman of South Carolina, and unwashed characters like the wise-cracking congressman from Kansas, "Sockless Jerry" Simpson. There were professional orators like the angry Mary Ellen Lease (her detractors called her "Mary Yellin' "), and homespun economic theorists like "Coin" Harvey and "General" Jacob Coxey, who believed so strongly in paper money that he named his son Legal Tender. The excesses of such people frightened off many Americans who might otherwise have lent a sympathetic ear to the farmers' complaints; others who might have been friendly observed the antics of the reformers with contempt and wrote off the whole movement as a joke.

Since neither of the major parties espoused the farmers' cause wholeheartedly, much of the protest found its way into various third-party organizations. At first, discontented elements concentrated on opposing the government's policy of retiring the paper money put in circulation during the Civil War. To save these greenbacks from extinction a Greenback (later Greenback-Labor) party sprang up. In 1878 its candidates polled a million votes, but decline followed as currency reformers turned to other methods of inflation.

Meanwhile the Patrons of Husbandry, better known as the Grange, originally a social organization for farm families, had begun to agitate in local politics against the middlemen who were draining off such a large percentage of the farmers' profits. In the seventies the Grangers became a power in the Middle West; in state after state they obtained the passage of laws setting maximum rates for railroads and prohibiting various forms of discrimination. The operations of grain elevators were also subjected to state regulation by "Granger Laws" in states such as Illinois, Iowa, Wisconsin, and Minnesota. The Grange abandoned political activity in the eighties, but other farm organizations quickly took its place. These coalesced first into the Northern Alliance and the Southern Alliance, and around 1890 the two Alliances joined with one another to become the Populist party.

Although William Jennings Bryan was a Democrat, he had grown up amid the agitations of the Granger movement. His father had even run for Congress in the seventies with Greenback party support. The aspirations and the general point of view of the midwestern farmers were young Bryan's own. Public men, he admitted late in life to the journalist Mark Sullivan, are "the creatures of their age. . . . I lived in the very center of the country out of which the reforms grew, and was quite naturally drawn to the people's side."

And they to his, one must add. Discontented farmers in his district were on the lookout for men who understood them and their problems. In 1888 the Republicans had carried the seat by 3,000 votes; now, in 1890, Bryan swept in with a lead of 6,713.

Bryan made an excellent record in his first Congress. He was a hard-working member, studying the technicalities of the tariff question for months before making his first important speech. But he saw that the tariff was rapidly being replaced by the money question as the crucial issue of the day. When he yielded the floor after completing his tariff speech, he collared a young Texas congressman named Joseph W. Bailey, who posed as a financial expert. Sitting on a sofa in the rear of the House chamber, he quizzed Bailey about the problem of falling prices. Bailey told him the tariff had little or no effect on the plight of the farmer; the whole difficulty arose from "an appreciation in value of gold." Interested, Bryan demanded a list of books on the subject and was soon deep in a study of the money question.

To a man like Bryan, studying the money question meant searching for some means of checking the deflationary trend that was so injurious to his farmer constituents. He quickly discovered that most farm-belt financial authorities felt this could best be done by providing the free coinage of silver. In 1873 the United States had gone on the gold standard, which meant that only gold was accepted for coinage at the mint. By going back to bimetallism, the amount of bullion being coined would be increased, and if the favorable ratio of sixteen to one between silver and gold were established, the production of silver for coinage would be greatly stimulated.

To press for the free coinage of silver at a ratio of sixteen to one with gold seemed less radical or dangerous than to demand direct inflation of the currency through the printing of greenbacks. Silver, after all, was a precious metal; coining it could not possibly lead to the sort of "runaway" inflation that had helped ruin the South during the Civil War. Debtors and other friends of inflation could also count on the powerful support of silver-mine interests. The free-coinage issue thus had a powerful political appeal. Despite the opposition of most conservative businessmen, the silverites were able, in 1878 and again in 1890, to obtain legislation providing for the coinage of *some* silver, although not enough to check the downward trend of prices.

Within a month after his tariff speech Bryan was calling for free coinage, and he stressed the issue in his successful campaign for reelection in 1892. But the new President, Democrat Grover Cleveland, was an ardent gold-standard man, and when a severe depression struck the country early in 1893, he demanded that the Silver Purchase Act of 1890, which had raised the specter of inflation in the minds of many businessmen, be repealed by Congress at once. In this way he committed his party to the resumption of the single gold standard.

Bryan refused to go along with this policy. Threatening to "serve my country and my God under some other name" than "Democrat" unless the Administration changed its mind, he resisted the repeal of the silver act in a brilliant extemporaneous speech. Cleveland carried the day for repeal, but Bryan emerged as a potential leader of the silver wing of the Democrats.

In 1894 he sought a wider influence by running for the United States Senate. In those days senators were still chosen by the state legislatures; to be elected Bryan would need the support of Nebraska's Populists as well as of his own party. He worked hard for fusion, but Populist support was not forthcoming. Though the Democrats backed Populist candidate Silas A. Holcomb for the governorship, the Populists refused to reciprocate and ran their own man for the Senate seat. The Republican candidate therefore won easily.

At this stage the Populists were trying hard to become a truly national party. Their program, besides demanding the free coinage of silver and various land reforms desired by farmers, called for government ownership of railroads, a graduated income tax, the direct election of U.S. senators, the eight-hour day, and a number of additional reforms designed to appeal to eastern workingmen and other dissatisfied groups. As early as 1892 their presidential candidate, James B. Weaver, had polled over a million votes; in 1894 the party won six seats in the Senate and seven in the House of Representatives. At least in Nebraska, the Populists were not yet ready to merge with the "conservative" Democratic organization.

Defeat for the Senate did not harm Bryan politically. He was still in his early thirties; to one so young, merely having run for the Senate brought considerable prestige. Also, he had conducted an intelligent and forceful campaign. Even so it was a defeat, certainly not calculated to lead him to the remarkable decision that he made after the Nebraska legislature had turned him down. This decision was to seek nomination for the Presidency of the United States itself!

The young man's "superlative self-assurance" (one might call it effrontery but for the fact that his daring plan succeeded) staggers the imagination. Many men within his party were far better known than he, and his state, Nebraska, was without major influence in Democratic affairs. With Cleveland and the national organization dead-set against free coinage and other inflationary schemes, Bryan's chances of capturing the nomination seemed infinitesimal. But if bold, his action was by no means foolish. Democratic voters were becoming more and more restive under Cleveland's conservative leadership. At least in Bryan's part of the nation, many thoughtful members of the party were beginning to feel that they must look in new directions and find new leaders if they were not to be replaced by the Populists as the country's second major party. Recognizing this situation before most politicians did, Bryan proceeded to act upon his insight with determination and dispatch.

First of all, he set out to make himself known beyond his own locality. Accepting the editorship of the Omaha *World-Herald* at a tiny salary in order to obtain a forum, he turned out a stream of editorials on the silver question, which he sent to influential politicians all over the country. He toured the South and West with his message, speaking everywhere and under all sorts of conditions: to close-packed, cheering throngs and to tiny groups of quiet listeners. His argument was simple but forceful, his oratory magnetic and compelling. Always he made sure to meet local leaders and to subject them to his genial smile, his youthful vigor, his charm, his sincerity. He did not push himself forward; indeed, he claimed to be ready to support any honest man whose program was sound. But he lost no chance to point out to all concerned his own availability. "I don't suppose your delegation is committed to any candidate," he wrote to a prominent Colorado Democrat in April of 1896. "Our delegation may present my name." When the Democratic convention finally met in Chicago, Bryan believed that he was known personally to more of the delegates than any other candidate.

Few delegates took his campaign seriously, however. At the convention, one senator asked Bryan who he thought would win out. Bryan replied characteristically that he believed he himself "had as good a chance to be nominated as anyone," and proceeded to tick off the sources of his strength: Nebraska, "half of the Indian Territory, . . ." but before Bryan could mention his other backers the senator lost interest and walked off with some of his cronies. The candidate, amiable and serene, took no offense. A majority of the delegates favored his position on silver. No one had a clear lead in the race. All he needed was a chance to plead his case.

The opportunity—Bryan called it an "unexpected stroke of luck," although he planned for it brilliantly—came when he was asked to close the debate on the platform's silver plank. When he came forward to address the jam-packed mob in the Chicago auditorium he was tense, but there was a smile on his face, and to observers he seemed the picture of calm self-confidence. He began quietly, but his voice resounded in the farthest corners of the great hall and commanded the attention of every delegate. He was conscious of his own humble position, he told the throng, but he was "clad in the armor of a righteous cause" and this entitled him to speak. As he went on, his tension evaporated and his voice rose. When he recounted the recent history of the struggle between the forces of gold and silver, the audience responded eagerly. "At the close of a sentence," he wrote later, "it would rise and shout, and when I began upon another sentence, the room was still as a church."

He spoke for silver as against gold, for the West over the East, for "the hardy pioneers who have braved all the dangers of the wilderness" as against "the few financial magnates who, in a back room, corner the money of the world."

> We have petitioned, and our petitions have been scorned; we have entreated, and our entreaties have been disregarded; we have begged, and they have mocked when our calamity came. We beg no longer; we entreat no more; we petition no more. *We defy them!*

The crowd thundered its agreement. Bryan proceeded. One after another he met the arguments of the party's Cleveland wing head on. Free silver would disturb the business interests? "Gold bugs" were defining the term too narrowly. Remember that wage earners, cross-roads merchants, and farmers were also businessmen. The cities favored the gold standard? Their prosperity really depended upon the prosperity of the great agricultural regions of the land, which favored bimetallism. "Burn down your cities and leave our farms," he said, "and your cities will spring up again as if by magic; but destroy our farms and the grass will grow in the streets of every city in the country."

Now Bryan was absolute master of the delegates. "I thought of a choir," he recalled afterward, "as I noted how instantaneously and in unison they responded to each point made." The crowd cheered because he was reflecting its sentiments, but also because it recognized, suddenly, its leader—handsome, confident, righteously indignant, yet also calm, restrained, and ready for responsibility. His mission accomplished, it was time to close, and Bryan had saved a marvelous figure of speech, tested in many an earlier oration, for his climax. "You shall not press down upon the brow of labor this crown of thorns," he warned, bringing his hands down suggestively to his temples; "you shall not crucify mankind upon a cross of gold." Dramatically he extended his arms to the side, the very figure of the crucified Christ.

Amid the hysterical demonstration that followed, it was clear that Bryan had accomplished his miracle. The next day, July 9, he was nominated for the Presidency on the fifth ballot.

The issue was clear-cut, for the Republicans had already declared for the gold standard and nominated the handsome, genial, and thoroughly conservative William McKinley. As a result, the Populists were under great pressure to go along with Bryan. While the Democrats had not adopted all the radical Populist demands, their platform contained a number of liberal planks in addition to that on free silver, including one calling for a federal income tax and another for stiffer controls of the railroad network. For the Populists to insist on nominating a third candidate would simply insure the election of the "gold bug" McKinley. Not every important Populist favored fusion; some were ready to concede defeat in 1896 and build their party for the future on broadly radical lines. "The Democratic idea of fusion," said Tom Watson of Georgia angrily, is "that we play Jonah while they play whale." But the rich scent of victory in the air was too much for the majority to resist. "I care not for party names," said "Sockless Jerry" Simpson bluntly; "it is the substance we are after, and we have it in William J. Bryan." Indeed, Bryan's friendly association with the Populists in earlier campaigns and his essentially Populistic views on most questions made it difficult for the party to oppose him. "We put him to school," one anti-Bryan Populist later remarked, "and he wound up by stealing the school-books." In any case, the Populist convention endorsed him; thus the silver forces united to do battle with the Republicans.

Both Bryan and McKinley men realized at once that this was to be a close and crucial contest. Seldom have the two great parties divided so clearly on fundamental issues; a showdown was inevitable; a major turning point in American history had been reached. Silver against gold was but the surface manifestation of the struggle. City against countryside, industry against agriculture, East against South and West, the nineteenth century against the twentieth—these were the real contestants in 1896.

After Bryan's nomination McKinley's manager, Mark Hanna, abandoned plans for a vacation cruise in New England waters and plunged into the work of the campaign. The situation was "alarming," he told McKinley. A "communistic spirit" was abroad, business was "all going to pieces." A mighty effort was called for. Hanna raised huge sums by "assessing" the great bankers, oil refiners, insurance men, and meat packers, using the threat of impending business chaos and wild inflation to loosen the purse strings of the tycoons. While McKinley, "the advance agent of prosperity," conducted a dignified and carefully organized campaign from his front porch in Canton, Ohio, 1,400 paid speakers beat the bushes for votes in every doubtful district. The Republican campaign committee distributed more than 120,000,000 pieces of literature printed in ten languages to carry its message to the voters. Boiler-plate editorials and other releases were sent free to hundreds of small-town newspapers. Hanna, Theodore Roosevelt said, "has advertised McKinley as if he were a patent medicine!" The Republican organization reached a peak of efficiency and thoroughness never before approached in a political contest; the campaign marked a methodological revolution that has profoundly affected every presidential contest since.

Bryan had little money, and no organization genius like Hanna to direct his drive. But he too effected a revolution that has left its mark on modern campaigning. McKinley's front porch technique was novel only in the huge number of visiting delegations that Hanna paraded across his man's lawn and the exaggerated care that the candidate took to avoid saying anything impolitic. It had always been considered undignified for a presidential nominee to go out and hunt for votes on his own. Bryan cast off this essentially hypocritical tradition at the very start. He realized that the concerted power of business and the press were aligned against him, and that his own greatest assets were his magnificent ability as a political orator and his personal sincerity and charm. His opponent could afford to sit tight; *he* must seek out the people everywhere if they were to receive his message. Between summer and November he traveled a precedent-shattering 18,000 miles, making more than 600 speeches and addressing directly an estimated 5,000,000 Americans. His secretary estimated that he uttered between 60,000 and 100,000 words every day during the campaign.

On the stump he was supurb. Without straining his voice he could make himself heard to a restless open-air throng numbered in the tens of thousands. He was equally effective at the whistle stops, outlining his case from the rear platform of his train while a handful of country people gazed earnestly upward from the roadbed. He was unfailingly pleasant and unpretentious. At one stop, while he was shaving in his compartment, a small group outside the train began clamoring for a glimpse of him. Flinging open the window and beaming through the lather, he cheerfully shook hands with each of these admirers. Neither he nor they, according to the recorder of this incident, saw anything unusual or undignified in the performance. Thousands of well-wishers sent him good luck charms and messages of encouragement. "If the people who have given me rabbits' feet in this campaign will vote for me, there is no possible doubt of my election," he said in one speech. It was because of this simple friendliness that he became known as "the Great Commoner."

Bryan was also unfailingly interesting. Even his most unsympathetic biographer admits that he spoke so well that at every stop the baggagemen from the campaign train would run back to listen to his talk—and this despite a schedule that called for as many as thirty speeches a day.

Such a campaign is an effective means of projecting an image of a candidate and his general point of view. It is not well suited for the making of complicated arguments and finely drawn distinctions; for that the McKinley approach was far superior. Wisely, for it was clearly the issue uppermost in the minds of most voters, Bryan hammered repeatedly at the currency question. He did not avoid talking about other matters: he attacked the railroads and the great business monopolists and the "tyranny" of the eastern bankers. He deplored the use of militia in labor disputes and of the injunction as a means of breaking strikes. He spoke in favor of income taxes, higher wages, and relief for hard-pressed mortgagees. But the silver issue was symbolic, and the Democratic position sound. There *was* a currency shortage; deflation *was* injuring millions of debtors and pouring a rich unearned increment into the pockets of bondholders. To say, as Henry Demarest Lloyd did at the time and as many liberal historians have since, that Bryan made free silver the "cowbird" of the reform movement, pushing out all other issues from the reform nest and thus destroying them, is an exaggeration and a distortion. All effective politicians stick to a small number of simple issues while on the stump; otherwise, in the hectic conflict of a hot campaign, they project no message at all. There is no reason to suspect that, if elected, Bryan would have forgotten about other reform measures and concentrated only on the currency.

For a time Bryan's gallant, singlehanded battle seemed to be having an effect on public opinion, and Republican leaders became thoroughly frightened. In addition to money, threats and imprecations now became weapons in the campaign. A rumor was circulated that Bryan was insane. The *New York Times* devoted columns to the possibility, and printed a letter from a supposed psychologist charging that he was suffering from "paranoia querulenta," "graphomania," and "oratorical monomania." "Men," one manufacturer told his workers, "vote as you please, but if Bryan is elected . . . the whistle will not blow Wednesday morning." According to the *Nation,* which was supporting McKinley, many companies placed orders with their suppliers "to be executed in case Mr. Bryan is defeated, and not otherwise." A Chicago company that held thousands of farm mortgages politely asked all its "customers" to indicate their presidential preferences—a not very subtle form of coercion but probably an effective one. In some cases men were actually fired because of their political opinions.

By the time election day arrived the McKinley managers were so confident of victory that Hanna began returning new contributions as no longer necessary. Nevertheless, a final monumental effort was made to get out the

William Jennings Bryan, orator and politician. (Library of Congress)

vote. Free transportation was provided to carry citizens to and from the polls, men were paid for time lost in voting, and in doubtful districts floaters and other disreputables were rounded up and paraded to the ballot boxes. Everywhere in the crucial North Central states the Hanna machine expended enormous efforts, and in these states the decision was made. McKinley carried them all and with them the nation. In the electoral college McKinley won by 271 to 176, but the popular vote was close—7,036,000 to 6,468,000. The change of a relative handful of votes in half a dozen key states would have swung the election to Bryan.

The victory, however, was McKinley's and conservatives all over America—and the world—echoed the sentiment of Hanna's happy telegram to the President-elect: GOD'S IN HIS HEAVEN, ALL'S RIGHT WITH THE WORLD! A watershed in the economic and social history of the United States had been crossed. The rural America of the nineteenth century was making way for the industrial America of the twentieth. Soon business conditions began to improve, agricultural prices inched upward, new discoveries of gold relieved the pressure on the money supply. While McKinley and Hanna (now senator from Ohio) ruled in Washington, the era of complacent materialism and easy political virtue that had entered American politics on the coattails of General Grant seemed destined to continue indefinitely. Reform, it appeared, was dead.

That these appearances were deceiving was due in considerable measure to William Jennings Bryan. Unchastened by defeat and always cheerful ("It is better to have run and lost than never to have run at all," he said), he maintained the leadership of his party. Consistently he took the liberal position on important issues. Despite his strong pacifism he approved of fighting Spain in 1898 in order to free Cuba. "Humanity demands that we should act," he said simply. He enlisted in the Army and rose to be a colonel, although he saw no action during the brief conflict. The sincerity of his motives was proved when the war ended, for he then fought against the plan to annex former Spanish colonies. Running for President a second time in 1900, he made resistance to imperialism an issue in the campaign along with free silver. If both of these were poorly calculated to win votes in 1900, they were nonetheless solidly in the liberal tradition. Bryan lost to McKinley again, this time by 861,459 votes, and leadership of the reform movement passed, after McKinley's assassination, to Theodore Roosevelt. But Bryan continued the fight. In 1904, battling almost alone against conservatives in his own party, he forced the adoption of a fairly liberal platform (including strong antitrust, pro-labor, and antitariff planks), and when the conservative Judge Alton B. Parker was nonetheless nominated for President, Bryan kept up his outspoken criticism. While remaining loyal to the Democratic party he announced boldly: "The fight on economic questions . . . is not abandoned. As soon as the election is over I shall . . . organize for the campaign of 1908."

In that campaign Bryan, once more the Democratic nominee, was once more defeated in his personal quest of the Presidency, this time by Roosevelt's handpicked successor, William Howard Taft. Immediately he announced that he would not seek the office again, thus throwing the field open to other liberals.

Although he thus abandoned formal leadership of the Democrats, Bryan continued to advocate reform. Throughout the Taft administration he campaigned up and down the country to bolster the liberal wing of his party. When the 1912 nominating convention met in Baltimore, he introduced and won approval of a highly controversial resolution denouncing Wall Street influence, and he stated repeatedly that he would not support any candidate who was under the slightest obligation to Tammany Hall. The platform, as one historian says, "was a progressive document, in the best Bryan tradition." In the end Bryan threw his support to Woodrow Wilson. While this alone did not account for Wilson's nomination, it was very important in his election, for it assured him the enthusiastic backing of millions of loyal Bryanites.

Nothing reveals Bryan's fine personal qualities better than his support of Wilson, for the former Princeton professor had opposed the Great Commoner since 1896, when he had called the Cross of Gold speech "ridiculous." In 1904 he had publicly demanded that the Bryan wing be "utterly and once and for all driven from Democratic counsels." As late as 1908 he had refused to appear on the same platform with Bryan. Mr. Bryan, he said, "is the most charming and lovable of men personally, but foolish and dangerous in his theoretical beliefs." During the campaign of that year he refused to allow Bryan to deliver a campaign speech on the Princeton campus.

By 1912 Wilson had become far more liberal and no longer opposed most of Bryan's policies; even so, had Bryan been a lesser man he would not have forgiven these repeated criticisms. But he was more concerned with Wilson's 1912 liberalism than with personal matters, despite the publication of an old letter in which Wilson had expressed the wish to "knock Mr. Bryan once and for all into a cocked hat!" He shrugged off the "cocked hat" letter, and when Wilson paid him a handsome public tribute they became good friends. Furthermore, during the 1912 campaign, Bryan campaigned vigorously for Wilson, making well over four hundred speeches within a period of seven weeks. When Wilson won an easy victory in November, Bryan reacted without a trace of envy or bitterness. "It is a great triumph," he declared, "Let every Democratic heart rejoice." A few months later he said in a speech in Chicago:

> Sometimes I have had over-sanguine friends express regret that I did not reach the presidency. . . . But I have an answer ready for them. I have told them that they need not weep for me. . . . I have been so much more interested in the securing of the things for which we have been fighting than I have been in the name of the man who held the office, that I am happy in the thought that this government, through these reforms, will be made so good that a citizen will not miss a little thing like the presidency.

Wilson made Bryan Secretary of State. He was needed in the administration to help manage his many friends in Congress. The strategy worked well, for Bryan used his influence effectively. His role was particularly crucial in the hard fight over the Federal Reserve bill, but his loyal aid was also important in passing income tax legislation and a new antitrust law and in other matters as well.

In managing foreign affairs Bryan was less successful, for in this field he was ill-prepared. Because of his frank belief in the spoils system, he dismissed dozens of key professional diplomats, replacing them with untrained political hacks. Naturally the Foreign Service was badly injured. His policy of not serving alcoholic beverages at official functions because of his personal convictions caused much criticism at home and abroad. "W. J. Bryan not only suffers for his principles and mortifies his flesh, as he has every right to do," the London *Daily Express* complained, "but he insists that others should suffer and be mortified." The Secretary's continuing Chautauqua lectures, at which he sometimes appeared on the same platform with vaudeville entertainers and freaks, were attacked by many as undignified for one who occupied such a high official position.

Bryan had answers to all these criticisms: the State Department had been overly snobbish and undemocratic; Wilson had agreed to his "grape juice" policy before appointing him; no one should be ashamed of speaking to the American people. He could also point to his "cooling-off treaties" with some twenty nations, which provided machinery for avoiding blow-ups over minor diplomatic imbroglios.

Unfortunately Bryan had but a dim understanding of Latin American problems and unwittingly fostered American imperialism on many occasions. His narrow-minded belief that he knew better than local leaders what was "good" for these small countries showed that he had no comprehension of cultural and nationalistic elements in other lands. Although well intended, his policies produced much bad feeling in South and Central America. Bryan did suggest lending Latin American nations money "for education, sanitation and internal development," a policy that anticipated our modern Point Four approach to underdeveloped areas. Wilson, however, dismissed the idea because he thought it, "would strike the whole country . . . as a novel and radical proposal."

When the World War broke out in 1914, Bryan, like his chief, adopted a policy of strict neutrality. America, he said, should attempt to mediate between the belligerents by suggesting "a more rational basis of peace." Bryan believed in real neutrality far more deeply than Wilson, who was not ready to face the possibility of a German victory. "We cannot have in mind the wishes of one side more than the wishes of the other side," Bryan warned the President after the latter had prepared a stiff note of protest against German submarine warfare. And when, after the sinking of the *Lusitania,* Wilson sent a series of threatening messages to Germany, Bryan resigned as Secretary of State. He never again held public office.

It would have been better for Bryan's reputation if he had died in 1915; instead he lived on for another decade, as amiable and well-intentioned as ever but increasingly out of touch with the rapidly changing times. He made no effort to keep up with the abrupt intellectual developments of the twentieth century, yet he was accustomed to speak his mind on current issues and continued to do so. There had always been those who had considered his uncomplicated faith in time-tested moral principles and in popular rule rather naïve; in the cynical, scientific, and amoral twenties only a relative handful of rural oldtimers saw much virtue in his homilies on the people's unfailing instinct to do always what was "right" and "good." In the world of Calvin Coolidge the old Populist fires no longer burned very brightly, and Bryan's anti-business bias seemed terribly old-fashioned. Many had considered him an anachronism even in Wilson's day; by Harding's he had simply ceased to count in politics. More and more he confined himself to religious questions. His ardent piety was heartwarming, but he was a smug and intolerant Fundamentalist whose ignorance of modern science and ethics did not prevent him from expounding his "views" on these subjects at length. The honest opinions of "the people," he believed, could "settle" scientific and philosophical questions as easily as political ones.

Advancing age, as well as increasing preoccupation with revealed religion, was making Bryan less tolerant. Never one to give much thought to reasoned counterarguments, he became, in the twenties, an outspoken foe of many aspects of human freedom. He defended prohibition, refused to condemn the Ku Klux Klan, and participated eagerly in the notorious Scopes anti-evolution trial in Dayton, Tennessee, with all its overtones of censorship and self-satisfied ignorance. The final great drama of Bryan's life occurred when Clarence Darrow mercilessly exposed his simple prejudices on the witness stand. Bryan complacently maintained, among other things, that Eve was actually made from Adam's rib and that Jonah had really been swallowed by the whale. The rural audience cheered, but educated men all over the world were appalled.

Throughout his lifetime, Bryan was subject to harsh and almost continual criticism, and at least superficially he failed in nearly everything he attempted. But he was too secure in his faith to be injured by criticism, and he knew that for over two decades his influence was greater than any of his contemporaries save Theodore Roosevelt and Wilson. His life was useful and happy, for he rightly believed that he had made a lasting contribution to his country's development. Nor is it fair to condemn him for his limited intelligence and superficial understanding of his times. Other political leaders of at best ordinary intellect have done great deeds, sometimes without appreciating the meaning of events they have helped to shape. Still, there was tragedy in Bryan's career—he was unable to grow.

In 1896 he was indeed the peerless leader, vital, energetic, dedicated, and, in a measure, imaginative. He saw the problems of Nebraska farmers, realized their wider implications, and outlined a reasonable program designed to deal with them. He was almost elected President as a result, despite his youth and inexperience. Suddenly he was a celebrity; thereafter he moved into a wider world and lived there at his ease. He did not abandon his principles, and he helped achieve many important reforms, for which we must always honor him, but he soon ceased to feed upon new ideas. In a sense, despite the defeats, life's rewards came to him too easily. His magnetic voice, his charm, his patent sincerity, the memory of the heroic fight of '96—these things secured his place and relieved him of the need to grapple with new concepts.

Although he was a man of courage, strength, and endurance, Bryan was essentially lax and complacent. He preferred baggy clothes, a full stomach, the easy, undemanding companionship of small minds. For years the momentum of 1896 carried him on, but eventually the speeding world left him far behind. Fortunately for his inner well-being, he never realized what had happened. A few days after Darrow had exposed his shallowness before the world, he died peacefully in his sleep, as serene and unruffled by events as ever.

7

Consumer Protection: The Pure Food and Drugs Act

by Gerald H. Carson

"Someone has said that all morality is based upon the assumption that somebody might be watching. In the milieu of late nineteenth-century business, nobody seemed to be watching." Thus writes Gerald H. Carson in the following essay about one of the Progressives' most successful pieces of legislation. Mr. Carson, a social historian who has written *The Old Country Store* and *The Social History of Bourbon*, successfully demonstrates how the Pure Food and Drugs Act of 1906 was a case study in progressivism.

The development of the act reflects the changing nature of American society at the turn of the century as the United States became more industrialized and more Americans consumed goods processed by others. Thus urbanized, they were frequently uncertain about the contents and effects of consumable items. The political discussions on the bill proposing to regulate the food and drugs industry illustrate the seemingly endless debate on regulation or deregulation of business. The act established a federal agency to watch the food and drugs industry and required labeling of contents of packaged goods. This neither destroyed the industry nor led to a government take-over of the business. Rather, the Pure Food and Drugs Act indicates the constructive effects of moderate governmental intervention in the public interest.

On a hot humid July morning in 1902, a burly 200-pound scientist and connoisseur of good food and drink sat hunched over his desk in a red brick building in Washington, D.C., and he planned deliberately to feed twelve healthy young men a diet containing borax. Dr. Harvey W. Wiley, chief chemist of the Department of Agriculture, had in mind a double objective: first, to determine the effects upon human beings of certain chemicals then commonly used to preserve processed foods; and, more broadly, to educate the public in the need for a federal "pure food" law. Food preparation was becoming industrialized and subject to more complicated processing; products were traveling longer distances, passing through many hands. Manufacturers, facing a novel situation, turned to dubious additives to make their products appear more appetizing or to preserve them. Borax compounds, the first object of Dr. Wiley's investigations, were used to make old butter seem like new.

Volunteers for the experiment were recruited from the Department of Agriculture. They pledged themselves to obey the rules. A small kitchen and dining room were fitted out in the basement of the Bureau of Chemistry offices with the assistant surgeon-general in attendance to see to it that the subjects of the experiment did not get too much borax, and Dr. Wiley to see that they got enough. A bright reporter, George Rothwell Brown, of the Washington *Post,* gave the volunteers an enduring handle, "the poison squad"; and before long the public began referring to Wiley, affectionately or otherwise according to the point of view, as "Old Borax."

Six of Dr. Wiley's co-operators at the hygienic table got a normal ration plus measured doses of tasteless, odorless, invisible boracic acid. The other six also enjoyed a wholesome diet, with equally tasteless, odorless, invisible borate of soda added to their menu. The resulting chemical and physiological data was quite technical. But the meaning was clear. The effects of borax included nausea and loss of appetite, symptoms resembling those of influenza and over-burdened kidneys. The feeding experiments continued over a five-year period. After the borax initiation, which made a popular sensation, the squad sub-sequently breakfasted, lunched, and dined on dishes containing salicylates sul-furous acid and sulfites, benzoates, formaldehyde, sulfate of copper, and saltpeter. Seldom has a scientific experiment stirred the public imagination as did Dr. Wiley's novel procedures in, as he said, "trying it on the dog."

"My poison squad laboratory," said Dr. Wiley, "became the most highly advertised boarding-house in the world."

A popular versifier wrote a poem about it, the "Song of the Pizen Squad." Lew Dockstader introduced a topical song into his minstrel show. The chorus closed with the prediction:

Next week he'll give them mothballs a la Newburgh or else plain:
O they may get over it but they'll never look the same!

The New York *Sun* sourly handed Wiley the title of "chief janitor and po-liceman of the people's insides," an expression of one line of attack which the opposition was to take—invasion of personal liberty.

The movement to protect the health and pocketbook of the consumer was directed no less at "the patent medicine evil" than it was at the chaotic sit-uation in the food manufacturing field. The "cures" for cancer, tuberculosis, "female weakness," the dangerous fat reducers and "Indian" cough remedies were a bonanza for their proprietors, and many an advertising wizard who knew little enough of drugs or materia medica came to live in a jigsaw mansion and drive a spanking pair of bays because he was a skillful manipulator of hypochondria and mass psychology. Slashing exposés in the popular maga-zines told of babies' soothing syrups containing morphine and opium, of people who became narcotic addicts, of the use of tonics that depended upon alcohol to make the patient feel frisky.

"Gullible America," said Samuel Hopkins Adams in an angry but thor-oughly documented series of articles, "will spend this year [1905] some sev-enty-five millions of dollars" in order to "swallow huge quantities of alcohol . . . narcotics . . . dangerous heart depressants . . . insidious liver stimu-lants."

The nostrum vendors at first looked upon the Food and Drugs Act as a joke. In time the manufacturers of Pink Pills for Pale People learned the hard way that they were living dangerously when they ignored the precept, "Thou shalt not lie on the label."

As public interest rose in "the food question," powerful groups took their places in the line of battle to contest the pure food and drug bills which appeared, and died, in Congress with monotonous regularity. On the one side were aligned consumer groups—the General Federation of Women's Clubs, the National Consumers' League, the Patrons of Husbandry, and the labor unions. With them stood food chemists who had had experience in state control work, the American Medical Association, important periodicals *(Collier's Weekly, Bok's Ladies' Home Journal, World's Work, The Independent, Cosmopolitan),* President Theodore Roosevelt, and Dr. Wiley.

In opposition were the food manufacturers and manufacturers of articles used in the adulteration of foods and drugs such as cottonseed oil, the proprietary medicine industry, the distillers, canners, *Leslie's Weekly* (to which Dr. Wiley was anathema), newspaper publishers opposed for business reasons, Chicago meat packers, and powerful lobbyists holed up at the Willard and the Raleigh Hotel; also an obdurate Senate, responsive to pressures from big business. Wiley, as the leading personality in the fight for a food bill, achieved the uncommon distinction of acquiring almost as many enemies as did President Roosevelt himself.

When the average member of Congress, newspaper publisher, or pickle manufacturer smelled socialism and deplored the effects of the proposed legislation upon business, he was only responding normally to two powerful stimuli: self-interest and the nostalgic memory of his lost youth. Most mature Americans of the 1890–1900 period were born on farms or in rural areas and knew the conditions of life of a scattered population. The close-knit farm family was the dominant economic unit. It raised, processed, cured, and stored what it ate, and there is abundant evidence that it ate more and better food than the common man of Europe had ever dreamed of tasting. There was no problem of inspection or of deceptive labels. No "Short-weight Jim" invaded the home kitchen or smokehouse. If the preparation was unsanitary, it was no one else's business. What wasn't raised locally was obtained by barter. There were adequate forces of control over that simple transaction—face-to-face bargaining, community of interest, fear of what the neighbors would say.

As to drugs and medicines, grandma could consult the "family doctor" book and compound her home remedies from roots, herbs, and barks gathered along the edge of forest, meadow, and stream: catnip for colic, mullein leaf for asthma, the dandelion for dyspepsia, and so on through the list of simples, essences, flowers, tinctures, and infusions, whose chief merit was that they did not interfere with the tendency of the living cell to recover.

When Americans were called to the cities by the factory whistle, a dramatic change took place in their food supply. No longer was there personal contact between the producer and consumer, nor could the buyer be wary even if he would. For how could a city man candle every egg, test the milk, inquire into the handling of his meat supply, analyze the canned foods which he consumed in increasing quantities?

Since foodstuffs had to stand up in their long transit from the plant to the home, it is not surprising that unhealthy practices developed. During the "embalmed beef" scandal, for example, there was a debate as to whether a little boric acid in fresh beef was after all only an excusable extension of the ancient and accepted use of saltpeter in corning beef. Analytical chemistry was called upon increasingly to make cheap foods into expensive ones, to disguise and simulate, to arrest the processes of nature. The food manufacturers raided the pharmacopœia. But the salicylic acid that was approved in the treatment of gout or rheumatism was received with mounting indignation on the dining room table where it proved to be a depressant of the processes of metabolism. It was objectionable on another ground too—that it led to carelessness in the selection, cleansing, and processing of foodstuffs.

It is difficult to picture today the vast extent of adulteration at the beginning of this century. More than half the food samples studied in the Indiana state laboratory were sophisticated. Whole grain flour was "cut" with bran and corn meal. The food commissioner of North Dakota declared that his state alone consumed ten times as much "Vermont maple syrup" as Vermont produced. The *Grocer's Companion and Merchant's Hand-Book* (Boston, 1883), warned the food retailer, in his own interest, of the various tricks used to alter coffee and tea, bread and flour, butter and lard, mustard, spices, pepper, pickles, preserved fruits, sauces, potted meats, cocoa, vinegar, and candies. A New York sugar firm was proud to make the point in its advertising of the 1880's that its sugar contained "neither glucose, muriate of tin, muriatic acid, nor any other foreign, deleterious or fraudulent substance whatever." The canned peas looked garden-fresh after treatment with $CuSO_4$ by methods known as "copper-greening." The pork and beans contained formaldehyde, the catsup benzoic acid. As a capstone of inspired fakery, one manufacturer of flavored glucose (sold as pure honey) carefully placed a dead bee in every bottle to give verisimilitude.

The little man of 1900 found himself in a big, big world, filled with butterine and mapleine.

This is not to suggest that the pioneer food manufacturer was as rascally as his contemporaries, the swamp doctor and the lightning rod peddler. What was occurring was less a collapse of human probity than an unexpected testing of human nature in a new context. Someone has said that all morality is based upon the assumption that somebody might be watching. In the milieu of late nineteenth-century business, nobody seemed to be watching. Thus the food crusade became necessary as a means of redressing the balance in the market which had turned so cruelly against the ordinary American and, indeed, against the honest manufacturer.

The ensuing controversy was symptomatic of the passing—painful, nostalgic to many, including no doubt many a big business senator—of the old, simple life of village and farm which was doomed by the expanding national life. It was, one feels, not solely in defense of the hake (sold as genuine codfish with boric acid as a preservative) that Senator George Frisbie Hoar of Massachusetts rose in the Senate to exalt "the exquisite flavor of the codfish, salted, made into balls, and eaten on a Sunday morning by a person whose theology is sound, and who believes in the five points of Calvinism."

The friends of food reform needed all the courage and public discussion they could muster. Since 1879, when the first federal bill was proposed, 190 measures to protect the consumer had been introduced in Congress, of which 49 had some kind of a subsequent history, and 141 were never heard of again. Meanwhile the states did what they could. About half of them had passed pure food laws by 1895. But there was no uniformity in their regulations. Foods legal in one state might be banned in another. Some of the laws were so loosely drawn that it was quite conceivable that Beechnut Bacon might be seized by the inspectors because no beechnuts were involved in its curing. Was Grape-Nuts misbranded because the great Battle Creek "brain food" had only a fanciful connection with either grapes or nuts? One bill actually proposed a numerical count of the contents of a package—the grains of salt, the cherries in a jar of preserves. What if Mr. Kellogg had to count every corn flake which went into his millions of packages?

Conflicts and foolish regulations could be ironed out over a period of time. The fatal flaw was that individual states had no power to get at the real problem: interstate traffic in the "patented" bitters, cancer cures, and strawberry jellies made out of dyed glucose, citric acid, and timothy seed.

The act which Wiley drew up was first introduced in 1902. It was successfully sidetracked in one legislative branch or the other for four years. The provisions were simple. In essence, it was a labeling act.

"Tell the truth on the label," Dr. Wiley said, "and let the consumer judge for himself."

Some of the legislators who opposed the act were states' rights Democrats, concerned about constitutional interpretation, who in the end fortunately saw the wisdom of sacrificing principle for expediency. Others were Old Guard Republicans who were special custodians of the *status quo* and highly sensitive to the sentiments of the business community: men like Senators Aldrich of Rhode Island (wholesale groceries), Kean of New Jersey (preserving and canning), Platt of Connecticut (home of the great Kickapoo Indian remedies), Hale and Frye of Maine, along whose rock-bound coast the familiar Maine herring became "imported French sardines," packaged in boxes with French labels.

The tactic in the Senate was one of unobtrusive obstruction and lip service to the idea of regulation. Open opposition was never much of a factor. "The 'right' to use deceptive labels," observed *The Nation,* "is not one for which

Workers in a meat packing plant in Chicago in 1905.
(Library of Congress)

impassioned oratory can be readily invoked." When a serious try was made to pass a general pure food law in 1902–3, Senator Lodge was able to direct the attention of the Senate to legislation more urgently needed, such as a Philippine tariff bill. In the last session of the 59th Congress (1904–5) the food bill was considered less pressing than a proposal to award naval commissions to a couple of young men who had been expelled from the Academy for hazing but still wanted very much to become officers in the United States Navy.

President Roosevelt finally decided to push the issue. "Mr. Dooley" offered a version of how it happened. "Tiddy," he said, was reading Upton Sinclair's novel, *The Jungle,* a grisly sociological tract on "Packingtown." "Tiddy was toying with a light breakfast an' idly turnin' over th' pages iv th' new book with both hands. Suddenly he rose fr'm th' table, an' cryin': 'I'm pizened,' begun throwin' sausages out iv th' window. Th' ninth wan sthruck Sinitor Biv'ridge on th' head an' made him a blond. It bounced off, exploded, an' blew a leg off a secret-service agent, an' th' scatthred fragmints desthroyed a handsome row iv ol' oak-trees. Sinitor Biv'ridge rushed in, thinkin' that th' Prisidint was bein' assassynated be his devoted followers in th' Sinit, an' discovered Tiddy engaged in a hand-to-hand conflict with a potted ham. Th' Sinitor fr'm Injyanny, with a few well-directed wurruds, put out th' fuse an' rendered th' missile harmless. Since thin th' Prisidint, like th' rest iv us, has become a viggytaryan. . . ." At any rate, in his annual message to Congress, December 5, 1905, Roosevelt recommended in the interest of the consumer and the legitimate manufacturer "that a law be enacted to regulate interstate commerce in misbranded and adulterated foods, drinks and drugs," and the bill was re-introduced in the Senate by Senator Weldon B. Heyburn of Idaho. Pressure from the American Medical Association, the graphic exposé of revolting conditions in the Chicago packing houses, and Roosevelt's skillful use of the report of an official commission which investigated the stockyards, finally forced a favorable vote in the Senate and then the House on the Pure Food and Drugs Bill. The meat inspection problem was, actually, a different matter. But an angry public was in no mood to make fine distinctions. Meat, processed foods, and fake medicines all tapped the family pocketbook, all went into the human stomach, and all smelled to high heaven in the spring of 1906. Roosevelt signed the bill into law on June 30, 1906.

The enforcement of the law was placed in the hands of Dr. Wiley. According to the Doctor, it was after the bill became law that the real fight began. Most food and drug manufacturers and dealers adjusted their operations to the new law, and found themselves in a better position because of it, with curtailment of the activities of fly-by-night competition and re-establishment of the consumers' confidence in goods of known quality. But there were die-hards like the sugar and molasses refiners, the fruit driers, whisky rectifiers, and purveyors of wahoo bitters, Peruna and Indian Doctor wonder drugs.

The administration of the Food and Drugs Act involved the Bureau of Chemistry in thousands of court proceedings, *United States* v. *Two Barrels of Desiccated Eggs, United States* v. *One Hundred Barrels of Vinegar;* and one merciful judge noted that Section 6 extended the protection of the act to our four-footed friends. Pure food inspectors had seized 620 cases of spoiled canned cat food. When the case of the smelly tuna fish turned up in the western district court of the state of Washington, the judge cited man's experience with cats throughout recorded time: "Who will not feed cats must feed mice and rats." He confirmed the seizure and directed an order of condemnation.

The law was subsequently strengthened both by legal interpretations and by legislative action, as experience developed needs not met by the original act. Government technicians worked with private industry in the solution of specific problems such as refrigeration and the handling of food. When Dr. Wiley retired from public service in 1912, a revolution had occurred in food processing in only six years' time. Yet the food industry had hardly begun to grow.

"The conditions created by the passage of the act," said Clarence Francis, former president and chairman of the board of General Foods Corporation, "invited responsible business men to put real money into the food business."

The next 25 years saw the decline of the barrel as a food container and its replacement by the consumer unit package; the setting of official standards for the composition of basic food products; and the banning of quack therapeutic mechanical devices such as the electric belt, whose galvanic properties were once presented so vividly to the "Lost Manhood" market. We still have with us in some measure the "horse beef" butcher and the "butterlegger." Tap water remains a tempting means of "extending" many foods. But there is no question about the general integrity of our food supply, the contribution to the national well-being of the original food law, as amended, and the readiness of today's food industry leaders to accept what is now called the Food, Drug, and Cosmetic Act as a proper blueprint of their obligation to the nation's consumers.

8

FDR: A Practical Magician
by John Kenneth Galbraith

On March 4, 1983, the United States marked the fiftieth anniversary of Franklin Delano Roosevelt's first inauguration. The perspective of fifty years allows us to make some reasonably safe assessments regarding FDR's politics and policies.

That he was "the dominant political figure of this century," as Professor Galbraith writes, is beyond question. His leadership during the severe crises of the Great Depression and World War II have assured his place among America's greatest presidents. The "Roosevelt Revolution," whether viewed as liberal or as essentially conservative, certainly has left a lasting legacy.

Thus, *what* Franklin D. Roosevelt accomplished is settled. *How* he was able to accomplish it is more difficult to discern. Professor Galbraith, who reminds us of his own affection for the man, is nonetheless perceptive in his analysis. By understanding the qualities of great presidential leadership, perhaps the nation and its future leaders can build upon those legacies which FDR left us a half-century ago.

That Franklin D. Roosevelt was, and preeminently so, the dominant political figure of this century—that he stood astride its first half like the Colossus itself—will not be in doubt. Nor are the reasons subject to serious dispute. It was his fate and fortune to face the two great tragedies of the time and to guide its greatest social achievement. The tragedies were, of course, the Second World War and the Great Depression, and few will quarrel as to the bearing of these two events on the Roosevelt transcendence. The world emerged better and in many ways stronger from both. We will never know, in either case, the disasters, even catastrophes, that might have been.

There can be equally little disagreement on Roosevelt's part in the most significant achievement of the age. It was Franklin D. Roosevelt who led the great transition in modern capitalism in the United States—the transition from an economic and social system in which participants were expected to bear the cost of their own helplessness or misfortune, earned or unearned, to one in which a compassionate protection tempered the inherent hardships and cruelties of the economy. Unemployment compensation, old-age pensions, lower-cost housing, varied support to agriculture, employment opportunity, and much more came together to compose this change that has earned the name the Roosevelt Revolution.

The revolution that Roosevelt brought about is both celebrated and not quite forgiven to this day. The poor are still thought by the stern to be unduly favored, with moral damage resulting. Under free enterprise, men, women, and children are meant to suffer; that suffering, like more income to the affluent, is essential as an incentive. No one would be more pleased than FDR at the success of the Roosevelt Revolution or less surprised at the deeply theological resistance it continues to engender.

There is general agreement, then, that the Depression, the war, and the great economic and social transformation of the first half of the twentieth century were central to the making of the Age of Roosevelt. Historians can often unite even on the obvious. What remains sharply in debate are the qualities of mind and personality that brought FDR, faced with such tragedy and such challenge, to such eminence. Never did history have so dense a pace as between 1932 and 1945. There was enough in those years to have overthrown a lesser man a dozen times. What allowed one leader so completely to dominate such a time?

Because love and loyalty have a blinding effect, the testimony of anyone who was there is somewhat flawed. The word of FDR's death, which reached me on that April evening in 1945, brought a sense of trauma I had never previously experienced in my life. I had felt a faith, affection, and commitment that, it seemed, would last forever. Not in the preceding twelve years had it occurred to me that a President might be wrong. Were a Roosevelt decision or action in conflict with my earlier views, I was always able to make the requisite adjustment and promptly did so. And it was the same for the others who proudly called themselves Roosevelt men. Thus my warning against too easily accepting us as witnesses. We are, needless to say, far, far better in our judgment of modern Presidents.

The ability to inspire loyalty and the compelling sweep of his personality were certainly important in the Roosevelt achievement. But important too was his enormous joy in combat. There are politicians who evade battle; there are those who invite it. The one who invites it, as did FDR, earns a loyalty from his followers not given to those political leaders whose instinct is to accommodation, appeasement, and retreat. Partly this is because there is pleasure for all participants in the contest, but it is also because there is no danger for the soldiers that retreat or surrender will leave them leaderless and exposed. This is not to say, of course, that Roosevelt never yielded; he was a master, as of much else, of the tactical withdrawal. But he never retreated because he was averse to the conflict; he never gave in because he sought to be loved by his enemies.

From this enjoyment of battle came the adversary tradition in American social and economic policy—the feeling of American business that government is inherently and intrinsically inimical or wrong. And in lesser measure the reverse. Not everyone will think this a good legacy. On more matters than not, government and business interests have a complementary role. Nor, in the longer, deeper view, is the conflict real.

Most of the Roosevelt Revolution, properly viewed, was conservative. It was intended to preserve the social tranquility and sense of belonging without

Franklin D. Roosevelt. (Library of Congress)

which capitalism could not have survived—and still will not survive. It protected values and institutions that were at risk. But the softening of the edges of capitalism and the transition to the welfare state were accomplished far more harmoniously in the other industrial lands than in the United States. They might, perhaps, have come more peacefully here too, with less enduring strain on the political fabric, but for the Roosevelt delight in his enemies—his commitment to the ancient Pulitzer injunction that one should not only comfort the afflicted but afflict the comfortable. Certainly this attitude added to the joy of all of us who were there. With what pleasure we made the President's enemies our own. How deeply we scorned those among us who were thought to have an instinct to appease. How unpleasant, on occasion, we must have been as people with whom to do business.

There is a myth, cultivated by Walter Lippmann among others, that Roosevelt was a man of words and not thought. That it was his practice to air ideas liberally, to test them on audiences casual and otherwise, is certainly true. Many, in consequence, came away in deep alarm as to the direction in which the President's mind seemed to be running. But the Roosevelt performance was distinctly different; there, ideas were linked to intensely practical, powerfully relevant action. The farm crisis in 1933 was thought to have many causes; his solution was to provide the farmers with cheap loans and organize them to produce less for higher prices. Whatever the reasons for unemployment, the obvious answer was for the government to provide jobs through the Public and Civil Works Administrations. The National Recovery Act (NRA), much belabored by economists then and since, recognized a basic characteristic of modern capitalism: wages and prices interact in the modern economy; prices can shove down wages, and lower wages and reduced purchasing power can allow and force further price reductions—deflation. The opposing dynamic—wages pressing up prices, prices pulling up wages—is a cause of inflation, as we know today—or should know. Then as now there was a strong practical case for direct intervention to arrest this malign process; there was a strong practical case for the NRA.

Unemployment compensation, old-age pensions, and public housing were eminently relevant to the problems they addressed. The mobilization of the American economy in World War II was the most successful exercise in economic management of modern times—a huge increase in production, no net reduction in aggregate civilian consumption, and all with no appreciable inflation. On none of these matters did the President fail to get alternative proposals—elaborate designs that substituted pretense and rhetoric for real solutions.

I do not suggest that FDR's ability to link ideas to effective action and to link initiative to desired result was infallible. In 1933, like our recent Presidents, he was briefly attracted to the magic of the monetarists—to the notion that the economy could be regulated in all its complexity by monetary witchcraft. But here, in brilliant contrast to his successors, he quickly repented. Roosevelt was, indeed, a man of many ideas, but it was his genius to select those that were most relevant to a firm and useful result.

Those who agree, at least in part, on the effectiveness of individual Roosevelt measures have another criticism of the President. They concede that these measures, or some of them, were a necessary response to diverse needs; they insist, however, that FDR was incapable of envisaging and embracing a comprehensive and internally consistent design. He had no all-inclusive theory of the state, the economy, and the social order. This is true; and it is something, I suggest, that no one can regret. Those scholars and politicians who have an overall plan are almost always more impressive in oratory than in action, and they can be callous as they pursue their plan relentlessly or await its effects. Coolidge and Hoover had such a design—and left the economy in all its complexity to the ultimately benign operation of laissez-faire. Those who suffered in the interim were the natural cost of the larger benefit. There is a similar plan in the minds of those who now speak so confidently of the "miracle of the market," of the pervasive wickedness of public regulation and the generally inimical character of the modern welfare state. The twentieth century has no more powerful lesson than the suffering that can be imposed by those, on both the right and the left, who are captured by a comprehensive design for social and economic policy. We remember and celebrate Roosevelt because, mercifully, he was exempt from cruel and confining theory. He moved from the needed result to the relevant action precisely because he was unencumbered by ideological constraint. That, no doubt, is another way of saying that Franklin D. Roosevelt was a superbly practical man.

This willingness to adapt, to change, and to act was at the basis of the Roosevelt success as a political leader, of his hold on the American people and through them directly on the Congress as well. No one can doubt his virtuosity in speech, in dealing with the press, and, above all, on the radio. But none of this talent would have survived and served for those twelve intense years had it not been associated with concrete action and visible result. We hear so much these days of the compelling television personality—the politician who has "mastered" this medium, allowing him to persuade workers, women, blacks, and the poor contrary to the viewers' need, interest, or fortune. I doubt that such a triumph of personality over underlying purpose is truly possible; certainly FDR's mastery of radio and the fireside chat would not have been effective had it been discovered that those stirring words were a disguise for social neglect and inaction.

The Roosevelt magic had yet another source. This was his ability to extend a sense of community, a community not confined by national frontiers and one to which all men and women of goodwill and good purpose could believe that they belonged.

When the President spoke of his commitment to economic betterment and social justice, of his resistance to the regressive world of the dictators and of his hope for a future in which the young would not face periodic slaughter—in which death would not be a statistic—he did not speak as a leader to followers, not even as a President to his people. He spoke as one involved in an effort in which all had a part, as a participant to fellow participants. It was this sense of a common effort with the President, membership in a common community, to which people responded.

The feeling was strongest in the United States, and it was made stronger by those who stood outside and saw it as a threat to the economic and social eminence that had once been their more or less exclusive possession. They could not resist, but they would not belong. Once again one sees Roosevelt's debt to his opposition. But this sense of community went far beyond national boundaries. He extended it to Latin America, where it was the essence of his avowal of the Good Neighbor policy. And to Britain, most notably in the months when she stood alone. And on to distant India with the commitment to Indian nationhood, which causes his name to be revered there to this day. But most of all this sense of community reached out to our immediate neighbor, Canada.

Recently, to illustrate this point, Thomas H. Eliot, a leading architect of the Social Security Act in the 1930s and a Roosevelt congressman from Massachusetts in the early forties, sent me a quotation I had not previously seen from the President's response to a welcoming speech made on his arrival in Canada for a visit. Roosevelt said: "While I was on my cruise last week, I read in a newspaper that I was to be received with all the honors customarily rendered to a foreign ruler. Your Excellency, I am grateful for the honors; but something within me rebelled at that word 'foreign.' I say this because when I have been in Canada I have never heard a Canadian refer to an American as a 'foreigner.' He is just an 'American.' And in the same way, across the border in the United States, Canadians are not 'foreigners.' They are 'Canadians.' I think that that simple little distinction illustrates to me, better than anything else, the relationship between the two countries."

It is one of the many legacies that we have from Franklin D. Roosevelt that we all belong, without exception, to a yet larger commonwealth. In this larger community there is a general concern for the economic well-being of all people and for the reality of social participation and social justice. Above all, there is a commitment to the negotiation, conciliation, and peaceful resolution of national differences on which, as another and somber legacy of the Roosevelt years, our very survival now depends.

9

How the Media Seduced and Captured American Politics

by Richard C. Wade

Ronald Reagan has been called a "Great Communicator" by some political analysts. The reasons behind this acclamation did not stem from the quality of the information the President dispensed. Rather, Reagan was effective in the *manner* in which he delivered his message, or at least many Americans of the television generation perceived him to be effective. Indeed, Reagan's background as a movie and TV celebrity may have been ideal for the age of the media campaign.

In the following essay, Richard C. Wade of the City University of New York traces the gradual expansion of the influence of television on American politics. Professor Wade's assessment of the effects of the media campaign are disturbing. Most troubling to him is the apparent correlation of the increased use of television campaigning with the decreasing number of voters who participate in our political system. As Wade notes, President Reagan's "landslide" in 1980 was delivered by "fewer than 20 percent of adults over eighteen years of age" in an election in which "just over half" of those registered actually voted.

Despite low voter turnout, inordinate campaign expenses, and the breakdown of traditional party functions, Dr. Wade does not despair. Instead he sees "no reason why the media revolution cannot . . . be made apt to democratic purposes." In order for that to happen, we must realize what has happened to our political system. Professor Wade has contributed to that realization with his timely observations.

Television has been accused of many things: vulgarizing tastes; trivializing public affairs; sensationalizing news; corrupting the young; pandering to profits; undermining traditional values. The indictments are no doubt too harsh, and they ignore the medium's considerable achievements over two decades. Yet even the severest critics have not noticed the way in which television first seduced and then captured the whole American political process.

The fact is that each year fewer people register to vote, and among those who do, an ever-shrinking number actually go to the polls. Since casting a free ballot constitutes the highest expression of freedom in a democracy, its declining use is a grave matter. How did we get ourselves into this perilous state?

Television's victory was not the result of a carefully planned and calculated assault on our political procedures; less still was it the conspiracy of a greedy and power-hungry industry. Rather it was a process in which each year witnessed a modest expansion of the electronic influence on American politics. A look at the presidential election of 1948, the first in the age of television, suggests both the magnitude and swiftness of the change. President Harry Truman ran a shoestring campaign sustained largely by his incumbency and the overconfidence of his opponent. Together the two candidates spent only about $15 million—the cost of a gubernatorial contest in New York three decades later. Both presidential candidates leaned heavily on their state and local parties for crowds and election-day support. Truman's whistle-stop tour of the country harked back to a century-old technique. Television covered the conventions but intruded no further. Radio handled the late returns, and the commentator H. V. Kaltenborn, who assumed historical patterns would hold true, waited for the rural vote to sustain his early prediction of a victory for New York governor Thomas E. Dewey.

Some of the possibilities of television emerged, however, in the next election. Sen. Robert Taft used time-honored, if somewhat questionable, tactics to line up a solid phalanx of Southern delegates at the 1952 Republican convention. Gen. Dwight Eisenhower's managers presented a more properly selected alternative set of delegates. Historically, disputes of this kind had been resolved behind closed doors and brought to the convention only for ratification. But Eisenhower strategists wanted to transform what had long been seen as a technical question into a moral one. They chose as their weapon televised committee hearings. For the first time, the public became privy to the vagaries of party rules. Viewers were let into the smoke-filled room. The result was a resounding defeat for Taft, and Eisenhower went into the convention with plenty of delegates and wearing the fresh, smiling face of reform.

A few months later Eisenhower's running mate, Richard Nixon, found himself entangled in a burgeoning scandal involving a private fund raised by large contributors to advance his political career. Though no law had been broken, the impropriety was clear, especially in a campaign based on cleaning up "the mess" in Washington. Eisenhower declared that anyone in public life should be as "clean as a hound's tooth," and many of his advisers told him to drop the young congressman.

A desperate Nixon decided to take his case directly to the public—through a half-hour paid telecast. He declared he had meant no wrongdoing, detailed the high costs facing a California congressman, noted his own modest means, and said he had always voted his own conscience on issues before the House. Most memorable, however, was his use of his dog, Checkers, as a kind of surrogate "hound's tooth." To sophisticates it seemed like a clip out of a daytime soap opera, but the public found it plausible enough. More important, it satisfied Dwight Eisenhower.

These two episodes revealed the ambiguity of the new medium. Until 1952, conventions had been closed party affairs run by the national committees. In fact, that is still their only legal function. But television put the voters on the convention floor. Both parties had to dispense with a lot of the traditional hoopla—endless floor demonstrations, marathon seconding speeches, visibly indulgent behavior by delegates—and keynote speakers had to project telegenic appeal as well as party service. To be sure, television introduced its own brand of hoopla. Cameras zoomed in on outrageous costumes, floormen interviewed colorful if not always important figures, and networks did the counting of the delegates before the issues or nominations actually got to the decisive stage.

The Nixon heritage was less complicated. The "Checkers" speech became shorthand for slick, calculated manipulation if not deception. Critics argued it demonstrated that a shrewd master of the medium could sell anything— not only commercial products but political candidates as well.

The presidential election of 1956 was essentially a rerun of the previous one, yet one episode demonstrated the increasing influence of television. With Stevenson's renomination by the Democrats a certainty, the networks faced a four-day yawn from their viewers. Salvation suddenly appeared in a contest over the Vice-Presidency. With no obvious choice and with Stevenson himself undecided, three senators moved into contention: Estes Kefauver of Tennessee, Hubert Humphrey of Minnesota, and John F. Kennedy of Massachusetts.

Chicago was awash with whispers of deals being concocted in smoke-filled rooms to designate a running mate, and to sustain his reform image, Stevenson threw open the choice to the convention. Suddenly there was theater. Kefauver had a second chance; Humphrey got his first; and Kennedy seemed to have no chance at all. A big scoreboard behind the podium recorded the voting from the floor. The Kentucky Derby never generated more excitement. As state by state announced the results, the lead fluctuated. At the last moment Humphrey released his delegates to the Tennessean who had contested Stevenson in a dozen primaries. Afterward only historians would remember that Kefauver had won, but Kennedy's performance gave the public its first impression of a man who would dominate his party—and the media—for almost a decade.

Four years later another national election provided television with one of its greatest moments: the Nixon-Kennedy debates. It was a strange event, and it is hard to say who won. A reading of the transcripts today reveals no surprises. Each candidate expressed views already known; each circled and jabbed; but there were no knockdowns. Yet millions saw the relative newcomer under the most favorable of circumstances, and even though the contrast was sharper visually than intellectually, there was a vague general feeling that JFK had got the better of it.

In all, the new medium lived up both to its responsibilities and its possibilities. For the first time, it had brought two presidential candidates to the same podium. The proceedings were overly elaborate, but the handling of the event was scrupulously fair and nonpartisan. And afterward it would become increasingly hard for candidates, even incumbents to avoid legitimate challenges on television.

The turbulence of the sixties can only be understood in the context of television's ubiquity. It brought its first war, Vietnam, into the living room from ten thousand miles away; it showed us racial explosions across urban

America; it covered the campus meetings that revealed the widest generation gap in American history; and it captured, in endless replays, the assassination of three of the country's most popular political leaders. And viewers were also voters. The decade of turbulence scrambled old allegiances and rendered old labels meaningless.

The year 1968 was a tide without a turning. Nixon's election ushered in a new era dominated by the paid commercial and an overall media strategy. Already what the press would call "image makers" or "media mavens" were on their way to becoming at least as important as campaign managers. Charles Guggenheim's twenty-five-minute TV film "A Man From New York," broadcast in the 1964 senatorial contest, purported to show that Robert Kennedy was not really from Massachusetts; four years later Guggenheim portrayed George McGovern as a bombardier in World War II to dispel the notion that he was a craven pacifist. More daringly, political manager David Garth ran John Lindsay for reelection in New York City with commercials in which the mayor admitted to endless small mistakes in office, the better to magnify presumed larger accomplishments.

Guggenheim and Garth were pioneers: the full media impact lay in the seventies, when it replaced more conventional activities. Its muscle was most obvious in determining the schedule of the candidate. Traditionally, managers had tried to get their stalwart in front of as many groups as possible. A heavy speaking schedule gave the candidate a chance to make his views known to disparate electorate, and if the newspapers covered the meetings, so much the better.

Now, every effort focused on television. Instead of sessions with political groups, the object was a contrived "event." The candidate showed up at a senior citizens' center and delivered a brief statement drawn from some position paper. Television news deadlines determined the timing; the campaign coverage of the previous week determined the issue. As election day approached, two or three of what Daniel Boorstin has called "pseudo events" highlighted the day's schedule. Nothing important was said, but the ninety-second exposure brought the candidate to the voter without the intercession of a party or political organization and showed him concerned about something that pollsters had discovered was on the public mind.

This direct appeal made parties increasingly superfluous. To be sure, they still had the critical line on the ballot; they still had enough registered members to make an endorsement worthwhile. But they were no longer the candidates' principal sponsor. Indeed, they could seldom guarantee a crowd. When that was needed, a few media celebrities could draw a larger audience than a politician's speech.

The parties also lost their traditional recruiting function. Formerly, the ambitious sought political office after a period of party service, often at lowly stations. Now the young headed directly toward electoral office with party registration their only evidence of loyalty. In fact, many considered a close affiliation with day-to-day party affairs to be the mark of a hack; a fresh, non-partisan face appealed more to the electorate than a veteran party standard-bearer. The spread of primaries at the expense of conventions opened the way to further end runs around the organization. In addition, state after state adopted laws designed to loosen the monopoly of parties over the nominating process, thus magnifying the importance of independents. In some states, for example, an eligible voter need only appear at the polls and declare himself at that moment either a Democrat or a Republican to be entitled to cast a ballot in a party primary.

Initially, reformers rejoiced at these trends, and the regular parties seemed to be the first casualties. But media politics knew no factional boundaries. Just as surely as it undermined traditional party practices, it also withered the voluntary base of reform politics. The parties depended on patronage, reformers on participation. What regulars would do as part of the job, independents would do from commitment. Yet a media campaign did not leave much for volunteers to do.

The new media managers cared little for traditional canvassing where party workers or volunteers went door to door to discover preferences, deliver literature, and argue the candidate's case. The foot soldiers were untrained in modern interviewing techniques; they worked at odd hours; they often returned with useless material; and even good campaigns could not provide full voter coverage. Large banks of telephones were more reliable. Paid operators called scientifically selected numbers; the message was uniform; computers swallowed the responses and spit out the printouts. Ironically, phone banks had originally been a volunteer activity. Supporters took home lists and made personal calls; but better management dictated closer control. The new system is expensive, and there is no way of knowing if phone canvassing, even confined to "prime" lists, is effective; but every campaign for high office finds it necessary.

Polling, too, is an indispensable part of the media campaign. This is not new, but its intensity is. "The calls go out every night randomly, 150 or more," wrote B. Brummond Ayres, Jr., in *The New York Times* in 1981, of the Reagan Presidency, "to homes across the country." The interviews last a half hour; they ask every kind of question bordering on the voter's interest and public matters. Then the computers whiz and calculators click; "earlier interviews are thrown into the mix" and "in a matter of hours President Reagan and the officials of the Republican National Committee have in hand the latest intelligence needed to tailor a speech, a program or a policy." Richard Werthlin's Washington firm is paid $900,000 a year for this "tracking" of the popular mood.

Previous Presidents relied on a handful of trusted advisers and erratic, and usually unsolicited, reports of party leaders and friends from across the country. But now all campaigns use polls. Indeed, despite their frequent and sometimes flagrant errors, the press and the media treat their results as news stories; columnists scatter ratings throughout their interpretations; analysts worry that their wide use has become a surrogate election, even affecting the actual outcome. Polls are, however, so much a part of the candidates' strategy that some state legislatures have moved against the release of selected parts and require the publication of the full survey. And one poll alone won't do. Anxious managers and candidates can hardly get enough of them, especially in the climactic weeks of the campaign. What is also important is that the survey is bought and requires no use of volunteers.

The media campaign is all business. There is none of the congenial chaos that characterized traditional politics. At headquarters a few people mill about numberless machines. Everything is computerized. Paid employees run the terminals; paid telephoners call numbers from purchased printouts; rented machines slap labels on direct-mail envelopes. Mercenaries grind out "position papers," and press releases are quickly dispatched to a computerized "key" list of newspapers, radio, television stations, columnists, and commentators. "What they have created," wrote the *New York Times* reporter Steven V. Roberts, "is an electronic party."

At the center of the effort is the purchasing of paid television commercials. They are the modern substitute for conventional campaigning. The candidate is not seen live; the message, in fact, is often delivered by a professional voice. The purpose is to project a candidate who is like the viewer, but better: one who arouses but does not agitate; one who elevates but does not disturb; one who exudes morality but not righteousness; one who conveys strength but not arrogance; one who is experienced but not cynical; one who has convictions but avoids controversy. Since such people are in as short supply in private life as in public affairs, a good deal of contrivance is demanded, and the commercial permits it.

The commercial does not seek truth but plausibility. It confines itself to a handful of "issues" that are the candidate's long suit and that are reiterated until the viewer is convinced that these are of paramount interest to other voters even if they are not so to him. The idea is to define the argument on the candidate's own terms. All this is done in the context of constant polling, telephone feedback, and it must be added, old-fashioned political instinct. As the campaign continues, one spot will be dropped, others altered, and still others emphasized.

The central fact about commercials is their cost. For maximum advantage they are artfully spliced into programs with large voting audiences. Since most advertisers head for the same viewers, the price is very high. In 1980 thirty seconds in the prime-time New York market cost $5,000; ninety seconds cost $15,000. Even in South Dakota these figures ran as high as $250 and $500.

The financial risks attendant on a media campaign are borne solely by the candidate, not by the media managers. Bookings for commercial spots have to be made far in advance and the money paid on the barrelhead. In the past, suppliers of campaign materials—printers, hotels, and airlines—were

John F. Kennedy conducting a press conference on Aug. 1, 1963. (Photograph by Abbie Rowe. National Archives.)

more tolerant. Some creditors had to wait years for their money and then settled on a percentage, often small, of the original bill.

But now media consultants get their money on schedule. The most common plea at a fund raiser as election day approaches is, "If we don't have the money by tomorrow noon, the candidate is off the air." This is shorthand for saying, "Unless you cough up, the election is over."

The media people have so convinced the public and political donors that the commercial is the campaign that only the penurious or uncommitted will resist. And the media's demand is insatiable. If the consultant's polls show the candidate is behind, then a large buy is crucial; if ahead, then the turnout is critical. In either case, the cameras roll and the candidate pays.

Worse still, the media's demand hits the candidate when he is most vulnerable. A whole career seems to ride on the outcome. Hence, the resources of the family are called in, friends enlisted, business and professional associates tapped. For a while this feeds the tube. But except for the personally very wealthy, the cupboard is soon bare. The only recourse is to go to "political givers," old and new. They have the capacity to underwrite the big loans to cover the up-front money. Yet their liability is very small. (State and federal laws restrict total spending and the amount of individual contributions; everything above those limits must be repaid.)

For the donors it is a cheap ante: they are ultimately repaid by the finance committee. After the election a few galas retire the victors' debt. For the losers, debt is a persistant nightmare.

Many people can afford political giving, but few do it. The result is a hectic and not always elevating courtship of a handful of wealthy people by the candidate and his finance committee. Some potential donors have only a dilettante's interest in politics, but most have interests that are more than marginally related to government. They expect what the trade euphemistically calls "access" to the winner.

The influence of money in American politics is, of course, not new. But the media has introduced a level of spending never known before. In the 1960 presidential campaigns about 10 percent of the budget went to television; by 1980 it had reached 80 percent. David Garth, the most successful practitioner of the new politics, succinctly summed up the present reality when he asserted that political effort outside commercials "is a waste of time and money." The result is that the inordinate power of money in American politics is larger now than it was a generation ago.

Nothing, perhaps, better illustrates today's sharp cleavage with past electioneering than Rep. Millicent Fenwick's 1982 campaign for the United States Senate seat from New Jersey. Now in her seventies, Fenwick grew up with the old politics. "I have a total amateur approach," she told *The New York Times,* reflecting her traditional reliance on volunteer activity. But she reluctantly admitted to hiring a television consultant, studying polls, and submitting to the new fund-raising imperative. "I have never used a television person before, and all this professionalism is not happy-making, being packaged by professionals as though you were some new kind of invention like the splash-free valve on a faucet." Yet soon Fenwick commercials began the "thematic" bombardment, polls suggested tactics, and fund raisers started scrambling. Ironically, she was defeated by a wealthy newcomer who had no reservations about television.

Perhaps an even more telling gauge of the transformation of the political process was Theodore White's bewilderment in covering the presidential election of 1980. Since 1960 he had been the country's premier chronicler of the summit contests. Now, baffled by the new system, and nearly certain it signaled democracy's decline, he left the campaign trail and went home to watch it all on television. Always the quintessential insider, he now felt himself irrelevant bric-a-brac from the age of Dwight Eisenhower. He decided, "I could sit at home and learn as much or more about the frame of the campaign as I could on the road." But in fact, Teddy White, without knowing it, was still at the center of things: all the strategy, all the organization, converged on the screen in front of him, coaxing the voters' acquiscence.

And the voters, more and more, choose to stay away. Ronald Reagan's 1980 presidential victory has been called the most decisive since Franklin Roosevelt's in 1932. Yet it drew the smallest voter turnout in modern history. Just over half the registered voters exercised their franchise that year, and fewer than 20 percent of adults over eighteen years of age gave the new President a "landslide." This decline in registration and voting and the ascendance of the media is no temporal coincidence. Increasingly politics has become a spectator sport, with the public watching without participating. The candidate moves in front of the voters on film, while the continued publication of polls keeps him abreast of the latest standings. Election day thus becomes a time for ratification rather than decision. Today many just don't bother. Worst of all, there are no signs that this trend will not continue. What if, someday, we give an election and no one comes?

The media, of course, is not wholly responsible for this imperilment. The public's disillusionment with politics and politicians is another cause, and it has happened before. The very size of the country and the aftereffects of the sixties' turbulence among the young create an air of alienation, discouragement, and irrelevance. But the media revolution is truly that, and in some form it is here to stay. Yet it is not immune to change. The convention system replaced caucuses a century and a half ago; primaries replaced conventions in most states in this century; and amendments, court decisions, and congressional legislation have immensely widened voter eligibility. The process has adjusted to changing technology in printing and to the democratization of the telephone and radio. There is no reason why the media revolution can not also be made apt to democratic purposes. But that is the task of the generation that is growing up in it, not those who suffered the shock of its introduction and present triumph.

10

I Am Not a Crook! Corruption in Presidential Politics

by Kenneth G. Alfers

President Richard Nixon's assertion in 1973 that he was "not a crook" was an astounding political statement. The very fact that he thought he needed to say it indicated the depth of suspicion regarding the conduct of Nixon and his staff. Beyond that, it is unlikely that the majority of Americans were about to believe such a statement. The unfolding Nixon scandals were causing increasing disillusionment with politics and were reconfirming widely held suspicions about politicians.

To this day, Nixon's defenders say that even if he did engage in wrongdoing, he was no worse than any other President—that is, "they all do it, don't they?" In fact, the historical evidence shows that the Nixon administration surpassed all others in the pervasiveness of its corruption. Furthermore, as the late Leon Jaworski, special prosecutor in the Watergate scandal, has said, there was no doubt that the former President was personally involved in many of the misdeeds of his presidency.

It is true that two other administrations were noted for their corruption—those of U.S. Grant and Warren Harding. The following essay compares those scandalous administrations with that of Nixon in the hope that knowledge of past corruption "can lessen the chance that it will be allowed to reach such proportions in the future." We may have to pay the price of vigilance, but we cannot afford corruption in presidential politics.

One of the most severe tests the U.S. political system can experience is the removal of the President for reasons of corruption. What makes political corruption so abhorrent is the fact that politicians are supposed to be representative of a particular district, state, or the nation as a whole. Unfortunately, the crooked politician may be more representative than it is sometimes realized. In "non-political" affairs there is often pressure to get ahead by any means necessary. Therefore, it might follow naturally that some politicians, who on the whole are usually little better or little worse than the rest of society, engage in illegal conduct. Even though they may be given the authority to act in the public interest, some of them may not rise above the drive for selfish, personal gain.

When political corruption reaches all the way to the President of the United States, the whole country justifiably takes an interest. The President is the one politician on whom all the voters can decide, and, therefore, all citizens feel that they have a stake in how the President conducts himself. As Head of State, the President does represent the United States at national and international functions. Thus, if a President engages in, or allows his administration to engage in, corrupt activities, the nation feels a sense of betrayal.

Three times within the last century the American presidency and, therefore, the American people, have been shaken by the exposure of widespread political corruption in the executive branch. First during the era of Reconstruction after the Civil War, later in the aftermath of the first World War, and more recently as the country emerged from the Vietnam War, the American people have had their faith in their national leaders severely tested. The nation weathered each storm without collapsing, but the damage has been great nevertheless. As historian Jarol B. Manheim has said, the nation emerged

> with its confidence shaken, its trust disabused, and its cynicism predominant. Indeed, in each instance the greatest cost of scandal has been, not the dollars lost through corrupt practices or the disservice to the national interest resulting from improper policies, but rather the decline in political interest and . . . support among the American population. The greatest cost of political corruption, in other words, has been to the political system itself. (Jarol B. Manheim, *Deja Vu: American Political Problems in Historical Perspective,* p. 96. For an analysis of the three presidential scandals discussed in this essay, read Chapter 4 of Manheim's book.)

By taking a closer look at the scandals attached to Presidents Grant, Harding, and Nixon, we can more fully understand how corruption ruined each man's presidency. We can attempt to understand the forces which led to their betrayal of public trust. We can examine what forces, both inside and outside the political system, exposed scandals to public scrutiny and brought about rectification. Finally, perhaps a fuller understanding of past corruption can lessen the chance that it will be allowed to reach such proportions in the future.

The Grant Administration

Ulysses S. Grant is often considered one of America's worst presidents, primarily because of the widespread political corruption which existed during his presidency.

Ironically enough, the scandal most often associated with the Grant era was not of his making. However, the uncovering of the so-called Credit Mobilier Scandal took place during his tenure and, therefore, was associated in the public mind with all the other misdeeds.

The Credit Mobilier was a railroad construction company established by the directors of the Union Pacific Railroad. The Union Pacific was interested in building a transcontinental railroad, especially since 1864 when the government offered a grant of 20 million acres of land and a loan of $55 million to encourage railroad construction. In effect, when the directors of the Union Pacific created the Credit Mobilier, there existed two corporations, separate but with identical ownership. Once they had this dual mechanism in place, the fraud commenced.

The Union Pacific proceeded to award construction contracts at inflated rates to the Credit Mobilier, which, of course, was owned by the very people who were letting the contracts. For example, a man named Oakes Ames, a shovel manufacturer and holder of Credit Mobilier stock, received a contract to build 667 miles of railroad for $42,000 a mile. This included a stretch of 238 miles *that had already been built*—at a cost of $27,000 per mile! The two companies kept a fantastic system of duplicate books, and between December 1867 to December 1868 the Credit Mobilier netted an estimated $40 to $50 million and paid a dividend of 595 percent.

Since these financial shenanigans involved government funds, it behooved the swindlers to keep the government out of its affairs. They accomplished this in two ways. First, they simply bribed the government commissioners whose jobs it was to oversee the construction of the railroad. Second, they distributed Credit Mobilier stock to members of Congress. They were aided in the latter pursuit by the above-mentioned Oakes Ames, who doubled as a member of the House of Representatives and sat on the Pacific Railroad Committee in the House. Ames put the matter quite succinctly in a letter later made public. "We want more friends in this Congress. There is no difficulty in getting men to look after their own property."

The scandal finally broke in 1872 when a suit was filed against the Credit Mobilier for delivery of stock which the plaintiff claimed to have purchased. Documents in the suit were leaked to the press, and the resulting outcry led to a congressional investigation. The disclosures in the investigation tainted several members of Congress and the Vice President. Two congressmen, Oates Ames and James Brooks, who sat on the U.P. Board of Directors, were censured. Vice President Schuyler Colfax was shown to have cashed-in twenty shares of Credit Mobilier stock, and he escaped impeachment proceedings by the fact that his term had almost expired anyway. But in the end the House white-washed the whole affair when the investigative report said that dishonest practices had been committed but that no one was guilty of them. A later governmental suit aimed at recovering some of the money was thrown out when the courts ruled that the government had no claim against the Credit Mobilier, since the Union Pacific, not the government, had let contracts to that company. Not surprisingly, the directors of the Union Pacific did not seek to recover funds from the directors of the Credit Mobilier!

President Grant was clearly not involved in the Credit Mobilier Scandal, but it became associated with him in two ways. First, Grant proclaimed total and badly misplaced confidence in Vice President Colfax's innocence. Second, the exposure of the Credit Mobilier Scandal coincided with disclosures of wrong-doing *within* the executive branch.

As Jarol Manheim has stated, "the President's own judgment was more clearly at issue in the second great scandal of the era, the Gold Conspiracy." Briefly stated, this scheme involved the attempt by two crafty businessmen of questionable ethics, Jay Gould and Jim Fisk, Jr., to corner the gold market by manipulating the government's policy regarding the price of gold. Gold was used as a medium of exchange for foreign and some domestic transactions, so there was a demand for the commodity which was in relatively short supply. The government attempted to regulate the price of gold and stabilize the economy by selling off some of its gold every month. Gould and Fisk sought to stop government sales after they had bought gold at a low figure. When scarcity drove the price up, they would sell!

To accomplish their objective, Gould and Fisk worked through an elderly real estate operator named Abel Corbin, who also happened to be President Grant's brother-in-law. Corbin introduced Gould and Fisk to the President, who was impressed by wealth and those who had it. Gould convinced the President that the economy would benefit from higher gold prices, which would result from reduced government sales. Grant went along with this reasoning and ordered the Secretary of Treasury to halt government sales. Grant then went on vacation, aboard a special train provided by Gould.

The conspirators now began to buy gold furiously, and soon they held contracts on roughly twice the available supply. The price of gold rose sharply. Grant, finally realizing what was happening, ordered the Treasury to sell $4 million in gold on September 24, 1869, a day that became known as "Black Friday." The price of gold fell drastically, leaving Fisk and a number of innocent businessmen facing bankruptcy. Gould had sold out before the crash when Corbin told him of Grant's decision to order the government sale. The public saw Grant as a slow-witted associate in an obvious scheme against the public interest. Their confidence in his judgment was considerably lessened.

Grant's naivete was further illustrated by the Whiskey Ring Scandal, which involved his personal secretary, Orville E. Babcock. The Whiskey Ring consisted of a sizable group of distillers, shippers, and government inspectors who conspired to deprive the government of tax revenues on whiskey produced in several large cities. When Babcock was implicated to the tune of $25,000 cash, plus diamonds, rare liquors, and other amenities, Grant went to extreme lengths to protect him. At Babcock's request, Grant tried to get him a trial before a friendly military tribunal. Failing at that, Grant issued an order that essentially denied the use of plea bargaining and trades of immunity for those aiding the government's case against Babcock. When the trial began, Grant filed a deposition assuring the jury of Babcock's integrity. The deposition, along with apparently perjured testimony of defense witnesses, led to Babcock's acquittal. Afterward, Grant dismissed from the government those who had played a leading role in prosecuting Babcock, including Treasury Secretary Benjamin H. Bristow.

As one historian phrased it, the Grant presidency was "The Era of Good Stealings." Further examples include the Treasury Scandal of 1873, in which James Sanborn made $213,500 by collecting delinquent taxes. Grant's Secretary of War, W. W. Belknap, augmented his $8,000 annual salary by selling appointments of War Department positions, most notably those as traders on

Indian posts, for as much as $20,000 apiece. Belknap resigned but was impeached by the House of Representatives anyway. He escaped conviction in the Senate only because most of those voting "not guilty" thought it improper to impeach someone who had already resigned.

Still other examples of political corruption under Grant can be cited. One instance involved presidential appointees to direct the customhouses in New York and New Orleans—the latter position being filled by one of Grant's brothers-in-law—who used their positions for personal and political gain. Another scandal involved the wife of George Williams, Grant's third Attorney General, who, apparently with her husband's advice and consent, accepted a bribe of some $30,000 to halt a suit in which her husband was involved. Grant's Secretary of Interior, Columbus Delano, resigned after being implicated in a scheme involving fraudulent land warrants for veterans. Finally, George M. Robeson, Secretary of the Navy, used his influence to help a Philadelphia grain dealer, as well as his own income.

The list of misdeeds could go on, but the point has been amply illustrated. The Grant Era was one of the most corrupt in U.S. history, although Grant himself was not dishonest. Rather, his weaknesses were in his inability to judge character and in his blind loyalty to unworthy appointees. He made possible and naively defended the indiscretions of others. That, more than anything else, earned for Grant his lowly position in American political history. Unfortunately, he would be joined by others.

The Harding Administration

It was another fifty years before political corruption permeated the executive branch as it did under Grant. That does *not* mean that political corruption did not exist. In fact, in the late nineteenth and early twentieth centuries it became almost an accepted fact that big industrialists kept politicians on retainer. John D. Rockefeller was said to have had the best state legislators and U.S. Senators that money could buy. However, the Presidents from Hayes through Wilson, although many of them were hardly more than adequate in performing their jobs, were not remembered for political corruption. It was not until Warren Gamaliel Harding became President in 1921 that the Chief Executive was again surrounded by scandal.

It was once said that Harding's only qualification for President was that he looked like one. A kind and friendly man, Harding had risen to the position of U.S. Senator prior to his presidential nomination. He had played along with the Ohio political machine, also known as the Ohio Gang, and was the available man when the Republicans sought to capitalize on the post-World War I disillusionment with Democrats Harding, like Grant, was to be "more guilty of poor judgment and misplaced loyalties than of any personal corruption. Still, in a president of the United States such characteristics can be fatal, and in Harding's case were quite literally so." (Manheim, p. 109)

Before considering the infamous Teapot Dome Scandal, let us take note of several other examples of political corruption during Harding's Presidency.

One scandal involved Charles R. Forbes, who headed the Veteran's Bureau. Forbes was an amiable fellow who could play poker, the type of man that Harding liked. He proceeded to use his position for personal gain and to help his friends and relatives. He made appointments—one of the appointees was his brother-in-law—to government jobs which hardly demanded any work. In fact, one employee picked up an annual salary of $4,800 for two hours of work each *year*. Forbes also connived with private business firms to swindle the government out of money appropriated for building veterans' hospitals. Furthermore, he conspired to dispose of "surplus" hospital goods at a considerable loss to the government and considerable gain to himself. When Forbes' misdeeds were exposed, Harding, like Grant in earlier times, stuck by his appointee. Finally, Forbes resigned, and after a Senate investigation and nine-week trial, he was sentenced to two years in jail and a $10,000 fine.

Another Harding appointee, Thomas W. Miller, was caught with his hand in the till. Miller was the Alien Property Custodian, whose job it was to oversee the settlement of claims on alien property seized during World War I. In one celebrated case, Miller ended up splitting some $441,000 with another Harding crony, Jess Smith, after approving a fraudulent transfer of $7 million worth of alien property. When the case was exposed, Miller was sentenced to eighteen months in prison, Attorney General Harry Daugherty refused to testify on grounds he might incriminate himself, and Jess Smith committed suicide. Smith had apparently decided that his career of dispensing government positions, immunity from government prosecutions, and access to government files could last no longer. Daugherty's Justice Department, popularly known as the "Department of Easy Virtue," was under constant suspicion for illegal acts ranging from the illegal sale of pardons and liquor permits to the operation of an espionage network which shadowed Congressmen in search of blackmail material. Harding's successor, Calvin Coolidge, requested Daugherty's resignation, something the loyal Harding would not do. Daugherty later stood trial twice on corruption charges, but the juries failed to convict him both times.

Another cabinet member was not so fortunate. Albert Fall, Harding's Secretary of Interior, became the first cabinet member to be sentenced to jail for engaging in illegal activities while holding public office. Fall's conviction resulted from his involvement in the Teapot Dome Scandal. Teapot Dome referred to a rock formation which set atop Naval Oil Reserve Number Three in Wyoming. The Teapot Dome Reserve and two others in California had been established prior to World War I as a safeguard for the preservation of oil possibly needed for military operations. When Fall took over the Interior Department he persuaded Harding to order the transfer of the oil reserves from the Navy Department to the Interior. Harding later wrote a letter to the Senate declaring that he not only approved the transfer but also all "subsequent acts" in the matter. Had he not died, such an admission may have brought about impeachment proceedings against Harding, for the "subsequent acts" of Albert Fall led to his imprisonment.

What Fall did was to lease to private oilmen E. L. Doheny and Harry Sinclair the rights to develop the naval oil reserves, with the government to receive a *portion* of the oil. He also improved his own finances in the process, receiving a $100,000 "loan" from Doheny and a payment of $68,000 from Sinclair. (Testimony on the Sinclair money received a humorous twist when Sinclair's secretary testified that he had been talking about "six or eight cows" not "sixty-eight thous." It seems that secretaries have to contrive some fabulous stories to cover misdeeds, *a la* Rosemary Woods with the Nixon tapes). When suspicions arose about the oil transfer and about Fall's new-found wealth, a congressional investigation was launched by Montana Senator Thomas J. Walsh. Similar to the Watergate Hearings fifty years later, other congressional business ground to a halt while the scandal was exposed.

The congressional hearings led to the appointment by President Coolidge of two special prosecutors and a lengthy series of trials which began in late 1926. By March, 1930, the trials were over, but the results were less than clear. The leases on the Teapot Dome and the other naval reserves were invalidated because they resulted from fraud, corruption, collusion, and conspiracy. But Fall and Doheny were acquitted on charges of conspiracy as were Fall and Sinclair in a second trial. However, Sinclair did serve brief sentences for contempt of Congress and contempt of court, and Fall was convicted of receiving a bribe from Doheny and was sentenced to a year in jail and a $100,000 fine. On the other hand, Doheny was acquitted of bribing Fall! The verdicts caused Senator George W. Norris to remark that it is "very difficult, if not impossible, to convict one hundred million dollars." Similarly, a historian has remarked that the decisions undermined faith in the courts and gave currency to the saying that "in America everyone is assumed guilty until proven rich."

Harding, who had also been the object of whispers that he maintained a mistress at the White House, was spared the full revelations of the scandals. His suspicions had been aroused, however, and he was heard to have grumbled about the disloyalty of his "god-damned friends." While returning from a speaking tour on the West Coast, he died of pneumonia and thrombosis on August 2, 1923. At the time, he was mourned sorrowfully and emotionally by a country unaware of the corruption yet to be disclosed. His reputation was subsequently tarnished, although like Grant, his personal honesty was not the issue. Rather, like his predecessor of fifty years earlier, his weakness in judgment and guidance submitted the country to its worst display of political corruption since Grant had left office.

Fortunately for the Republicans, Calvin Coolidge was President when most of the revelations about the Harding scandals became public. Coolidge had the image of a Puritan ascetic, and no one questioned his integrity. Years later, FDR was accused of abusing his powers of patronage, Truman was criticized for tolerating influence peddling, Eisenhower was said to be too protective of aide Sherman Adams, and some referred to LBJ as "Landslide" Lyndon for his suspicious victory in a 1948 Senate race. "But fifty years passed before another major scandal . . . the most centralized and most pernicious of all, shook the nation to its very foundations and forced the de facto impeachment of a president of the United States. That scandal was Watergate, and the president was Richard Milhous Nixon." (Manheim, p. 119)

The Nixon Administration

The name Watergate originally referred to a posh apartment and office complex in Washington, D.C., which housed the headquarters of the Democratic National Committee. On June 17, 1972, five men were arrested for breaking into those headquarters, and from that day on Watergate became the name for the most scandalous of all presidential corruptions. The burglars had in their possession cameras, electronic bugging devices, several crisp new $100 bills in sequential order, and notebooks which included the names of E. Howard Hunt and G. Gordon Liddy, the latter a counsel to the Committee to Reelect the President (CREEP). Questions were thus raised about the connection between the Nixon White House, whose press secretary, Ron Ziegler, termed the affair "a third-rate burglary," and the burglars. By the time those questions were answered several years later, some sixty-three people were charged with crimes associated with the Nixon presidency, fifty-four of them were convicted or pleaded guilty, and the President himself resigned in disgrace.

Obviously, the break-in itself did not seem to merit such an extensive list of guilty parties. Had matters been handled openly at the time the break-in occurred, the fallout would not have been so great. However, the White House decided to cover up any connection between the President and the burglary. Elements of the cover-up included payment of "hush-money," frequent lies by the President and his spokesmen (the White House referred to these as "misstatements" or as "inoperative" remarks), misuse of the Justice Department, and manipulation of the Central Intelligence Agency.

Very few of the details of the cover-up were revealed before Richard Nixon had defeated George McGovern in the 1972 presidential election. During the summer following that election a Senate committee, chaired by Senator Sam Ervin of North Carolina, began investigating campaign practices. Television viewers took more than a casual interest as John W. Dean, former counsel to President Nixon, traced an elaborate White House plot to cover up the Watergate Affair, a cover-up that was denied by two top White House aides, H. R. Haldeman and John Ehrlichman. With Dean standing virtually alone, the committee needed corroboration. It got that and more when a White House assistant, Alexander P. Butterfield, revealed that a taping system in the President's office had probably recorded Dean's conversations, and all others, held in that office. The Senate Committee and Special Prosecutor Archibald Cox, who had been named earlier by Nixon to handle Watergate-related prosecutions, went after a whole series of relevant tapes. Nixon refused to turn them over on the grounds of executive privilege. A lengthy political and legal battle

The Senate Select Committee on Watergate chaired by
Sen. Sam Ervin. (Photograph by Don White. Instructional
Resources Corp.)

was now joined, with the first turning point occurring on Saturday, October 20, 1973, when President Nixon fired Cox and accepted the resignations of Attorney General Elliot Richardson and Deputy Attorney General William Ruckelshaus, who had both refused Nixon's order to dismiss Cox. Known as the "Saturday Night Massacre," this event caused a massive public outcry of indignation aimed at the President. It was becoming more obvious to the public that Nixon, indeed, must have something to hide. (See Manheim, pp. 121–122)

Numerous revelations throughout the Watergate investigation added to Nixon's problems. At the end of 1972 it was revealed that even though Nixon had become a millionaire while in office, he had paid less than $1,000 in income taxes in 1970 and 1971. Meanwhile, when the White House agreed to release tapes subpoenaed by the special prosecutor, it announced that two critical tapes were missing and one had an eighteen and one-half minute gap where a presidential discussion of Watergate should have been. In March, 1974, seven presidential aides and election officials were indicted for their roles in the cover-up, and seven for involvement in a break-in at the office of the psychiatrist for Daniel Ellsberg, who had been implicated in releasing sensitive Pentagon documents to the press. On April 29, 1974, Nixon went before a national television audience to announce that he was releasing more than a thousand pages of edited transcripts of presidential conversations. Contrary to his hopes, the transcripts only deepened public outcry, for they revealed the tone of the White House conversations as being "cynical, amoral, vindictive, self-serving, and conspiratorial." (Thomas A. Bailey and David M. Kennedy, *The American Pageant,* Sixth Edition, p. 914) In July the Supreme Court ordered Nixon to release the tapes themselves, and the discrepancies with the transcripts became obvious.

Finally, the House Judiciary Committee voted impeachment of the President of the United States. The Committee approved three articles of impeachment: the first charged the President with obstruction of justice; the second charged Nixon with abuse of the power of his office; the third accused him of conduct "subversive of constitutional government" by ignoring lawful subpoenas for tapes and other written documents. Most observers thought at least the first article would be approved by the full House of Representatives and, therefore, necessitate a trial in the Senate.

The House vote and the Senate trial never happened. On August 5, 1974, Nixon released three subpoenaed tapes of conversations he had with aides soon after the Watergate break-in. The "smoking gun" that skeptics had wanted had been found, for the tapes left no doubt that Nixon had been deeply involved in the cover-up all along. What congressional support he had left now collapsed, and on August 8, 1974, Nixon told a national television audience that he was resigning the following day. Had he not resigned he likely would have become the first U.S. President to have been impeached by the House and removed from office after conviction in the Senate. (Incidentally, resignation also allowed Nixon to receive his full retirement benefits.)

Nixon's closest associates, former Attorney General John Mitchell and presidential advisers H. R. Haldeman and John Ehrlichman, were convicted of Watergate-related crimes and sentenced to prison. John Dean, White House counsel and star witness in the Watergate investigation, pleaded guilty to charges of participating in the cover-up and served four months in jail. Charles Colson, a political adviser and reputed "hatchet man" in the White House, served six months in jail for obstruction of justice. Jeb Stuart Magruder, a high official on Nixon's campaign staff, was jailed for seven months for obstruction of justice. G. Gordon Liddy, who presented the burglary plans to Mitchell, spent more than four years in jail. E. Howard Hunt, who recruited the burglars, served thirty-two months.

The Watergate break-in, the cover-up, the resignation of Richard Nixon, and the imprisonment of his aides did not constitute the whole story of the Nixon scandals. Ten months before Nixon resigned, his Vice-President, Spiro Agnew, stepped down from his position. Agnew had come under investigation from a Baltimore grand jury investigating charges of kickbacks and tax fraud in Maryland. When evidence of his guilt seemed overwhelming, Agnew pleaded no contest to a charge of income tax evasion and resigned. Nixon, under terms of the Twenty-fifth Amendment, appointed Gerald R. Ford as Vice-President, who then became President following Nixon's resignation. A few weeks after

Nixon's departure, Ford pardoned the former President for any misdeeds he may have committed while President.

There were other scandals in the Nixon years as well. Richard G. Kleindienst, Mitchell's successor as Attorney General, pleaded guilty to a charge of obstructing prosecution of an antitrust suit against International Telephone and Telegraph (ITT). There were a number of charges related to illegal campaign contributions, which led to guilty pleas from former Nixon attorney Herbert Kalmback and former Treasury Secretary Maurice Stans, who was director of fund-raising activities for CREEP. Still other illegalities involved the so-called "dirty tricks" of the 1972 campaign and the actions of the White House "plumbers."

The list of guilty parties in the Nixon scandals could go on, but it is clear that political corruption reached new depths under Nixon. The pervasiveness of wrongdoing outstripped even that of the Grant and Harding eras. Like his predecessors in corruption, Nixon had encouraged a political atmosphere which led to disregard of the law. Unlike his predecessors, Nixon was personally involved in direct abuse of presidential power.

There are some other interesting similarities in a retrospective glance at the three periods of corruption. Each occurred during a Republican administration. In each instance, the reflexive response of the President was to deny scandal and to cover it up and protect associates. Congressional hearings and special legal procedures outside the executive-controlled Justice Department were significant in bringing the corruption into the open. This supports the importance of the system of checks and balances within the constitutional framework. The press also played an important role in each case, most notably in the Nixon scandals. The dogged reporting of Carl Bernstein and Bob Woodward of the Washington *Post* will be long-remembered as an example of the press's role in exposing wrongdoing in public office.

Three additional considerations deserve comment. First, all three crises in the presidency followed extended periods of national turmoil and each followed costly wars. Secondly, each scandalous administration followed a period in which the powers of the presidency were expanded. The development of this "imperial presidency" contributed to Richard Nixon's view that the President of the United States was above the law. Grant and Harding were not seeking personal power, but their trusting nature allowed subordinates to take advantage of the presidency for financial gain. Nixon's offense was greater than the two earlier Presidents in this sense, for he sought to acquire and maintain illegal political power as well as financial gain. Finally, each period of corruption resulted in a breakdown of trust between the American people and their government. The losses here cannot be measured, but they are nevertheless real and extremely significant.

There is some scandal in almost every presidential administration and in almost every session of Congress, but the massive scale of corruption during the Grant, Harding, and Nixon eras reached shocking proportions. It seems that there is a regular pattern of a fifty-year interval between such extensive political abuses. Perhaps by keeping in mind the forces which brought about the scandals, by keeping a vigilant watch on the activities of political leaders, and by making sure that their own sense of proper conduct serves as a model for politicians, the American people can prevent such abuses of political power from happening again.

11

Whatever Became of Jimmy Carter?

by Tom Wicker

The collapse of the imperial presidency of Richard Nixon opened the White House Doors for Jimmy Carter, whom Tom Wicker calls "the least imperial of Presidents." Despite the opening, however, President Carter was not able to solidify his following and inspire confidence in his leadership. In 1980, the majority of American voters rejected him in favor of Ronald Reagan. For years after that, President Reagan blamed ex-president Carter for most of the country's problems. As Mr. Wicker says, Carter became "not only a defeated but a widely disdained President, figuring hardly at all in his country's or his party's affairs."

But was he as bad a President as many people seem to think? Tom Wicker, a highly respected columnist for *The New York Times,* presents a perceptive analysis of Jimmy Carter's strengths and weaknesses in the following article. He provides us with a needed corrective on President Carter's record. Moreover, he raises some intriguing questions about "presidential leadership, American politics, the press, even the people themselves."

He was one of the most intelligent men ever to occupy the White House, and perhaps the hardest worker. He achieved the presidency—the first person from a southern state to do so since before the Civil War—by a Horatio Algerish rise from political obscurity. A voracious student of domestic and foreign problems, intimately familiar with their minutest details, he was an efficient administrator who usually answered memorandums in writing the day he received them. At his frequent news conferences he was knowledgeable, candid— even grammatical. Honestly self-searching, willing to confess error, he was the least imperial of Presidents, a man of considerable moral courage who often made great decisions largely on the merits of the case—as most Americans profess to believe a President always should.

Yet—to some extent *therefore*—the voters turned on James Earl Carter Jr. in 1980 as if in a paroxysm of exasperation and drove him from office after only one term. They did so in spite of the Camp David accords and the Egyptian-Israeli treaty, the Panama Canal treaties, the negotiation of SALT II, the normalization of relations with China, the reestablishment of human rights as a principal factor in American foreign policy, the most extensive environmental-protection program seen before or since, and four restrained budgets with relatively manageable deficits.

That record would win respect and re-election for most Presidents. But nearly four years after he left office, Jimmy Carter is not only a defeated but a widely disdained President, figuring hardly at all in his country's or his party's affairs.

Early this year I began to wonder about Jimmy Carter's near-total absence from the 1984 presidential campaign. How could a President who had entered office as such a fresh face, on such a wave of new hopes, have been so quickly banished? How could an able, conscientious man with a solid record of achievement be so thoroughly repudiated? Or so widely considered a weak and vacillating leader, while his easy-going, ill-informed successor—with no list of successes objectively comparable to Carter's—is favored for reelection as a leader who is "standing tall"? What, if anything, might the answers say about presidential leadership, American politics, the press, even the people themselves?

Ultimately, I flew to Atlanta to ask all that of Jimmy Carter. Before I left New York, I learned he hadn't changed in one regard; he was still a man of precision and punctuality, and his secretary warned me seriously to be on time.

I arrived well ahead of time at his rather formal, but light and roomy, office in the Robert Woodruff Library of Emory University; Carter came in right on the dot, having walked across campus with his secret service protectors from an early-morning undergraduate lecture on Soviet-American relations.

Neat in his blue suit, trim, polite, his smile and teeth flashing as always, Carter still had in his blue eyes the look that became known in the 1976 campaign as "steely." I think now that *frosty* would be a better word. He appeared only a little older than the man who'd left the White House, considerably older than the one who'd entered it. I sensed that he still didn't like to play what one of the Georgia boys on his staff used to call "grab-ass with the press."

Though flinching from none of my questions—which, in sum, asked why and how he'd failed—Carter was more reticent, somewhat more defensive, less willing to concede fault even in hindsight, than most of his old colleagues had been. Only in discussing what he saw as Ronald Reagan's favorable treatment in the press—in comparison with his own—did Carter relax his obvious self-restraint.

"Reagan condemned Washington more than I did, and he's not considered an alien," he complained, his tone sharpening. "He often says things patently untrue at news conferences. I'd have been drummed out of office for that."

I think his complaint has merit; and there's little doubt that bad luck and misunderstanding and some nearly insurmountable difficulties plagued him in Washington. But my rummagings through a past that struck me somehow as more remote than four years ago, rummagings that often seemed like the turning of yellowed pages from another epoch, suggested what he must find hardest to accept; that Jimmy Carter also has himself to blame, and perhaps not least, for the unhappy fate of his presidency.

Entering in 1977 an office significantly weakened by Lyndon Johnson and Vietnam, by Richard Nixon and Watergate, any new President also would have encountered a world changing in many ways Americans had not found congenial—their new vulnerability, for example, to what many called "raggedy-assed" oil sheiks in the faraway Middle East.

Reaction had long been building against the dominance of the post–New Deal Democratic party and its drift toward bigger government and more numerous federal programs, aptly symbolized by Lyndon Johnson's "Great Society." Carter had discovered that reaction—before many more-experienced politicians—and capitalized on it in his winning 1976 campaign.

But he had not converted a party whose three previous nominees had been Johnson, Hubert Humphrey, and George McGovern. He had seized only its titular leadership. The Democrats, moreover, were roughly divided between old New Dealers, conventionally liberal at home and toughly anticommunist abroad, and social and peace activists who wanted easier relations with the Soviet Union and social programs instead of military spending.

Jimmy Carter was not quite of either faction; he was more détente-minded than the New Dealers, but his fiscal policies were too conservative for the party's left wing. He was never seen as anti-Soviet enough to gain the confidence of the more hawkish Democrats; and as the years went by, his fiscal policies further alienated the New Left. So did the military-spending increases he finally approved.

A former naval officer and a reluctant spender at most, Carter was suspicious of military waste; in his first year he cut $2.5 billion from the Pentagon budget (and Congress cut $2 billion more). But by 1978 he had been forced to accept a 3 percent increase, since that had been set as a goal by all the NATO countries—a goal Carter privately regarded as a "conspiracy of defense ministers." Later, mostly to win votes from hawkish senators for ratification of SALT II, he reluctantly agreed to 5 percent annual growth in the Pentagon budget, beginning in 1981.

Thus, Jimmy Carter actually laid out a major course—increased U.S. military appropriations—along which Ronald Reagan pushed much further; which meant that to the left wing of the Democratic party, Carter appeared not only to be moving away from détente but to be sacrificing needed social spending to the insatiable demands of the military. These were dominant themes in Edward Kennedy's insurgent campaign against him in 1980.

Nor did Carter have the fealty of the "party in waiting"—those experienced bureaucrats, veterans of the Kennedy and Johnson administrations and of congressional staff service who had whiled away the Nixon-Ford years in law offices, faculty positions, foundations, and the like, waiting for a Democratic Restoration. These Democrats were first in line to man the new administration.

Save for his Georgia-based White House staff, Carter—the one-term governor and newcomer to Washington—had little choice but to take them on. He had never played on the larger national stage; his business experience was peanuts, his acquaintance slight. He had the limitations of the life he'd led, which was one reason he surrounded himself with Georgians he knew well and trusted—Bert Lance, Charlie Kirbo, Hamilton Jordan—a process one admirer described this way: "Carter carried his cocoon with him."

But when the new President welcomed aboard the "party in waiting," he found that it had its own agenda—more federal programs for everything from job training to sex education. Carter resisted. After all, Lyndon Johnson had had only a small deficit and negligible inflation when he launched the Great Society; Carter inherited a deficit of over $65 billion and 4.9 percent inflation. How could he deliver the traditional liberal "wish list"? But the Democrats largely staffing his administration—as one of his closest associates put it—"overran him."

That had two damaging consequences: the Carter administration became more associated with the political legacy of the Great Society—"social engineering," big spending—than Carter ever wanted or intended; and the "party in waiting," far from accepting and supporting him, found good reason—in his resistance and in their failure to understand *his* goals—for covertly opposing him.

Thus, when troubles came Jimmy Carter had no reserves of party support to call upon, no deep pool of long association, old friendships, or common endeavor to draw from.

"Jimmy Carter," a diplomat who served under him and other Presidents (including Reagan) told me in 1983, "was the victim of his own virtues. He made important decisions more often on the basis of what he thought was right, without regard to political consequences, than any President I've seen."

My diplomat friend was not speaking entirely in praise, although he did admire Carter's courage and intelligence. But he knew, as many other experienced politicians and government servants—even some journalists—know, that political success is not necessarily or always a matter of being morally right, even when a leader can be sure of what *is* right. Lincoln, Roosevelt, all the most successful Presidents rarely acted "without regard to political consequences."

Jimmy Carter often did, contrary to public opinion of him. Even after reaching "the pinnacle of politics," Carter never conceded that he had to be what his chief domestic adviser, Stuart Eizenstat, called "the nation's chief politician": responsible less for being morally right than for persuading Congress and the American people—in Harry Truman's phrase—"to do what they ought to do without persuasion."

But Carter "didn't like to horse-trade," Eizenstat recalls. "He thought it was a perversion of the process. He felt that people should make decisions on the basis of merit and high ideals. The last way to get his support was to say something would be politically advantageous."

In his sunny Atlanta quarters I asked Carter whether he still believed the voters would reward a man who "did the right thing" regardless of politics.

Carter hesitated. When he finally answered, it was as if to prove he'd been right all along:

"I imposed a grain embargo on Russia after the invasion of Afghanistan. That was just before the Iowa caucuses, in a grain state. They still voted for me over Kennedy."

So, he added, with apparent modesty but firmly, "I hope the answer to your question is yes." If he were ever again in office, he said, "political consequences" still would not be high on his list of considerations. Then, after another pause: "No way I could do it differently."

An admirable statement? Yes, in human terms, but arrogant too, and politically disdainful—arrogant because it implied that Jimmy Carter would always know the right thing to do and would never fear doing it, and disdainful of the skill and knowledge with which a President can shape political consequences for the most positive effect on his highest goals.

Carter, of course, was not without political instincts, nor was he always "above politics." I watched his 1976 campaign closely; sensing changing public attitudes, he told me long before the event that he would defeat George Wallace in the Florida primary. I didn't believe him, but he knew what he was talking about. That year, he was called "fuzzy on the issues"—a calculated strategy for letting different voting blocs each think he was *their* man. In 1980 he had no compunction about making such serious charges as that Reagan would divide the country, whites from blacks, North from South.

Nevertheless, in the White House, Carter, in more ways than one, was indeed "the victim of his own virtues." A major reason for his unpopularity and ultimate defeat, for example, surely was one of those virtues—his willingness to take on tough issues, problems that sooner or later had to be settled but that were sure political losers for the President who braved them:

• **The energy crisis.** Coming between the two great "oil shocks" of the 1970s, the 1976 campaign was not one in which the so-called energy crisis figured strongly. Nevertheless, the new President pledged to present Congress, within ninety days, with a "comprehensive energy policy" designed to reduce American reliance on imported oil; that goal was so important, he told Americans, that the struggle to reach it was the "moral equivalent of war."

It might have been, but he could hardly have set himself a harder, more thankless task. The unnecessary ninety-day deadline gave him too little time to consult Congress on what the traffic would bear, even had he been inclined to do so. And a truly "comprehensive" policy was bound to demand sacrifices from consumers, offend powerful energy interests and their many supporters in Congress, put Democratic members of Congress in the uncomfortable position of defying either their constituents or their President, and—in short—please practically no one.

But Carter pushed ahead. His energy bill was more than a hundred pages long and occupied Congress for eighteen months of controversy and confusion. Much of it was ultimately enacted, but none without bitter struggle and a mighty toll on Carter's political capital.

• **The Panama Canal treaties.** That astute Washington political preceptor Clark Clifford once observed that Carter's effort to win ratification of new Panama Canal treaties properly belonged in a second term—when a President had a record of accomplishment to build upon, and no reelection campaign to lose.

Panama's desire for greater control of the Canal and a new relationship with the U.S. had been hanging fire throughout the Johnson, Nixon, and Ford years; the public and Congress had stubbornly resisted what became known as "the giveaway" of one of the prized symbols of the nation's power. Polls showed that only 8 percent of Americans favored "any change" in the Canal's status when Carter took office, he recalled in our interview.

Some of his advisers, he said, shared Clifford's "strong inclination" to postpone the issue to a second term. But he and Secretary of State Cyrus Vance didn't think the matter could wait that long; Panamanian sensitivity and impatience were such that a popular uprising might have come at any time, with what Vance had told me would have been "serious consequences in the hemisphere and far broader consequences elsewhere in the Third World."

Besides, "it was not my nature," Carter told me, to duck a tough fight. The decision was made, he said—no trace of a second thought in his voice—"deliberately, by me," to go for a new treaty at once. So tough was the legislative battle, however, so strong public opposition, that Howard Baker—the Senate Republican leader and a crucial treaty supporter—later told Carter, "If I keep on voting right, I'll never come back to the Senate."

Winning the Panama vote, Carter said, was "almost a political miracle." If so, its political price was extremely great, and Jimmy Carter paid it in hard coin—particularly in his political base, where opposition to the treaties was powerful. In 1980 the man who had led the fight against the Canal "giveaway"—Ronald Reagan—carried nine southern states that had backed Carter, the southerner, in 1976.

• **The Middle East.** Harold Brown is sure of it. The seeming triumph at Camp David, the former Defense Secretary told me, "was Jimmy Carter's personal effort based on his personal beliefs. His commitment brought it about. Otherwise, Sadat's visit to Jerusalem would not have caused anything to happen."

"He was the architect," Sol Linowitz, Carter's Panama negotiator and later an adviser on the Middle East, agreed. And Carter went ahead, Linowitz pointed out, against the warnings of most of his Middle East experts. And for thirteen days at Camp David the President of the United States went back and forth between Sadat and Begin—two profoundly opposed and suspicious men, each representative of a historical idea as much as a nation or a political position—gradually, agonizingly bringing them to agreement on the return of the Sinai to Egypt and the framework for an Egyptian-Israeli peace treaty. Presidents Theodore Roosevelt and Woodrow Wilson had acted as peacemakers, too, but never so directly as Carter.

"The only reason he could do that was his intense preparation," Lloyd Cutler, Carter's White House counsel, told me years later. "He literally mastered the subject in every detail. You can't conceive of Ronald Reagan doing that."

Later, when the painfully arranged "peace process" at Camp David seemed to be breaking down, Carter went to Jerusalem and Cairo and brought to fruition the first peace treaty ever concluded between an Arab state and Israel. But the effort he put into Middle East peacemaking brought him little by way of political payoff.

To many American Jews his efforts appeared to be unwelcome "pressure on Israel" that risked its security. His later disputes with Begin over the West Bank settlements further soured the American political atmosphere. Carter's poll standing actually declined after his return from the Middle East, and in 1980 more Jews voted against him—for Reagan, for John Anderson—than for him.

So it seemed to go for Jimmy Carter. When he "normalized" relations with China, the logical follow-up to Richard Nixon's "opening," he was attacked—not least by Reagan—for deserting Taiwan. The negotiation of SALT II was concluded only after détente was dead and hawkish opposition had been aroused by the Soviet military buildup of the 1970s; then the Soviet invasion of Afghanistan ended any chance for treaty ratification. Even the grain embargo Carter had proudly cited to me cost him dearly among farmers as Reagan, the hard-line anticommunist, expediently promised to lift the embargo.

He was always a curious mixture of modesty and self-assurance—as he remained during my Atlanta interview. He had what some who know him well consider "real insecurities" that he tried to overcome with his gift for assimilating information. One of those friends suggested to me that, partially as a result, Jimmy Carter "didn't know what he didn't know. So he didn't aim high enough in the people he had around him. He didn't reach out soon enough to people beyond his experience—he didn't know he needed to."

Carter came to the White House with the view that Congress much resembled the Georgia legislature—"a bunch of corrupt rednecks," as one Georgian put it—with which he had warred continually as governor. So he approached Congress "with a certain meanness, when what you want in Washington is a little tit for tat. Some experience in the Senate would have taught him that." But Carter's *actual* experience had taught him, instead, that legislators had to be forced, not led.

The problem, however, was more than inexperience. Numerous previous administration officials told me that Carter had regarded most members of Congress as thoroughgoing politicians interested only in political gain, in comparison to his own willingness to rise above political pressures to serve the public interest—a willingness that had led *him,* for example, though at grievous cost, to proceed with trucking deregulation over the powerful opposition of the southern truckers who had supported him in 1976.

Assuming such a high posture, Carter, as Washington quickly learned, didn't "drink with the boys" in traditional political fashion. In contrast, the far more relaxed Reagan has established just such good off-hours relations with some of his strongest antagonists—Speaker Tip O'Neill, to take a good example. Nor did Carter ever really accept the "stroking"—the praise, preferment, and occasional political spoils—by which most Presidents try to bind congressional followers to their program.

Understanding Congress so poorly, Carter needed nothing more than he needed an experienced liaison man; instead, he named one of his Georgia loyalists, Frank Moore—who, members of Congress soon saw, knew little more about Capitol Hill and its denizens than the President did. By common estimate, it took two years for Moore to get on top of his job, by which time Carter's congressional relations were beyond repair.

The Washington press, for much the same reasons as Congress, also had little love for Jimmy Carter, despite the openness of his administration and his articulate, informative—and frequent!—news conferences. Reporters, a skeptical crew, tend to regard any politician who openly displays his or her religious faith—as Carter constantly did—as merely angling for the votes of churchgoing Americans. And when the phrase "I'll never tell you a lie" became part of Carter's 1976 campaign litany, experienced reporters knew that no President can afford to tell the truth, the whole truth, and nothing but the truth, all the time. Disliking what they saw as Carter's posturing, many determined to catch him in a lie and expose it. Some never stopped trying.

For his part, Carter hardly put himself out to win over the press corps, which he suffered no more gladly than he did Congress. More than three years after he left Washington, Carter's resentment of the press—despite his southern cordiality to me—was unmistakable. He could not, he said, remember "a columnist wholeheartedly supportive of me," while he called James J. Kilpatrick, George F. Will, and William F. Buckley Jr. "almost spokesmen" for Ronald Reagan.

Carter even outlined a sort of class theory of press discrimination, which suggested that Franklin Roosevelt and John Kennedy had represented the "eastern establishment" and Reagan a new "western establishment" of wealth and influence, so they'd been treated well by a press respectful of their status; but he lumped himself with Richard Nixon and Lyndon Johnson as "true outsiders" who had suffered in the press for having no establishment position.

Undoubtedly the cool relations between reporters and Carter colored press reports on his administration, if only subconsciously. When I asked him how much responsibility he thought the press bore for his failure to win reelection, he smiled his familiar thin smile, displaying no amusement at all, and said softly, "A lot."

Despite such problems, the record shows that Jimmy Carter accomplished a great deal in four years. But he *appeared* far less successful than he was, and not only because of poor relations with the press and television.

He had taken office with a diverse, ambitious agenda but had, as one of his most loyal aides ruefully put it, "no master plan, no order of priority. He went for all the laundry list at once. There was no building from one to another, no building up a picture of mounting triumph." When I asked Carter if, in retrospect, he agreed, he conceded with characteristic precision (but without admitting the point): "I had a long agenda of specific domestic and foreign policy goals, and we pursued all of them, if not simultaneously then sequentially."

But he also pointed out to me that one of his early congressional successes—a 1977 economic program that he said had later created many thousands of jobs—had been lost sight of in the controversy then developing over his energy proposals and the Panama Canal. In fact, by the estimate of Stuart Eizenstat, 90 percent of Carter's economic program, including a small tax cut, was passed by Congress in 1977.

Carter nevertheless got a quick reputation for "lack of leadership," because Congress at the same time was balking at such politically difficult Carter initiatives as the energy program, hospital cost containment, and welfare reform. And once a President's "image" has been set in his first few months— FDR's "hundred days" is the classic example—that image attains a life of its own, persisting sometimes far beyond any real evidence for it.

SALT II, for another example, probably could have been negotiated, possibly even ratified, in Carter's first hundred days, on the basis of the Ford-Brezhnev agreement reached at Vladivostok in November 1974. Important Republicans—Ford, Henry Kissinger, Howard Baker—were committed to those agreements, and the Senate probably would have ratified such a SALT quickly. If at the outset Carter had focused only on the treaty and on his economic program, a perfectly supportable position, he might well have earned an enduring reputation for strong leadership and direction—as Reagan did in the first half of 1981 by pushing through his promised budget and tax cuts and military-spending increases.

But rather than taking a quick SALT triumph—as well as obtaining a useful treaty—Carter abandoned the Vladivostok agreements and sent Secretary of State Vance to Moscow with an entirely new proposal for greater arms reductions.

The Soviets, nonplussed by the new proposals and suspicious of such an unorthodox approach, sent Vance packing and set the SALT negotiations back a year or more. Carter got neither the leadership credit he might have had nor, ultimately, the treaty that had been within his grasp.

Carter simply had too many programs going at once. At one point Speaker O'Neill sent word to the White House that ten or fifteen pending Carter bills were too many—to which three or four did the President give priority? Mr. Mondale and Hamilton Jordan were assigned to pare the list to essentials. They did, but when the President reviewed their work, he restored most of the items they'd eliminated.

Some of the many Carter initiatives inevitably seemed contradictory— for example, hospital cost control on the one hand, deregulation of airlines and trucking on the other. And as a consequence, Pat Caddell's polls showed, the Carter administration and its leader "never projected a coherent image," a clear public sense of where they were taking the country. Carter himself developed a reputation, mostly undeserved, for vacillation—beginning with his withdrawal in 1977 of the fifty-dollar-per-taxpayer rebate he had proposed as a stimulus to the economy.

That decision can now be seen as a justified reevaluation of policy, in light of a more rapid economic recovery than had been expected. But there is a thin line, not always recognized by the public, between a "flip-flop" and "reevaluations" such as these:

• In early 1980 the U.S. delegate to the UN Security Council, Donald McHenry, cast a vote supporting a resolution hostile to Israel. The next day Carter ordered the vote reversed, calling it an error caused by a mix-up in McHenry's instructions. Critics called this "flip-flop" a craven bid for Jewish votes in the forthcoming New York primary; but Sol Linowitz and others insist the original vote *was* a genuine mistake that Carter could not be dissuaded from correcting.

• After first calling upon the NATO governments to accept the neutron bomb, Carter abruptly canceled its production. This, too, appears to have been a painful but genuine reevaluation—"a midnight call of conscience," in Lloyd Cutler's plausible opinion. But it caused consternation in the alliance and further worsened the hostile relations between Carter and Helmut Schmidt of West Germany—two men of superior intellect and high confidence in their own virtues.

In all these "flip-flops," however his judgment may be questioned, Carter appears in retrospect less vacillating than strong-willed enough to ignore the advice of subordinates and change his mind publicly, whatever the political damage. Surely that's preferable to blind consistency; but the net political consequence—characteristically ignored, in all these cases, by Jimmy Carter— was a reputation for what Harold Brown called "Hamlet-like indecision." Watching that reputation grow, Brown concluded that Americans "associate agonized self-searching with a lack of leadership." Jimmy Carter's fate suggests Brown was right.

But Carter, now watching events from Georgia, is not alone in wondering why Ronald Reagan, too, is not more vigorously charged with "flip-flops"— for example, in withdrawing the Marines from Lebanon after he said it would be disastrous, even a "surrender," to do so; or in running up the biggest deficits in history, after promising a balanced budget in his 1980 campaign.

One answer is suggested by what Hedley Donovan, a Time Inc. executive who also served in the Carter White House, called Carter's "capacity for detail—which in many cases was excessive." He "got into the machinery too much." The result, said Andrew Young, of the "engineer's view of the world" was that "every detail of the bridge was in place, but he didn't tell the American people where it was going." By immersing himself in the details of programs and policies—often a strength—Carter so closely associated himself with them that when he decided to make changes, he was seen as indecisive; and when programs failed, he was identified with the failure.

He couldn't, at least didn't, talk well in slogans and simplicities. In speeches and at news conferences he overexplained, if anything, in an effort not to be simplistic, ignoring a cardinal political rule: If you can't put it on a bumper sticker, don't bring it up.

Reagan, in contrast, has a real talent for reducing complexities to bumper-sticker size. As a leader, he delegates authority, appears uninvolved in detail, but has nevertheless set a clear direction for his administration—reducing the size of government, building up the military. On that broad front he appears generally consistent—as it is not easy to do when a leader takes responsibility for details, as Carter did for that mistaken UN vote. Without such a general policy "framework" as Reagan has established, as one insider reflects today, "every compromise on detail seems to be a change with the wind."

Another result of Reagan's kind of leadership, according to polls, is that a public that does not strongly support many of his programs seems to like him personally. In his case, what he *does* and what he *is* are apparently judged separately. It may tell much about the two Presidents, personally and politically, that when Carter's attempt to rescue the hostages from Iran failed, he went on television himself to give the public the bad news; when Reagan had to withdraw the Marines from Lebanon, he let a State Department spokesman issue an announcement.

So by 1980 some of the reasons Jimmy Carter had been elected became reasons for his defeat. The nonpolitical outsider of 1976 was seen as an inept and vacillating amateur; the new face from beyond Washington couldn't seem to get along with Congress; the earnest, religious peanut farmer appeared aloof and self-righteous. His solid record of accomplishment was obscured by the seemingly aimless variety and scope of his enterprises, too many of which were sound but unpopular. No wonder a woman in a Los Angeles audience rose in the fall of 1980 to ask his White House aide, Anne Wexler, what many an American probably wanted to know:

"Why can't you make me feel good about my President?"

By then, of course, dominating all other reasons why few felt good about Jimmy Carter was the state of the economy—inflation, unemployment, and interest rates all going up—and the plight of the American hostages in Iran. Most analysts think these two issues, more than any others, destroyed in 1980 whatever chance remained for Carter to be reelected.

There's little question that he botched the economy. After campaigning against the "Ford recession," he overstimulated in 1977 and 1978—even after dropping the fifty-dollar rebate—failing to recognize what Eizenstat called "the sleeping giant" of inflation. After the giant woke up in 1978, Carter shifted his emphasis. But even before his inauguration he had pledged not to use wage and price controls, as Nixon had in 1972, or even to ask for standby authority to do so. When voluntary guidelines and "jawboning" predictably failed to halt inflation, he had no alternative but slowdown and recession—the harsh medicine to which he turned, too late, in 1980.

There was misfortune in all this, but miscalculation too. Some economic analysts argue that Carter could have fought inflation more effectively had it not been for what Hedley Donovan called "a tendency to blame it all on oil prices and an attitude that there was nothing the Carter administration could do about it—the whole Western world was being hit." In this view, Carter subtly conveyed a defeatist attitude on inflation that was depressing to investors and markets and counterproductive to Carter's guidelines and jawboning.

Iran was another matter. Carter can be faulted for admitting the shah to the United States for medical treatment, the decision that precipitated the seizure of the hostages; but that decision can be defended, too, on humanitarian grounds and because no one, in 1979, could have foreseen the length, complexity, and gravity of the Iranian response.

There's little need here to rehash Carter's yearlong efforts to free the hostages—except perhaps to report Cyrus Vance's considered judgment, long after the crisis, that "the situation had to run its course." The Ayatollah Khomeini was using the hostages to pull Iran together and establish his own control, in the chaos left by the shah's abdication, so Khomeini, Vance believes, had no intention of freeing the hostages, no matter what Carter did, until the Khomeini government was firmly established—and he didn't.

But the American public's initial rally-round-the-President support for Carter's efforts to recover the hostages gradually gave way to frustration. That frustration exploded into hostility when, on the last Sunday before the election of 1980, he went on television once again—unwisely interrupting a pro football game—to say that the latest possibility of winning the hostages' freedom had fizzled, as had all the others.

Every member of the Carter administration I talked to, from Secretary of State Vance on down, believed that if Carter had taken strong military action against Iran—even if the result had been failure, or a number of dead hostages, or a prolonged war risking Soviet involvement—he would have been reelected. Yet the same men and women unanimously agreed that Carter was

124

right not to take such action. And they proudly pointed out that—too late to influence the election—he finally did bring the hostages home, all of them, alive.

It was, said Zbigniew Brzezinski, "testimony to the strength of Carter's character" that he did not bomb Iran or declare war but negotiated patiently throughout the year while his reelection chances were trickling away. But what kind of testimony about the American people is it that this peaceful, patient course contributed so much to his defeat?

Carter, with his usual high-mindedness, is charitable on the point. He had never resented, he told me, other people's "personifying" him with the hostage issue. Rather, he thought that the public's long tolerance for his policy of negotiation was "a sign of American greatness" and "a vivid demonstration of proper priorities: we value human life and freedom, and we wouldn't forget about those people."

He conceded, however—with no apparent bitterness—that the television image of "Americans with white bandages around their eyes" may have been the cause of his defeat. Actually, I believe the true political effect of the hostage issue was that it contributed fatally to the public conclusion that Jimmy Carter was not a strong leader.

Carter's physical appearance and manner may have furthered the idea that he was weak. Slight of stature, he was usually depicted by cartoonists as a miniature figure. James Reston, a Scotsman, used to refer to him in *The New York Times* rather affectionately as "Wee Jimmy"—until the White House asked him to stop. When Carter took up running, he lost weight and his features came to look haggard; a picture of him close to collapse in a road race near Camp David not only failed to win the joggers' vote but damaged him seriously. Americans don't like to think of their President gasping for breath; they'd rather see Ronald Reagan astride a horse.

Carter's high voice didn't improve his weak delivery of speeches, nor did the involuntary, quirky smile that too often played around his lips, for no apparent reason. He didn't look or sound like many Americans' concept of a President—particularly in contrast to the tall and handsome Reagan, with his polished television manner. Carter didn't look *strong*.

But surely his defeat, and the years since, sharply raise the question, What is the American voters' idea of strength? Reagan's defeat of seven hundred Cubans in the invasion of Grenada? His surrogate army of contras trying to overthrow the recognized government of Nicaragua? His denunciation of the Soviets' "evil empire"? Two hundred billion dollars in deficits?

In pursuit of Reagan's failed policy in Lebanon, 262 Marines died. During Jimmy Carter's entire four years in office not one American died in combat, anywhere (those who were killed in the Iranian desert in the aborted rescue attempt of April 1980 are considered accident victims).

Carter's kind of strength even cleared the way for his successor, in at least two significant instances. Reagan's current problems in Central America would be compounded twice over, in perhaps every country of the region, had not Carter pushed through the Panama Canal "giveaway"—of which Ronald Reagan was the most vociferous opponent.

And had Carter not continued, even after his resounding defeat, to seek the release of the hostages—succeeding in literally his last hours in office—Reagan at the outset of his administration would have had to concentrate on the Ayatollah Khomeini and the Iranian mobs, rather than on the tax and budget cuts that established his leadership reputation.

For my part, I think of Carter's years with exasperation, disappointment, a sense of opportunities lost. Even crediting Carter's substantial achievements, I can't help thinking that so much ability, so much dedication, such high goals, should have produced far more and been rewarded with the respect and appreciation of the American people.

One reason that didn't happen was Carter's persistent inability or refusal to supplement his virtues with the realization that his was a political office—"preeminently," Franklin Roosevelt said, "a place of political leadership." Carter failed to grasp, nor does he grant today, that a President's highest task is not the making of morally correct judgments, but *politics*—moving the nation, by the political consequences of his words, deeds, and character, toward goals a diverse people may not always share or understand.

But I think the people failed *him* too. They didn't see or credit the strength of his restraint and the courage of his convictions. They didn't recognize that a President could be strong and courageous—on Iran, on Panama, on human rights—without boastful rhetoric or military posturing or the waste of lives. And when they had the kind of President so many say they want—one who tries to be "above politics"—they summarily threw him out of office.

Perhaps the people just didn't hear from him what they wanted to be told, what they wanted to believe about themselves. After the traumas of Vietnam and Watergate and OPEC, perhaps once-confident Americans became fearful about their destiny and needed the kind of reassurance that a military buildup and a muscle-flexing leader can give. Maybe they began to wonder, as Andy Young suggested to me, " 'Is God still on our side?' And Reagan says, 'Yes, God is still on our side.' He says it so well, and Carter didn't say it at all."

Part III

Diplomacy and War during America's Second Century

Recognition that the United States is a superpower, taken for granted by Americans living in the 1980s, is a relatively recent historical development. When the nation celebrated its centennial in 1876, the United States was not playing an active role in the world arena. For the most part, U.S. forays of diplomatic activity prior to 1898 concerned boundary settlements or the occasional acquisition of additional territory. Besides, as we have seen, domestic issues were sufficient to occupy most of the national attention. Thus, almost until the end of the nineteenth century, the United States remained isolationist in the diplomatic and military sense of that term.

The Spanish-American War in 1898 proved to be a significant turning point in the rise of the United States to world power status. For the first time, U.S. troops were sent overseas to engage in armed combat—every generation since has faced a similar prospect. In addition, the results of the Spanish-American War put the United States in a position to engage in imperialism.

For two decades following the Spanish-American War, the United States remained activist in world affairs. Intervention became common in Latin America. From Cuba to Panama, from the Dominican Republic to Mexico, the United States flexed its newly developed muscles. Involvement in World War I seemed a logical extension of a mission "to make the world safe for democracy." Tragically, the results of that war insured neither democracy nor avoidance of future wars.

When the United States pulled back from world leadership in 1919–1920 by refusing to join the League of Nations, many Americans probably hoped for a return to the "good old days" of non-involvement in world affairs. However, the United States could not avoid some very persistent issues—communism, disarmament, relations with Latin America, and aggression. Of course, the ultimate act of aggression against the United States, the Japanese attack on Pearl Harbor, finally brought the nation into World War II.

That war was a crucial factor in thrusting the United States into what appears to be a permanent position of involvement in world affairs. Realistically, the United States was simply too powerful, both militarily and economically, to avoid entanglements. The containment policy served as a philosophical framework for resistance to communism, which has been reflected in foreign aid programs, the Korean and Vietnam Wars, and the alarming arms race.

Recent reassessments of American foreign policy have dealt with questions similar to those faced at the end of the nineteenth century: Should the United States intervene directly in the internal affairs of another country? What principles should the United States uphold? To what extent are U.S. principles valid for other nations? Where is the line drawn between principle and practicality? What are the costs and benefits of being a world power? Reasonable answers to these questions depend upon an understanding of American foreign policy during the past century.

Part III

Diplomacy and War during America's Second Century

12

The Needless War with Spain

by William E. Leuchtenburg

Secretary of State John Hay called it "a splendid little war." Indeed, if in 1898 the United States was going to engage in an overseas war for the first time in its history, this was the sort of war to have. The Spanish-American War was short, the casualties were light, and the spoils of victory were great.

However, the Spanish-American War cannot be so easily dismissed. As William E. Leuchtenburg, Professor of History at the University of North Carolina, observes in the following essay, "We entered a war in which no vital American interest was involved, and without any concept of its consequences." Why, then, did we enter the war? What bearing did the consequences of it have on twentieth-century American foreign policy? Professor Leuchtenburg, who has gained distinction for *The Perils of Prosperity, 1914–1932* and the prize-winning *Franklin Roosevelt and the New Deal*, provides an enlightening account of how apparently "minor" factors can propel a nation into war.

The United States in the 1890's became more aggressive, expansionistic, and jingoistic than it had been since the 1850's. In less than five years, we came to the brink of war with Italy, Chile, and Great Britain over three minor incidents in which no American national interest of major importance was involved. In each of these incidents, our secretary of state was highly aggressive, and the American people applauded. During these years, we completely overhauled our decrepit Navy, building fine new warships like the *Maine*. The martial virtues of Napoleon, the imperial doctrines of Rudyard Kipling, and the naval theories of Captain Alfred T. Mahan all enjoyed a considerable vogue.

There was an apparently insatiable hunger for foreign conquest. Senator Shelby M. Cullom declared in 1895: "It is time that some one woke up and realized the necessity of annexing some property. We want all this northern hemisphere, and when we begin to reach out to secure these advantages we will begin to have a nation and our lawmakers will rise above the grade of politicians and become true statesmen." When, in 1895, the United States almost became involved in a war with Great Britain over the Venezuelan boundary, Theodore Roosevelt noted: "The antics of the bankers, brokers and anglo-maniacs generally are humiliating to a degree. . . . Personally I rather hope the fight will come soon. The clamor of the peace faction has convinced me that this country needs a war." The Washington *Post* concluded: "The taste of Empire is in the mouth of the people. . . ."

In the early nineteenth century, under the leadership of men like Simon Bolivar, Spain's colonies in the New World had launched a series of successful revolutions; of the great Spanish empire that Cortes and Pizarro had built, the island of Cuba, "the Ever Faithful Isle," was the only important Spanish possession to stay loyal to the Crown. Spain exploited the economy of the island mercilessly, forcing Cubans to buy Spanish goods at prices far above the world market, and Madrid sent to Cuba as colonial officials younger sons who had no interest in the island other than making a quick killing and returning to Spain. High taxes to support Spanish officialdom crippled the island; arbitrary arrests and arbitrary trials made a mockery of justice; and every attempt at public education was stifled.

The island of Cuba had been in a state of political turbulence for years when in 1894 the American Wilson-Gorman Tariff placed duties on Cuban sugar which, coupled with a world-wide depression, brought ruin to the economy of the island. The terrible hardship of the winter was the signal for revolution; on February 24, 1895, under the leadership of a junta in New York City headed by José Martí, rebels once more took the field against Spain. At first, the American people were too absorbed with the Venezuelan crisis to pay much attention to another revolt in Cuba. Then, in September, 1895, came the event which changed the course of the Cuban rebellion: William Randolph Hearst, a young man of 32 who had been operating the San Francisco *Examiner* in a sensational fashion, purchased the New York *Morning Journal,* and immediately locked horns with Joseph Pulitzer and the *World* in a circulation war that was to make newspaper history.

Hearst capitalized on the fact that the American people had only the most romantic notions of the nature of the Cuban conflict. The rebels under General Máximo Gómez, a tough Santo Domingan guerrilla fighter, embarked on a program of burning the cane fields in the hope not only of depriving the government of revenue but also of so disrupting the life of the island that the government would be forced to submit. Although there were some noble spirits in the group, much of the rebellion had an unsavory odor; one of the main financial supports for the uprising came from American property owners who feared that their sugar fields would be burned unless protection money was paid.

While Gómez was putting Cuba to the torch, American newsmen were filing reports describing the war in terms of nonexistent pitched battles between the liberty-loving Cubans and the cruel Spaniards. The war was presented, in short, as a Byronic conflict between the forces of freedom and the forces of tyranny, and the American people ate it up. When Hearst bought the *Journal* in late 1895, it had a circulation of 30,000; by 1897 it had bounded to over 400,000 daily, and during the Spanish-American War it was to go well over a million.

The sensational newspapers had influence, yet they represented no more than a minority of the press of the country; and in the South and the Middle West, where anti-Spanish feeling became more intense, the representative newspaper was much more conservative. Certainly the yellow press played a tremendous part in whipping up sentiment for intervention in Cuba, but these feelings could not be carried into action unless American political leaders of both parties were willing to assume the terrible responsibility of war.

By the beginning of 1896 the rebels had achieved such success in their guerrilla tactics that Madrid decided on firmer steps and sent General Don Valeriano Weyler y Nicolau to Cuba. When Weyler arrived in February, he found the sugar industry severely disrupted and the military at a loss to meet the rebel tactic of setting fire to the cane fields. Weyler declared martial law and announced that men guilty of incendiarism would be dealt with summarily; he was promptly dubbed "The Butcher" by American newspapermen.

By late 1896 Weyler still had not succeeded in crushing the insurrection, and his measures became more severe. On October 21 he issued his famous *reconcentrado* order, directing the "reconcentration" of the people of Pinar del Río in the garrison towns, and forbidding the export of supplies from the towns to the countryside. Reasoning that he could never suppress the rebellion so long as the rebels could draw secret assistance from people in the fields, Weyler moved the people from the estates into the towns and stripped the countryside of supplies to starve out the rebellion. Since many of the people had already fled to the towns, the *reconcentrado* policy was not as drastic as it appeared; yet the suffering produced by the policy was undeniable. Lacking proper hygienic care, thousands of Cubans, especially women and children, died like flies.

When William McKinley entered the White House in 1897, he had no intention of joining the War Hawks. "If I can only go out of office . . . with the knowledge that I have done what lay in my power to avert this terrible calamity," McKinley told Grover Cleveland on the eve of his inauguration, "I shall be the happiest man in the world." McKinley came to power as the "advance agent of prosperity," and business interests were almost unanimous in opposing any agitation of the Cuban question that might lead to war. Contrary to the assumptions of Leninist historians, it was Wall Street which, first and last, resisted a war which was to bring America its overseas empire.

The country had been gripped since 1893 by the deepest industrial depression in its history, a depression that was to persist until the beginning of 1897. Each time it appeared recovery might be on its way, a national crisis had cut it off: first the Venezuelan boundary war scare of December, 1895, then the bitter free silver campaign of 1896. What business groups feared more than anything else was a new crisis. As Julius Pratt writes: "To this fair prospect of a great business revival the threat of war was like a specter at the feast."

McKinley was not a strong President, and he had no intention of being one. Of all the political figures of his day, he was the man most responsive to the popular will. It was his great virtue and, his critics declared, his great weakness. Uncle Joe Cannon once remarked: "McKinley keeps his ear to the ground so close that he gets it full of grasshoppers much of the time." If McKinley was not one of our greatest Presidents, he was certainly the most representative and the most responsive. Anyone who knew the man knew that, although he was strongly opposed to war, he would not hold out against war if the popular demand for war became unmistakable. "Let the voice of the people rule"—this was McKinley's credo, and he meant it.

The threat to peace came from a new quarter, from the South and West, the strongholds of Democracy and free silver. Many Bryanite leaders were convinced that a war would create such a strain on the currency system that the opposition to free silver would collapse. Moreover, with the opposition to war strongest in Wall Street, they found it easy to believe that Administration policy was the product of a conspiracy of bankers who would deny silver to the American people, who would deny liberty to the people of Cuba, who were concerned only with the morality of the countinghouse. Moreover, Bryan was the spokesman for rural Protestantism, which was already speaking in terms of a righteous war against Spain to free the Cubans from bondage. These were forces too powerful for McKinley to ignore. McKinley desired peace, but he was above all, a Republican partisan, and he had no intention of handing the Democrats in 1900 the campaign cry of Free Cuba and Free Silver.

While McKinley attempted to search out a policy that would preserve peace without bringing disaster to the Republican party, the yellow press made his job all the more difficult by whipping up popular anger against Spain. On February 12 the *Journal* published a dispatch from Richard Harding Davis, reporting that as the American steamship *Olivette* was about to leave Havana Harbor for the United States, it was boarded by Spanish police officers who searched three young Cuban women, one of whom was suspected of carrying messages from the rebels. The *Journal* ran the story under the headline, "Does Our Flag Protect Women?" with a vivid drawing by Frederic Remington across one half a page showing Spanish plainclothes men searching a wholly nude woman. War, declared the *Journal,* "is a dreadful thing, but there are things more dreadful than even war, and one of them is dishonor." It shocked the country, and Congressman Amos Cummings immediately resolved to launch a congressional inquiry into the *Olivette* outrage. Before any steps could be taken, the true story was revealed. The *World* produced one of the young women who indignantly protested the *Journal's* version of the incident. Pressured by the *World,* the *Journal* was forced to print a letter from Davis explaining that his article had not said that male policemen had searched the women and that, in fact, the search had been conducted quite properly by a police matron with no men present.

The *Olivette* incident was manufactured by Hearst, but by the spring of 1897 the American press had a new horror to report which was all too true. Famine was stalking the island. Cuba had been in a serious economic state when the rebellion broke out in 1895; two years of war would, under any circumstances, have been disastrous, but the deliberate policies pursued both by the insurgents and by the government forces made the situation desperate. It was a simple matter for Hearst and Pulitzer reporters to pin the full responsibility on Weyler.

By the middle of July, McKinley had formulated a policy which he set down in a letter of instructions to our new American minister to Spain, General Stewart L. Woodford. The letter emphasized the need of bringing the Cuban war to an end and said that this could be done to the mutual advantage of both Spain and the Cubans by granting some kind of autonomy to Cuba. If Spain did not make an offer to the rebels and if the "measures of unparalleled severity" were not ended, the United States threatened to intervene.

On August 8 an Italian anarchist assassinated the Spanish premier; and when Woodford reached Madrid in September, a new government was about to take over headed by Señor Sagasta and the Liberals, who had repeatedly denounced the "barbarity" of the previous government's policy in Cuba. Sagasta immediately removed General Weyler, and the prospects for an agreement between the United States and Spain took a decided turn for the better.

While Woodford was carrying on skillful diplomatic negotiations for peace in Madrid, the Hearst press was creating a new sensation in this country with the Cisneros affair. Evangelina Cisneros was a young Cuban woman who had been arrested and imprisoned in the Rocojidas in Havana, guilty, according to the American press, of no other crime than protecting her virtue from an unscrupulous Spanish colonel, an aide to Butcher Weyler. The Rocojidas, Hearst's reporters told American readers, was a cage where the innocent beauty was herded with women criminals of every type, subject to the taunts and vile invitations of men who gathered outside.

When it was reported that Señorita Cisneros, whose father was a rebel leader, was to be sent for a long term to a Spanish penal colony in Africa or in the Canaries, the *Journal* launched one of the most fabulous campaigns in newspaper history. "Enlist the women of America!" was the Hearst war cry, and the women of America proved willing recruits. Mrs. Julia Ward Howe signed an appeal to Pope Leo XIII, and Mrs. Jefferson Davis, the widow of the president of the Confederacy, appealed to the queen regent of Spain to "give Evangelina Cisneros to the women of America to save her from a fate worse than death." When the *Journal* prepared a petition on behalf of Señorita Cisneros, it obtained the names of Mrs. Nancy McKinley, the mother of the President, and Mrs. John Sherman, the wife of the secretary of state, as well as such other prominent ladies as Julia Dent Grant and Mrs. Mark Hanna.

It was a startling coup for Mr. Hearst, but he had not yet even begun to display his ingenuity. On October 10, 1897, the *Journal* erupted across its front page with the banner headline: "An American Newspaper Accomplishes at a Single Stroke What the Best Efforts of Diplomacy Failed Utterly to Bring About in Many Months." Hearst had sent Karl Decker, one of his most reliable correspondents, to Havana in late August with orders to rescue the Cuban Girl Martyr "at any hazard"; and Decker had climbed to the roof of a house near the prison, broken the bar of a window of the jail, lifted Evangelina out, and, after hiding her for a few days in Havana, smuggled her onto an American steamer. Decker, signing his dispatch to the *Journal* "Charles Duval," wrote: "I have broken the bars of Rocojidas and have set free the beautiful captive of monster Weyler. Weyler could blind the Queen to the real character of Evangelina, but he could not build a jail that would hold against *Journal* enterprise when properly set to work." The Cuban Girl Martyr was met at the pier by a great throng, led up Broadway in a triumphal procession, taken to a reception at Delmonico's where 120,000 people milled about the streets surrounding the restaurant, and hailed at a monster reception in Madison Square Garden. The Bishop of London cabled his congratulations to the *Journal,* while Governor Stephens of Missouri proposed that the *Journal* send down 500 of its reporters to free the entire island.

On October 23 Sagasta announced a "total change of immense scope" in Spanish policy in Cuba. He promised to grant local autonomy to the Cubans immediately, reserving justice, the armed forces, and foreign relations to Spain. On November 13 Weyler's successor, Captain-General Blanco, issued a decree modifying considerably the *reconcentrado* policy, and on November 25 the queen regent signed the edicts creating an autonomous government for the island. In essence, Madrid had acceded to the American demands.

While Woodford was conducting negotiations with a conciliatory Liberal government in Madrid and while there was still hope for peace, the fatal incident occurred which made war virtually inevitable. On January 12, 1898, a riot broke out in Havana, and Spanish officers attacked newspaper offices. The nature of the riot is still not clear; it was over in an hour, and it had no anti-American aspects. If the United States now sent a naval vessel to Havana, it might be buying trouble with Spain. Yet if a riot did break out and Americans were killed, the Administration would be stoned for not having a ship there to protect them. For several days McKinley wavered; then he ordered the *Maine* to Havana, but with the explanation that this was a courtesy visit demonstrating that so nonsensical were the rumors of danger to American citizens that our ships could again resume their visits to the island.

As the *Maine* lay at anchor in Havana Harbor, the rebels, with a perfect sense of timing, released a new propaganda bombshell. In December, 1897, in a private letter, Señor Enrique Dupuy de Lôme, the Spanish minister at Washington, had set down his opinions of President McKinley's annual message to Congress: "Besides the ingrained and inevitable bluntness *(groseria)* with which it repeated all that the press and public opinion in Spain have said about Weyler," De Lôme wrote, "it once more shows what McKinley is, weak and a bidder for the admiration of the crowd, besides being a would-be politician *(politicastro)* who tries to leave a door open behind himself while keeping on good terms with the jingoes of his party." De Lôme added: "it would be very advantageous to take up, even if only for effect, the question of commercial relations, and to have a man of some prominence sent here in order that I may make use of him to carry on a propaganda among the Senators and others in opposition to the junta."

De Lôme had, to be sure, written all this in a private letter (which was stolen by an insurgent spy in the Havana post office), not in his official capacity, and his characterization of McKinley was not wholly without merit, but it was a blunder of the highest magnitude. Not only had De Lôme attacked the President, but he had gone on to suggest that the negotiations then going on over a commercial treaty were not being conducted in good faith. Throughout the letter ran precisely the tone which Hearst had been arguing expressed the Spanish temper—a cold, arrogant contempt for democratic institutions. The State Department immediately cabled Woodford to demand the recall of the Spanish minister, but Madrid had the good fortune of being able to tell Woodford that De Lôme, informed of the disaster the night before, had already resigned.

A week after the publication of the De Lôme indiscretion, at 9:40 on the night of February 15, 1898, came the terrible blow which ended all real hope for peace. In the harbor of Havana, the *Maine* was blown up by an explosion of unknown origin. In an instant, the ship was filled with the sounds of shrieking men and rushing water. The blast occurred in the forward part of the ship where, a half hour before, most of the men had turned in for the night; they were killed in their hammocks. Of the 350 officers and men on board, 260 were killed. By morning the proud *Maine* had sunk into the mud of Havana Harbor.

"Public opinion should be suspended until further report," Captain Sigsbee cabled to Washington, but even Sigsbee could not down his suspicions. The *Maine* had gone to a Spanish possession on a courtesy call, and the *Maine* now lay at the bottom of Havana Harbor. What could it mean but war? "I would give anything if President McKinley would order the fleet to Havana tomorrow," wrote Theodore Roosevelt. "The *Maine* was sunk by an act of dirty treachery on the part of the Spaniards." Volunteers lined up for war service, even though there was no one to enlist them; in New York 500 sharpshooting Westchester businessmen volunteered as a unit for the colors. The *Journal* reported: "The Whole Country Thrills With War Fever."

The cause of the explosion of the *Maine* has never been finally established. That Spain deliberately decided to blow up the *Maine* is inconceivable, although it is possible that it might have been the work of unauthorized Spanish extremists. The one group which had everything to gain from such an episode was the rebels; yet it seems unlikely that either they or Spanish hotheads could have carried out such an act and remained undetected. The most likely explanation is that it was caused by an explosion of internal origin; yet the evidence for this is not conclusive. In any event, this was the explanation that the Navy in 1898 was least willing to consider since it would reflect seriously on the care with which the Navy was operating the *Maine*.

The move toward war seemed relentless. On March 9 Congress unanimously voted $50,000,000 for war preparations. Yet the days went by and there was no war, in part because important sectors of American opinion viewed

Hearst's stores of the atrocious conditions on the island with profound skepticism. Senator Redfield Proctor of Vermont decided to launch his own investigation into conditions on the island. On March 17, after a tour of Cuba, Proctor made one of the most influential speeches in the history of the United States Senate.

Proctor, who Roosevelt reported was "very ardent for the war," had not generally been regarded as a jingo, and no man in the Senate commanded greater respect for personal integrity. Proctor declared that he had gone to Cuba skeptical of reports of suffering there, and he had come back convinced. "Torn from their homes, with foul earth, foul air, foul water, and foul food or none, what wonder that one-half have died and that one-quarter of the living are so diseased that they can not be saved?" Proctor asked. "Little children are still walking about with arms and chest terribly emaciated, eyes swollen, and abdomen bloated to three times the natural size. . . . I was told by one of our consuls that they have been found dead about the markets in the morning, where they had crawled, hoping to get some stray bits of food from the early hucksters."

The question of peace or war now lay with McKinley. The Spaniards, Woodford had conceded, had gone about as far as they could go; but with the *Maine* in the mud of Havana Harbor, with the country, following Proctor's speech, crying for war, how much longer could McKinley hold out? The jingoes were treating his attempt to preserve peace with outright contempt; McKinley, Roosevelt told his friends, "has no more backbone than a chocolate éclair."

"We will have this war for the freedom of Cuba," Roosevelt shouted at a Gridiron Dinner on March 26, shaking his fist at Senator Hanna, "in spite of the timidity of the commercial interests." Nor was McKinley permitted to forget the political consequences. The Chicago *Times-Herald* warned: "Intervention in Cuba, peacefully if we can, forcibly if we must, is immediately inevitable. Our own internal political conditions will not permit its postponement. . . . Let President McKinley hesitate to rise to the just expectations of the American people, and who can doubt that 'war for Cuban liberty' will be the crown of thorns the free silver Democrats and Populists will adopt at the elections this fall?"

On March 28 the President released the report of the naval court of inquiry on the *Maine* disaster. "In the opinion of the court the *Maine* was destroyed by the explosion of a submarine mine, which caused the partial explosion of two or more of the forward magazines," the report concluded. Although no one was singled out for blame, the conclusion was inescapable that if Spain had not willfully done it, Spain had failed to provide proper protection to a friendly vessel on a courtesy visit in its waters. Overnight a slogan with the ring of a child's street chant caught the fancy of the country:

Remember the Maine!
To hell with Spain!

"I have no more doubt than that I am now standing in the Senate of the United States," declared Henry Cabot Lodge, "that that ship was blown up by a government mine, fired by, or with the connivance of, Spanish officials."

Desiring peace yet afraid of its consequences, McKinley embarked on a policy of attempting to gain the fruits of war without fighting. On March 29 Woodford demanded that Spain agree to an immediate armistice, revoke the reconcentration order, and co-operate with the United States to provide relief; Spain was given 48 hours to reply. On March 31 Spain replied that it had finally revoked the reconcentration orders in the western provinces; that it had made available a credit of three million pesetas to resettle the natives; that it was willing to submit the *Maine* controversy to arbitration; and that it would grant a truce if the insurgents would ask for it. In short, Spain would yield everything we demanded, except that it would not concede defeat; the appeal for a truce would have to come from the rebels. Since the rebels would not make such an appeal, since they were confident of ultimate American intervention, the situation was hopeless; yet Spain had come a long way. Woodford cabled to Washington: "The ministry have gone as far as they dare go to-day. . . . No Spanish ministry would have dared to do one month ago what this ministry has proposed to-day."

For a week the Spaniards attempted to cling to their last shreds of dignity. On Saturday, April 9, Madrid surrendered. Driven to the wall by the American demands, the Spanish foreign minister informed Woodford that the government had decided to grant an armistice in Cuba immediately. Gratified at achieving the final concession, Woodford cabled McKinley: "I hope that nothing will now be done to humiliate Spain, as I am satisfied that the present Government is going, and is loyally ready to go, as fast and as far as it can."

It was too late. McKinley had decided on war. Spain had conceded everything, but Spain had waited too long. Up until the very last moment, Spanish officials had feared that if they yielded to American demands in Cuba, it might mean the overturn of the dynasty, and they preferred even a disastrous war to that. Proud but helpless in the face of American might, many Spanish officials appeared to prefer the dignity of being driven from the island in a heroic defensive war to meek surrender to an American ultimatum. In the end they surrendered and promised reforms. But they had promised reforms before—after the Ten Years' War which ended in 1878—and they had not kept these promises. Throughout the nineteenth century, constitutions had been made and remade, but nothing had changed. Even in the last hours of negotiations with the American minister, they had told Woodford that the President had asked the Pope to intervene, when the President had done nothing of the sort. Even if their intentions were of the best, could they carry them out? Spain had had three full years to end the war in Cuba and, with vastly superior numbers of troops, had not been able to do it. And the insurgents would accept nothing from Madrid, not even peace.

Theodore Roosevelt and the Rough Riders in Cuba in 1898. (Library of Congress)

On Monday, April 11, McKinley sent his message to Congress, declaring that "the forcible intervention of the United States as a neutral to stop the war, according to the large dictates of humanity and following many historical precedents" was "justifiable on rational grounds." The fact that Spain had met everything we had asked was buried in two paragraphs of a long plea for war. It took Congress a full week to act. On Monday night, April 18, while the resolution shuttled back and forth between the two chambers and the conference room, congressmen sang "The Battle Hymn of the Republic" and "Dixie" and shook the chamber with the refrain of "Hang General Weyler to a Sour Apple Tree." At three o'clock the next morning the two houses reached an agreement—the United States recognized the independence of Cuba, asserted that we would not acquire Cuba for ourselves, and issued an ultimatum to Spain to withdraw within three days. On April 20 President McKinley signed the resolution. War had come at last. But not quite. Although hostilities had begun, not until four days later did Congress declare war. When it did declare war, it dated it from McKinley's action in establishing a blockade four days before. To the very end, we protested our peaceful intentions as we stumbled headlong into war.

We entered a war in which no vital American interest was involved, and without any concept of its consequences. Although McKinley declared that to enter such a war for high purposes, and then annex territory, would be "criminal aggression," we acquired as a result of the war the Philippines and other parts of an overseas empire we had not intended to get and had no idea how to defend. Although we roundly attacked Spain for not recognizing the rebel government, we, in our turn, refused to recognize the rebels. Although we were shocked by Weyler's policies in Cuba, we were soon in the unhappy position of using savage methods to put down a rebel uprising in the Philippines, employing violence in a measure that easily matched what Weyler had done.

It would be easy to condemn McKinley for not holding out against war, but McKinley showed considerable courage in bucking the tide. McKinley's personal sympathy for the Cubans was sincere; only after his death was it revealed that he had contributed $5,000 anonymously for Cuban relief. It would be even easier to blame it all on Hearst; yet no newspaper can arouse a people that is not willing to be aroused. At root lay the American gullibility about foreign affairs, with the penchant for viewing politics in terms of a simple morality play; equally important were the contempt of the American people for Spain as a cruel but weak Latin nation and the desire for war and expansion which permeated the decade. The American people were not led into war; they got the war they wanted. "I think" observed Senator J. C. Spooner, "possibly the President could have worked out the business without war, but the current was too strong, the demagogues too numerous, the fall elections too near."

13

Woodrow Wilson and the League of Nations
by Thomas A. Bailey

If Theodore Roosevelt was the realist in foreign affairs, then Woodrow Wilson was the idealist. Wilson's deep belief in democracy was at the heart of his missionary diplomacy. His idealism also led him to elevate World War I to a struggle "to make the world safe for democracy" and to make it the war "to end all wars." Tragically, Wilson's idealism, as well as his own frail body, were crushed in the ruins of the "Great War."

Wilson believed that a League of Nations could successfully deal with world problems and maintain the peace. He went to Europe to assure that his League was written into the Treaty of Versailles. But having accomplished that, he was unable to secure ratification of the Treaty by the U.S. Senate. In the process, Wilson himself collapsed.

Thomas A. Bailey is Professor Emeritus of History at Stanford University and a renowned Wilson scholar. Among his numerous books are *Woodrow Wilson and the Lost Peace* and *Woodrow Wilson and the Great Betrayal*. In the following essay he stresses the roles of personality, partisanship, and the refusal of political leaders to compromise as key elements in the Senate votes rejecting ratification of the Treaty and the League. As Bailey concludes, "the American people were one war short of accepting leadership in a world organization for peace."

The story of America's rejection of the League of Nations revolves largely around the personality and character of Thomas Woodrow Wilson, the twenty-eighth President of the United States. Born in Virginia and reared in Yankee-gutted Georgia and the Carolinas, Wilson early developed a burning hatred of war and a passionate attachment to the Confederate-embraced principle of self-determination for minority peoples. From the writings of Thomas Jefferson he derived much of his democratic idealism and his invincible faith in the judgment of the masses, if properly informed. From his stiff-backed Scotch-Presbyterian forebears, he inherited a high degree of inflexibility; from his father, a dedicated Presbyterian minister, he learned a stern moral code that would tolerate no compromise with wrong, as defined by Woodrow Wilson.

As a leading academician who had first failed at law, he betrayed a contempt for "money-grubbing" lawyers, many of whom sat in the Senate, and an arrogance toward lesser intellects, including those of the "pygmy-minded" senators. As a devout Christian keenly aware of the wickedness of this world, he emerged as a fighting reformer, whether as president of Princeton, governor of New Jersey, or President of the United States.

As a war leader, Wilson was superb. Holding aloft the torch of idealism in one hand and the flaming sword of righteousness in the other, he aroused the masses to a holy crusade. We would fight a war to end wars; we would make the world safe for democracy. The phrase was not a mockery then. The American people, with an amazing display of self-sacrifice, supported the war effort unswervingly.

The noblest expression of Wilson's idealism was his Fourteen Points address to Congress in January, 1918. It compressed his war aims into punchy, placard-like paragraphs, expressly designed for propaganda purposes. It appealed tremendously to oppressed peoples everywhere by promising such goals as the end of secret treaties, freedom of the seas, the removal of economic barriers, a reduction of arms burdens, a fair adjustment of colonial claims, and self-determination for oppressed minorities. In Poland university men would meet on the streets of Warsaw, clasp hands, and soulfully utter one word, "Wilson." In remote regions of Italy peasants burned candles before poster portraits of the mighty new prophet arisen in the West.

The fourteenth and capstone point was a league of nations, designed to avert future wars. The basic idea was not original with Wilson; numerous thinkers, including Frenchmen and Britons, had been working on the concept long before he embraced it. Even Henry Cabot Lodge, the Republican senator from Massachusetts, had already spoken publicly in favor of a league of nations. But the more he heard about the Wilsonian League of Nations, the more critical of it he became.

A knowledge of the Wilson-Lodge feud is basic to an understanding of the tragedy that unfolded. Tall, slender, aristocratically bewhiskered, Dr. Henry Cabot Lodge (Ph.D., Harvard), had published a number of books and had been known as the scholar in politics before the appearance of Dr. Woodrow Wilson (Ph.D., Johns Hopkins). The Presbyterian professor had gone further in both scholarship and politics than the Boston Brahmin, whose mind was once described as resembling the soil of his native New England: "naturally barren but highly cultivated." Wilson and Lodge, two icy men, developed a mutual antipathy, which soon turned into freezing hatred.

The German armies, reeling under the blows of the Allies, were ready to give in by November, 1918. The formal armistice terms stipulated that Germany was to be guaranteed a peace based on the Fourteen Points, with two reservations concerning freedom of the seas and reparations.

Meanwhile the American people had keyed themselves up to the long-awaited march on Berlin; eager voices clamored to hang the Kaiser. Thus the sudden end of the shooting left inflamed patriots with a sense of frustration and letdown that boded ill for Wilson's policies. The red-faced Theodore Roosevelt, Lodge's intimate of long standing, cried that peace should be dictated by the chatter of machine guns and not the clicking of typewriters.

Wilson now towered at the dizzy pinnacle of his popularity and power. He had emerged as the moral arbiter of the world and the hope of all peoples for a better tomorrow. But regrettably his wartime sureness of touch began to desert him, and he made a series of costly fumbles. He was so preoccupied with reordering the world, someone has said, that he reminded one of the base-ball player who knocks the ball into the bleachers and then forgets to touch home plate.

First came his brutally direct appeal for a Democratic Congress in Oc-tober, 1918. The voters trooped to the polls the next month and, by a narrow margin, returned a Republican Congress. Wilson had not only goaded his par-tisan foes to fresh outbursts of fury, but he had unnecessarily staked his pres-tige on the outcome—and lost. When the Allied leaders met at the Paris peace table, he was the only one not entitled to be there, at least on the European basis of a parliamentary majority.

Wilson next announced that he was sailing for France, presumably to use his still enormous prestige to fashion an enduring peace. At this time no Pres-ident had ever gone abroad, and Republicans condemned the decision as evi-dence of a dangerous Messiah complex—of a desire, as former President Taft put it, "to hog the whole show."

The naming of the remaining five men to the peace delegation caused partisans further anguish. Only one, Henry White, was a Republican, and he was a minor figure at that. The Republicans, now the majority party, com-plained that they had been good enough to die on the battlefield; they ought to have at least an equal voice at the peace table. Nor were any United States senators included, even though they would have a final whack at the treaty. Wilson did not have much respect for the "bungalow-minded" senators, and if he took one, the logical choice would be Henry Cabot Lodge. There were already enough feuds brewing at Paris without taking one along.

Doubtless some of the Big Business Republicans were out to "get" the President who had been responsible for the hated reformist legislation of 1913–14. If he managed to put over the League of Nations, his prestige would soar to new heights. He might even arrange—unspeakable thought!—to be elected again and again and again. Much of the partisan smog that finally suffocated the League would have been cleared away if Wilson had publicly declared, as he was urged to do, that in no circumstances would be run again. But he spurned such counsel, partly because he was actually receptive to the idea of a third term.

The American President, hysterically hailed by European crowds as "Voovro Veelson," came to the Paris peace table in January, 1919, to meet with Lloyd George of Britain, Clemenceau of France, and Orlando of Italy. To his dismay, he soon discovered that they were far more interested in im-perialism than in idealism. When they sought to carve up the territorial booty without regard for the colonials, contrary to the Fourteen Points, the stern-jawed Presbyterian moralist interposed a ringing veto. The end result was the mandate system—a compromise between idealism and imperialism that turned out to be more imperialistic than idealistic.

Wilson's overriding concern was the League of Nations. He feared that if he did not get it completed and embedded in the treaty, the imperialistic powers might sidetrack it. Working at an incredible pace after hours, Wilson headed the commission that drafted the League Covenant in ten meetings and some thirty hours. He then persuaded the conference not only to approve the hastily constructed Covenant but to incorporate it bodily in the peace treaty. In support of his adopted brain child he spoke so movingly on one occasion that even the hard-boiled reporters forgot to take notes.

Wilson now had to return hurriedly to the United States to sign bills and take care of other pressing business. Shortly after his arrival the mounting Republican opposition in the Senate flared up angrily. On March 4, 1919, 39 senators or senators-elect—more than enough to defeat the treaty—published a round robin to the effect that they would not approve the League in its existing form. This meant that Wilson had to return to Paris, hat in hand, and there weaken his position by having to seek modifications.

Stung to the quick, he struck back at his senatorial foes in an indiscreet speech in New York just before his departure. He boasted that when he brought the treaty back from Paris, the League Covenant would not only be tied in but so thoroughly tied in that it could not be cut out without killing the entire pact. The Senate, he assumed, would not dare to kill the treaty of peace outright.

At Paris the battle was now joined in deadly earnest. Clemenceau, the French realist, had little use for Wilson, the American idealist. "God gave us the ten commandments and we broke them," he reportedly sneered. "Wilson gave us the Fourteen Points—we shall see." Clemenceau's most disruptive demand was for the German Rhineland; but Wilson, the champion of self-determination, would never consent to handing several million Germans over to the tender mercies of the French. After a furious struggle, during which Wilson was stricken with influenza, Clemenceau was finally persuaded to yield the Rhineland and other demands in return for a security treaty. Under it, Britain and America agreed to come to the aid of France in the event of another unprovoked aggression. The United States Senate short-sightedly pigeonholed the pact, and France was left with neither the Rhineland nor security.

Two other deadlocks almost broke up the conference. Italy claimed the Adriatic port of Fiume, an area inhabited chiefly by Yugoslavs. In his battle for self-determination, Wilson dramatically appealed over the head of the Italian delegation to the Italian people, whereupon the delegates went home in a huff to receive popular endorsement. The final adjustment was a hollow victory for self-determination.

The politely bowing Japanese now stepped forward to press their economic claims to China's Shantung, which they had captured from the Germans early in the war. But to submit 30,000,000 Chinese to the influence of the Japanese would be another glaring violation of self-determination. The Japanese threatened to bolt the conference, as the Italians had already done, with consequent jeopardy to the League. In the end, Wilson reluctantly consented to a compromise that left the Japanese temporarily in possession of Shantung.

The Treaty of Versailles, as finally signed in June, 1919, included only about four of the original Fourteen Points. The Germans, with considerable justification, gave vent to loud cries of betrayal. But the iron hand of circumstance had forced Wilson to compromise away many of his points in order to salvage his fourteenth point, the League of Nations, which he hoped would iron out the injustices that had crept into the treaty. He was like the mother who throws her younger children to the pursuing wolves in order to save her sturdy first-born son.

Bitter opposition to the completed treaty had already begun to form in America. Tens of thousands of homesick and disillusioned soldiers were pouring home, determined to let Europe "stew in its own juice." The wartime idealism, inevitably doomed to slump, was now plunging to alarming depths. The beloved Allies had apparently turned out to be greedy imperialists. The war to make the world safe for democracy had obviously fallen dismally short of the goal. And at the end of the war to end wars there were about twenty conflicts of varying intensity being waged all over the globe.

The critics increased their clamor. Various foreign groups, including the Irish-Americans and the Italian-Americans, were complaining that the interests of the old country had been neglected. Professional liberals, for example the editors of the *New Republic,* were denouncing the treaty as too harsh. The illiberals, far more numerous, were denouncing it as not harsh enough. The Britain-haters, like the buzz-saw Senator James Reed of Missouri and the acid-penned William R. Hearst, were proclaiming that England had emerged with undue influence. Such ultra-nationalists as the isolationist Senator William E. Borah of Idaho were insisting that the flag of no superstate should be hoisted above the glorious Stars and Stripes.

When the treaty came back from Paris, with the League firmly riveted in, Senator Lodge despaired of stopping it.

"What are you going to do? It's hopeless," he complained to Borah. "All the newspapers in my state are for it." The best that he could hope for was to add a few reservations. The Republicans had been given little opportunity to help write the treaty in Paris; they now felt that they were entitled to do a little rewriting in Washington.

Lodge deliberately adopted the technique of delay. As chairman of the powerful Senate Committee on Foreign Relations, he consumed two weeks by reading aloud the entire pact of 264 pages, even though it had already been printed. He then held time-consuming public hearings, during which persons with unpronounceable foreign names aired their grievances against the pact.

Lodge finally adopted the strategy of tacking reservations onto the treaty, and he was able to achieve his goal because of the peculiar composition of the Senate. There were 49 Republicans and 47 Democrats. The Republicans consisted of about twenty "strong reservationists" like Lodge, about twelve "mild reservationists" like future Secretary of State Kellogg, and about a dozen

President Woodrow Wilson. (Library of Congress)

"irreconcilables." This last group was headed by Senator Borah and the no less isolationist Senator Hiram Johnson of California, a fiery spellbinder.

The Lodge reservations finally broke the back of the treaty. They were all added by a simple majority vote, even though the entire pact would have to be approved by a two-thirds vote. The dozen or so Republican mild reservationist were not happy over the strong Lodge reservations, and if Wilson had deferred sufficiently to these men, he might have persuaded them to vote with the Democrats. Had they done so, the Lodge reservations could have all been voted down, and a milder version, perhaps acceptable to Wilson, could have been substituted.

As the hot summer of 1919 wore on, Wilson became increasingly impatient with the deadlock in the Senate. Finally he decided to take his case to the country, as he had so often done in response to his ingrained "appeal habit." He had never been robust, and his friends urged him not to risk breaking himself down in a strenuous barnstorming campaign. But Wilson, having made up his mind, was unyielding. He had sent American boys into battle in a war to end wars; why should he not risk his life in a battle for a League to end wars?

Wilson's spectacular tour met with limited enthusiasm in the Middle West, the home of several million German-Americans. After him, like baying bloodhounds, trailed Senators Borah and Johnson, sometimes speaking in the same halls a day or so later, to the accompaniment of cries of "Impeach him, impeach him!" But on the Pacific Coast and in the Rocky Mountain area the enthusiasm for Wilson and the League was overwhelming. The high point—and the breaking point—of the trip came at Pueblo, Colorado, where Wilson, with tears streaming down his cheeks, pleaded for his beloved League of Nations.

That night Wilson's weary body rebelled. He was whisked back to Washington, where he suffered a stroke that paralyzed the left side of his body. For weeks he lay in bed, a desperately sick man. The Democrats, who had no first-rate leader in the Senate, were left rudderless. With the wisdom of hindsight, we may say that Wilson might better have stayed in Washington, providing the necessary leadership and compromising with the opposition, insofar as compromise was possible. A good deal of compromise had already gone into the treaty, and a little more might have saved it.

Senator Lodge, cold and decisive, was now in the driver's seat. His Fourteen Reservations, a sardonic parallel to Wilson's Fourteen Points, had been whipped into shape. Most of them now seem either irrelevant, inconsequential, or unnecessary; some of them merely reaffirmed principles and policies, including the Monroe Doctrine, already guaranteed by the treaty or by the Constitution.

But Wilson, who hated the sound of Lodge's name, would have no part of the Lodge reservations. They would, he insisted, emasculate the entire treaty. Yet the curious fact is that he had privately worked out his own set of reservations with the Democratic leader in the Senate, Gilbert M. Hitchcock, and these differed only in slight degree from those of Senator Lodge.

As the hour approached for the crucial vote in the Senate, it appeared that public opinion had veered a little. Although confused by the angry debate, it still favored the treaty—but with some safe-guarding reservations. A stubborn Wilson was unwilling to accept this disheartening fact, or perhaps he was not made aware of it. Mrs. Wilson, backed by the President's personal physician, Dr. Cary Grayson, kept vigil at his bedside to warn the few visitors that disagreeable news might shock the invalid into a relapse.

In this highly unfavorable atmosphere, Senator Hitchcock had two conferences with Wilson on the eve of the Senate voting. He suggested compromise on a certain point, but Wilson shot back, "Let Lodge compromise!" Hitchcock conceded that the Senator would have to give ground but suggested that the White House might also hold out the olive branch. "Let Lodge hold out the olive branch," came the stern reply. On this inflexible note, and with Mrs. Wilson's anxiety mounting, the interview ended.

The Senate was ready for final action on November 19, 1919. At the critical moment Wilson sent a fateful letter to the Democratic minority in the

Senate, urging them to vote down the treaty with the hated Lodge reservations so that a true ratification could be achieved. The Democrats, with more than the necessary one-third veto, heeded the voice of their crippled leader and rejected the treaty with reservations. The Republicans, with more than the necessary one-third veto, rejected the treaty without reservations.

The country was shocked by this exhibition of legislative paralysis. About four fifths of the senators professed to favor the treaty in some form, yet they were unable to agree on anything. An aroused public opinion forced the Senate to reconsider, and Lodge secretly entered into negotiations with the Democrats in an effort to work out acceptable reservations. He was making promising progress when Senator Borah got wind of his maneuvers through an anonymous telephone call. The leading irreconcilables hastily summoned a council of war, hauled Lodge before them, and bluntly accused him of treachery. Deeply disturbed, the Massachusetts Senator said: "Well, I suppose I'll have to resign as majority leader."

"No, by God!" burst out Borah. "You won't have a chance to resign! On Monday, I'll move for the election of a new majority leader and give the reasons for my action." Faced with an upheaval within his party such as had insured Wilson's election in 1912, Lodge agreed to drop his backstage negotiations.

The second-chance vote in the Senate came on March 19, 1920. Wilson again directed his loyal Democratic following to reject the treaty, disfigured as it was by the hateful Lodge reservations. But by this time there was no other form in which the pact could possibly be ratified. Twenty-one realistic Democrats turned their backs on Wilson and voted Yea; 23 loyal Democrats, mostly from the rock-ribbed South, joined with the irreconcilables to do the bidding of the White House. The treaty, though commanding a simple majority this time of 49 Yeas to 35 Nays, failed of the necessary two-thirds vote.

Wilson, struggling desperately against the Lodge reservation trap, had already summoned the nation in "solemn referendum" to give him a vote in favor of the League in the forthcoming presidential election of 1920. His hope was that he could then get the treaty approved without reservations. But this course was plainly futile. Even if all the anti-League senators up for re-election in 1920 had been replaced by the pro-League senators, Wilson would still have lacked the necessary two-thirds majority for an unreserved treaty.

The American people were never given a chance to express their views directly on the League of Nations. All they could do was vote either for the weak Democratic candidate, Cox, who stood for the League, and the stuffed-shirt Republican candidate, Harding, who wobbled all over the map of the League arguments. If the electorate had been given an opportunity to express itself, a powerful majority probably would have favored the world organization, with at least some reservations. But wearied of Wilsonism, idealism, and self-denial, and confused by the wordy fight over the treaty, the voters rose up and swept Harding into the White House. The winner had been more anti-League than pro-League, and his prodigious plurality of 7,000,000 votes condemned the League to death in America.

What caused this costly failure of American statesmanship?

Wilson's physical collapse intensified his native stubbornness. A judicious compromise here and there no doubt would have secured Senate approval of the treaty, though of course with modifications. Wilson believed that in any event the Allies would reject the Lodge reservations. The probabilities are that the Allies would have worked out some kind of acceptance, so dire was their need of America's economic support, but Wilson never gave them a chance to act.

Senator Lodge was also inflexible, but prior to the second rejection he was evidently trying to get the treaty through—on his own terms. As majority leader of the Republicans, his primary task was to avoid another fatal split in his party. Wilson's primary task was to get the pact approved. From a purely political point of view, the Republicans had little to gain by engineering ratification of a Democratic treaty.

The two-thirds rule in the Senate, often singled out as the culprit, is of little relevance. Wilson almost certainly would have pigeonholed the treaty if it had passed with the Lodge reservations appended.

Wilson's insistence that the League be wedded to the treaty actually contributed to the final defeat of both. Either would have had a better chance if it had not been burdened by the enemies of the other. The United Nations, one should note, was set up in 1945 independently of any peace treaty.

Finally, American public opinion in 1919–20 was not yet ready for the onerous new world responsibilities that had suddenly been forced upon it. The isolationist tradition was still potent, and it was fortified by postwar disillusionment. If the sovereign voters had spoken out for the League with one voice, they almost certainly would have had their way. A treaty without reservations, or with a few reservations acceptable to Wilson, doubtless would have slipped through the Senate. But the American people were one war short of accepting leadership in a world organization for peace.

14

Pearl Harbor: Who Blundered?

by Colonel T. N. Dupuy

Prior to the outbreak of World War II, the United States tried to apply some of the "lessons" of history. Basically, policymakers attempted to avoid the factors which had brought the United States into World War I. But this war was different—the enemies were even more fearful and the stakes were even greater. It was unlikely that the United States could have avoided World War II, but any lingering hopes along those lines were shattered when the Japanese attacked Pearl Harbor on December 7, 1941.

Military historian Trevor N. Dupuy has called the attack "the worst disaster in the military annals of the United States." How could it have happened? Indeed, who blundered? Without subscribing to any conspiracy theory and by providing his readers with an accurate chronicle of events, Colonel Dupuy shows in his essay that there were many failures leading up to Pearl Harbor. Even though the "lessons" of history must be analyzed carefully and applied judiciously, Dupuy hopes that another such "day of infamy" can be avoided if we truly understand what went wrong at Pearl Harbor.

Precisely at 7:55 A.M. on Sunday, December 7, 1941, a most devastating Japanese aerial attack struck the island of Oahu, Territory of Hawaii. When it was all over, the battleships of our Pacific Fleet, moored by pairs in their Pearl Harbor base, had received a mortal blow. Our army air strength in Hawaii—the Japanese found its planes ranged neatly wing to wing on airfield ramps—was a tangled mass of smoking wreckage.

The worst disaster in the military annals of the United States had ushered us into World War II. As in most wars, the political and diplomatic background was so complex and confused as to defy definitive analysis—though this has not prevented historians and others from making the attempt. But as to the disaster itself, the military record is clear.

A well-planned and brilliantly executed surprise attack by Japanese carrier-based aircraft was launched against the major American bastion in the Pacific. The United States government, its senior military leaders, and its commanders in Hawaii had had sufficient information to be adequately warned that an attack was possible, and had had time to be prepared to thwart or to blunt the blow. The information was largely ignored; the preparations were utterly inadequate.

Someone had blundered. Who? And how?

At the moment of the attack four professional military men filled posts of vital importance. In Washington, General George C. Marshall, Chief of

Staff, was responsible for the entire United States Army and all of its installations. In a nearby office sat his Navy counterpart, Admiral Harold R. Stark, Chief of Naval Operations. On the Hawaiian island of Oahu, Lieutenant General Walter C. Short commanded the Hawaiian Department, the Army's most vital overseas outpost. Commanding the United States Pacific Fleet was Rear Admiral Husband E. Kimmel; his headquarters was also on Oahu, overlooking the great Navy base at Pearl Harbor.

Marshall, product of the Virginia Military Institute, had a well-deserved reputation for brilliant staff work under Pershing in France in World War I. Later he had taken a prominent part in developing the Army's Infantry School at Fort Benning, Georgia. Short, a graduate of the University of Illinois, had entered the Army from civilian life in 1901. Early in 1941 he had been chosen by Marshall to command the Hawaiian Department.

Both Stark and Kimmel had graduated from the United States Naval Academy at Annapolis—Stark in 1903, Kimmel a year later. Both had risen to their high positions in the Navy following exemplary command and staff service at sea and on shore. Close personal friends, both were highly respected by their naval colleagues.

The thinking and attitudes of these four men were shaped by two decades of unanimous opinion among American soldiers and sailors that someday Japan would clash with the United States in a struggle for predominance in the vast Pacific Ocean. All accepted without question the basic elements of U.S. doctrine for the defense of the Pacific in such a war.

The doctrine was that the United States Navy—and in particular its Pacific Fleet—was the essential element to American success in a Pacific war. Immobilization or destruction of that fleet would be the greatest damage Japan could inflict on the United States. Upon the Army lay the responsibility for furthering the offensive powers of the fleet by protecting its great Pearl Harbor base; by safeguarding the Panama Canal, the Navy's life line from the Atlantic to the Pacific; and by defending the advanced Philippine delaying position, which in military opinion was likely to be Japan's initial target.

Since 1939 the top military authorities of the nation, including President Franklin D. Roosevelt, had understood the almost inexorable logic of events that pointed to our eventual involvement either in the conflict which Hitler had begun in Europe or that in Asia between Japan and China—or both. And under Roosevelt's skillful guidance the nation, albeit grudgingly, was very slowly building up its military strength.

As 1941 rolled along, it became apparent, even to the man in the street, that the most pressing danger lay in the Far East. Our diplomatic relations with Japan were worsening; by November they appeared to be almost at the breaking point. The long-continued diplomatic bickering between the two nations on a variety of subjects had resulted in the arrival in Washington of a special envoy, Saburo Kurusu, who—with Ambassador Kichisaburo Nomura—had on November 20 presented the State Department with a document that was practically an ultimatum.

Japan would acquiesce to our government's demands that she withdraw from Indochina only upon "establishment of an equitable peace in the Pacific area" and, further, upon "supply to Japan [by the U.S. of] a required quantity of oil."

In 1940, our cipher experts had cracked the Japanese secret codes—a cryptoanalytical procedure known in the War Department as "Magic." Hence our government knew that the envoys had received instructions to press for American acceptance of this "final proposal" by November 25. The ambassadors had been warned that for reasons "beyond your ability to guess" this was essential, but that if the "signing can be completed by the 29th" the Imperial Japanese government would wait. "After that things are automatically going to happen."

It was also known through Magic radio intercepts that a large proportion of Japanese military strength—land, sea, and air—was concentrating in the Indochina and South China Sea areas. No evidence of aircraft carriers had been found, however, either in those areas or in the Japanese mandated islands. Intelligence agencies, monitoring Japanese radio traffic, considered it probable that the carriers were still in their home waters, but they were not certain.

On this basis Marshall, Stark, and their respective staffs concluded that the Japanese were preparing to strike in Southeast Asia; this threat, of course, included the Philippine Commonwealth. Accordingly our Army and Navy commanders in the Philippines and at Guam had been specifically warned. The commanders in Hawaii, Panama, Alaska, and on the West Coast were kept informed of important developments.

This was the situation as Marshall and Stark saw it early on November 25. From that time on events succeeded one another with increasing rapidity, both in Washington and in Hawaii. This is how they unfolded:

Washington, Tuesday, November 25

Marshall and Stark attended a "War Council" meeting with the President, Secretary of State Cordell Hull, Secretary of War Henry L. Stimson, and Secretary of the Navy Frank Knox. Were the Japanese bluffing? Hull thought not; rejection of their terms would mean war. "These fellows mean to fight," he told the group. "You [Marshall and Stark] will have to be prepared."

Adequate preparation could not be guaranteed by either service chief. The great draft army was still only a partly disciplined mass. The Navy, better prepared for an immediate fight, was still far from ready for an extended period of combat. Marshall urged diplomatic delay. If the State Department could hold war off for even three months, the time gained would be precious, especially in the Philippines, where Douglas MacArthur's newly raised Commonwealth Army was only partly organized and equipped.

Perhaps the State Department's formula—*modus vivendi* they called it— which had been sent by cable to our British, Chinese, Australian, and Dutch allies for comment—would gain the needed time. This was a proposal for a three-month truce in Sino-Japanese hostilities, during which the United States, in return for Japan's withdrawal from southern Indochina, would make limited economic concessions to her.

It was evident to all concerned that otherwise hostilities were almost certain to break out within a few days. The President, noting Japan's proclivity for attacking without a declaration of war, impressed on all concerned that if war came, it must result from an initial blow by Japan. How, then, asked Roosevelt, could the United States permit this without too much danger to itself?*

That evening Stark wrote a lengthy warning to Kimmel in Hawaii, informing him that neither the President nor the Secretary of State "would be surprised over a Japanese surprise attack," adding that while "an attack upon the Philippines would be the most embarrassing thing that could happen to us . . . I still rather look for an advance into Thailand, Indochina, Burma Road areas as the most likely." Marshall reviewed the incoming and outgoing messages to overseas commanders, and busied himself with the almost numberless duties of his most important task: preparing our Army for combat.

Honolulu, Tuesday, November 25

Kimmel and Short had more than a passing interest in the status of our negotiations with Japan. Admiral Kimmel had been kept informed of the increasingly strained relations by frequent frank and newsy letters from Admiral Stark. One of these, dated November 7, had said in part: "Things seem to be moving steadily towards a crisis in the Pacific. . . . A month may see, literally, most anything. . . . It doesn't look good."

---

*The claim has been advanced—notably by Rear Admiral Robert A. Theobald in *The Final Secret of Pearl Harbor* (Devin-Adair, 1954)—that President Roosevelt abetted the Japanese surprise "by causing the Hawaiian Commanders to be denied invaluable information from decoded Japanese dispatches concerning the rapid approach of the war and the strong probability that the attack would be directed at Pearl Harbor." He did so, according to now-retired Admiral Kimmel in a recent interview with United Press International, to "induce the Japanese to attack Pearl Harbor and thus permit him to honor his secret commitments to Great Britain and the Netherlands with the full support of the American people."

The report of the Army Pearl Harbor Board, submitted to the Secretary of War on October 20, 1944, apportioned a share of the blame for the surprise to the War and Navy Departments and their top military officers in Washington. Even so, the service inquiries concluded that General Short and Admiral Kimmel had sufficient information to realize that war was imminent and had no excuse for inadequate security measures. They were not court-martialed, despite their requests, largely for political reasons. In this they were grievously wronged, for they had a right to be heard in their own defense. On the other hand, although I am not an apologist for the late President Roosevelt, it is simply ridiculous to suggest that he, who loved the Navy perhaps more than did any of our Presidents, would deliberately offer the Pacific Fleet as a sacrifice to entice Japan into war, and that this scheme was abetted by other responsible military men and statesmen. So many people would have known of such a nefarious plot that it would in fact have been impossible to muffle it.—T.N.D.

Admiral Kimmel undoubtedly was thinking of that letter when he reread the official radio message which he had received the day before, November 24:

Chances of favorable outcomes of negotiations with Japan very doubtful. . . . A surprise aggressive movement in any direction including attack on Philippines or Guam is a possibility. Chief of Staff has seen this dispatch, concurs and requests action addressees to inform senior Army officers their areas. Utmost secrecy necessary in order not to complicate an already tense situation or precipitate Japanese action.

Admiral Kimmel promptly sent a copy of the message to General Short. He had standing instructions to show such messages to the Army commander: the most critical messages from Washington were usually sent over Navy channels because the Army code was considered to be less secure. The Admiral saw no need for further action. After receiving a warning message on October 16 he had taken some measures for a partial alert and reported those promptly to Stark, who replied: "OK on the disposition which you made."

Admiral Kimmel and General Short had a cordial personal relationship, despite subsequent widespread but unfounded allegations to the contrary. They had frequently discussed, officially and personally, the possibility of a surprise Japanese attack and the measures to be taken to prepare for it and to thwart it if it should come. These plans had been approved in Washington. The Navy was responsible for long-range reconnaisance up to 700 miles, while the Army, with its land-based aircraft, was responsible for inshore reconnaissance for a distance up to twenty miles from shore. The Army's new radar would provide additional reconnaissance and air-warning service for a distance of up to 130 miles from Oahu. Periodically the commanders held joint maneuvers to test the plans and the readiness of their forces to carry them out.

They commanded large forces which might soon be called upon to fight, and it was essential that they maintain an intensive training schedule to assure the highest possible standard of combat efficiency. This was a formidable task, since many of their officers and men were inexperienced and untrained, having only recently been brought into our rapidly expanding armed forces. At the same time, as outpost commanders, both Short and Kimmel were well aware of their responsibilities for assuring the security of the fleet and of the island of Oahu.

Moreover, each commander assumed the other knew his business; each assumed the other's command was running on a full-time status. Each felt— as shown by later testimony—that to probe into the other's shop would be an unpardonable and resented intrusion. As a result, the liaison essential to any sort of joint or concerted operation—the daily constant and intimate exchange of details of command operations between Army and Navy staffs—was almost nonexistent. Each commander, then, was working in a partial vacuum.

On the single island of Oahu were concentrated most of the 42,857 troops that comprised the units of General Short's department. Carrying out the intensive training schedule was the bulk of two infantry divisions, less one regiment scattered in detachments on the other islands of the group. Also on Oahu were most of the antiaircraft and coast defense units of the Coast Artillery Command, and more than 250 aircraft of the Army's Hawaiian air force. Some of these aircraft, aloft on routine training exercises, were being tracked by the inexperienced crews of six Army mobile radar units newly installed at different points on the island.

There was comparable activity at the great Pearl Harbor Navy Yard, on the southern coast of the island, close by the bustling metropolis of Honolulu. Quite a few vessels of the U.S. Pacific Fleet were in port. Here Kimmel, the fleet's commander in chief, had his headquarters, from which he and his staff closely supervised the intense training programs of their ships in Hawaiian waters. The fleet comprised eight battleships, two aircraft carriers (with a total of 180 planes), sixteen cruisers, forty-five destroyers, twelve submarines, and slightly more than 300 land-based aircraft. In addition another battleship, an aircraft carrier, four cruisers, and various smaller vessels were temporarily absent, many being in mainland yards for repairs.

The Navy Yard itself was the principal installation of the Fourteenth Naval District; both base and the district were commanded by Rear Admiral Claude C. Bloch, who was a direct subordinate of Kimmel both as base commander and as a Pacific Fleet staff officer—a setup which bred no little confusion and which was not helped by the fact that Bloch was Kimmel's senior in the service, though not in command. Kimmel properly held Bloch responsible for the functioning and local security of all the land-based installations of the fleet in Hawaii, while he himself devoted his principal attention to the readiness of the fleet to function offensively at sea. He considered Bloch to be Short's naval counterpart, so far as local protection of the fleet in Hawaii was concerned. Formal co-ordination of Army and Navy activities in Hawaii and nearby Pacific areas, however, was done at conferences—fairly frequent—between Kimmel and Short.

[On November 25 (Washington date line), Vice Admiral Chuichi Nagumo's First Air Fleet—six aircraft carriers and 414 combat planes, escorted by two battleships, two heavy cruisers and one light, and nine destroyers—put to sea from Tankan Bay in the southern Kurile Islands. Eight tank ships trailed it. Screening the advance were twenty-eight submarines which had left Kure a few days earlier.

This powerful naval striking force had long been preparing for a surprise attack on the United States Pacific Fleet at Pearl Harbor. It did not, however, have a final directive to carry it out. The First Air Fleet was to leave the Kurile Islands and steam slowly east into the North Pacific to await orders either to attack or, if negotiations with the United States reached a conclusion satisfactory to Japan, to return home.]

Washington, Wednesday, November 26

Before attending a meeting of the Army-Navy Joint Board, both General Marshall and Admiral Stark had learned that Secretary of State Hull, with the full approval of the President, had made a momentous decision.

During the evening of the twenty-fifth and the early hours of the twenty-sixth, the State Department received the comments of our allies on the *modus vivendi* reply to the Japanese ultimatum. The British, Australians, and Dutch gave lukewarm approval to the proposal for a three-month truce, though in a personal message to the President, Prime Minister Winston Churchill remarked pointedly, "What about Chiang Kai-shek? Is he not having a very thin diet?"

Chiang, in fact, had protested violently against the truce proposal, which, with its relaxation of economic pressure on Japan, could only work to the psychological and military disadvantage of China. The protest, as well as information gleaned from more intercepted messages indicating that the Japanese would accept nothing less than complete agreement to their demands of November 20, caused Secretary Hull to doubt the wisdom of the *modus vivendi*. Obviously, these concessions were inadequate to satisfy Japanese demands, yet, because they would seem like American appeasement they would strike a major blow to Chinese morale.

Hull therefore recommended a different reply, which the President approved. After a calm but firm restatement of the principles which had guided the American negotiations, the new note proposed, in essence: withdrawal of Japanese military forces from China and Indochina, recognition of the territorial integrity of those countries, unqualified acceptance of the National Government of China, and, finally, negotiation of a liberal U.S.-Japanese trade treaty once the other conditions had been met.

At 5 P.M. on November 26 Secretary Hull met with the two Japanese ambassadors and presented this reply to them. Special envoy Kurusu read the note, then commented that his government would "throw up its hands" and that the American position practically "put an end to the negotiations."

By frequent phone calls, Secretary Hull had kept both Stimson and Knox informed of these rapid developments, and the two service secretaries had passed on the information to their senior military subordinates. So it was that when they met at a Joint Board conference that same day, Marshall and Stark were well aware of the course of the events still in progress at the State Department. Agreeing that war was now almost certain, they both felt that it was incumbent upon them to remind the President once more of the dangerous weakness of the Army and the Navy and particularly the grave danger of disaster in the Philippines if war were to break out before further reinforcements of men and matériel could reach General MacArthur. They directed their subordinates to have ready for their signatures the next day a joint memorandum to the President which would urge avoidance of hostilities for as long as possible consistent with national policy and national honor.

Late in the afternoon General Marshall held a conference with Major General Leonard T. Gerow, Chief of the War Plans Division, to discuss what should be done the next day, November 27. Marshall had planned to be in North Carolina that day to observe the final phases of the largest maneuvers in the Army's peacetime history; he felt he should carry out that intention, despite his concern about a report that a large Japanese troop convoy had moved into the South China Sea. The two officers discussed the grave implications of the growing Japanese concentrations in the Southeast Asia region. Even though he intended to be back at his desk on the twenty-eighth, General Marshall authorized Gerow to send overseas commanders a warning in his name if further information next day—the twenty-seventh—should point to the possibility of a surprise Japanese attack.

Honolulu, Wednesday, November 26

Admiral Kimmel received a report from the radio intelligence unit in Hawaii of a strong concentration of Japanese submarines and carrier aircraft in the Marshall Islands. This implied, but did not definitely prove, that some Japanese carriers were there as well. This information was perhaps inconsistent with a somewhat more definite report from the Philippines saying that radio traffic indicated all known Japanese carriers to be in home waters. Neither Admiral Kimmel nor members of his staff saw any need to inform General Short of these reports.

Short, meanwhile, had received an official message directing him to send two long-range B-24 bombers—due from the mainland—to photograph and observe the Japanese bases of Truk in the Caroline Islands and Jaluit in the Marshalls, reporting the number and locations of all Japanese naval vessels. He was to make sure both planes were "fully equipped with gun ammunition." But neither mission was ever flown: only one B-24 reached Short, and it was not properly equipped.

[On the high seas, their bleak rendezvous at Tankan far astern, Nagumo's task force was steaming eastward. Radio silence was absolute. High-grade fuel kept smoke to a minimum. No waste was thrown overboard to leave telltale tracks; blackout on board was complete. Only the Admiral and a handful of his staff knew their orders; the rest of the command buzzed with speculation like so many hornets.]

Washington, Thursday, November 27

General Gerow, summoned to Mr. Stimson's office, found Secretary Knox and Admiral Stark already there. The Secretary of War felt the time had come to alert General MacArthur in the Philippines. He told his listeners that Secretary Hull had warned him no peaceful solution was apparent. "I have washed my hands of it," Hull had said, "and it is now in the hands of you and Knox, the Army and the Navy."

Stimson added word of a telephone discussion with the President, who, agreeing that an alert order be sent out, desired all commanders to be cautioned that Japan must commit the first overt act of war. All four in Stimson's office then prepared drafts of alert messages to be sent to General MacArthur and Admiral Hart in the Philippines and to Army and Navy commanders in Hawaii, Panama, and on the West Coast.

Early in the afternoon Gerow sent out the warning:

> Negotiations with Japan appear to be terminated to all practicable purposes with only the barest possibilities that the Japanese Government might . . . offer to continue.

The message then reiterated Mr. Roosevelt's desire that Japan commit the first overt act. But this, it was pointed out,

> should not repeat not be construed as restricting you to a course . . . that might jeopardize your defense. *Prior to hostile Japanese action you are directed to undertake such reconnaissance and other measures as you deem necessary* [italics supplied], but these measures should be carried out so as not repeat not to alarm civil population or disclose intent. Report measures taken. . . .

The message further directed that, should hostilities occur, commanders would undertake offensive tasks in accordance with existing war plans. It concluded with the caution that dissemination of "this highly secret information" should be limited to the essential minimum.

Stark's message to Navy commanders (as well as to our special naval observer in London, who was to advise the British) was sent at the same time; it opened bluntly: "This dispatch is to be considered a war warning." It related the end of negotiations and the expectation that "an aggressive move" might come within the next few days. Then, in contrast to the more general Army warning, it added the information that known military activities of the Japanese indicated they probably intended to launch "an amphibious expedition against either the Philippines, Thai or Kra peninsula or possibly Borneo." Like the Army warning, it directed execution of existing war plans in the event of hostilities. Naval commanders in the continental United States, Guam, and Samoa were cautioned to take antisabotage measures.

If read together, these two messages definitely pointed a finger at Southeast Asia as the expected enemy target. This, of course, in no way excuses any of the subsequent actions of our commanders in Hawaii, whose paramount responsibility was the security of their post. But it must have influenced their thinking.

Honolulu, Thursday, November 27

The official warnings from Washington confirmed to Short and Kimmel the seriousness of the international situation. Short, who noted that he was expected to report the measures he was taking, sent the following reply: "Report Department alerted to prevent sabotage. Liaison with the Navy."

The Hawaiian Department plans provided for three kinds of alert. Number 1, which was what Short had ordered, was to guard against sabotage and uprisings—long a preoccupation of all Hawaiian commanders because of the high proportion of Japanese in the Islands. Number 2 included security against possible isolated, external air or naval attacks. Number 3 was a full-scale deployment for maximum defense of the Islands, and particularly of Oahu—heart of the military organization. Only in the two higher stages of alert was ammunition to be distributed to the antiaircraft batteries; in Alert No. 1 all ammunition was to be kept stored in the dumps. Under Alert No. 1, planes would be parked closely for easy guarding; under the others they would be dispersed.

General Short felt he was confirmed in his concern over sabotage when his intelligence officer—or G-2—presented a message from the War Department G-2, warning that "subversive activities may be expected."

In obedience to the instruction to make such reconnaissance as he might "deem necessary," Short did, however, order his newly installed radar stations to operate daily from 4 A.M. to 7 A.M.; these were the dawn hours when surprise attack was most likely. Further reconnaissance, he felt, was the Navy's responsibility. He didn't know that Kimmel was having troubles of his own in attempting any sustained offshore reconnaissance. Nor was Kimmel aware that Short's radar was operating only on a curtailed basis.

Kimmel pondered over what steps he should take. Though he was already alerted to some extent, he knew that for the moment he could do little in the way of "defensive deployment" in his war plan tasks—most specifically, raids into the Japanese mandated islands. Should he then prepare for an attack against Oahu? The Washington message implied that this was not a probability. Even so, he didn't have sufficient planes for a 360 degree, distant reconnaissance from Oahu.

In compliance with instructions from Washington, Kimmel was sending some Marine planes to Wake and Midway islands. He decided that the two carrier task forces he was ordering to carry out this instruction could, en route, conduct long-range searches to the west, over the direct route from Japan to Oahu.

Task Force 8, under Vice Admiral William F. Halsey, including the carrier *Enterprise* and three cruisers, was leaving that day. In conference with Halsey before departure, Kimmel showed him the "war warning" message. Halsey asked how far he should go if he met any Japanese ships while searching. "Use your common sense," was Kimmel's reply. Halsey, it is understood, commented that these were the best orders he could receive, adding that if he found as much as one Japanese sampan, he would sink it. Kimmel, by making no further comment, apparently acquiesced.

Pending the arrival of Halsey at Wake, Kimmel sent orders to a patrol plane squadron based on Midway to proceed to Wake and return, searching ocean areas and covering a 525-mile area around Wake itself.

Kimmel felt that he had done all he could in that line without completely halting fleet training and exhausting the pilots of his relatively weak air command. But he did order immediate attack on any and all unidentified submarines discovered in the vicinity of Oahu and other fleet operating zones. Neither then nor later, apparently, did he check on the local security measures undertaken by Admiral Bloch's command, nor did he suggest any co-ordination between Bloch and Short.

[Nagumo's force was steady on a course laid between the Aleutians and Midway Island, the carriers in two parallel rows of three each. Battleships and cruisers guarded the flanks, destroyers screened wide, and submarines were scouting far ahead.]

Washington, Friday, November 28

General Marshall, back from his North Carolina inspection, was briefed by Gerow on the previous day's happenings. He read and approved the joint memorandum, already signed by Admiral Stark, which urged on the President the need for gaining time, particularly until troops—some already at sea and nearing Guam, others about to embark on the West Coast—could reach the Philippines. He also approved the warning message Gerow had sent to the overseas commanders.

At noon he attended the President's "War Council" meeting at the White House. The implications of a large Japanese amphibious force, known to be sailing southward through the South China Sea, were discussed. British Malaya, the Netherlands East Indies, and the Philippines were potential targets, the invasion of which would immediately involve us in war. But unless Congress should previously declare war, the United States could not attack this force. It was agreed that the President should send a message to Emperor Hirohito urging him to preserve peace, and that Mr. Roosevelt should also address Congress, explaining the dangers being created by this Japanese aggressive action. The President then left for a short vacation at Warm Springs, Georgia, directing his advisers to have the two documents prepared in his absence.

Marshall, back at his desk, thumbed through a sheaf of radio replies to the "war warning" message. Lieutenant General John L. DeWitt, commanding on the Pacific Coast, reported instituting a harbor alert at San Francisco and similar precautions in Alaska in liaison with naval authorities. He requested permission to direct air as well as ground deployment of his far-flung command. It was a long message, contrasting sharply with Short's succinct report of sabotage defense measures in Hawaii. But the Chief of Staff didn't pay much attention; it would be Gerow's job to handle any necessary responses. So Marshall initialed most of the messages and then forgot about them.

Short's message, however, was not initialed by Marshall. He would later testify he had no recollection of ever having seen it, although it bore the routine rubber stamp, "Noted by Chief of Staff."

159

As for Admiral Stark, he was pushing off a long message to Navy commanders on the West Coast, and to Admiral Kimmel, quoting the Army alert message of the twenty-seventh, including its admonition that Japan must commit the first "overt act."

Honolulu, Friday, November 28

Kimmel read Stark's long quote of the Army's alert message. He was particularly interested in its stress that "if hostilities cannot . . . be avoided the United States desires that Japan commit the first overt act." This appeared to confirm his decision of the previous day: limiting defensive deployment to one patrol squadron cruising from Wake to Midway and sending carrier task forces for local defense of those outposts.

Admiral Kimmel received several other interesting reports. The U.S.S. *Helena* reported contact with an unidentified submarine. An intelligence estimate based on radio intercepts indicated Japanese carriers were still in their own home waters. Another report on intercepted Japanese messages established a "winds code," by means of which Japan would notify its diplomatic and consular representatives abroad of a decision to go to war: "cast wind rain" meant war with the United States; "north wind cloudy," war with Russia; "west wind clear," war with England and invasion of Thailand, Malaya, and the Dutch East Indies.

It was all very interesting. However, the Admiral never thought of mentioning any of these reports during his conference with General Short that day. They discussed mutual responsibility for security of Wake and Midway—in light of the mixed Army-Navy garrisons at both places. But neither thought of asking the other what action he had taken on the November 27 warnings, nor did either volunteer any information on matters he considered to be of interest to his own individual service only.

[Admiral Nagumo's fleet spent the day in attempts to refuel in a plunging sea—an operation which, as it turned out, would continue for several days under almost heartbreaking conditions of bad weather.]

Washington, Saturday, November 29

Both General Marshall and Admiral Stark received Magic copies of more intercepted Japanese messages. One of these from Premier Tojo in Tokyo to the ambassadors in Washington was quite ominous:

> The United States' . . . humiliating proposal . . . was quite unexpected and extremely regrettable. The Imperial Government can by no means use it as a basis for negotiations. Therefore . . . in two or three days the negotiations will be de facto ruptured. . . . However, I did not wish you to give the impression that the negotiations are broken off. Merely say to them that you are awaiting instructions. . . . From now on, do the best you can.

To Marshall and Stark this was clear evidence indeed that the Japanese were stalling for time only long enough to get their forces ready to attack in the Indonesia-Southeast Asia area. It seemed now only a question of time, as more reports streamed in about Japanese convoys moving into the South China Sea.

For a good part of the morning Stark and Marshall were working closely with Secretaries Knox and Stimson in preparing and revising drafts of the presidential messages to Congress and to Emperor Hirohito, in accordance with the agreement at the previous day's meeting of the War Council. Finally, about noon, the two secretaries were satisfied, and their proposed drafts were sent to Secretary Hull.

Late in the afternoon both read with considerable interest reports of a warlike speech which Premier Tojo had delivered that day (November 30, Tokyo time). The twenty-ninth had been the deadline established in the messages from Tokyo to the ambassadors. The speech, while warlike, failed to give any indication of Japanese intentions.

Honolulu, Saturday, November 29

Things were generally quiet on Oahu and in the outlying waters, as the Army and Navy both began a weekend of relaxation after five days of strenuous training. There was considerable bustle, however, at the Army's headquarters at Fort Shafter, as well as at Navy headquarters at nearby Pearl Harbor. General Short approved a message in reply to the latest sabotage warning from Washington, outlining in detail the security measures which had been taken. Admiral Kimmel received another message from Washington reminding him once more that he was to be prepared to carry out existing war plans in the event of hostilities with Japan. Thus, once again, the two commanders were reminded of the alert messages they had received on the twenty-seventh, and once again they found themselves satisfied with the actions they had then taken.

[In the North Pacific Admiral Nagumo's fleet continued refueling.]

Washington, Sunday, November 30

General Marshall, returning from his usual Sunday morning horseback ride at Fort Myer, found another intercepted Japanese message awaiting him; the Foreign Ministery was cautioning its envoys in Washington to keep talking and "be careful that this does not lead to anything like a breaking-off of negotiations." He agreed with G-2's conclusion that the Japanese were stalling until their South China Sea assault was ready.

Stark, at his desk, was called that morning by Secretary of State Hull, gravely concerned about Premier Tojo's warlike speech. The Secretary told him he was going to urge the President's return from Warm Springs. A later call from Hull informed Stark that President Roosevelt would be back Monday morning; Stark must see the President and report on the naval developments in the Far East.

Honolulu, Sunday, November 30

General Short, in light of his instructions "not to alarm the civil population," must have been annoyed to read the Honolulu *Advertiser* headlines that morning: "Hawaii Troops Alerted." There wasn't anything he could do about it, however; even the limited nature of his Alert No. 1 would draw newspaper attention in a critical time such as this. He also read that "Leaders Call Troops Back in Singapore—Hope Wanes as Nations Fail at Parleys" and "Kurusu Bluntly Warned Nation Ready for Battle."

Kimmel ordered a squadron of patrol planes to Midway, to replace temporarily the squadron which he had ordered to reconnoiter about Wake. He was also interested in an information copy of a Navy Department message to Admiral Hart, commanding our Asiatic Fleet at Manila, directing him to scout for information as to an intended Japanese attack on the Kra Isthmus of Thailand, just north of Malaya.

Kimmel didn't think that war could be delayed much longer. He wrote on the top of a piece of paper the words—"Steps to be taken in case of American-Japanese war within the next twenty-four hours," an *aide-memoire* of the orders he must issue to his fleet.

[The Japanese First Air Fleet was still engaged in the arduous refueling job, while continuing its eastward course at slow speed.]

Washington, Monday, December 1

A busy day. Stark learned from his intelligence staff that the Japanese Navy had changed service radio frequencies and call letters for all units afloat—a normal prewar step. He went to the White House with Secretary Hull and briefed the President.

In the afternoon both Stark and Marshall digested an unusual number of important Magic intercepts of Japanese messages. Japan's Foreign Minister was urging his ambassadors to prevent the United States "from becoming unduly suspicious," emphasizing that it was important to give the impression to the Americans that "negotiations are continuing." Tokyo also had ordered its diplomatic offices in London, Hong Kong, Singapore, and Manila "to abandon the use of code machines and to dispose of them." Japan's ambassador at Bangkok reported his intrigues to maneuver Thailand into a declaration of war on Great Britain.

But most significant was an exchange between Japan's ambassador to Berlin and his foreign office. The ambassador reported that Foreign Minister von Ribbentrop had given him Hitler's unequivocal assurance that "should Japan become engaged in a war against the United States, Germany, of course, would join the war immediately." Tojo promptly told the ambassador to inform the German government that "war may suddenly break out between the Anglo-Saxon nations and Japan through some clash of arms. . . . This war may come quicker than anyone dreams."

162

And how quickly would that be? This was the question which sprang immediately to the minds of Admiral Stark and General Marshall, the men responsible for readying the armed forces of the United States for the coming clash of arms. They had no way of knowing that the answer lay in a brief uncoded message picked up by several American radio intelligence intercept stations just a few hours earlier. "Climb Mount Niitaka," was the message. No significance could be attached to it, so it never came to the attention of Marshall or Stark. Nor would it have meant anything to either of them.

Honolulu, Monday, December 1

Kimmel and Short held another routine conference. Presumably they discussed at some length the grave international situation. Supplementing the cryptic but alarming official intelligence reports and warnings were the headlines blazoning the Honolulu newspapers.

But neither Kimmel nor Short in their conversation discussed local security precautions or a possible threat to Oahu. Politely but inconclusively they continued discussion of the divided responsibility at Wake and Midway. Kimmel never thought to mention to Short that he had received another Washington warning about the "winds code" and that he had also been informed of the change in Japanese military frequencies and call letters. It never occurred to Kimmel that Short might not have been told about either matter.

Routine training continued in Army posts. General Short was quite pleased that his limited alert—which the War Department had apparently approved—had not interfered noticeably with training programs.

["Climb Mount Niitaka!"

Admiral Nagumo sucked in his breath as the message was laid before him this day. This was it; the prearranged code which meant "Proceed with attack."

Obedient to the signal flags broken out aboard the flagship, the gray ships came foaming about to a southeasterly course, vibrating to the thrust of increased propeller speed. Inside the steel hulls the mustered crews, learning the news, cheered, quaffed sake, and burned incense to the spirits of their ancestors.]

Washington, Tuesday, December 2

Additional Magic intercepts indicated further Japanese preparations for war, with the enemy's known offensive weight still massing in Southeast Asia.

Honolulu, Tuesday, December 2

Kimmel, discussing intelligence reports with his staff, noted the change in Japanese radio frequencies as related in the Navy Department's fortnightly intelligence summary, received late the previous day. The gist of it was that Tokyo was preparing for "operations on a large scale."

Then Kimmel called for intelligence estimates on the location of Japanese aircraft carriers. Captain Edwin T. Layton, his intelligence officer, gave estimated locations for all except Divisions 1 and 2—four carriers.

"What!" exclaimed Kimmel, "you don't know where [they] are?"

"No, sir, I do not. I think they are in home waters, but—"

Sternly, but with a suspicion of a twinkle in his eyes, Kimmel delivered himself of a masterpiece of unconscious irony.

"Do you mean to say they could be rounding Diamond Head and you wouldn't know it?"

The conference ended after a discussion on the difficulty of locating a force operating under sealed orders while preserving radio silence.

Short met Kimmel that day again. They continued debate over jurisdiction at Wake and Midway.

[Nagumo's fleet was steadily driving south toward Oahu. In prearranged code—unintelligible to American Magic interceptors—Tokyo had confirmed the target date: "X-Day will be 8 December"—December 7, Honolulu time.]

Washington, Wednesday, December 3

Along with the other recipients of Magic information, General Marshall and Admiral Stark noted but attached no particular significance to a pair of intercepted messages made available to them that day.

One, dated November 15, was already old; its translation had been deferred for several days in order to take care of messages considered more urgent. It referred to an earlier message directing the Japanese consulate at Honolulu to make periodic reports on the location of American warships in Pearl Harbor, and requested the Honolulu consulate to step up these reports to twice a week.

No particular importance was attributed to this by Admiral Stark or his senior naval intelligence officers, since the Japanese had long been making efforts to obtain information about the activities and number of ships in harbor at other naval bases on the West Coast and at Panama. The fact that the Japanese wanted more complete data, including exact locations of specific vessels in Pearl Harbor, was assumed to be merely an indication of their thoroughness in evaluating intelligence on America's main Pacific combat force.

The other message was a reply by Prime Minister Tojo to the suggestion of his ambassadors at Washington that peace could perhaps be preserved through a high-level conference—they had proposed former Premier Prince Konoye as the Japanese envoy and Vice President Henry Wallace or Presidential Assistant Harry Hopkins for the United States—at "some midway point, such as Honolulu." "Tojo's response, that "it would be inappropriate for us to propose such a meeting," seemed a less significant indication of Japan's immediate intentions than the continuing reports of her movements in and near Indochina.

Honolulu, Wednesday, December 3

Admiral Kimmel noted the continuing and surprising lack of information on Japanese carriers contained in the latest daily radio intelligence summary, which stated that "carrier traffic is at a low ebb."

That day, too, he received Admiral Stark's letter of November 25. He agreed with Stark's view that "an attack on the Philippines" might be embarrassing, but that "an advance into Thailand, Indochina, Burma Road area [was] most likely."

In the afternoon Short and Kimmel conferred. They soon got into a grim discussion of what they could do to carry out assigned war plans when and if war broke out. Both were thinking, of course, of planned naval and air raids into the Marshall Islands and of security measures for Wake and Midway. There was no mention of like measures for Oahu. Nor did Admiral Kimmel think to mention to General Short his latest intelligence reports about the burning of Japanese codes or the missing aircraft carriers.

[Nagumo's planners on the high seas were busy marking on their charts of Pearl Harbor the exact locations of six of the U.S. battle fleet—the Penn-sylvania, Arizona, California, Tennessee, Maryland, and West Virginia. The data came from Honolulu, relayed by radio through Imperial Navy Head-quarters in Tokyo.]

Washington, Thursday, December 4

A mixed bag of Magic intercepts available to both Stark and Marshall gave clear indication of Japanese intentions to go to war. Instructions came to Ambassador Nomura to completely destroy one of the two special machines for secret coding, but to hold the other and its cipher key—which should be in his personal possession—"until the last minute." One intercepted message, considered to be relatively insignificant, was to the Japanese consul at Honolulu; he was to "investigate completely the fleet-bases in the neighborhood of the Hawaiian military reservation."

Stark and Marshall concerned themselves with routine activities.

Honolulu, Thursday, December 4

Admiral Kimmel conferred with two of his senior task-force commanders, scheduled to sail the next day on combined training-alert missions. One, under Vice Admiral Wilson Brown, was to proceed to Johnson Island, 700 miles southwest of Oahu, on a joint Navy-Marine bombardment and landing exercise. The other, under Rear Admiral T. H. Newton, included the carrier *Lexington*. This force was to go to Midway Island, fly off a squadron of Marine planes to reinforce the local garrison, and then rendezvous with Brown at Johnson Island. En route the *Lexington's* planes would conduct routine scouting flights.

Kimmel's intention was that, should war break out, these forces would be available for raids into the Marshall Island group in accordance with existing war plans. Both task-force commanders understood their war-plan missions; both were aware in general of the tense international situation. Kimmel, therefore, felt he was under no obligation to inform either of Washington's November 27 "war warning" message.

The net naval situation on Oahu now was that the entire carrier force of the Pacific Fleet was either at sea or about to steam and that the approaches to the island from the west would be scouted for several days to come.

Kimmel felt that these steps would ensure a reconnaissance search of a large portion of the central Pacific Ocean, as extensive as his limited aircraft strength would permit. But, from the Hawaiian Islands north to the Aleutians, both sea and air were still bare of American reconnaissance.

Kimmel and Short did not meet that day.

[Admiral Nagumo, watching the intermittent refueling being carried on during the day, was intrigued to learn from Honolulu, via Tokyo, that watchful Japanese eyes were "unable to ascertain whether air alert had been issued. There are no indications of sea alert. . . ."]

Washington, Friday, December 5

Both War and Navy departments were busy compiling data for President Roosevelt on Japanese sea, land, and air strength concentrating in French Indochina and adjacent areas. In an intercepted Japanese message from Washington, Ambassador Nomura told Tokyo that in case of Japanese invasion of Thailand, joint military action by Great Britain and the United States "is a definite certainty, with or without a declaration of war." Another, from Tokyo, reiterated the previous instructions about destruction of codes and coding machines.

Admiral Stark, conferring with staff officers, decided no further warning orders need be sent to overseas naval commanders; the message of November 27 was adequate. All concurred.

Honolulu, Friday, December 5

General Short read with interest a cryptic message from G-2 in Washington to his intelligence officer, directing him to get in touch with the Navy immediately "regarding broadcasts from Tokyo reference weather." So Lieutenant Colonel George W. Bicknell, assistant G-2, gave the General all facts obtainable from his own office and from Kimmel's headquarters. Short was informed by Kimmel of the departure of the two naval task forces of Admirals Brown and Newton.

[While pilots and squadron leaders on board Nagumo's fleet studied and restudied their coming roles, the ships—900 miles north of Midway and 1,300 miles northwest of Oahu—slid slowly down the North Pacific rollers, still far beyond the range of any American search plane.]

Washington, Saturday, December 6

Reports of increasing Japanese concentration and movements in Indochina, South China, and the South China Sea absorbed Stark and Marshall, as well as all the other members of the War Cabinet from the President down. Mr. Roosevelt, the service chiefs were glad to learn, had decided that he would personally warn Emperor Hirohito that further aggressions might lead to war and urge the Japanese ruler that withdrawal of his forces from Indochina "would result in the assurance of peace throughout the whole of the South Pacific area."

Late in the afternoon Magic plucked out of the air thirteen parts of a fourteen-part memorandum from Tokyo to the Japanese envoys. This much of the message summarized negotiations from the Japanese viewpoint, concluding that the American note of November 26 was not "a basis of negotiations." The envoys were instructed to handle it carefully, since "the situation is extremely delicate."

Distribution of this intercept was curious. Decoding was completed after office hours. General Sherman A. Miles, Army G-2, saw no need to disturb either the Secretary of War, General Marshall, or General Gerow at their homes. (In passing it might be mentioned that one didn't disturb General Marshall at home without extremely good reason.) Some Navy people saw the message. Stark, who was at the theater, learned of it when he returned home and found that he was expected to call the White House. The President had received the intercept, as had the State Department. The details of the conversation are not known, but presumably the President told Stark, as he had earlier said to Harry Hopkins: "This means war!"

Honolulu, Saturday, December 6

In the daily radio intelligence summary received that morning from Washington, Admiral Kimmel was again struck by lack of information on the location of Japanese carriers. In other dispatches, however, there was considerable information about different kinds of Japanese activity. He received a copy of Admiral Hart's message reporting on the movement of the two convoys south of Indochina. And he received a message from Washington authorizing him, "in view of the international situation and the exposed position of our outlying Pacific Islands," to order the destruction of classified documents at these islands, "now or under later conditions of greater emergency." Neither the Admiral nor any member of his staff saw any need to pass on any information to the Army. Presumably General Short was getting it all through Army channels.

Carefully checking the reported locations of all fleet units and projecting their planned routes for the next twenty-four hours, Admiral Kimmel again made his daily revision of his personal check-list memorandum: "Steps to be taken in case of American-Japanese war within the next twenty-four hours."

Over at Fort Shafter, Army headquarters, the daily staff conference was as usual presided over by Colonel Walter C. Phillips, chief of staff. General Short did not normally attend these meetings. Bicknell, assistant G-2, who seems to have been on his toes those days, reported the Japanese consulate in Honolulu was busily burning and destroying secret papers, significant in light of similar reports throughout the world already noted in the intercepts. The chief of staff and G-2 reported this information later to General Short.

And so Oahu drifted into another weekend: a time of relaxation for both Army and Navy. Short, however, was interrupted by Bicknell early that evening at his quarters while he and his G-2—Colonel Kendall Fielder—and their wives were about to drive to a dinner dance.

Bicknell, with some sense of urgency, reported that the local FBI agent had passed to him and to Navy intelligence a transcript of a suspicious long-distance telephone message. A Japanese named Mori, talking to someone in Tokyo, mentioned flights of airplanes, searchlights, and the number of ships in Pearl Harbor, along with cryptic reference to various flowers—apparently part of some sort of code.

Both the FBI man and Bicknell were alarmed at the implications of this flower code. Neither Short nor Fielder, however, was disturbed. Short, before they hurried to the car where their wives awaited them impatiently, told Bicknell he was, perhaps, "too intelligence-conscious." In any event they could talk about it again in the morning.

The district intelligence officer of the Navy decided that the transcript should be studied further by a Japanese linguist and so put the FBI report away until Monday morning. Admiral Kimmel was not informed.

[Nagumo's fleet, the wallowing tankers now left behind, was churning southward at twenty-four-knot speed. By 6 A.M. next day it would be 230 miles north of Oahu with its planes thrusting skyward. And at dawn, five midget two-man submarines—disgorged from five large Japanese submarines gathered offshore that night—poked their way around Diamond Head, Pearl Harbor-bound.]

Washington, Sunday, December 7

By 8 A.M. the last part of the Japanese memorandum—Part Fourteen—had been intercepted, transcribed, and was ready for distribution. Both Army and Navy intelligence officers were slightly surprised at its mild tone: "The Japanese Government regrets . . . that it is impossible to reach an agreement through further negotiations."

Stark got it in his office. Marshall was taking his Sunday morning recreational ride at Fort Myer: the message would await his arrival—usually at about 11 A.M. All others concerned got it. Meanwhile two other messages had been intercepted by Magic, and Colonel Rufus Bratton, executive officer in G-2, was so upset by them he tried vainly to get them to the Chief of Staff.

One of the messages ordered the embassy to destroy immediately its one remaining cipher machine plus all codes and secret documents. The other read:

"Will the Ambassador please submit to the United States Government (if possible to the Secretary of State) our reply to the United States at 1 P.M. on the 7th, your time."

It will be remembered that General Marshall did not take kindly to interruptions in his off-duty hours. So, despite the limited area of his ride—an automobile or motorcycle from Fort Myer headquarters could have intercepted him in fifteen minutes at most—not until his return to his quarters at ten-thirty did Marshall learn that an important message was awaiting him. He reached his office in the Munitions Building at about 11:15, to find General Gerow, General Miles, and Colonel Bratton there. Bratton handed him the three intercepted messages—the memorandum, the instructions to destroy codes and papers, and the instruction to deliver the Japanese answer at 1 P.M. precisely. Marshall read quickly but carefully, as was usual with him. Then—

"Something is going to happen at one o'clock," he told the officers. "When they specified a day, that of course had significance, but not comparable to an hour."

He immediately called Stark, who had read all three messages. A warning should be sent at once to all Pacific commanders, Marshall felt. Stark hesitated; he felt all had already been alerted. Marshall stated that in view of the "one o'clock" item he would apprise Army commanders anyway.

Hanging up, he reached for a pencil and drafted his instruction to DeWitt, Western Defense Command; Andrews, Panama Command; Short, Hawaiian Command; and MacArthur, Philippine Command. It took him about three minutes. He read it to the group:

"The Japanese are presenting at 1 P.M. E.S.T. today, what amounts to an ultimatum. Also they are under orders to destroy their code machine immediately. Just what significance the hour set may have, we do not know, but be on alert accordingly."

As he was ordering Bratton to send it out at once, Stark telephoned back. Would Marshall please include in his dispatch the "usual expression to inform the naval officer?" Marshall quickly added the words "Inform naval authorities of this communication." He sent Bratton on his way, instructing him to return as soon as the message had been delivered to the message center.

Bratton was back in five minutes; he had delivered the message personally to the officer in charge of the message center, Colonel French.

Marshall, obviously more perturbed than any of those present had ever before seen him, asked Bratton how much time would be consumed in enciphering and dispatching the message. Bratton didn't know. So back he was rushed to find out.

Marshall, it developed, was pondering whether or not he should telephone a warning—especially to MacArthur. Time was running out; not much more than one hour remained. Marshall had a "scrambler" phone on his desk, which permitted secure long-distance conversations with similar phones in the head-quarters of overseas commanders; eavesdroppers would hear only unintelligible gibberish. Marshall, however, must have had some private reservations as to the efficacy of the scrambler mechanism, and apparently feared that the Japanese might have some way of deciphering the conversation. A telephone call which could not be kept secret might precipitate Japanese action; it would almost certainly indicate we had broken their secret code. Would it be worth it?

Bratton reported back that the process would take about thirty minutes.

"Thirty minutes until it is dispatched, or thirty minutes until it is received and decoded at the other end?"

Business of rushing back to the message center again, while the big office clock ticked away. Bratton, charging back, announced that the message, decoded, would be in the hands of the addressees in thirty minutes. It was now precisely noon. In Hawaii it was only 6:30 A.M. Marshall, satisfied, made no further follow-up.

Had he done so he would have found out that Colonel French at the message center was having some troubles. To San Francisco, Panama, and Manila the warning sped without delay. But the War Department radio, so Colonel French was informed, had been out of contact with Hawaii since 10:20 that morning. French decided to use commercial facilities: Western Union to San Francisco, thence commercial radio to Honolulu. This was a normal procedure; usually it would mean but little further delay. French never dreamed of disturbing the Chief of Staff by reporting such trivia. So Marshall's warning was filed at the Army Signal Center at 12:01 P.M. (6:31 A.M. in Hawaii); teletype transmission to San Francisco was completed by 12:17 P.M. (6:47 A.M. in Hawaii), and was in the Honolulu office of RCA at 1:03 P.M. Washington time (7:33 A.M. in Hawaii). Since that was too early for teletype traffic to Fort Shafter, RCA sent it by motorcycle messenger. He would, as it turned out, be delayed through extraordinary circumstances.

Honolulu, Sunday, December 7

Extraordinary circumstances had become almost commonplace on and near Oahu as early as 3:42 A.M. At that hour the mine sweeper *Condor,* conducting a routine sweep of the harbor entrance, sighted a submarine periscope. This was a defensive area where American submarines were prohibited from operating submerged. The *Condor* flashed a report of the sighting to the destroyer *Ward,* of the inshore patrol. For two hours the *Ward* searched the harbor entrance in vain; meanwhile the *Condor* and another mine sweeper had entered the harbor at about 5 A.M.; for some reason the antisubmarine net, opened to permit the entrance of the mine sweepers, was not closed.

At 6:30 the U.S.S. *Antares*—a repair ship towing a steel barge—was approaching the harbor entrance when she sighted a suspicious object, which looked like a midget submarine. The *Antares* immediately notified the *Ward.*

At 6:55 a Navy patrol plane sighted the same object and dropped two smoke pots on the spot. The *Ward* hastened to the scene, spotting the sub—her superstructure just above the surface—at 6:40, and promptly opened fire. At the same time the patrol plane dropped bombs or depth charges. The submarine keeled over and began to sink, as the *Ward* dropped more depth charges. Shortly after 6:50 the destroyer sent a coded message that it had attacked a submarine in the defensive sea area.

At about 7:40 Admiral Kimmel received a telephone call from the staff duty officer, reporting the *Ward*-submarine incident. Kimmel replied, "I will be right down." Quickly he completed dressing and left for his headquarters.

Meanwhile, the Army's six mobile radar stations on Oahu had been on the alert since 4 A.M. in compliance with General Short's Alert No. 1 instructions. At 7 A.M. five of these stations ceased operations, in accordance with these same instructions. At the remote Opana station at the northern tip of the island, Privates Joseph Lockard and George Elliott kept their set on while waiting for the truck which was to pick them up to take them to breakfast. Lockard, an experienced radar operator, planned to use this time to give Elliott a bit more instruction. At this moment an unusual formation appeared at the edge of the screen; Lockard checked the machine, found it operating properly, and at 7:02 A.M. concluded that a large number of aircraft, approximately 130 miles distant, was approaching Oahu from the north. For fifteen minutes Lockard and Elliott observed the approach of the formation, debating whether they should report it. Finally, at 7:20, Lockard called the radar information center. The switchboard operator informed him that the center had closed down twenty minutes before, that everyone had left except one Air Corps officer, First Lieutenant Kermet Tyler. Lockard reported the approaching flight to Tyler, who thought for a moment; the flight was undoubtedly either a naval patrol, a formation of Hickam Field bombers, or—most likely—a number of B-17's due from the mainland. "Forget it," he told Lockard.

Twenty minutes later—about 7:50—there was a bustle of activity on the decks of the ninety-four vessels of the Pacific Fleet in Pearl Harbor. It was almost time for morning colors on each vessel, and white-garbed sailors were briskly preparing for the daily flag-raising ceremony. Except for one destroyer, moving slowly toward the entrance, each ship was motionless at its moorings.

At 7:55 boatswains' whistles piped, and the preparatory signal for the colors ceremony was hoisted on each ship. At the same moment a low-flying plane, approaching over the hills to the northeast, swooped low over Ford Island, in the middle of the harbor. A bomb dropped on the seaplane ramp, close by the eight battleships moored next to the island. As the plane zoomed upward, displaying the red sun emblem of Japan, it was followed closely by others. By 9:45 some 260 Japanese planes had flashed that emblem over Oahu, and when the dreadful 110 minutes were over, 2,403 Americans—mostly sailors on the battleships—were dead or dying; 1,178 more had been wounded; the battle force of the Pacific Fleet had been destroyed, with four battleships sunk or capsized and the remaining four damaged, while several smaller vessels were sunk or damaged severely. The Japanese lost twenty-nine planes, five midget submarines, and less than a hundred men.

One small further incident is pertinent to our assessment of United States leadership in high places just before Pearl Harbor.

The Nisei RCA messenger boy carrying General Marshall's message speedily found himself involved in trouble. Not until 11:45 could he thread his way through traffic jams, road blocks, and general confusion to reach the Fort Shafter signal office, which was itself swamped in traffic by this time.

Not until 2:58 P.M. Hawaiian time—9:58 that evening in bewildered Washington—was the message decoded and placed on Short's desk. He rushed a copy to Admiral Kimmel, who read it, remarked—perhaps unnecessarily—that it was not of the slightest interest any more, and dropped it into the wastebasket.

It had been a pretty long thirty minutes.

Who was responsible?

No disaster of the magnitude of Pearl Harbor could have occurred without the failure—somewhere and somehow—of leadership. A total of eight separate official investigations searched for scapegoats, and found them. The disaster remained a political football long after the last three of these investigations. And much confusion and argument still exist.

Yet through this welter of discord, some facts and conclusions stand out. Today, nearly thirty years later, in another time of crisis, they hold important lessons.

It makes no difference, in assessing responsibility, that exceptional Japanese military skill, shrouded by deceit and assisted by almost incredible luck, accomplished its mission. Nor, indeed, does it matter that—as adjudicated in the always brilliant light of afterthought—Japan might well have inflicted defeat upon our Pacific Fleet and our Army forces in Hawaii regardless of how well alerted they may have been on December 7, 1941.

It makes no difference, so far as responsibility for the disaster itself was concerned, whether the war could have been prevented by wiser statesmanship or more astute diplomacy—though this would have required a wholehearted and unified national determination which did not exist in America in 1941 and the years before. It makes no difference that on December 7 the President and the Secretary of State—like the civilian Secretaries of War and Navy—had their eyes fixed on the Japanese threat in Southeast Asia. They had repeatedly warned the military men that war had probably become unavoidable.

What *does* matter is that the civilian statesmen—however deft or clumsy, shrewd, or shortsighted—performed their difficult tasks of diplomacy and of administration confident that the military men would carry out their professional responsibilities by doing everything humanly possible to prepare for a war so clearly impending. They had every right to expect that—within the limits of scanty means available—the Armed Forces would be ready for any contingency.

172

The explosion of the U.S.S. *Shaw* during the Japanese attack on Pearl Harbor, Dec. 7, 1941. (Library of Congress)

The confidence and expectations of civilian leadership and of the nation were tragically dashed that Sunday almost thirty years ago.

Military failures were responsible for Pearl Harbor.

In Washington the most important of these were the following:

1. The War Department staff, over which General Marshall presided, was at the time a complicated but "one-man" shop, where delegation of responsibility was the exception rather than the rule. When Marshall was absent, the operational wheels tended to freeze. This situation was to some extent due to cumbersome organization, to some extent due to the personality of the Chief of Staff.

2. General Marshall, in a letter to General Short on February 7, 1941, stressed that "the risk of sabotage and the *risk involved in a surprise raid by air and submarine* [italics supplied] constitute the real perils of the [Hawaiian] situation." Yet, although definitely warning General Short on November 27 of the threat of war, and ordering him to report the measures he would take in response, Marshall did not check up on those measures; moreover, he was unaware that Short had done no more than to take routine precautions against sabotage. And General Gerow, heading the War Plans Division of General Marshall's General Staff—as he testified later in taking full responsibility for this slip—had not made any

provision for following up operational orders. The net result was that both Marshall and Short remained the whole time in blissful ignorance of a vital misinterpretation of orders.

3. Marshall and Admiral Stark—and indeed all members of their staffs who knew the situation—permitted themselves to be hypnotized by the concrete evidence of the aggressive Japanese build-up in Southeast Asia which threatened our Philippines outpost. This theme, it will be remembered, ran as background to nearly all the warnings sent Hawaii. Thus succumbing to the illusory diagnosis of "enemy probable intentions," both top commanders ignored the danger implicit in our inability to locate at least four Japanese carriers.

4. Finally, on December 7, having indicated his full realization of the significance of the "one o'clock" intercept—that less than two hours now separated peace and war—and having decided not to use his "scrambler" telephone, Marshall failed to require surveillance and positive report on the delivery of his final warning.

These certainly were grave lapses in leadership. Yet in fairness, it should be noted that the consequences might not have been disastrous if all subordinate commanders had taken adequate security measures on the basis of the instructions, information, and warnings which they had received. To General Marshall's credit one must also chalk up his ability to profit by his mistakes. In less than three months after Pearl Harbor, he completely reorganized the War Department, decentralizing the mass of relatively minor administrative and executive matters that choked major strategical and tactical decisions. His newly created Operations Division of the General Staff—which he aptly termed his "command post"—ensured co-ordinated action and direction of Army activities in theaters of war all around the globe. On Oahu the situation was less ambiguous: military leadership at the top failed utterly.

Almost three decades later, with war clouds still lowering over most of the world, the story of the Pearl Harbor disaster has more significance than mere passing memorials to the brave men who lost their lives that day. If the lessons are heeded, our surviving descendants may never again have to commemorate another "day of infamy."

15

The Cold War

by Charles L. Mee, Jr.

Most Americans living today have spent most, if not all, of their lives under the specter of the Cold War. Tension and hostility between the United States and the Soviet Union, who were wartime allies, has been so severe since 1945 that the two major powers have dealt with each other as enemies. Fortunately, the two sides have not challenged each other directly in an all-out shooting confrontation. Rather, the Cold War has been fought on the periphery in limited wars and has been marked by bitter rhetoric aimed at the other side.

In the United States, the Soviet Union is usually held responsible for initiating and sustaining the Cold War. Likewise, the Russian people are told that U.S. actions frequently leave the Soviet leaders no choice but to pursue a hard line in opposition to American policy. Thus, the value of the following essay is enhanced, for what Charles L. Mee, Jr., has done is to present a finely balanced view of the origins of the Cold War. Mr. Mee, a former editor of *Horizon* magazine and author of *Meeting at Potsdam,* takes us back to the final days of World War II and clearly delineates the needs of Harry Truman and Joseph Stalin. All the ingredients of the Cold War—"distrust, suspicion, anxiety, fear"—were present even before the final defeat of Japan. The use of the atomic bombs to end that war added to the "harshness and provocation" coming from both sides. Finally, Mr. Mee analyzes the effects of the Cold War on the American people—effects still being felt four decades after World War II ended.

On April 12, 1945, Franklin Roosevelt died, and soon afterward Vyascheslav M. Molotov, the Russian foreign minister, stopped by in Washington to pay his respects to Harry Truman, the new President. Truman received Molotov in the Oval Office and, as Truman recalled it, chewed him out "bluntly" for the way the Russians were behaving in Poland. Molotov was stunned. He had never, he told Truman, "been talked to like that in my life."

"Carry out your agreements," Truman responded, "and you won't get talked to like that."

That's a good way to talk, if you want to start an argument. . . .

In Europe, Germany surrendered to the Allies on May 8. On May 12, Prime Minister Winston Churchill sent Truman an ominous cable about the Russians: "An iron curtain is drawn down upon their front," Churchill said, and, moreover, "it would be open to the Russians in a very short time to advance if they chose to the waters of the North Sea and the Atlantic." On May 17, Churchill ordered his officers not to destroy any German planes. In fact, Churchill kept 700,000 captured German troops in military readiness, prepared to be turned against the Russians.

That, too, is a good way to behave, if you are looking for trouble. . . .

Joseph Stalin said little: he did not advance his troops to the Atlantic, but he planted them firmly throughout eastern Europe and, in violation of previous agreements with the British and Americans, systematically crushed all vestiges of democratic government in Poland, Hungary, Czechoslovakia, Bulgaria, Rumania, Yugoslavia, and Finland. In truth, not quite: the Finns had managed to salvage a few bits and scraps of democratic usage for themselves. At dinner one night in the Kremlin, Andrei Zhdanov, one of Stalin's propagandists, complained that the Russians should have occupied Finland. "Akh, Finland," said Molotov, "that is a peanut."

And that, too, is a nice way to behave, if you are trying to stir up a fight. . . .

Most people, most of the time, want peace in the world, and they imagine that most politicians, being human, share the same wishes. At the end of a war, presumably, the desire for peace is most intense and most widely shared. Lamentably, that is not always the case. At the end of World War II the Russians, as Churchill remarked, feared "our friendship more than our enmity."

The Russians had both immediate cause and long-standing historical reasons for anxiety.

"From the beginning of the ninth century," as Louis Halle, a former State Department historian, has written, "and even today, the prime driving force in Russia has been fear. . . . The Russians as we know them today have experienced ten centuries of constant, mortal fear. This has not been a disarming experience. It has not been an experience calculated to produce a simple, open, innocent, and guileless society." Scattered over a vast land with no natural frontiers for protection, as Halle remarks, the Russians have been overrun "generation after generation, by fresh waves of invaders. . . . Lying defenseless on the plain, they were slaughtered and subjugated and humiliated by the invaders time and again."

Thus the Russians sought to secure their borders along eastern Europe. The czars attempted this, time and again: to secure a buffer zone, on their European frontier, a zone that would run down along a line that would later be called the Iron Curtain.

Yet, at the end of World War II, Stalin's fears were not just fears of outsiders. World War II had shown that his dictatorship was not only brutal but also brutally inept; he was neither a great military leader nor a good administrator; and the Russian soldiers returning from the Western Front had seen much evidence of Western prosperity. Stalin needed the Cold War, not to venture out into the world again after an exhausting war, but to discipline his restless people at home. He had need of that ancient stratagem of monarchs— the threat of an implacable external enemy to be used to unite his own people in Russia.

Churchill, on the other hand, emerged from World War II with a ruined empire irretrievably in debt, an empire losing its colonies and headed inevitably toward bankruptcy. Churchill's scheme for saving Great Britain was suitably inspired and grand: he would, in effect, reinvent the British Empire; he would establish an economic union of Europe (much like what the Common Market actually became); this union would certainly not be led by vanquished Germany or Italy, not by so small a power as the Netherlands, not by devastated France, but by Great Britain. To accomplish this aim, unfortunately, Churchill had almost nothing in the way of genuine economic or military power left; he had only his own force of persuasion and rhetoric. He would try to parlay those gifts into American backing for England's move into Europe. The way to bring about American backing was for Churchill to arrange to have America and Russia quarrel; while America and Russia quarreled, England would—as American diplomats delicately put it—"lead" Europe.

Truman, for his part, led a nation that was strong and getting stronger. Henry Luce, the publisher of the influential *Time* and *Life* magazines, declared that this was to be the beginning of "the American century"—and such a moment is rarely one in which a national leader wants to maintain a status quo. The United States was securing the Western Hemisphere, moving forcefully into England's collapsing "sterling bloc," acquiring military and economic positions over an area of the planet so extensive that the sun could never set on it.

The promise was extraordinary, the threat equally so. The United States did not practice Keynesian economics during the 1930's. It was not Roosevelt's New Deal that ran up the enormous federal deficit or built the huge, wheezing federal bureaucracy of today. War ran up the deficit; war licked the depression; war made the big federal government. In 1939, after a decade of depression, after the Civilian Conservation Corps, the Public Works Administration, the Civil Works Administration, the Agricultural Adjustment Act, the Social Security Act, and all the rest of the New Deal efforts on behalf of social justice, the federal budget was $9 billion. In 1945 it was $100 billion.

American prosperity was built upon deficit spending for war. President Truman knew it, and maintained deficit spending with the Cold War. Eventually, with the Truman Doctrine and the Marshall Plan, the encouragement of American multinational companies, and a set of defense treaties that came finally to encompass the world, he institutionalized it. The American people might find this easier to damn if they had not enjoyed the uncommon prosperity it brought them.

In October, 1944, Churchill visited Stalin in Moscow. The need then, clearly, was for cooperation among the Allies in order to win the war—and it appeared at the time that the cooperativeness nurtured during the war could be continued afterward. Each had only to recognize the other's vital interests. Churchill commenced to outline those interests to be recognized for the sake of the postwar cooperation.

"I said," Churchill recalled, " 'Let us settle about our affairs in the Balkans. Your armies are in Rumania and Bulgaria. We have interest, missions, and agents there. Don't let us get at cross-purposes in small ways. So far as Britain and Russia are concerned, how would it do for you to have ninety per cent predominance in Rumania, for us to have ninety per cent of the say in Greece, and go fifty-fifty about Yugoslavia?' "

Churchill wrote this out on a piece of paper, noting, too, a split of Bulgaria that gave Russia 75 per cent interest, and a fifty-fifty split of Hungary. He pushed the piece of paper across the table to Stalin, who placed a check mark on it and handed it back. There was a silence. "At length I said, 'Might it not be thought rather cynical if it seemed we had disposed of these issues, so fateful to millions of people, in such an offhand manner? Let us burn the paper.' 'No, you keep it,' said Stalin."

Such casual and roughshod "agreements" could hardly be the last word on the matter; yet, they signified a mutual recognition of one another's essential interests and a willingness to accommodate one another's needs—while, to be sure, the smaller powers were sold out by all sides. At this same time, in October, 1944, and later on in January, 1945, Roosevelt entered into armistice agreements with Britain and Russia that gave Stalin almost complete control of the internal affairs of the ex-Nazi satellites in eastern Europe. As a briefing paper that the State Department prepared in the spring of 1945 for President Truman said, "spheres of influence do in fact exist," and "eastern Europe is, in fact, a Soviet sphere of influence."

In short, the stage was set for postwar peace: spheres of influence had been recognized; a tradition of negotiation has been established. Yet, the European phase of World War II was no sooner ended than symptoms of the Cold War began to appear. The Big Three no longer needed one another to help in the fight against Hitler, and the atomic bomb would soon settle the war against Japan.

Toward the end of May, 1945, Harry Hopkins arrived in Moscow to talk with Stalin, to feel out the Russians now that the war in Europe had ended, and to prepare the agenda for discussion at the Potsdam Conference that would be held in Germany in mid-July. The United States had a problem, Hopkins informed Stalin, a problem so serious that it threatened "to effect adversely the relations between our two countries." The problem was, Hopkins said, Poland: "our inability to carry into effect the Yalta Agreement on Poland."

But, what was the problem? Stalin wanted to know. A government had been established there, under the auspices of the occupying Red Army, a government that was, naturally, "friendly" to the Soviet Union. There could be no problem—unless others did not wish to allow the Soviet Union to ensure a friendly government in Poland.

"Mr. Hopkins stated," according to the notes taken by his interpreter, Charles Bohlen, "that the United States would desire a Poland friendly to the Soviet Union and in fact desired to see friendly countries all along the Soviet borders.

"Marshal Stalin replied if that be so we can easily come to terms in regard to Poland."

But, said Hopkins, Stalin must remember the Declaration on Liberated Europe (signed at the Yalta Conference in February, 1945) and its guarantees for democratic governments; there was a serious difference between them; Poland had become the issue over which cooperation between Russia and America would flourish or fail.

Evidently Stalin could not understand this demand; apparently he could not believe that Americans were sincerely so idealistic. Did not America, after all, support a manifestly undemocratic dictatorship in Franco's Spain? "I am afraid," Averell Harriman, the U.S. ambassador to the Soviet Union, cabled home to Truman, "Stalin does not and never will fully understand our interest in a free Poland as a matter of principle. He is a realist in all of his actions, and it is hard for him to appreciate our faith in abstract principles. It is difficult for him to understand why we should want to interfere with Soviet policy in a country like Poland, which he considers so important to Russia's security, unless we have some ulterior motive."

And indeed, Russia's sphere of influence was recognized, it seemed, only so that it might serve as a bone of contention. Poland, Czechoslovakia, Bulgaria, Rumania, Hungary, all became bones of contention. It is not clear that any one of the Big Three deeply cared what happened to these eastern European countries so long as the countries served as useful pawns. Hopkins insisted that Stalin must recognize freedom of speech, assembly, movement, and religious worship in Poland and that all political parties (except fascists) must be "permitted the free use, without distinction, of the press, radio, meetings, and other facilities of political expression." Furthermore, all citizens must have "the right of public trial, defense by counsel of their own choosing, and the right of habeas corpus."

Of course, Stalin said, of course, "these principles of democracy are well known and would find no objection on the part of the Soviet Government." To be sure, he said, "in regard to the *specific* [italics added] freedoms mentioned by Mr. Hopkins, they could only be applied in full in peace time, and even then with certain limitations."

In the latter two weeks of July, 1945, the Big Three gathered at Potsdam, just outside of Berlin, for the last of the wartime conferences. They discussed the issues with which the war in Europe had left them, and with which the war in the Far East would leave them when it came to an end. They discussed spheres of influence, the disposition of Germany, the spoils of war, reparations, and, of course, eastern Europe.

At one of the plenary sessions of the Potsdam Conference, they outlined the spheres of influence precisely, clearly, and in detail during a discussion of the issue of "German shares, gold, and assets abroad." To whom did these items belong? What, for instance, did Stalin mean when he said "abroad"?

STALIN: ". . . the Soviet delegation . . . will regard the whole of Western Germany as falling within your sphere, and Eastern Germany, within ours."

Truman asked whether Stalin meant to establish "a line running from the Baltic to the Adriatic." Stalin replied that he did.

STALIN: "As to the German investments, I should put the question this way: as to the German investments in Eastern Europe, they remain with us, and the rest, with you. . . ."

TRUMAN: "Does this apply more specifically: the German investments in Europe or in other countries as well?"

STALIN: "Let me put it more specifically: the German investments in Rumania, Bulgaria, Hungary, and Finland go to us, and all the rest to you."

FOREIGN MINISTER ERNEST BEVIN: "The German investments in other countries go to us?"

STALIN: "In all other countries, in South America, in Canada, etc., all this is yours. . . ."

SECRETARY OF STATE JAMES BYRNES: "If an enterprise is not in Eastern Europe but in Western Europe or in other parts of the world, that enterprise remains ours?"

STALIN: "In the United States, in Norway, in Switzerland, in Sweden, in Argentina [general laughter], etc.—all that is yours."

A delegation of Poles arrived at Potsdam to argue their own case before the Big Three. The Poles, struggling desperately and vainly for their land, their borders, their freedoms, did not seem to understand that their fate was being settled for reasons that had nothing to do with them. They wandered about Potsdam, trying to impress their wishes on the Big Three. "I'm sick of the bloody Poles," Churchill said when they came to call on him. "I don't want to see them. Why can't Anthony [Eden] talk to them?" Alexander Cadogan, Permanent Undersecretary for Foreign Affairs, found the Poles at Eden's house late one night and "had to entertain them as best I could, and went on entertaining them—no signs of A. He didn't turn up till 11:30. . . . So then we got down to it, and talked shop till 1:30. Then filled the Poles (and ourselves) with sandwiches and whiskies and sodas and I went to bed at 2 A.M." Altogether, it had been an agreeable enough evening, although in general, Cadogan confided to his diary, he found the Poles to be "dreadful people. . . ."

Germany, too, provided a rich field for contention. The answer to the German question became a simple but ticklish matter of keeping Germany sufficiently weak so that it could not start another war and yet, at the same time, sufficiently strong to serve as a buffer against Russia, or, from Russia's point of view, against the Western powers. To achieve this delicate balance, the Big Three haggled at Potsdam over a complex set of agreements about zones of authority, permissible levels of postwar industry, allocation of resources of coal and foodstuffs, spoils of war reparations, and other matters. The country as a whole was divided into administrative zones in which Allied commanders had absolute veto powers over some matters, and, in other respects, had to defer to a central governmental council for measures to be applied uniformly to Germany.

Out of all these careful negotiations came the astonishing fact that Germany was established as the very center and source of much of the anxiety and conflict of the Cold War. How this could have happened is one of the wonders of the history of diplomacy. The discussions and bargaining at Potsdam among Churchill, Truman, and Stalin, and among the foreign ministers, and on lower levels, among economic committees and subcommittees, is maddeningly tangled; but, once all of the nettlesome complexities are cleared away, the postwar arrangement for Germany can be seen with sudden and arresting clarity. The Big Three agreed to have a Germany that would be politically united—but, at the very same time, economically divided. They agreed, then, to create a country that could never be either wholly united nor entirely divided, neither one Germany nor two Germanies, but rather a country that would be perpetually at war with itself, and, since its two halves would have two patrons, would keep its two patrons in continuous conflict. Whether this postwar arrangement for Germany was intentional or inadvertent, it was certainly a diplomatic tour de force. In 1949, with the formation of the West German and East German governments, the contradictions of the Potsdam policy became overt.

Eastern Europe, Germany, and the atomic bomb were the three most striking elements of the early Cold War. It was while he was at the Potsdam Conference that President Truman received news that the test of the bomb at Alamogordo had been successful. By that time the bomb was no longer militarily necessary to end the war against Japan; the Japanese were near the end and were attempting to negotiate peace by way of their ambassador to Moscow. After the bomb was dropped, Truman would maintain that it had avoided the invasion of the Japanese mainland and so saved a million American lives. But was that true?

General Henry (Hap) Arnold, chief of the Army Air Forces, said, before the atomic device was dropped on Japan, that conventional bombing would end the war without an invasion. Admiral Ernest J. King, chief of U.S. naval operations, advised that a naval blockade alone would end the war. General Eisenhower said it was "completely unnecessary" to drop the bomb, and that the weapon was "no longer mandatory as a measure to save American lives." Even General George Marshall, U.S. chief of staff and the strongest advocate at that late hour for the bomb's use, advised that the Japanese at least be forewarned to give them a chance to surrender. Diplomats advised Truman that he need only have Russia sign his proclamation calling for Japanese surrender; the Russians had not yet declared war against Japan, and so the Japanese still had hopes that the Russians would help them negotiate peace; if Russia signed the proclamation, the Japanese would see that their last chance was gone and would surrender. None of this advice was followed.

After the war, the United States Strategic Bombing Command issued a study confirming the advice Truman had been getting before he gave the order to drop the atomic bomb: "Japan would have surrendered even if the atomic bombs had not been dropped, even if Russia had not entered the war, and even if no invasion had been planned or contemplated." Then why was it dropped?

Admiral William Leahy, Truman's top aide, was unable to offer the puzzled British chiefs of staff a better explanation than that it was "because of the vast sums that had been spent on the project," although he commented that in using the bomb, the Americans "had adopted an ethical standard common to the barbarians of the Dark Ages."

However that may be, its use must have been chilling to Stalin; doubly chilling if Stalin realized that the United States had used the bomb even when it was not militarily necessary. Indeed, according to Secretary of State James Byrnes, that was the real reason why the bomb was used after all—"to make Russia," as he said, "more manageable in Europe." Perhaps it is because that constituted a war crime—to kill people when it is not militarily necessary is a war crime according to international accord—that Truman insisted to his death, and in obstinate defiance of all other opinion, that it was militarily necessary.

The bomb may have been dropped, too, in order to end the war against Japan without Russian help. The Russians had promised to enter the war in the Far East exactly three months after the war in Europe ended—which it did on May 8. Truman's aim was not merely to end the war against Japan, but to end it before August 8.

When word reached Potsdam that the atomic bomb had been successfully tested, Truman was enormously pleased. When the news was passed along to Churchill, the prime minister was overcome with delight at the "vision—fair and bright indeed it seemed—of the end of the whole war in one or two violent shocks." Churchill understood at once that "we should not need the Russians," and he concluded that "we seemed suddenly to have become possessed of a merciful abridgment of the slaughter in the East and of a far happier prospect in Europe. I have no doubt that these thoughts were present in the minds of my American friends."

The problem was what to tell the Russians. Presumably, as allies of the Americans and British, they needed to be told of this new weapon in which Truman and Churchill placed such tremendous hopes. Yet, if the Russians were told, they might rush to enter the war against Japan and so share in the victory. "The President and I no longer felt that we needed [Stalin's] aid to conquer Japan," Churchill wrote. And so Stalin must be told about the existence of the bomb—and at the same time he must not be told. In short, Truman and Churchill decided, Stalin must be informed so casually as not to understand that he was being informed of much of anything.

On July 24, after one of the sessions of the Potsdam Conference, Truman got up from the baize-covered table and sauntered around to Stalin. The President had left his interpreter, Charles Bohlen, behind and relied on Stalin's personal translator-signifying that he had nothing important to say, just idle, end-of-the-day chit-chat.

"I was perhaps five yards away," Churchill recalled, "and I watched with the closest attention the momentous talk. I knew what the President was going to do. What was vital to measure was its effect on Stalin. I can see it all as if it were yesterday."

"I casually mentioned to Stalin," Truman wrote in his memoirs, "that we had a new weapon of unusual destructive force. The Russian Premier showed no special interest. All he said was that he was glad to hear it and hoped we would make 'good use of it against the Japanese.' "

"I was sure," Churchill said, "that [Stalin] had no idea of the significance of what he was being told . . . his face remained gay and genial and the talk between these two potentates soon came to an end. As we were waiting for our cars I found myself near Truman. 'How did it go?' I asked. 'He never asked a question,' he replied."

According to the Russian General Shtemenko, the ploy worked: the Russian Army staff "received no special instructions" after this meeting. According to Marshall Georgi K. Zhukov, commander of the Russian zone of occupation in Germany, Stalin returned from the meeting and told Molotov about Truman's remarks. Molotov "reacted immediately: 'Let them. We'll have to talk it over with Kurchatov and get him to speed things up.' I realized they were talking about research on the atomic bomb."

Whatever the case, whether Stalin realized what he had been told at the time, or only in retrospect, the nuclear arms race began, in effect, at Potsdam, on July 24, 1945, at 7:30 P.M.

Distrust, suspicion, anxiety, fear—all were intensified at Potsdam, and to them were added harshness and provocation, from all sides. During the next few months the agreements that had been reached were violated, or used as the bases for accusations of duplicity and bad faith. Many of the questions raised at Potsdam had been postponed and delegated to a Council of Foreign Ministers that was established to deal with these questions, and new ones, as they arose. The first meeting of the council was set for September, 1945. James Brynes, before he left Washington to attend the meeting, had chatted with Secretary of War Henry Stimson. "I found that Byrnes was very much against any attempt to cooperate with Russia," Stimson noted in his diary. "His mind is full of his problems with the coming meeting of foreign ministers and he looks to have the presence of the bomb in his pocket, so to speak, as a great weapon to get through the thing. . . ." The British Chancellor of the Exchequer, Rt. Hon. Hugh Dalton, asked Foreign Minister Ernest Bevin how things were going, once the meeting started. "Like the strike leader said," Bevin replied, "thank God there is no danger of a settlement."

Not everyone was so quick or so eager to encourage the start of the Cold War. Henry Stimson was very much the elder statesman in 1945; he had spent more than fifty years in assorted government positions, and he foresaw dread consequences in Truman's developing policies toward Russia. Stimson had long thought that America should be tough with the Soviet Union, but he now believed that toughness was turning into harshness and harshness into provocativeness. In a memo that he wrote Truman in the autumn of 1945, he focused his thoughts around one of the most vexing problems of the postwar world:

". . . I consider the problem of our satisfactory relations with Russia as not merely connected with but as virtually dominated by the problem of the atomic bomb. Except for the problem of the control of that bomb, those relations, while vitally important, might not be immediately pressing. . . . But with the discovery of the bomb, they became immediately emergent. These relations may be perhaps irretrievably embittered by the way in which we approach the solution of the bomb with Russia. For if we fail to approach them now and merely continue to negotiate with them having this weapon rather ostentatiously on our hip, their suspicions and their distrust of our purposes and motives will increase. . . .

"The chief lesson I have learned in a long life is that the only way you can make a man trustworthy is to trust him; and the surest way to make him untrustworthy is to distrust him and show your distrust."

Men like Stimson—and Henry Wallace, then Secretary of Commerce—were allowed, or forced, to resign. Others, those who tended to believe in an aggressive attitude toward Russia, were spotted, and promoted—young men such as John Foster Dulles and Dean Rusk. George Kennan, then in the American embassy in Moscow, was discovered after he sent a perfervid 8,000-word cable back to Washington: "We have here a political force committed fanatically to the belief that with U.S. there can be no permanent modus vivendi, that it is desirable and necessary that the internal harmony of our society be disrupted, our traditional way of life be destroyed, the international authority of our state be broken. . . ." In his memoirs, Kennan says that he now looks back on his cable "with horrified amusement." At the time, however, he was ideal for Truman's use, and he was recalled from Moscow and made chairman of the State Department's Policy Planning Committee, or as the *New York Times* called him, "America's global planner."

At Potsdam, the Big Three had all agreed to remove their troops from Iran. They set a deadline of March 2, 1946, and, as the deadline approached, the British announced that they would be leaving. The Russians, however, let it be known that they were somewhat reluctant to leave until they had made an agreement with the Iranians for an oil concession, and, regardless even of that agreement, Stalin rather thought he would like to withdraw only from central Iran and keep some troops in northern Iran. Not all these matters were immediately clarified and so, on March 1, 1946, Stalin announced that Russian soldiers would remain in Iran "pending clarification of the situation."

President Truman, meanwhile, invited Winston Churchill to deliver an address in March, 1946, at Fulton, Missouri: "A shadow has fallen upon the scenes so lately lighted by the Allied victory," said the former prime minister. "Nobody knows what Soviet Russia and its Communist international organization intends to do in the immediate future, or what are the limits, if any, to their expansive and proselytising tendencies. . . . From Stettin in the Baltic to Trieste in the Adriatic [the line, as Churchill neglected to mention, to which he and Truman had agreed at Potsdam], an iron curtain has descended across the Continent. Behind that line lie all the capitals of the ancient states of Central and Eastern Europe . . . in what I must call the Soviet sphere . . . this is certainly not the Liberated Europe we fought to build up. Nor is it one which contains the essentials of permanent peace."

In Moscow, a well-rehearsed Russian reporter quizzed Stalin.

QUESTION: "How do you appraise Mr. Churchill's latest speech in the United States?"

STALIN: "I appraise it as a dangerous act, calculated to sow the seeds of dissension among the Allied states and impede their collaboration."

QUESTION: "Can it be considered that Mr. Churchill's speech is prejudicial to the cause of peace and security?"

STALIN: "Yes, unquestionably. As a matter of fact, Mr. Churchill now takes the stand of the warmongers, and in this Mr. Churchill is not alone. He has friends not only in Britain but in the United States of America as well."

During the winter of 1946–47, a succession of snowstorms hit Britain. Coal was already in short supply; factories had already closed for lack of fuel that winter. With the blizzards came rationing, first of electricity and then of food; finally heat was cut off. Britain, as Louis Halle wrote, "was like a soldier wounded in war who, now that fighting was over, was bleeding to death." The empire was at last dying.

In Washington, on February 21, 1947, a Friday afternoon, First Secretary H. M. Sichel of the British embassy delivered two notes to Loy Henderson at the State Department. Until that moment, Britain had been the principal support for the economy of Greece and the provider for the Turkish Army. The first of Sichel's notes said that Britain could no longer support Greece; the second said Britain could no longer underwrite the Turkish Army. "What the two notes reported," Halle observed, "was the final end of the *Pax Britannica*."

The following week, on February 27, Truman met with congressional leaders in the White House. Undersecretary of State Dean Acheson was present at the meeting, and Truman had him tell the congressmen what was at stake. Acheson spoke for ten minutes, informing the legislators that nothing less than the survival of the whole of Western civilization was in the balance at that moment; he worked in references to ancient Athens, Rome, and the course of Western civilization and freedoms since those times. The congressmen were silent for a few moments, and then, at last, Senator Arthur Vandenberg of Michigan, a prominent Republican who had come to support an active foreign policy, spoke up. All this might be true, Vandenberg said; but, if the President wished to sell his program to the American people, he would have to "scare hell out of the country." It was at that moment that the Cold War began in earnest for the United States.

Atomic bomb test in the South Pacific. (Library of Congress)

It would be nice to be able to say that one nation held back from the nattering and abusiveness, that one seemed reluctant to start a conflict with its former allies, that one tried to compose the differences that had predictably arisen at the end of the war, that this one was the first to make a provocative move or charge and that one was last—but in truth all three leaped into the fray with such haste and determination that the origins of the Cold War are lost in a blur of all three sides hastening to be first in battle.

It is difficult to know the effects the Cold War had upon the Russian people in these years. But America paid heavy costs. When a nation has an actively internationalist, interventionist foreign policy, political power in that country tends to flow to the central government, and, within the central government, to the executive branch. That there was, in recent times, the creation of an "imperial presidency" in the U.S. was no quirk or happenstance; it was the natural outgrowth of the Cold War. From the imperial presidency, from the disorientation of the constitutional system of checks and balances, Watergate, proteiform and proliferating spy organizations, the impotence and decadence of Congress—all these were almost inevitable. That is why George Washington, a profoundly sophisticated man, advised Americans to avoid foreign entanglements; and that is why Americans who prize their freedom have always been a peace-loving people.

16

The U.S. and Castro, 1959–1962

by Hugh Thomas

One of the most intriguing diplomatic relationships during the last quarter-century has been that of the United States and Fidel Castro. That relationship grew out of the special connection between Cuba and the United States which dates at least as far back as the Spanish-American War. In the following article, Hugh Thomas, formerly Professor of History at the University of Reading and author of *Cuba: The Pursuit of Freedom,* provides the proper perspective for understanding U.S.-Cuban relations.

Between 1898 and the 1930s, the United States dominated Cuba with its military and economic presence on the island. That dominance instilled an anti-Americanism in Cuban nationalist intellectuals which eventually helped spawn a communist revolution. Before that revolution occurred, the United States had found itself in a familiar but still uncomfortable position of supporting non-communist dictators who gradually lost popular support. Then, when Fidel Castro made his first moves against Fulgencio Batista, U.S. policy was "ambiguous." When Castro consolidated his power and proclaimed Cuba to be a "socialist state," Cuba became one of the key focal points of the larger Cold War between the United States and the Soviet Union. Despite various U.S. attempts to dislodge him, Castro remained in power into the 1980s, when American attention was again increasingly drawn to the whole Caribbean/Central American region. To understand contemporary developments there, one must understand the relationship between the U.S. and Castro.

One of the perplexing mysteries of the mid-twentieth century is why Cuba, a rich island with long and close ties to the United States, became a communist state. It did so in an unprecedented and unexpected way—without Soviet military help, without enduring a destructive civil war (deaths during Castro's revolution against Batista probably did not reach two thousand), and without the leadership of Cuba's Communist party, which played at best a minor role in such fighting as there was. By Latin American standards, Cuba, furthermore, was not economically backward. Indeed, in terms of per capita income, she was as wealthy as any country in Latin America except Venezuela and Argentina, and in some ways—as in her communications network—was more advanced and technologically sophisticated than Venezuela. She was, finally, as closely connected with the United States as it was possible to be without actually being part of the Union—the Cuban peso and the U.S. dollar, for instance, having been for many years interchangeable at par.

There was, to be sure, a dark side to life in Cuba before Castro. The political history of the island during the generations that followed the gaining of independence from Spain in 1898 had been characterized by electoral fraud, corruption, and bouts of tyranny. Political gangsterism had been rife. The economy had depended largely on the trade in sugar, which, while enriching many, left a large minority of the population chronically underemployed, unemployed, or destitute. Health and educational facilities were inadequate in Havana, the capital, and often nonexistent in the countryside. Neither the judiciary nor the civil service was free from political manipulation and intimidation. Relations between the whites and the black and mulatto minority were uneasy and became worse in the 1950's. The dictator of those latter years, Fulgencio Batista, indulged police brutality and military corruption and inefficiency. A typical story of Batista's last days concerns one of his communiqués, which announced that he was spending twelve hours a day with his generals, conducting the war against Castro. In fact, he and his commanders were whiling away the time playing canasta.

Partly because of adverse changes in the world sugar market and partly because of the growth, since the world depression, of strong, venal, and restrictionist trade unions, the country's economy had become stagnant. The unions frequently were charged with holding back the modernization of the sugar industry: Julio Lobo, the last great sugar merchant of old Cuba, for example, had a cane-cutting machine delayed at customs for two years and finally had to send it back to the United States. Though Cuba's previous history had been one of ready acceptance of technical innovations soon after their invention (Cuba had had a steam engine in 1798 and railways in 1833), the country, during the several years prior to Castro's accession to power, had become one of Latin America's least inviting prospects for foreign investment.

Still, such weaknesses do not necessarily make a country easy prey to communism. Venezuela had similar extremes of wealth and poverty in 1959. She relied more on oil for her stability than Cuba did on sugar, and she had less experience with democracy than Cuba had had. Yet when Pérez Jiménez, her last dictator, fell in 1958, the Venezuelan people were able to establish what became the most effective democracy in Latin America. A stagnant economy usually does not cause a revolution. Furthermore, the Communist party in Cuba was neither strong nor adventurous. Its middle-aged leaders did not seem unhappy about what appeared to be their remoteness from power. Communism in 1959, particularly after Khrushchev had explained the crimes of Stalin three years before, seemed a spent force.

Was it, perhaps, the United States that was responsible for what happened in Cuba in 1959 and subsequently? Since this view is widely held, it needs to be considered under two heads: first, the impact of the United States on Cuba during the sixty years between the Spanish-American War and Castro's revolution; and second, the interrelationship of the two countries during the second dictatorship of Batista (1952–1958) and the first two years of Castro's rule (1959–1960).

During the first third of the twentieth century, the United States dominated Cuba so thoroughly that the island was a U.S. protectorate in all but name. Prior to 1898, while the island was still a Spanish colony, the United States had become Cuba's most important trading partner and had invested some thirty million dollars in her economy. American intervention in the Cuban rebellion against Spain, from 1895 to 1898, led inexorably to the Spanish-American War, but in voting for that war, the U.S. Senate stipulated that it did not wish American occupation of Cuba after hostilities. Nevertheless, minds changed, and after the peace that secured Cuba's freedom from Spain, the United States insisted on three years of military occupation. Cuba became a nominally independent republic only in 1902. Even then, the Platt Amendment to the U.S. acceptance of Cuban independence, introduced by Republican Senator Orville Platt of Connecticut, gave the United States the right to intervene militarily in the island under certain circumstances: if civil war erupted on the island and if Cuba were not kept clean and free from dangerous disease. The Platt Amendment also placed restrictions on the Cuban government's capacity to incur debts and to embark on treaties with a third power, and enabled the United States to establish naval bases on the island—which it did at Guantánamo, to help secure the Panama Canal. These terms were as severe on Cuba as were those that the treaties of Versailles and St. Germain imposed on defeated Germany and Austria in 1919—and were as strongly resented.

A Cuban constituent assembly was prevailed upon to accept the Platt Amendment as part of the first constitution of "independent" Cuba. In 1906 the United States took advantage of its rights under the amendment, and another three years of occupation followed. The United States threatened to intervene again in both 1912 and 1917, each time with direct consequences to Cuba's internal political affairs. In the 1920's, General Enoch Crowder, the U.S. envoy to Havana, was given full powers to reorganize Cuba's finances, and in the same decade the United States recognized and supported General Gerardo Machado, even when he made himself a dictator. This support ended in 1933, when Sumner Welles, President Franklin D. Roosevelt's new ambassador to Cuba, helped inspire Machado's fall. The following year Welles assisted in the overthrow of a progressive Cuban government under Dr. Grau San Martin, which prepared the way for a new, only partially veiled tyranny under General Batista.

The Platt Amendment was abolished in 1934, but even so, the United States would not have hesitated to impose its own candidate on Cuba during World War II, had it been deemed necessary. It was not required: General Batista (who in 1940 was elected president—reasonably honestly) might have been a "son-of-a-bitch," but he was "our son-of-a-bitch," in FDR's words. Threats of U.S. intervention lasted longer. Probably the FBI knew of, and possibly may have encouraged, a plot to overthrow Dr. Grau San Martin in his second presidency in 1947.

The United States, meanwhile, had built up an economic position on the island as important as its political one. Investments in sugar mills gave U.S.

companies control of 60 per cent of Cuban sugar production by the 1920's. American companies also had large landholdings. Cuban tobacco was marketed through U.S. merchants. U.S. companies, or their Cuban subsidiaries, controlled electricity, telephones, and other public utilities. Cuba was even sometimes represented in diplomacy affecting sugar by American citizens with Cuban interests. U.S. dominance over Cuban cultural life was almost equally strong.

Some benefits for Cuba naturally followed from this close relationship. Had it not been for American intervention in 1898, Cuba would not so soon have become free from Spain. The U.S. interest in Cuba raised the Cuban standard of living to half that of the United States by 1925. U.S. military doctors with the occupying forces made possible the conquest of yellow fever, for many generations the scourge of Havana (though it had been a Cuban of Scottish ancestry, Dr. Carlos Finlay, who first discovered that yellow fever is carried by mosquitoes). The building by a U.S. company of a railway along the length of the island was an achievement from which Cuba will always benefit. American investments in sugar mills were carried out with an iron determination to make profits and to ensure a supply of sugar for the United States in time of war, but those investments transformed the Cuban economy and gave it the shape that it now has. The close contacts established in North America by upper-class Cubans also meant that their children could easily be educated in the United States.

But this close association meant, too, that the United States was an all-too-useful scapegoat in Cuba when things went wrong. The United States habitually was blamed for the corruption of the elections, for the establishment of Machado's and Batista's dictatorships, for unemployment, and for poverty. From the Cuban point of view, U.S. behavior there was often characterized by a patronizing superiority toward local politicians, culture, and traditions, which was irritating even (or particularly) when it was justified. While many Americans went to Cuba believing that they were bringing prosperity, others took with them ideas of tax evasion, philistinism, and money grubbing. A substantial part of the quite large Cuban middle class became *depayse:* not only were people from that class educated in the United States, but they spent their years of exile, during the eras of dictatorship, in the United States, and even when preaching nationalism, Cuban politicians were often preparing their people to ask for a loan from the American government.

Cuban nationalism therefore, naturally, took an anti-American turn. The benefits which the Americans brought were easily forgotten. Cubans in 1898 argued that the United States had cheated them of victory over Spain; they attacked the Platt Amendment; and each new incident of intervention or threatened intervention created new waves of resentment. Historians at the University of Havana told students that each opportunity for national regeneration had been thwarted by "dollar diplomacy." It was into this tradition that Castro and the intellectuals of his generation were born.

The anti-Americanism of Cuban nationalist intellectuals burned strongly in the 1950's, though, by then, the Platt Amendment was long dead and U.S. economic domination of the country was much less notable than it had been twenty years before. But nationalists often dwell on past wrongs, and Sumner Welles's treatment of Dr. Grau San Martin was remembered as if it had happened only yesterday. (Grau San Martin, when he ultimately reached office, had abused his position scandalously to enrich himself and his friends, but he still represented in Cuba the memory of a revolution that the United States seemed to have betrayed in 1934.)

Thus, if one considers the sweep of Cuban history since the beginning of the century, the United States in a sense can be regarded as the unwitting author of the communist revolution in Cuba. The revolution was like a child's rage at a disliked guardian who had taken over in 1898 from the real parents, the Spaniards, after a war of ambiguous implications. But in the short term, during the years leading up to Castro's revolution, the United States played a much less obvious part.

The United States, as far as is known, was not involved in Batista's second *coup d'etat* in 1952, but U.S. intelligence was active thereafter in Cuba. The CIA, for example, helped Batista set up an anticommunist agency in the Cuban government, the BRAC *(Buro Para Represion de las Actividades Communistas).* "I was the father of the BRAC," Arthur Gardner, the U.S. Ambassador to Cuba from 1953 to 1957, told me in 1962. Also in the 1950's, Latin American radicals took notice of the CIA's involvement in a *coup d'etat* that toppled Colonel Jacobo Arbenz's nationalist, but communist-supported, government in Guatemala. Che Guevara, the Argentinian who was subsequently one of Castro's most devoted followers, was in Guatemala at that time, and he obviously drew his own clear, harsh conclusions as to what the U.S. reaction might be to a new nationalist revolution elsewhere in Latin America or the Caribbean. Meanwhile Batista remained, till 1958, a favorite client of American businessmen and of many policymakers in Washington.

The attitude of the U.S. government toward Castro's movement against Batista was ambiguous at first. On the one hand, there were those officials who believed that Castro always had been a communist and should therefore be destroyed as soon as possible. This group included Ambassador Gardner; his successor, Earl T. Smith, who was ambassador from 1957 to 1959; and Admiral Arleigh Burke, the U.S. Chief of Naval Operations. Gardner suggested to Batista in 1957 that he should try to have Castro secretly murdered in the hills, where the civil war already had begun. Though Batista replied, "No, no, we couldn't do that, we're Cubans," there *was* at least one attempt on Castro in the Sierra Maestra, and presumably it was Batista's doing.

But many members of the American government took a different line: Roy Rubottom, Assistant Secretary of State for Latin American Affairs, had high hopes for Castro, as did the State Department's Director of the Office of Caribbean and Mexican Affairs, William Wieland. These friendly attitudes were shared by some officials within the CIA. Indeed, the second-ranking representative of the CIA in Havana had an open row with Ambassador Smith on the subject of whether Castro was, or was not, a communist, in 1957, and both J. C. King (Chief of Western Hemisphere Affairs of the CIA) and Lyman B. Kirkpatrick (Inspector General of the CIA) were, for a time, hopeful that Castro might turn out to be a liberal.

The United States thus presented a divided front toward Castro. He, in turn, was able to employ, to good effect, these divisions among both American policymakers and various molders of public opinion. A notable example was his use of the visit to Cuba of Herbert Matthews, a high-minded correspondent of the *New York Times,* in February 1957. Castro saw Matthews in a remote part of the mountains and persuaded him that he was a moderate, nationalist reformer and that he had much more of a following than was really the case. Matthews' reporting was friendly to Castro and helped to create in the United States widespread sympathy for the rebellion. That sympathy, in March, 1958, enabled Rubottom and his friends in the State Department to ensure an embargo on the sale of arms to Cuba, an action as important for its psychological effect upon Batista as for its actual disservice to the Cuban army. Until then, Batista had assumed that the United States automatically would support him even if he used against his internal enemies American arms that had been supplied to him for "hemisphere defense."

By the end of 1958, Batista's position had begun to disintegrate, due largely to the corruption and inefficiency of his army rather than to the military skill of Castro—though it would be foolish to underestimate Castro's ability to make the most of a propaganda advantage in Cuba. The U.S. government made an attempt to get Batista to resign and hand over power to a junta of generals, which, in the words of the CIA's Kirkpatrick, seemed then to offer the United States "the best possibility of bringing peace" and avoiding "a blood bath." The task of trying to persuade Batista to agree to this plan was entrusted to William Pawley, an American with long-established business interest in Cuba (he had founded Cubana Airlines and was a personal friend of Batista's). Pawley's mission failed, possibly because Rubottom had told him to avoid saying that he was acting in the name of President Eisenhower. A week later, however, Ambassador Earl Smith, with the greatest personal reluctance, told Batista that the United States government judged he had no alternative save to leave, that the State Department thought he could now only be a hindrance to its hastily devised plans for a transition. Batista agreed, partly because he now had a great deal of money outside of Cuba, and partly because his heart was not in the fight, though he complained at the same time that the United States was carrying out still another act of intervention—and one which did, indeed, seem like a repetition of Sumner Welles's intervention in 1933 against Machado.

Before Batista finally left Cuba, one of his generals, Cantillo, tried to reach an armistice with Castro and even attempted to make himself the leader of a caretaker government. At the same time, the CIA was busy bribing the jailer of another officer, Colonel Ramón Barquín, a nationally respected enemy of Batista, to let him out of prison so he could assist in the formation of a new government. These and other last-minute plans all came to nothing. Batista's army was crumbling fast, and public enthusiasm for Castro and his allies was growing enormously, as Barquín and Cantillo in the end recognized. Batista left Cuba in the early morning hours of January 1, 1959. The U.S. government then realized that it had to choose between allowing Castro to take power and "sending in the Marines." The latter course was favored by Admiral Burke and probably by Allen Dulles, the Director of the CIA, but nothing was done. In the meantime, men and women from Castro's organization took over the maintenance of public order in the Cuban cities. Castro himself was in Havana by January 8, 1959. A new, progressive government was formed. In the beginning, Castro did not figure in this. Even when he did take over as prime minister, in February, the majority of the members of his government were well known to be liberals.

American reactions continued to be ambiguous, but in the Eisenhower administration those willing to give Castro the benefit of the doubt were predominant. The new ambassador to Havana, Philip Bonsal, concluded before arriving in Havana in February that "Castro was not a communist" and, at a meeting of the U.S. ambassadors in the Caribbean region on April 11, 1959, commented privately that Castro was a "terrific person, physically and mentally, he was far from crazy [and] he was not living on pills." Most press comments in the United States early in 1959 thought much the same.

There was, of course, some expressed hostility to the new Cuba in the United States, and Castro exploited it to strengthen his position with the reawakened Cuban public opinion. For example, when Senator Wayne Morse of Oregon and various American newspapers and newsmagazines protested against the public trial of Batista's police, Castro suggested that their opposition constituted another variation on the theme of intervention. He also made the most of his visit to the United States in April, 1959, as the guest of the American Society of Newspaper Editors, to arouse further support for himself among the American people. Many Americans were even angry that President Eisenhower refused to meet him on that occasion, preferring to leave the task to Vice President Nixon.

The transition in Cuba from an open to a closed society, after that visit, came fast. In early 1959 Castro was still talking of the desirability of an "entirely democratic revolution." The Cuban revolution would be as "autochthonous as Cuban music," with no place for extremists or communists. In May, 1959, however, a classical agrarian reform, taking over large estates and giving land to squatters and peasants, was promulgated. This inspired a curt but polite U.S note of protest, demanding compensation for all dispossessed landowners, Cuban and American alike. The reform caused a political upheaval in the countryside, though accounts of what happened are hard to find. Certainly it was then that the first resistance to Castro began to be organized by Cubans of the Right. Some politicians began to criticize Castro for failing to call elections. But Castro himself was busy directing abortive expeditions against the dictatorships in the Dominican Republic, Nicaragua, and Haiti.

In May, also, Castro dismissed several liberal ministers from his cabinet and had his first clash with the Cuban judiciary over a habeas corpus case. A month later the chief of the Cuban air force fled to the United States and told the Internal Security Subcommittee of the Senate that communism was beginning to take over in Cuba. A few weeks after that, in mid-July, Castro hounded out of office his own nominee as President of Cuba, Judge Manuel Urrutia, accusing him of treason and anticommunist expressions. Others who, like Hubert Matos, the military chief of the province of Camagüey, continued to criticize communism in public were shortly afterward arrested. Most of the other liberal cabinet members were then dismissed or were cowed into humiliating betrayals of their old faiths. The attitude of those who remained in office, like that of many liberals caught up in other revolutionary circumstances, is easy to condemn but important to judge objectively. The Cuban liberals who stayed with Castro in 1959 (like Raúl Roa, the Foreign Minister; Osvaldo Dorticós, President of Cuba for many years; Armando Hart, the Minister of Education; and Regino Boti, the Minister of Economics) were clearly men whose dedication to liberal ideology was not as firm as was their previously submerged desire for a strong nationalist state, which would break absolutely with a past in which none of them personally had been very successful.

Next, the truant former chief of Cuba's air force flew over Havana in a U.S. B-25 bomber converted to a cargo carrier, dropping pamphlets on the city. Antiaircraft guns fired at his plane, and some of their shell fragments fell to the ground and killed a few Cubans—an event that heralded a several months exchange of insults between Cuba and the United States. In February, 1960, only a year after Castro had taken power, Anastas Mikoyan, Deputy Premier of the Soviet Union, arrived in Havana to conclude the first commercial arrangement between Russia and Cuba, and in March, President Eisenhower gave his approval to the training of Cuban exiles by the CIA for a possible invasion of the island. In the course of the first half of 1960, the independence of the judiciary, press, trade unions, and university was destroyed, and the flight of middle-class Cubans and liberals began in earnest. By then, a clash with the United States was inevitable.

In June, 1960, the Cubans asked U.S. oil refiners to process Russian, and not Venezuelan, oil. They refused. Castro retaliated by nationalizing the refineries. Eisenhower then cut off the U.S. sugar quota, an arrangement by which the United States bought a substantial portion of Cuba's sugar at a price higher than that of the world market. In return, Castro expropriated the U.S. sugar mills and all public utilities owned by the United States in Cuba. Eisenhower responded with a ban on all U.S. exports to Cuba, save medicines and some foodstuffs. The Cubans immediately took over all the remaining large private enterprises. In January, 1961, the U.S. embassy was withdrawn. Something like a new civil war had broken out by this time in the hills of Escambray in southern Cuba. In April the CIA's force of exiles landed at the Bay of Pigs. Immediately after the failure of that ill-starred invasion, Castro, on May 1, 1961, proclaimed Cuba a "socialist state" and decreed that there would be no more elections. The revolution, he announced, had given every Cuban a rifle, not a vote.

From this summary of events, despite the unfolding drama of 1960 and 1961, it will be seen that the real decisions concerning the direction the revolution would take were made in 1959, between May and October, and probably in June or July. Castro and Guevara on separate occasions mentioned that time was crucial, and it was then, also, that leading figures were first ousted or arrested for anticommunism. When the mere expression of anticommunism becomes a crime, it is a sure sign of what line a government wishes to pursue. By that time, the possibilities of achieving a humane or open regime in Cuba were over.

A proper interpretation of what happened, and why, must consider Castro's personality, first and foremost. Castro had a strong hold over Cuban opinion in 1959, and his position as "maximum leader" of the revolution was unquestioned. Marxism belittles the role of individuals in history. But in the establishment of regimes based on Marx's philosophy, individuals, from Lenin to Castro, have played decisive parts. Castro's motives, therefore, need to be investigated, so far as it is possible, in examining why the revolution in Cuba took the course it did.

Some would say that this question presents no real problems. Earl Smith, Arthur Gardner, and some others thought that Castro had been a communist for years. William Pawley claimed to have heard Castro, during riots in Bogotá in 1948, proclaim on the Colombian radio: "This is Fidel Castro from Cuba. This is a communist revolution. . . ." This interpretation of Castro's early loyalties has had corroboration from Castro himself. In a speech in Havana in December, 1961, he said that he had been an apprentice Marxist-Leninist for many years; "I absolutely believe in Marxism! Did I believe on 1 January [1959]? I believed on 1 January. . . ." More recently in a taped interview in Cuba with American television reporter Barbara Walters, in mid-1977, Castro said (though the section was excised from what was shown the U.S. viewing audience): "I became a communist before reading a single book by Marx, Engels, Lenin, or anyone. I became a communist by studying capitalist political economy. . . . When I was a law student in the third year at the University of Havana. . . . I became what could be called a utopian communist. Then I was introduced to Marxist literature. . . ." In another U.S. television interview, shown by CBS on June 10, 1977, he recalled his meeting with Vice President Nixon in April, 1959, and said that at the time, "I was a communist. I personally was a communist." In 1961, moreover, he had explained that if he had admitted in the Sierra Maestra how extreme his opinions really were, he would have been killed then and there.

196

Castro, therefore, had lent the support of his own authority to what may be described as a "conspiracy theory" in explanation of the Cuban revolution. Some other points can be added. For example, Fidel Castro's brother and intimate adviser, Raúl, had been an overt member of the Cuban Communist Youth Movement since 1953. Fidel Castro had influential communist friends at Havana University between 1945 and 1948, most of whom did well in the communist regime after 1961 (for instance, Lionel Soto, in 1976 Ambassador to London and an Adviser on Cuba's African policy; Flavio Bravo, Deputy Prime Minister in 1977; and Alfredo Guevara, for years head of the Cuban Film Institute). Though perhaps not actually a member of the Communist party, much less a Soviet agent (as some members of the FBI suggested), Castro—so the conspiracy theory runs—must always have been in touch with the party.

When the communist leaders in Cuba realized that Castro was likely to win the war against Batista, they began to help him and accordingly were welcomed into the large alliance over which he presided, and which they attempted to take over from the moment that he and they arrived in Havana. Naturally (again, according to the conspiracy theory), Castro welcomed communist support, and this was why, save for making a few liberal gestures in early 1959, he failed to create an organized movement, with membership and branches, or to name a day for elections, or even to clarify the attitude of his revolution toward the democratic Constitution of 1940.

Such a conspiracy theory, however, does not really explain Castro satisfactorily. In 1961 he had good reason to want to assure the communists that he had been a Marxist for many years, since at that time he was being challenged by old-time Cuban communists like Aníbal Escalante. In 1977 he may have found it convenient to tell the world, and particularly the Third World, that he was a "utopian communist" in his university days, but at the same time, it is probable that he is not now averse to obscuring memories of exactly what he was doing at the university. Marxist or not, he was mixed up in the political gangsterism that stained the University of Havana at the time, and on a number of occasions between 1947 and 1949 he was implicated in murder charges. The Cuban Communist party in the 1940's and 1950's, moreover, was not an organization very attractive to a young man interested in power, and Castro was obviously that. Castro always believed in direct action, and the party's leaders were something of an early version of the sober, cautious Eurocommunists of the 1970's. In the mid-1950's, the public arguments between the Castroists and the communists over the desirability of an "armed struggle" did not sound like shadowboxing. The Communist party, it has been noted, did not play much of a part in the fight against Batista. Its leaders, indeed, were friendly with Batista's ministers, some of them having collaborated with Batista during World War II, even serving as ministers in his government. The head of the Cuban party dedicated a book to Batista's Minister of the Interior as late as 1956. The CIA thought that the Communist party numbered about seventeen thousand in 1958, which would have made it the largest organized party in Cuba, but its electoral showing always had been dismal.

On the whole, it seems likely that Castro—whose speeches even today do not read as if they were being delivered by one who thinks much of Marx (there is scarcely a word of Marxist jargon in them)—wanted to found a radical, nationalist, populist movement which would embark on action, rather than join the passive and ineffective Communist party. Thus, the 26 July Movement (which was named for Castro's first blow against Batista, a raid on the Moncada barracks at Santiago de Cuba on July 26, 1958) grew quickly from its original few dozen, attracting idealists, fighters and opportunists, ex-political gangsters, as well as philanthropists. It no doubt always had the sympathy of some communists, but not of the party's leadership until 1958.

By the time Castro reached Havana, the 26 July Movement had grown to tens of thousands. No one will ever know how many there actually were in the movement, since no membership cards were ever issued: anyone could grow a beard and call himself a *fidelista* in early 1959. There was no congress of the movement, few officers, and no agreement on policy. Castro must have kept his eyes open toward the communists from the start, since Russia, the headquarters of the communist world, would be an alternative to the United States as a buyer of sugar and a supplier of arms. No doubt Raúl Castro, as a real communist, and Che Guevara, a long-time communist sympathizer, had been quick to point this out to Fidel. Even so, the thrust of the movement that Castro headed was in the beginning primarily nationalist and not communist, nor even particularly socialist. Castro told Rómulo Betancourt, the democratic President of Venezuela, in early 1959 that he was determined above all to have a row with the United States in order to purge Cuba of many past humiliations at the hands of the "monster of the north," as the United States had been termed by José Martí, the Cuban nationalist hero of the 1890's who was one of the chief inspirational figures of Castro's revolution.

In slightly different circumstances, in a different generation, with a different international posture by the world communist movement, Castro perhaps could have lurched as easily toward the Right, as toward the Left—say, toward Peronism or fascism. Fascist techniques were used so much during the early days of the Cuban revolution in 1959 and 1960 that, indeed, that useful term "fascist left" might have been coined to apply to it. Castro's cult of heroic leadership, of endless struggle, of exalted nationalism had characterized all fascist movements in Europe. The emotional oratory, the carefully staged mass meetings, the deliberate exacerbation of tension before the "leader" spoke, the banners, and the mob intimidation—all these Castroist techniques recalled the days of Nazism. Castro's movement gained its initial support less from the organized workers than from the same rootless petty bourgeois classes that supported fascism in Europe in the 1920's. As in Hitler's Germany, the workers joined the movement late, only after they saw that it was beginning to be successful and would be in power for a long time.

The temptation, however, for Castro to turn the movement toward communism must have been strong in 1959, since he knew that would be the course which would most infuriate the United States. It was risky to be sure, but he was, above all, the man for risks. As for the old communists, they had in their ranks, as Castro later put it to the *New York Times's* Herbert Matthews, "men who were truly revolutionary, loyal, honest and trained. I needed them." Castro, no doubt, was surprised by the ease with which the old institutions collapsed before him. They did so because they had been compromised by their support of, or association with, the discredited Batista. Castro could not have known how feeble the liberal response would be, since his own movement had been built partly on liberal enthusiasm. But he did know that if he lost the liberals, he would require a disciplined bureaucracy in their place—"I need them." That was a true comment on Castro's association with the communists in 1959.

There is also another simple, but essential point to make: everything in Castro's past life suggested that if he were faced with having to choose between *fidelismo* (which would, in the end, imply adopting the rule of law and a risk of losing an election) and communism (which could give him an opportunity to remain in power for a long time), he would choose the latter. The brutality of communist regimes in practice never seemed to trouble him. In February, 1959, he made it perfectly clear that air force officers who had fought for Batista *had* to be found guilty of war crimes; a verdict of innocence, first returned, was rejected. Whatever hesitation Castro did display in 1959 was caused, surely, by anxiety lest an alliance with the communists might give power to them and their secretary-general, and not to himself. He needed to make certain that he could ride the tiger personally before he let it out of its cage. In this, he was showing himself primarily not the communist, but the Latin American *caudillo* that he really always has been.

Castro began to make use of the communists in the armed forces from the moment he arrived in Havana. Guevara made sure that the files of BRAC, Batista's anticommunist police section, were seized immediately after victory. The BRAC's director was shot without a trial as soon as Castro's men reached the capital. A prominent communist, Armando Acosta, was made commander of the old fortress of La Punta in Havana as early as January 5, 1959—before Castro himself was in the city. Communist "instructors" moved into the army at once. Other communists were utilized from the start in the Institute of Agrarian Reform, which was established in May, 1959. By the end of that year, communists also were being appointed to ministries that were being abandoned by regular civil servants and *fidelistas*.

A careful study of available memoirs (those of Eisenhower, Lyman Kirkpatrick of the CIA, Ambassador Bonsal, and others), as well as testimony given to the Senate Internal Security Subcommittee in 1960–61 and to the Church Committee in 1975, provides no suggestion of any CIA or other U.S. action against Cuba during 1959. Of course, there was right-wing Cuban opposition to the Revolution, but the evidence is that the American government, the only serious enemy Castro had to face from then on, did not know how to deal with the apparently unique nationalist movement founded by Castro, and so did nothing the first year. The earliest material unearthed by the Church Committee concerning a U.S. interest in overthrowing Castro was a recommendation in December, 1959, by J. C. King, still the head of the Western Hemisphere Division of the CIA, to his chief, Allen Dulles, that, since a "far left" dictatorship existed in Cuba, "thorough consideration [should] be given to the elimination of Fidel Castro." The committee went on to report that the first discussion in the White House (among a so-called special group of advisers) of any idea of a "covert program" to topple Castro occurred on January 13, 1960. There was some sabotage carried out in western Cuba by Cuban exiles in 1959, but the neglect in controlling such actions by Castro's enemies does not prove that there was a concerted effort by the U.S. government to overthrow Castro.

The dictator of the Dominican Republic, General Leonidas Trujillo, did launch an unsuccessful invasion of Cuba in the summer of 1959, but again there is no proof of any American involvement in that hopeless venture. When the ex-commander of the Cuban air force flew over Havana to drop pamphlets in October, 1959, Castro must have known perfectly well that the Cubans killed during the episode died from fragments of shells fired from the ground at the plane. But Castro described the flight as an attempt to "bomb" Cuba into submission, speaking, as Ambassador Bonsal accurately put it, "in a manner reminiscent of Hitler at his most hysterical. . . . There was the same blatant disregard for truth, the same pathological extremes of expression, gesticulation and movement." (Ambassador Bonsal's judgment of Castro thus had changed, as had the revolution itself, during 1959.) Evidence may yet be produced to prove that the CIA, the FBI, or some other agency of the U.S. government was active against Castro in 1959. But if it was, it is inconceivable that the activity was on a scale, or of a subtlety, adequate to divert a resourceful leader, such as Castro has since shown himself to be, from a chosen democratic course—from one, say, of re-establishing the Constitution of 1940. Cuba, or rather Castro, surely chose a path deliberately in 1959, and however much that path may have been determined by memory of old historical vendettas, it was certainly not affected one way or the other by current American policy.

The stability of the system that has continued since 1961 in Cuba is a contrast to the volatile days before 1959. Yet there have been curious developments. A revolution which once had as one of its chief aims the end of complete reliance on a sugar economy has laid emphasis on that crop more than ever before. The failure of the Cuban revolution to export its example to Latin America in the 1960's was, in the 1970's, compensated for by the dispatch of an expeditionary force to Africa. From providing the world before 1959 with sugar, cigars, and popular dances, Cuba, since the revolution, has provided it with *guerrilleros*. Cuba, at one remove, also gave President Nixon the hard core of disciplined "plumbers" who made Watergate. The Cuban connection with the stories associated with the murder of President Kennedy cannot quite be shaken off. Neither the far Left nor the far Right of U.S. politics would be what they are were it not for Cuba. This is a modern expression of an old U.S. tradition. Many will have forgotten that Cuba was an obsessive question in American politics in the decade before the Civil War. The Southern states' desire to increase the number of slave states by purchasing Cuba from Spain was indeed one of the causes of that struggle. During Cuba's two wars of independence, in the 1870's and 1890's, the island was a major problem in U.S. politics. It has been so once or twice in the twentieth century, too, never more so than between 1959 and 1962. Geography, as well as history, strongly suggests that she will one day play that part again.

17

Machismo in the White House: LBJ and Vietnam

by Larry L. King

The effects of the Vietnam War have rippled through American society for the past two decades. Physical and emotional scars from that war will survive at least as long as the generation which fought the war. In the context of American foreign policy, the war forced a reassessment of the containment policy.

The tragedy of Vietnam is indelibly linked to the tragedy of President Lyndon Baines Johnson. Having assumed power upon the assassination of President John F. Kennedy, President Johnson established himself quickly as an effective leader on the domestic front. However, his determination to pursue the Vietnam War brought him down.

Larry L. King holds the Stanley Walker Journalism Award and is the author of numerous books and plays, including "The Best Little Whorehouse in Texas." Mr. King's description of LBJ is especially insightful as he describes the shaping of the President's personality and how he made the Vietnam War his war.

He was an old-fashioned man by the purest definition. Forget that he was enamored of twentieth-century artifacts—the telephone, television, supersonic airplanes, spacecraft—to which he adapted with a child's wondering glee. His values were the relics of an earlier time; he had been shaped by an America both rawer and more confident than it later would become; his generation may have been the last to believe that for every problem there existed a workable solution: that the ultimate answer, as in old-time mathematics texts, always reposed in the back of the book. He bought the prevailing American myths without closely inspecting the merchandise for rips and snares. He often said that Americans inherently were "can-do" people capable of accomplishing anything they willed; it was part of his creed that Americans were God's chosen: why otherwise would they have become the richest, the strongest, the freest people in the history of man? His was a God, perhaps, who was a first cousin to Darwin: Lyndon B. Johnson believed in survival of the fittest, that the strong would conquer the weak, that almost always the big 'uns ate the little 'uns.

There was a certain pragmatism in his beliefs, a touch of fatalism, even a measure of common sense. Yet, too, he could be wildly romantic. Johnson truly believed that any boy could rise to become President, though only thirty-five had. Hadn't he—a shirt-tailed kid from the dusty hard-scrabble precincts of the Texas outback—walked with kings and pharaohs while reigning over

Men of the 25th Infantry Division of the U.S. Army on patrol in South Vietnam. (Photograph by SP4 Bohdan Zakroszeny. U.S. Army.)

what he called, without blushing, the Free World? In his last day, though bitter and withering in retirement at his rural Elba, he astonished and puzzled a young black teen-ager by waving his arms in windmill motions and telling the youngster, during a random encounter, "Well, maybe someday all of us will be visiting *your* house in Waco, because you'll be President and your home will be a national museum just as mine is. It'll take a while, but it'll happen, you'll see. . . ." Then he turned to the black teenager's startled mother: "Now, you better get that home of yours cleaned up spick-and-span. There'll he hundreds of thousands coming through it, you know, wanting to see the bedroom and the kitchen and the living room. Now, I hope you get that dust rag of yours out the minute you get home."

Doris Kearns, the Harvard professor and latter-day L.B.J. confidante, who witnessed the performance, thought it to be a mock show: "almost a vaudeville act." Dr. Johnson peddling the same old snake oil. Perhaps. Whatever his motives that day, Lyndon Johnson chose his sermon from that text he most fervently believed throughout a lifetime; his catechism spoke to his heart of American opportunity, American responsibility, American good intentions, American superiority, American destiny, American infallibility. Despite a sly personal cynicism—a suspicion of others, the keen, cold eye of a man determined not to be victimized at the gaming tables—he was, in his institutional instincts, something of a Pollyanna. There *was* such a thing as a free lunch;

there *was* a Santa Claus; there *was,* somewhere, a Good Fairy, and probably it was made up of the component parts of Franklin Roosevelt, Saint Francis, and Uncle Sam.

These thoroughly American traits—as L.B.J. saw them—comprised the foundation stone upon which he built his dream castle; he found it impossible to abandon them even as the sands shifted and bogged him in the quagmire of Vietnam. If America was so wonderful (and it *was;* he had the evidence of himself to prove it), then he had the obligation to export its goodness and greatness to the less fortunate. This he would accomplish at any cost, even if forced to "nail the coonskin to the wall." For if Lyndon B. Johnson believed in God and greatness and goodness, he also believed in guts and gunpowder.

All the history he had read, and all he had personally witnessed, convinced him that the United States of America—if determined enough, if productive enough, if patriotic enough—simply could not lose a war. As a boy his favorite stores had been of the minutemen at Lexington and Concord, of the heroic defenders of the Alamo, of rugged frontiersmen who'd at once tamed the wild land and marauding Indians. He had a special affinity for a schoolboy poem proclaiming that the most beautiful sight his eyes had beheld was "the flag of my country in a foreign land." He so admired war heroes that he claimed to have been fired on "by a Japanese ace," though no evidence supported it; he invented an ancestor he carelessly claimed had been martyred at the Alamo; at the Democratic National Convention in 1956 he had cast his state's delegate votes for the Vice-Presidential ambitions of young John F. Kennedy, "that fighting sailor who bears the scars of battle."

On a slow Saturday afternoon in the 1950's, expansive and garrulous in his posh Senate majority-leader quarters, Johnson discoursed to a half dozen young Texas staffers in the patois of their shared native place. Why—he said—you take that ragtag bunch at Valley Forge, who'd have given them a cut dog's chance? There they were, barefoot in the snow and their asses hanging out, nothing to eat but moss and dead leaves and snakes, not half enough bullets for their guns, and facing the soldiers of the most powerful king of his time. Yet they sucked it up, wouldn't quit, lived to fight another day—and won. Or you take the Civil War, now: it had been so exceptionally bloody because you had aroused Americans fighting on *both* sides; it had been something like rock against rock, or like two mean ol' pit bull-dogs going at each other with neither of them willing to be chewed up and both of 'em thinking only of taking hunks out of the other. He again invoked the Alamo: a mere handful of freedom-loving men standing against the Mexican hordes, knowing they faced certain death, but they'd carved their names in history for all time, and before they got through with ol' General Santa Anna he thought he'd stumbled into a nest of stinging scorpions or bumble-bees.

Fifteen years later Johnson would show irritation when Clark Clifford suggested that victory of Vietnam might require a sustaining commitment of twenty to thirty years. No—L.B.J. said—no, no, the thing to do was get in and out quickly, pour everything you had into the fight, land the knockout blow: hell, the North Vietnamese *had* to see the futility of facing all that American muscle. If you really poured it on 'em, you could clean up that mess within six months. We had the troops, the firepower, the bombs, the sophisticated weaponry, the oil—everything we needed to win. Did we have the resolve? Well, the Texas Rangers had a saying that you couldn't stop a man who just kept on a-coming. And that's what we'd do in Vietnam, Clark, just keep on a-coming. . . .

Always he talked of the necessity to be strong; he invoked his father's standing up to the Ku Klux Klan in the 1920's, Teddy Roosevelt's carrying that big stick, F.D.R.'s mobilizing the country to beat Hitler and Tojo. He liked ol' Harry Truman—tough little bastard and his own man—but, listen, Harry and Dean Acheson had lost control when they failed to properly prosecute the Korean War. They lost the public's respect, lost control of General MacArthur, lost the backing of Congress, lost the *war* or the next thing to it. Next thing you know, they got blamed for losing China and then there was Joe McCarthy accusing them of being soft on communism and everybody believed it. Well, it wouldn't happen to him, nosir. *He* hadn't started the Vietnam war—Jack Kennedy had made the first commitment of out-and-out combat troops, don't forget—but *he* wouldn't bug out no matter how much the Nervous Nellies brayed. Kennedy had proved during the Cuban missile crisis that if you stood firm then the Reds would back down. They were playground bullies, and he didn't intend to be pushed around any more than Jack Kennedy had. When a bully ragged you, you didn't go whining to the teacher but gave him some of his own medicine.

Only later, in exile, when he spoke with unusual candor of his darker parts, did it become clear how obsessed with failure Lyndon Johnson always had been. As a preschool youngster he walked a country lane to visit a grandfather, his head stuffed with answers he knew would be required ("How many head of cattle you got, Lyndon? How much do they eat? How many head can you graze to the acre?") and fearing he might forget them. If he forgot them, he got no bright-red apple but received, instead, a stern and disapproving gaze. L.B.J.'s mother, who smothered him with affection and praise should he perform to her pleasure, refused to acknowledge his presence should he somehow displease or disappoint her. His father accused him of being a sleepyhead, a slow starter, and sometimes said every boy in town had a two-hour head start on him. Had we known these things from scratch, we might not have wondered why Lyndon Johnson seemed so blind for so long to the Asian realities. His personal history simply permitted him no retreats or failures in testings.

From childhood L.B.J. experienced bad dreams. As with much else, they would stay with him to the grave. His nightmares were of being paralyzed and unable to act, of being chained inside a cage or to his desk, of being pursued by hostile forces. These and other disturbing dreams haunted his White House years; he could see himself stricken and ill on a cot, unable even to speak—

like Woodrow Wilson—while, in an adjoining room, his trusted aides squabbled and quarreled in dividing his power. He translated the dreams to mean that should he for a moment show weakness, be indecisive, then history might judge him as the first American President who had failed to stand up and be counted.

These deep-rooted insecurities prompted Lyndon Johnson always to assert himself, to abuse staff members simply to prove that he held the upper hand, to test his power in small or mean ways. Sometimes, in sending Vice President Hubert Humphrey off on missions or errands with exhortations to "get going," he literally kicked him in the shins. "Hard," Humphrey later recalled, pulling up his trouser leg to exhibit the scars to columnist Robert Allen. Especially when drinking did he swagger and strut. Riding high as Senate majority leader, Johnson one night after a Texas State Society function, at the National Press Club in Washington—in the spring of 1958—repaired to a nearby bar with Texas Congressmen Homer Thornberry and Jack Brooks. "I'm a powerful sumbitch, you know that?" he repeatedly said. "You boys realize how goddamn *powerful* I am?" Yes, Lyndon, his companions uneasily chorused. Johnson pounded the table as if attempting to crack stout oak: "Do you know Ike couldn't pass the Lord's Prayer in Congress without me? You understand that? Hah?" Yes, Lyndon. "Hah? Do you? Hah?" An observer thought he never had seen a man more desperate for affirmations of himself.

Johnson always was an enthusiastic Cold Warrior. He was not made uncomfortable by John Foster Dulles' brinkmanship rhetoric about "rolling back" communism or of "unleashing" Chiang Kaishek to free the Chinese mainland. He was, indeed, one of the original soldiers of the Cold War, a volunteer rather than a draftee, just as he had been the first member of Congress to rush to the recruiting station following Pearl Harbor. Immediately after World War II he so bedeviled House Speaker Sam Rayburn about his fears of America dismantling its military machine that Rayburn appointed him to the postwar Military Policy Committee and to the Joint Committee on Atomic Energy. L.B.J. early had a preference for military assignments in Congress; he successfully campaigned for a seat on the House Naval Affairs Committee in the 1930's and, a decade later, the Senate Armed Services Committee. He eventually chaired the Senate Preparedness Committee and the Senate Space Committee. Perhaps others saw the exploration of outer space in scientific or peaceful terms. Johnson, however, told Senate Democrats that outer space offered "the ultimate position from which total control of the earth may be exercised. Whoever gains that ultimate position gains control, total control, over the earth."

Lyndon Johnson was a nagger, a complainer, a man not always patient with those of lesser gifts or with those who somehow inconvenienced him in the moment. Sometimes he complained that the generals knew nothing but "spend and bomb"; almost always, however, he went along with bigger military spending and, in most cases, with more bombing or whatever other military action the brass proposed. This was his consistent record in Congress, and he generally affirmed it as President.

On November 12, 1951, Senator Johnson rattled his saber at the Russians:

> We are tired of fighting your stooges. We will no longer sacrifice our young men on the altar of your conspiracies. The next aggression will be the last. . . . We will strike back, not just at your satellites, but at you. We will strike back with all the dreaded might that is within our control, and it will be a crushing blow.

Even allowing for those rhetorical excesses peculiar to senatorial oratory, those were not the words of a man preoccupied with the doctrine of peaceful coexistence. Nor were they inconsistent with Johnson's mind-set when he made public demand—at the outbreak of the Korean War, in June, 1950—that President Truman order an all-out mobilization of all military reserve troops, national guard units, draftees, and even civilian manpower and industry. In a Senate debate shortly thereafter Senator Johnson scolded colleagues questioning the Pentagon's request for new and supplementary emergency billions: "Is this the hour of our nation's twilight, the last fading hour of light before an endless night shall envelop us and all the Western world?"

His ties with Texas—with its indigenous xenophobic instincts and general proclivities toward a raw yahooism—haunted him and, in a sense, may have made him a prisoner of grim political realities during the witch-hunting McCarthy era. "I'm damn tired," he said, "of being called a Dixiecrat in Washington and a Communist in Texas"; it perfectly summed up those schizophrenic divisions uneasily compartmentalizing his national political life and the more restrictive parochial role dictated by conditions back home. He lived daily with a damned-if-I-do-and-damned-if-I-don't situation. Texas was a particularly happy hunting ground for Senator Joe McCarthy, whose self-proclaimed anticommunist crusade brought him invitation after invitation to speak there; the Texas legislature, in the 1950's controlled beyond belief by vested interests and showing the ideological instincts of the early primates, whooped through a resolution demanding that Senator McCarthy address it despite the suggestion of State Representative Maury Maverick, Jr., that the resolution be expanded to invite Mickey Mouse. Both Johnson's powerful rightist adversaries and many of his wealthy Texas benefactors were enthusiastic contributors to the McCarthy cause.

Privately Johnson groused to intimates of McCarthy's reckless showboat tactics and particularly of the Texas-directed pressures they brought down on him: why, Joe McCarthy was just a damn drunk, a blowhard, an incompetent who couldn't tie his own shoelaces, probably the biggest joke in the Senate. But—L.B.J. reminded those counseling him to attack McCarthy—people believed him, they were so afraid of the Communists they would believe anything. McCarthy was as strong as horseradish. There would come a time when the hysteria died down, and then McCarthy would be vulnerable; such a fellow was certain to hang himself in time. But right now anybody openly challenging McCarthy would come away with dirty hands and with his heart broken. "Touch pitch," he paraphrased the Bible, "and you'll be defiled." By temperament a man who coveted the limelight and never was bashful about claiming credit for popular actions, Johnson uncharacteristically remained in the background when the U.S. Senate voted to censure McCarthy in late 1954. Though he was instrumental in selecting senators he believed would be effective and creditable members in leading the censure effort, Johnson's fine hand was visible only to insiders.

Johnson believed, however—and probably more deeply than Joe McCarthy—in a worldwide, monolithic Communist conspiracy. He believed it was directed from Moscow and that it was ready to blast America, or subvert it, at the drop of a fur hat. L.B.J. never surrendered that view. In retirement he suggested that the Communists were everywhere, honeycombing the government, and he told surprised visitors that sometimes he hadn't known whether he could trust even his own staff. The Communists (it had been his first thought on hearing the gunshots in Dallas, and he never changed his mind) had killed Jack Kennedy; it had been their influence that turned people against the Vietnam war. One of L.B.J.'s former aides, having been treated to that angry lecture, came away from the Texas ranch with the sad and reluctant conclusion that "the Old Man's absolutely paranoid on the Communist thing."

In May, 1961, President Kennedy dispatched his Vice President to Asia on a "fact-finding" diplomatic trip. Johnson, who believed it his duty to be a team player, to reinforce the prevailing wisdom, bought without qualification the optimistic briefings of military brass with their charts and slides "proving" the inevitable American victory. "I was sent out here to report the *progress* of the war," he told an aide, as if daring anyone to give him anything other than good news. Carried away, he publicly endowed South Vietnam's President Ngo Dinh Diem with the qualities of Winston Churchill, George Washington, Andrew Jackson, and F.D.R. Visiting refugee camps, he grew angry at Communist aggressions "against decent people" and concluded: "There is no alternative to United States leadership in Southeast Asia. . . . We must decide whether to help to the best of our ability or throw in the towel . . . [and] . . . pull back our defenses to San Francisco and a 'Fortress America' concept." He believed then—and always would—in the "domino theory" first stated by President Eisenhower. Even after announcing his abdication, he continued to sing the tired litany: if Vietnam fell then the rest of Asia might go, and then Africa, and then the Philippines. . . .

When Lyndon Johnson suddenly ascended to the Presidency, however, he did not enter the Oval Office eager to immediately take the measure of Ho Chi Minh. Although he told Ambassador Henry Cabot Lodge that "I am not going to be the President who saw Southeast Asia go the way China went," he wanted, for the moment, to keep the war—and, indeed, all foreign entanglements—at arm's length. His preoccupation was with his domestic program; here, he was confident, he knew what he was doing. He would emulate F.D.R.

in making people's lives a little brighter. To aides he eagerly talked of building schools and houses, of fighting poverty and attaining full employment, of heating the economy to record prosperity. The honeymoon with Congress—he said—couldn't last; he had seen Congress grow balky and obstinate, take its measure of many Presidents, and he had to assume it would happen again. Then he would lean forward, tapping a forefinger against someone's chest or squeezing a neighboring knee, and say: "I'm like a sweetheart to Congress right now. They love me because I'm new and courting 'em and it's kinda exciting, like that first kiss. But after a while the new will wear off. Then Congress will complain that I don't bring enough roses or candy and will accuse me of seeing other girls." The need was to push forward quickly: pass the Civil Rights bill in the name of the martyred John F. Kennedy, then hit Capitol Hill with a blizzard of domestic proposals and dazzle it before sentiment and enthusiasms cooled. Foreign affairs could wait.

Lyndon Johnson at that point had little experience in foreign affairs. Except for showcase missions accomplished as Vice President, he had not traveled outside the United States save for excursions to Mexico and his brief World War II peregrinations. He probably had little confidence in himself in foreign affairs; neither did he have an excessive interest in the field. "Foreigners are not like the folks I am used to," he sometimes said—and though it passed as a joke, his intimates felt he might be kidding on the level.

Ambassadors waiting to present their credentials to the new President were miffed by repeated delays—and then angrily astonished when L.B.J. received them in groups and clumps, seemingly paying only perfunctory attention, squirmng in this chair, scowling or muttering during the traditional ceremonies. He appeared oblivious to their feelings, to their offended senses of dignity. "Why do *I* have to see them?" the President demanded. "They're Dean Rusk's clients, not mine."

Defense Secretary Robert McNamara was selected to focus on Vietnam while L.B.J. concocted his Great Society. McNamara should send South Vietnam equipment and money as needed, a few more men, issue the necessary pronouncements. But don't splash it all over the front pages, don't let it get out of hand, don't give Barry Goldwater Vietnam as an issue for the 1964 campaign. Barry, hell, he was a hip shooter; he'd fight Canada or Mexico—or, at least, give that impression—so the thing to do was sit tight, keep the lid on, keep all Vietnam options open. Above all, "Don't let it turn into a Bay of Pigs." Hunker down; don't gamble.

The trouble—Johnson said to advisers—was that foreign nations didn't understand Americans or the American way; they saw us as "fat and fifty, like the country-club set"; they didn't think we had the steel in our souls to act when the going got rough. Well, in time they'd find out differently. They'd learn that Lyndon Johnson was not about to abandon what other Presidents had started; he wouldn't permit history to write that he'd been the only American President to cut and run; he wouldn't sponsor any damn Munichs. But for right now—cool it. Put Vietnam on the back burner and let it simmer.

But the Communists—he later would say—wouldn't permit him to cool it. There had been that Gulf of Tonkin attack on the United States destroyer *Maddox,* in August of 19-and-64, and if he hadn't convinced Congress to get on record as backing him up in Vietnam, why, then, the Reds would have interpreted it as a sign of weakness and Barry Goldwater would have cut his heart out. And in February of 19-and-65, don't forget, the Vietcong had made that attack on the American garrison at Pleiku, and how could he be expected to ignore that? There they came, thousands of 'em, barefoot and howling in their black pajamas and throwing homemade bombs: it had been a damned insult, a calculated show of contempt. L.B.J. told the National Security Council: "The worst thing we could do would be to let this [Pleiku] thing go by. It would be a big mistake. It would open the door to a major misunderstanding." Twelve hours later American aircraft—for the first time—bombed in North Vietnam; three weeks later L.B.J. ordered continuing bombing raids in the north to "force the North Vietnamese into negotiations"; only a hundred and twenty days after Pleiku, American forces were involved in a full-scale war and seeking new ways to take the offensive. Eight Americans died at Pleiku. Eight. Eventually fifty thousand plus would die in Asia.

Pleiku was the second major testing of American will within a few months, in L.B.J.'s view. Then in the spring of 1965 rebels had attacked the ruling military junta in the Dominican Republic. Lives and property of U.S. citizens were endangered, as Johnson saw it, but—more—this might be a special tactic by the Reds, a dry run for bigger mischief later on in Vietnam. The world was watching to see how America would react. "It's just like the Alamo," he lectured the National Security Council. "Hell, it's like you were down at that gate, and you were surrounded, and you damn well needed somebody. Well, by God, I'm going to *go*—and I thank the Lord that I've got men who want to go with me, from McNamara right down to the littlest private who's carrying a gun."

Somewhat to his puzzlement, and certainly to his great vexation, Lyndon Johnson would learn that not everybody approved of his rushing the Marines into the Dominican Republic, and within days building up a twenty-one-thousand-man force. Attempting to answer criticism, he would claim thousands of patriots "bleeding in the streets and with their heads cut off," paint a false picture of the United States ambassador cringing under his desk "while bullets whizzed over his head," speak of howling Red hordes descending on American citizens and American holdings, and, generally, open what later became known as the Credibility Gap.

By now he had given up on his original notion of walking easy in Vietnam until he could put the Great Society across. Even before the three major testings of Tonkin Gulf, the Dominican Republic, and Pleiku, he had said—almost idly—"Well, I guess we have to touch up those North Vietnamese a little bit." By December, 1964, he had reversed earlier priorities: "We'll beat the Communists first, then we can look around and maybe give something to the poor." Guns now ranked ahead of butter.

Not that he was happy about it. Though telling Congress "This nation is mighty enough, its society is healthy enough, its people are strong enough to pursue our goals in the rest of the world while still building a Great Society here at home," he knew, in his bones, that this was much too optimistic an outlook. He privately fretted that his domestic program would be victimized. He became touchy, irritable, impatient with those who even timorously questioned America's increasing commitment to the war. Why should *I* be blamed— he snapped—when the Communists are the aggressors, when President Eisenhower committed us in Asia in 1954, when Kennedy beefed up Ike's efforts? If he didn't prosecute the Vietnam war now, then later Congress would sour and want to hang him because he hadn't—and would gut his domestic programs in retaliation. He claimed to have "pounded President Eisenhower's desk" in opposing Ike's sending two hundred Air Force "technicians" to assist the French in Indochina (though those who were present recalled that only Senators Russell of Georgia and Stennis of Mississippi had raised major objections). Well, he'd been unable to stop Ike that time, though he *had* helped persuade him against dropping paratroopers into Dien Bien Phu to aid the doomed French garrison there. And after all that, everybody now called Vietnam Lyndon Johnson's war. It was unfair. "The only difference between the Kennedy assassination and mine is that I am alive and it [is] more torturous."

Very well; if it was his war in the public mind, then he would personally oversee its planning. "Never move up your artillery until you move up your ammunition," he told his generals—a thing he'd said as Senate majority leader when impatient liberals urged him to call for votes on issues he felt not yet ripe. Often he quizzed the military brass, sounding almost like a dove, in a way to resemble courtroom cross-examinations. He forced the admirals and generals to affirm and reaffirm their recommendations as vital to victory. Reading selected transcripts, one might make the judgment that Lyndon Johnson was a most reluctant warrior, one more cautious than not. The evidence of Johnson's deeds, however, suggests that he was being a crafty politician—making a record so that later he couldn't be made the sole scapegoat. He trusted McNamara's computers, perhaps more than he trusted men, and took satisfaction when their print-outs predicted that X amount of bombing would damage the Vietcong by Y, or that X number of troops would be required to capture Z. Planning was the key. You figured what you had to do, you did it, and eventually you'd nail the coonskin to the wall.

He devoutly believed that all problems had solutions: in his lifetime alone we'd beaten the Great Depression, won two world wars, hacked away at racial discrimination, made an industrial giant and world power of a former agrarian society, explored outer space. This belief in available solutions led him, time and again, to change tactics in Vietnam and discover fresh enthusiasm for each new move; he did not pause, apparently, to reflect upon why given tactics, themselves once heralded as practical solutions, had failed and had been abandoned. If counterinsurgency failed, you bombed. If bombing wasn't wholly effective, then you tried the enclave theory. If *that* proved disappointing, you sent your ground troops on search-and-destroy missions. If, somehow, the troops couldn't find the phantom Vietcong in large numbers (and therefore couldn't destroy them), you began pacification programs in the areas you'd newly occupied. And if *this* bogged down, you beefed up your firepower and sent in enough troops to simply outmuscle the rice-paddy ragtags: napalm 'em, bomb 'em, shoot 'em. Sure it would work. It always had. Yes, surely the answer was there somewhere in the back of the book, if only you looked long enough. . . .

He sought, and found, assurances. Maybe he had only a "cow-college" education, perhaps he'd not attended West Point, he might not have excessive experience in foreign affairs. But he was surrounded by good men, what David Halberstam later would label "the best and the brightest," and certainly these were unanimous in their supportive conclusions. "He would look around him," Tom Wicker later said, "and see in Bob McNamara that [the war] was technologically feasible, in McGeorge Bundy that it was intellectually respectable, and in Dean Rusk that it was historically necessary." It was especially easy to trust expertise when the experts in their calculations bolstered your own gut feelings—when their computers and high-minded statements and mighty hardware all boiled down to reinforce your belief in American efficiency, American responsibility, American destiny. If so many good men agreed with him, then what might be wrong with those who didn't?

He considered the sources of dissatisfaction and dissent: the liberals—the "red-hots," he'd often sneeringly called them, the "pepper pots"—who were impractical dreamers, self-winding kamikazes intent on self-destruction. He often quoted an aphorism to put such people in perspective: "Any jackass can kick down a barn, but it takes a carpenter to build one." He fancied, however, that he knew all about these queer fellows. For years, down home, Ronnie Dugger and his *Texas Observer* crowd, in L.B.J.'s opinion, had urged him to put his head in the noose by fighting impossible, profitless fights. They wanted him to take on Joe McCarthy, slap the oil powers down, kick Ike's rear end, tell everybody who wasn't a red-hot to go to hell. Well, he'd learned a long time ago that just because you told a fellow to go to hell, he didn't necessarily have to go. The liberals didn't understand the Communists. Bill Fulbright and his bunch—the striped-pants boys over at the State Department and assorted outside pepper pots—thought you could *trust* the Communists; they made the mistake of believing the Reds would deal with you honorably when—in truth— the Communists didn't respect anything but force. You had to fight fire with fire; let them know who had the biggest guns and the toughest heart.

Where once he had argued the injustice of Vietnam being viewed as "his" war, Lyndon Johnson now brought to it a proprietary attitude. This should have been among the early warnings that L.B.J. would increasingly resist less than victory, no matter his periodic bombing halts or conciliatory statements inviting peace, because once he took a thing personally, his pride and vanity and ego knew no bounds. Always a man to put his brand on everything (he wore monogrammed shirts, boots, cuff links; flew his private L.B.J. flag when in residence at the L.B.J. ranch; saw to it that the names of Lynda Bird Johnson and Luci Baines Johnson and Lady Bird Johnson—not Claudia, as she had been named—had the magic initials L.B.J.), he now personalized and internalized the war. Troops became "my" boys, those were "my" helicopters, it was "my" pilots he prayed might return from their bombing missions as he paid nocturnal calls to the White House situation room to learn the latest from the battlefields; Walt Rostow became "my" intellectual because he was hawkish on L.B.J.'s war. His machismo was mixed up in it now, his manhood. After a cabinet meeting in 1967 several staff aids and at least one cabinet member— Stewart Udall, Secretary of the Interior—remained behind for informal discussions; soon L.B.J. was waving his arms and fulminating about his war. Who the hell was Ho Chi Minh, anyway, that he thought he could push America around? Then the President did an astonishing thing: he unzipped his trousers, dangled a given appendage, and asked his shocked associates: "Has Ho Chi Minh got anything like that?"

By mid-1966 he had cooled toward many of his experts: not because they'd been wrong in their original optimistic calculations so much as that some of them had recanted and now rejected *his* war. This Lyndon Johnson could not forgive: they'd cut and run on him. Nobody had deserted Roosevelt, he gloomed, when he'd been fighting Hitler. McGeorge Bundy, deserting to head the Ford Foundation, was no longer the brilliant statesman but merely "a smart kid, that's all." Bill Moyers, quitting to become editor of *Newsday,* and once almost a surrogate son to the President, suddenly became "a little puppy I rescued from sacking groceries"—a reference to a part-time job Moyers held while a high-school student. George Ball, too, was leaving? Well, he'd always been a chronic beller-acher. When Defense Secretary McNamara doubted too openly (stories of his anguish leaked to the newspapers), he found it difficult to claim the President's time; ultimately he rudely was shuttled to the World Bank. Vice President Hubert Humphrey, privately having second thoughts, was not welcomed back to high councils until he'd muffled his dissent and shamelessly flattered L.B.J. Even then Johnson didn't wholly accept his Vice President; Hubert, he said, wasn't a real man, he cried as easily as a woman, he didn't have the weight. When Lady Bird Johnson voiced doubts about the war, her husband grumbled that *of course* she had doubts; it was *like* a woman to be uncertain. *Has Ho Chi Minh got anything like that?*

Shortly after the Tet offensive began—during which Americans would be shocked by the Vietcong temporarily capturing a wing of the American embassy in Saigon—the President, at his press conference of February 2, 1968, made such patently false statements that even his most loyal friends and supporters were troubled. The sudden Tet offensives had been traumatic, convincing many Americans that our condition was desperate, if not doomed. For years the official line ran that the Vietcong could not hang on: would shrink by the attritions of battle and an ebbing of confidence in a hopeless cause; stories were handed out that captured documents showed the enemy to be of low morale, underfed, ill-armed. The Vietcong could not survive superior American firepower; the kill ratio favored our side by 7-to-1, 8-to-1, more. These and other optimisms were repeated by the President, by General Westmoreland, by this ambassador or that fact-finding team. Now, however, it became apparent that the Vietcong had the capability to challenge even our main lair in Asia—and there to inflict serious damage as well as major embarrassments.

It was a time demanding utmost candor, and L.B.J. blew it. He took the ludicrous position that the Tet offensive (which would be felt for weeks to come) had abysmally failed. Why, we'd known about it all along—had, indeed, been in possession of Hanoi's order of battle. Incredible. To believe the President one had also to believe that American authorities had simply failed to act on this vital intelligence, had wittingly and willingly invited disaster. The President was scoffed at and ridiculed; perhaps the thoughtful got goose bumps in realizing how far Lyndon Johnson now lived from reality. If there was a beginning of the end—of Johnson, of hopes of anything remotely resembling victory, of a general public innocence of official razzmatazz—then Tet, and that press conference, had to be it.

Even the stubborn President knew it. His Presidency was shot, his party ruined and in tatters; his credibility was gone; he could speak only at military bases, where security guaranteed his safety against the possibility of mobs pursuing him through the streets as he had often dreamed. The nightmare was real now. Street dissidents long had been chanting their cruel "Hey, Hey, L.B.J. / How Many Kids Did You Kill Today"; Senator Eugene McCarthy soon would capture almost half the vote in the New Hampshire primary against the unpopular President. There was nothing to do but what he'd always sworn he would not do: quit. On March 31, 1968, at the end of a televised speech ordering the end of attacks on North Vietnam in the hope of getting the enemy to the negotiation table, Johnson startled the nation by announcing: ". . . I do not believe that I should devote an hour or a day of my time to any personal partisan causes or to any duties other than the awesome duties of this office— the Presidency of your country. Accordingly, I shall not seek, and I will not accept, the nomination of my party for another term. . . ."

"In the final months of his Presidency," former White House aide Eric Goldman wrote, "Lyndon Johnson kept shifting in mood. At times he was bitter and petulant at his repudiation by the nation; at times philosophical, almost serene, confidently awaiting the verdict of the future." The serenity always was temporary; he grew angry with Hubert Humphrey for attempting to disengage himself from the Johnson war policy and, consequently, refused to make more than a token show of support for him. He saw Richard Nixon win on a pledge of having "a secret plan" to end the war—which, it developed, he did not have.

In his final White House thrashings—and in retirement—Lyndon Johnson complained of unfinished business: he had wanted to complete Vietnam peace talks, free the crew of the *Pueblo,* begin talks with the Russians on halting the arms race, send a man to the moon. But the war—he would say in irritation—the war had ruined all that; the people hadn't rallied around him as they had around F.D.R. and Woodrow Wilson and other wartime Presidents; he had been abandoned—by Congress, by cabinet members, by old friends; no other President had tried so hard or suffered so much. He had a great capacity for self-pity and often indulged it, becoming reclusive and rarely issuing a public statement or making public appearances. Doris Kearns has said that she and others helping L.B.J. write his memoirs, *The Vantage Point,* would draft chapters and lay out the documentation—but even then Lyndon Johnson would say no, no, it wasn't like that, it was like *this;* and he would rattle on, waving his arms and attempting to justify himself, invoking the old absolutes, calling up memories of the Alamo, the Texas Rangers, the myths and the legends. He never seemed to understand where or how he had gone wrong.

Part IV
Social Issues during America's Second Century

Compared to the more familiar topics of economic, political, and diplomatic/military history, the area of social history is a relatively new field to most students of United States history. This additional dimension to the study of the past can provide us with a badly needed perspective on the social issues facing contemporary America.

The status of minorities has always been a topic of particular significance in the United States. This nation was founded on the principle of equality, but that concept was difficult to achieve in reality. The struggle of minority groups to attain equal opportunity has tested the American social fabric as have few other issues. As described in the following articles, Indians, Blacks, and women all faced discrimination during America's second century. How that discrimination was applied to these groups and how they resisted it are two of the common threads running through the readings.

Two other major social issues are addressed in this section: Urbanization and the Environment. In many ways, urbanization was a by-product of the industrialization process. By the 1920s, for the first time in U.S. history, most Americans lived in urban areas. The lure of the city was more than just economic—its culture and excitement, including big-time sporting events like boxing, also attracted immigrants and rural Americans. Unfortunately, urban problems, or, as Lincoln Steffens, an early twentieth century journalist and social reformer termed it, the "shame of the cities," also became apparent. Soon urban crusaders like Jane Addams began to address some of those problems.

Americans have become more conscious of their environment in recent years. Unfortunately, that awareness was often brought about by suffering the effects of carelessness and/or waste. For a people whose national characteristics had largely been molded by abundance, the prospect of living with less instead of more was unsettling at best. Understanding the historical development of environmental issues, as well as other aspects of the American experience, is a necessary first step for preparing any reasonable agenda for the future.

18

Reluctant Conquerors: American Army Officers and the Plains Indians

by Thomas C. Leonard

For generations, the Plains Indians had been able to avoid being overwhelmed by non-Indian settlers. Many potential settlers had moved further west to California in the hopes of finding fabulous wealth in the gold mines. Others found the Plains area itself to be unfavorable for permanent settlement. Then, at the end of the Civil War, patterns of settlement changed. Liberal federal land policies, the transcontinental railroads, steel plows, barbed wire, and windmills all combined to induce non-Indians into the mythical "Great American Desert." Thus, in the quarter-century after the Civil War, the Plains Indians faced a fate similar to other tribes in other regions of the United States.

Given the circumstances, some Indians chose to fight. What followed was the last period of Indian "wars" in American history. The ensuing battles between the Plains Indians and U.S. Cavalry troops were usually portrayed at the time, and for decades afterward, as a struggle between savagery and "civilization." Professor Thomas C. Leonard of the University of California, Berkeley, author of *Above the Battle: War-Making in America from Appomattox to Versailles,* shows that it was not quite that simple. As Professor Leonard himself says, an account of the relationship between American army officers and the Plains Indians "throws a revealing light on a history that is still too often falsified with glib stereotypes."

The white man's peace at Appomattox in 1865 meant war for the Plains Indians. In the next quarter century six and a half million settlers moved west of the Missouri River, upsetting a precarious balance that had existed between two million earlier pioneers and their hundred thousand "hostile" red neighbors. The industrial energy that had flowed into the Civil War now pushed rail lines across traditional hunting grounds. Some twenty-five thousand soldiers were sent west to meet insistent demands for protection coming from stockmen and miners spread out between the Staked Plains of Texas and the Montana lands watered by the Powder, Bighorn, and Yellowstone rivers.

It is ironic that the men who carried the wounds of the struggle to maintain the union of their own society now were ordered to dismember the culture of the native Americans. These Indian fighters today have been knocked out of that false gallery of heroes created by western novels and movies. On the centennial of the Battle of the Little Bighorn a granite mountain outside of Custer, South Dakota, is being carved into the shape of the Sioux warrier leader Crazy Horse. Times have changed, and a second look at the Army's

Indian fighters is in order. They have a complex story to tell, one filled with an ambivalence about their enemy as well as about the civilians who sent them to fight.

The officer corps did not relish their double assignment of pushing Indians back from lands claimed by whites and, for good measure, "redeeming" native Americans from "barbarism"—for Christian civilization. In the letter books and official reports that these men kept so meticulously on the frontier there is a continual lament: civilian officials and opinion makers only cut budgets and issued contradictory directions. The rules of war demanded restraint and a fine regard for the enemy's rights, but it seemed as if the same civilians who interpreted these rules wanted quick work on the battlefield. The United States government itself broke the treaties that promised the Indians land, yet expected the Army to keep the peace through mutual trust.

At the same time that western settlers were clamoring for protection, their land grabs were provoking Indian retaliation. Not incidentally, army officers endured the torture of the annual congressional debate over how much their pay should be cut and seethed as western bankers charged 12 to 40 per cent to convert their government paper into the coin they needed on the frontier. "Friends" of the Indian—with their talk of a "conquest by kindness"—were a special annoyance. Eastern philanthropists like Edward A. Lawrence damned the officers when blood was shed and were among those who chillingly approved the "swift retribution" meted out to General Custer by the Sioux. Frontier forts rarely had the long, timbered stockades beloved by Hollywood set designers—but perhaps many officers longed for a massive wall, high enough to repel civilians as well as Indians.

By 1870 General William T. Sherman doubted he could fight with honor on the plains; from the west and the east, he wrote, "we are placed between two fires." But Sherman may have been envied by another proud Civil War hero, General Philip H. Sheridan, who mused upon a shattered reputation as he watched whole frontier towns—wanting the extermination of Indians—turn out to hang him in effigy.

To officers so provoked, action seemed the thing to sweep away the complications of the Indian problem; to strike at the red man again and again appeared not only the quickest way to dry up civilian complaints but the just way to punish an incomprehensibly wild enemy. Sheridan pleaded with Sherman for authority to act upon the appalling reports that crossed his desk each week:

> Since 1862 at least 800 men, women, and children have been murdered within the limits of my present command, in the most fiendish manner; the men usually scalped and mutilated, their [he omits the word] cut off and placed in their mouth; women ravished sometimes fifty and sixty times in succession, then killed and scalped, sticks stuck in their persons, before and after death.

Sheridan said it was now a question of who was to remain alive in his district, red or white. As for himself: "I have made my choice." It was, in fact, Sheridan who first enunciated the judgment that would become the epitaph of so many native Americans: "The only good Indians I ever saw were dead."

Sheridan's choice, made in passion, proved extraordinarily complicated to carry out, for the fact is that the Indian fighters were troubled by various kinds of respect for their enemy. In the first place, no commander in the West could conceal his admiration for the red man's fighting skill. "Experience of late years," one reported to his colleagues, "has most conclusively shown that our cavalry cannot cope with the Indian man for man." Though these seasoned veterans and heroes reported a very favorable official casualty ratio, in more candid moments they pronounced that Indian fighting was the most difficult combat American soldiers had ever faced.

It followed that so high an estimate of the enemy's ability undermined the Army's pride in its own competence. Sheridan berated the inefficiency that made campaigns in the West "a series of forlorn hopes," and Sherman wrote in so many words to the Secretary of War what had silently haunted his fellow officers: ". . . it seems to be impossible to force Indians to fight at a disadvantage in their own country. Their sagacity and skill surpasses that of the white race." It further followed that victory against such valiant opponents was bittersweet. Both Sheridan and Sherman confessed to pity and compassion for the native Americans they had set out to destroy. As Sheridan wrote:

> We took away their country and their means of support, broke up their mode of living, their habits of life, introduced disease and decay among them and it was for this and against this they made war. Could anyone expect less?

Few officers escaped a sort of wistful appreciation of their primitive enemy in what they took to be his insatiable appetite for war—and not a few admired precisely this unrestrained aggressiveness. Indeed, peaceful assimilation seemed not good enough for the Indians. One of Sheridan's favorite generals sought a large audience to explain the temptations of the Indian culture:

> To me, Indian life, with its attendant ceremonies, mysteries, and forms, is a book of unceasing interest. Grant that some of its pages are frightful, and, if possible, to be avoided, yet the attraction is none the weaker. Study him, fight him, civilize him if you can, he remains still the object of your curiosity, a type of man peculiar and undefined, subjecting himself to no known law of civilization, contending determinedly against all efforts to win him from his chosen mode of life.
>
> If I were an Indian, I often think I would greatly prefer to cast my lot among those of my people who adhered to the free open plains rather than submit to the confined limits of a reservation, there to be the recipient of the blessed benefits of civilization, with its vices thrown in without stint or measure.

Two years after he published this gratuitous advice, General George A. Custer met the object of his interest for the last time at the Little Bighorn.

General Nelson A. Miles, one of the officers who chased the Sioux after Custer's fall, had a personal reason for revenge: an Indian had taken a point-blank shot at him during an awkward moment in a peace parley. But Miles's reflections show the remarkable extent to which men like him overcame their anger with the enemy. The general spoke of the Indian's "courage, skill, sagacity, endurance, fortitude, and self-sacrifice of a high order" and of "the dignity, hospitality, and gentleness of his demeanor toward strangers and toward his fellow savages." Miles was inclined to think that lapses from this standard meant only that Indians had "degenerated through contact with the white man." Writing on this subject, he did not show the personal arrogance and pride that was the despair of his military superiors. Miles viewed Custer's fall in 1876 as a chastising message for the nation's centennial. He quoted Longfellow: ". . . say that our broken faith / wrought all this ruin and scathe, / In the Year of a Hundred Years."

Miles was not an eccentric in the sympathies he expressed. Colonel John Gibbon, for example, the man who discovered the mutilated bodies of the soldiers who had fallen with Custer at the Little Bighorn, seemed, during his subsequent chase of the Sioux, more angry at the "human ghouls" in the Army who had disturbed some Sioux graves than at the warriors who had killed his colleagues. Such desecrations, he thundered, "impress one with the conviction that in war barbarism stands upon a level only a little lower than our boasted civilization." By Gibbon's lights, the record of white hostility and treachery would force any man to fight: "Thus would the savage in us come to the surface under the oppression which we know the Indian suffers." Like so many Indian fighters who addressed the perennial "Indian question," Gibbon raised more questions about his own culture than he answered about his enemy's.

To these soldiers the courage and bearing of the red man suggested a purer way of life before the coming of the white man, and the military frequently searched for Greek and Roman analogies to suggest the virtues of its enemies. Heathens though they were, they had nobility. Even the Indians' faults might be excused by their manifestly lower stage of cultural evolution.

General George Crook was in a good position to speak of the red men's virtues, for as a fighting man he resembled them. In the field he dispensed with the army uniform and seemed only at ease when he was free of all cumbersome marks of civilization. Crook left one post, he tells us, "with one change of underclothes, toothbrush, etc., and went to investigate matters, intending to be gone a week. But I got interested after the Indians and did not return there again for over two years."

In the harsh campaigns in the Southwest, Crook taught his men to move over the land like Apaches, and when white men failed him, he was adept in recruiting Indians for army service. Frederic Remington observed Crook's methods and saw they made officers less "Indian fighters" than "Indian thinkers." "He's more of an Indian than I am," marveled one Apache. Crook repaid such compliments; back at West Point to deliver a graduation address, he may have shocked many with this observation:

With all his faults, and he has many, the American Indian is not half so black as he has been painted. He is cruel in war, treacherous at times, and not over cleanly. But so were our forefathers. His nature, however, is responsive to treatment which assures him that it is based upon justice, truth, honesty, and common sense. . . .

Crook hesitated to condemn even the most ferocious Apaches, because he respected their spirit and believed that "we are too culpable as a nation, for the existing condition of affairs."

In the view of many officers the weaknesses of their own culture were more glaring than the faults of their enemy. "Barbarism torments the body; civilization torments the soul," one colonel concluded. "The savage remorselessly takes your scalp, your civilized friend as remorselessly swindles you out of your property." Indeed, many of the officers who led the fight for civilization seemed to accept Indian culture on its own terms. Colonel Henry B. Carrington—one of the field officers who supplied Sheridan with maddening accounts of Indian outrages—was an interesting case study. Carrington's official report of the eighty fallen soldiers under his command in the Fetterman fight in Wyoming in 1866 provided grisly reading:

> Eyes torn out and laid on the rocks; teeth chopped out; joints of fingers cut off; brains taken out and placed on rocks, with members of the body; entrails taken out and exposed; hands and feet cut off; arms taken out from sockets; eyes, ears, mouth, and arms penetrated with spearheads, sticks, and arrows; punctures upon every sensitive part of the body, even to the soles of the feet and the palms of the hand.

Yet Carrington's own response to this carnage was not vengeful but reflective, even scholarly. A year later Margaret Carrington, the colonel's wife, published *Ab-sa-ra-ka,* a study of the region the Army had fought to control. In her book she treated this Indian act of warfare with impressive open-mindedness, never directly condemning it. She did note that "the noblest traits of the soldiers were touchingly developed as they carefully handled the mutilated fragments" from the battlefield—but she also praised the Indian: "In ambush and decoy, *splendid.*" Close observers, she wrote, overcame anger to become reconciled, even sympathetic, to "the bold warrior in his great struggle."

As he took charge of enlarged sections of *Ab-sa-ra-ka* in the 1870's Colonel Carrington expanded on this theme of noble resistance. To him the Barbarities of the *whites,* in their "irresponsible speculative emigration," overshadowed the red "massacre" of Fetterman's men. Carrington confessed, like Custer, "if I had been a red man as I was a white man, I should have fought as bitterly, if not as brutally, as the Indian fought." And standing before the American Association for the Advancement of Science in 1880 to read his official report of the Fetterman mutilations again, Carrington explained to the scientists that the Indian's disposition of enemies was intended to disable his foe in the afterlife, and so was quite understandable. Nor did he disparage the red man's values, but rather closed his address by suggesting some inadequacies on the other—his own—side: "From 1865 until the present time, there has not been a border campaign which did not have its impulse in the aggressions of a white man."

Few men in the West raised more unusual questions about both cultures than Captain John Bourke. He entered the campaigns, he wrote later, "with the sincere conviction that the only good Indian was a dead Indian, and that the only use to make of him was that of a fertilizer." But the notebooks of this odd, inquiring soul reveal a man haunted by the details of the enemy's life. Mastering several Indian languages, Bourke produced an impressive series of monographs on native religious ceremonies, and in 1895 he became president of the American Folklore Society. Learning proved corrosive to his early cultural pride, and at the end of his army service he was willing to admit that "the American aborigine is not indebted to his pale-faced brother, no matter what nation or race he may be, for lessons in tenderness and humanity."

Admittedly, Captain Bourke's appreciation of native culture was more complex than the respect paid by other Indian fighters. Acknowledging the red man's fighting prowess and noble character, Bourke was more deeply interested in Indian snake ceremonies and scatological rites—mysteries thoroughly repulsive to most white sensibilities. Indeed, his interest in these ceremonies was as intense and sustained as were his protestations of "horror" during each "filthy" and "disgusting" rite. He put all this scholarship and his rather prurient curiosity to work in *Scatologic Rites of All Nations,* where he observed such "orgies" throughout the development of Western civilization, even surviving in nations of what he called "high enlightenment." Here was no sentimental accommodation with Indian culture but a panoramic reminder to the white race of its own barbaric past. Thus the Indians' vices, no less than their virtues, set up a mirror before the advancing Christian whites.

It did not, of course, deter the whites. However noble their image of the savage may have been, it is important to recognize in all of these Indian fighters a fundamental conviction that the price of civilization was not too high. Aware as they were of the ambiguities of their mission, their sympathies and remorse never swayed them from their duty, and no officer of tender conscience was provoked to resign his commission.

How were such mixed emotions sustained? In point of fact, the military's apologia for the red man answered certain professional and psychological needs of the workaday Army. The Army, for both noble and ignoble reasons, wanted to assume control of the administration of Indian affairs that had been held by civilians—a few good words for the long-suffering red man smoothed the way to this goal. Further, by praising the Plains Indians as relentless and efficient warriors the military justified its own ruthless strategy—and setbacks. Nor was frontier ethnology exactly disinterested; close study of the Indians often yielded military advantage for white men. And while empathy for the enemy clearly made the assignment to "redeem" the Indian more painful, there were some emotional satisfactions to be derived from even the most generous attitudes toward the Indians' way of life.

In some instances an officer's respect for the primitive unfettered aggressiveness happily loosened his own. Thus General George Schofield, commander of the Department of the Missouri, could confess that "civilized man . . . never feels so happy as when he throws off a large part of his civilization and reverts to the life of a semi-savage." When Schofield acted on his own advice on a long hunting trip, he returned invigorated, recording that "I wanted no other occupation in life than to ward off the savage and kill off his food until there should no longer be an Indian frontier in our beautiful country." One of Sherman's aides reached a similar ominous conclusion after saluting the red man's way of life. This officer was deeply impressed by his colleagues' glowing reports of the nobility of Indian religion, and, he mused,

> There is no doubt the Indians have, at times, been shamefully treated. . . .
> And there is no doubt a man of spirit would rebel. . . . However, it is useless to moralize about the Indians. Their fate is fixed, and we are so near their end, it is easy to see what that fate is to be. That the Indian might be collected, and put out of misery by being shot deliberately, (as it would be done to a disabled animal), would seem shocking, but something could be said in favor of such procedure.

This puzzling mixture of aggression and regret is less surprising if we take into account the ways, according to contemporary psychologists, that anger and frustration can give rise to these contrasting emotions. The officer corps was enraged by much of what it saw happening to America. The Indians' tactics seemed horrible yet ingenious. Their culture was repellent, but also alluring for its integrity. At the same time, evident in the reports and memoirs of these officers is a disturbing sense of having been abandoned by their own unworthy civilization. Army training and experience prevented these men from acting out their anger, and some anger was instead internalized and expressed in the mourning and guilt they exhibited so frequently. Their appreciation of the native Americans for what they had been was combined with a determination to punish a society for what it refused to become. Their fight for civilized settlement as it should be was troubled by their anger that some virtues, retained by the Indians, were slipping away from the white man.

If we appreciate the military's doubts—of its mandate, of its justice, of its ability, as well as of its commitments to civilization, duty, and progress—the tragedy of the West does not go away. It deepens. Was there an escape from the emotional trap in which the Army found itself? To refuse to win the West would have required a conversion to primitivism hard to imagine inside the ranks of army life and scarcely imaginable in ordinary men living ordinary lives outside of the Army. But the career of one lieutenant in the Nez Perce war illustrates that such a transformation was possible.

Charles Erskine Scott Wood (1852–1944) served on General O. O. Howard's staff, and it was he who took down the very moving speech of the defeated Chief Joseph. Wood's reflections on the Nez Perce campaign, published in the early 1880's, struck the conventional balance between remorse and pride. Surveying the shameful record of white treaty violations, he warned his army colleagues that retribution might follow. Yet there seemed to be no other pos-

U.S. cavalryman on the battlefield at Wounded Knee, S.D., on Jan. 1, 1891. (Smithsonian Institution)

sible outcome—"forces" were "silently at work, beyond all human control," against the red man's survival. Wood, a gifted literary man, proceeded to join the somewhat crowded celebration of the culture he had worked to destroy, hymning the vividness and nobility of the Indian, qualities that seemed poignant by their passing. But in all this he declined to attack directly the civilization that had corrupted and supplanted the Indians', and his fashionable sympathy sounded much like General Custer's.

But Wood was, in time, to change greatly. He quit the Army, entered the Columbia Law School, and began to cause trouble. Not satisfied with the state of letters or the law in his time, Wood allied himself with the radical Industrial Workers of the World and searched for a literary form to express his increasingly anarchistic temperament. The fruit of this veteran's singular rehabilitation was a long experimental poem, *The Poet in the Desert,* an affecting personal renunciation of "civilization" and a call for the revolt of the masses against privilege. Wood, with booming voice and flowing white beard, was in the twentieth century rather like Father Time—reminding Americans of sins against the Indians. He knew:

> *I have lain out with the brown men*
> *And know they are favored.*
> *Nature whispered to them her secrets,*
> *But passed me by.*

226

I sprawled flat in the bunch-grass, a target
For the just bullets of my brown brothers betrayed.
I was a soldier, and, at command,
Had gone out to kill and be killed.

We swept like fire over the smoke-browned tee-pees;
Their conical tops peering above the willows.
We frightened the air with crackle of rifles,
Women's shrieks, children's screams,
Shrill yells of savages;
Curses of Christians.
The rifles chuckled continually.
A poor people who asked nothing but freedom,
Butchered in the dark.

Wood's polemic is more straightforward than many that are asserted today on behalf of the native Americans. He learned—and his colleagues in the Army demonstrated—that respect and compassion for another culture are very unsure checks on violence. And Wood's life points out one of the costs of war that Americans have generally been spared: in a prolonged campaign the victor can emerge attracted to his enemy's faith. Our frontier officers had put a civil war behind them and were not ready to turn against their society to save the red man. But their thoughtfully expressed ambivalence toward their task of winning the West throws a revealing light on a history that is still too often falsified with glib stereotypes.

19

Ride-in: A Century of Protest Begins

by Alan F. Westin

The historical experience of black Americans has provided perhaps the most severe test for the principle of equality in the United States. Achieving the constitutional guarantees of freedom and basic civil rights consumed most of this nation's first century. Achieving equality of opportunity in a society which remained racist and discriminatory in its economic, political and social institutions absorbed much of the second century.

It has become commonplace to say that blacks have made more gains in the last three decades than at any other time since Reconstruction. In fact, the civil rights era of the late 1950s and 1960s is often referred to as the "Second Reconstruction." The fact that a "Second Reconstruction" was necessary to *restore* basic civil rights to black Americans should raise numerous questions about black history during America's second century.

In the following essay, Professor Alan F. Westin of Columbia University, a specialist in constitutional history, makes an important contribution to our understanding of what went wrong with civil rights for blacks. The Supreme Court decision to emasculate the Civil Rights Act of 1875 not only wiped away some of the gains of Reconstruction but also ushered in an era of blatant legal discrimination in the United States. The fact that we are still attempting to recover from the effects of that decision made a century ago underscores the realization that history is a very binding force.

It began one day early in January when a Negro named Robert Fox stepped aboard a streetcar in Louisville, Kentucky, dropped his coin into the fare box, and sat down in the white section of the car. Ordered to move, he refused, and the driver threw him off the car. Shortly after, Fox filed a charge of assault and battery against the streetcar company in the federal district court, claiming that separate seating policies were illegal and the driver's actions were therefore improper. The district judge instructed the jury that under federal law common carriers must serve all passengers equally without regard to race. So instructed, the jury found the company rules to be invalid and awarded damages of fifteen dollars (plus $72.80 in legal costs) to Mr. Fox.

Immediately there was sharp criticism of the Fox decision from the city and state administrations, both Democratic; the company defied the court's ruling and continued segregated seating. After several meetings with local federal officials and white attorneys co-operating with them, Louisville Negro leaders decided to launch a full-scale "ride-in." At 7 P.M. on May 12, a young Negro boy boarded a streetcar near the Willard Hotel, walked past the driver, and took a seat among the white passengers. The driver, under new company regulations, did not attempt to throw him off but simply stopped the car, lit a cigar, and refused to proceed until the Negro moved to "his place." While the governor, the Louisville chief of police, and other prominent citizens looked on from the sidewalks, a large crowd which included an increasingly noisy mob of jeering white teen-agers gathered around the streetcar.

Before long, there were shouts of "Put him out!" "Hit him!" "Kick him!" "Hang him!" Several white youths climbed into the car and began yelling insults in the face of the young Negro rider. He refused to answer—or to move. The youths dragged him from his seat, pulled him off the car, and began to beat him. Only when the Negro started to defend himself did the city police intervene: they arrested him for disturbing the peace and took him to jail.

This time the trial was held in Louisville city court, not the federal court. The magistrate ruled that streetcar companies were not under any obligation to treat Negroes exactly as they treated whites, and that any federal measures purporting to create such obligations would be "clearly invalid" under the constitutions of Kentucky and the United States. The defendant was fined, and the judge delivered a warning to Louisville Negroes that further ride-ins would be punished.

But the ride-in campaign was not halted that easily. In the following days, streetcar after streetcar was entered by Negroes who took seats in the white section. Now the drivers got off the cars entirely. On several occasions, the Negro riders drove the cars themselves, to the sound of cheers from Negro spectators. Then violence erupted. Bands of white youths and men began to throw Negro riders off the cars: windows were broken, cars were overturned, and for a time a general race riot threatened. Moderate Kentucky newspapers and many community leaders deplored the fighting; the Republican candidate for governor denounced the streetcar company's segregation policies and blamed the violence on Democratic encouragement of white extremists.

By this time, newspapers across the country were carrying reports of the conflict, and many editorials denounced the seating regulations. In Louisville, federal marshals and the United States attorney backed the rights of the Negro riders and stated that federal court action would be taken if necessary. There were even rumors that the President might send troops.

Under these threats, the streetcar company capitulated. Soon, all the city transit companies declared that "it was useless to try to resist or evade the enforcement by the United States authorities of the claim of Negroes to ride in the cars." To "avoid serious collisions," the company would thereafter allow all passengers to sit where they chose. Although a few disturbances took place in the following months, and some white intransigents boycotted the streetcars, mixed seating became a common practice. The Kentucky press soon pointed with pride to the spirit of conciliation and harmony which prevailed in travel facilities within the city, calling it a model for good race relations. Never again would Louisville streetcars be segregated.

The event may have a familiar ring, but it should not, for it occurred almost one hundred years ago, in 1871. The streetcars were horse-drawn. The

President who considered ordering troops to Louisville was ex-General Grant, not ex-General Eisenhower. The Republican gubernatorial candidate who supported the Negro riders, John Marshall Harlan, was not a post-World War II leader of the G.O.P. but a former slaveholder from one of Kentucky's oldest and most famous political families. And the "new" Negroes who waged this ride-in were not members of the Congress of Racial Equality and the National Association for the Advancement of Colored People, or followers of Dr. Martin Luther King, but former slaves who were fighting for civil rights in their own time, and with widespread success.

And yet these dramatic sit-ins, ride-ins, and walk-ins of the 1870's are almost unknown to the American public today. The standard American histories do not mention them, providing only thumbnail references to "bayonet-enforced" racial contacts during Reconstruction. Most commentators view the Negro's resort to direct action as an invention of the last decade. Clearly, then, it is time that the civil-rights struggle of the 1870's and 1880's was rescued from newspaper files and court archives, not only because it is historically important but also because it has compelling relevance for our own era.

Contrary to common assumptions today, no state in the Union during the 1870's, including those south of the Mason-Dixon line, required separation of whites and Negroes in places of public accommodation. Admission and arrangement policies were up to individual owners. In the North and West, many theatres, hotels, restaurants, and public carriers served Negro patrons without hesitation or discrimination. Some accepted Negroes only in second-class accommodations, such as smoking cars on railroads or balconies in theatres, where they sat among whites who did not have first-class tickets. Other northern and western establishments, especially the more exclusive ones, refused Negro patronage entirely.

The situation was similar in the large cities of the southern and border states. Many establishments admitted Negroes to second-class facilities. Some gave first-class service to those of privileged social status—government officials, army officers, newspapermen, and clergymen. On the other hand, many places of public accommodation, particularly in the rural areas and smaller cities of the South, were closed to Negroes whatever their wealth or status.

From 1865 through the early 1880's, the general trend in the nation was toward wider acceptance of Negro patronage. The federal Civil Rights Act of 1866, with its guarantee to Negroes of "equal benefit of the laws," had set off a flurry of enforcement suits—for denying berths to Negroes on a Washington-New York train; for refusing to sell theatre tickets to Negroes in Boston; and for barring Negro women from the waiting rooms and parlor cars of railroads in Virginia, Illinois, and California. Ratification of the Fourteenth Amendment in 1868 had spurred more challenges. Three northern states, and two southern states under Reconstruction regimes, passed laws making it a crime for owners of public-accommodation businesses to discriminate. Most state and federal court rulings on these laws between 1865 and 1880 held in favor of Negro rights, and the rulings built up a steady pressure on owners to relax racial bars.

Nevertheless, instances of exclusion and segregation continued throughout the 1870's. To settle the issue once and for all (thereby reaping the lasting appreciation of the Negro voters), congressional Republicans led by Senator Charles Sumner pressed for a federal statute making discrimination in public accommodations a crime. Democrats and conservative Republicans warned in the congressional debates that such a law would trespass on the reserved powers of the states and reminded the Sumner supporters that recent Supreme Court decisions had taken a narrow view of federal power under the Civil War amendments.

After a series of legislative compromises, however, Sumner's forces were able to enact the statute; on March 1, 1875, "An Act to Protect all Citizens in their Civil and Legal Rights" went into effect. "It is essential to just government," the preamble stated, that the nation "recognize the equality of all men before the law, and . . . it is the duty of government in its dealings with the people to mete out equal and exact justice to all, of whatever nativity, race, color, or persuasion, religious or political. . . ."

Section 1 of the act declared that "All persons within the jurisdiction of the United States shall be entitled to the full and equal enjoyment of the accommodations . . . of inns, public conveyances on land or water, theaters and other places of public amusement; subject only to the conditions and limitations established by law, and applicable alike to citizens of every race or color. . . ." Section 2 provided that any person violating the act could be sued in federal district court for a penalty of $500, could be fined $500 to $1,000, or could be imprisoned from thirty days to one year. (A separate section forbade racial discrimination in the selection of juries.)

Reaction to the law was swift. Two Negro men were admitted to the dress circle of Macauley's Theatre in Louisville and sat through the performance without incident. In Washington, Negroes were served for the first time at the bar of the Willard Hotel, and a Negro broke the color line when he was seated at McVicker's Theatre in Chicago. But in other instances, Negroes were rejected despite "Sumner's law." Several hotels in Chattanooga turned in their licenses, became private boardinghouses, and accepted whites only. Restaurants and barber shops in Richmond turned away Negro customers.

Suits challenging refusals were filed en masse throughout the country. Perhaps a hundred were decided in the federal district courts during the late 1870's and early 1880's. Federal judges in Pennsylvania, Texas, Maryland, and Kentucky, among others, held the law to be constitutional and ruled in favor of Negro complainants. In North Carolina, New Jersey, and California, however, district judges held the law invalid. And when other courts in New York, Tennessee, Missouri, and Kansas put the issue to the federal circuit judges, the judges divided on the question, and the matter was certified to the United States Supreme Court.

But the Supreme Court did not exactly rush to make its ruling. Though two cases testing the 1875 act reached it in 1876 and a third in 1877, the Justices simply held them on their docket. In 1879, the Attorney General filed a brief defending the constitutionality of the law, but still the Court reached no decisions. In 1880, three additional cases were filed, but two years elapsed before the Solicitor General presented a fresh brief supporting the statute. It was not until late in 1883 that the Supreme Court passed upon the 1875 act, in what became famous as the *Civil Rights Cases* ruling. True, the Court was badly behind in its work in this period, but clearly the Justices chose to let the civil-rights cases "ripen" for almost eight years.

When they finally came to grips with the issue, six separate test suits were involved. The most celebrated had arisen in New York City in November of 1879. Edwin Booth, the famous tragedian and brother of John Wilkes Booth, had opened a special Thanksgiving week engagement at the Grand Opera House. After playing *Hamlet, Othello,* and *Richelieu* to packed houses, he was scheduled to perform Victor Hugo's *Ruy Blas* at the Saturday matinee on November 22.

One person who had decided to see Booth that Saturday was William R. Davis, Jr., who was later described in the press as a tall, handsome, and well-spoken Negro of twenty-six. He was the business agent of the *Progressive-American,* a Negro weekly published in New York City. At 10 o'clock Saturday morning, Davis' girl friend ("a bright octoroon, almost white," as the press put it), purchased two reserved seats at the box office of the Grand Opera House. At 1:30 P.M., Davis and his lady presented themselves at the theatre, only to be told by the doorkeeper, Samuel Singleton, that "these tickets are no good." If he would step out to the box office, Singleton told Davis, his money would be refunded.

It is unlikely that Davis was surprised by Singleton's action, for this was not the first time he had encountered such difficulties. Shortly after the passage of the 1875 act, Davis had been refused a ticket to the dress circle of Booth's Theatre in New York. He had sworn out a warrant against the ticket seller, but the failure of his witness to appear at the grand jury proceedings had led to a dismissal of the complaint. This earlier episode, as well as Davis' activity as a Negro journalist, made it probable that this appearance at the Opera House in 1879 was a deliberate test of the management's discriminatory policies.

Though Davis walked out of the lobby at Singleton's request, he did not turn in his tickets for a refund. Instead, he summoned a young white boy standing near the theatre, gave him a dollar (plus a dime for his trouble), and had him purchase two more tickets. When Davis and his companion presented these to Singleton, only the lady was allowed to pass. Again Davis was told that his ticket was "no good." When he now refused to move out of the doorway, Singleton called a policeman and asked that Davis be escorted off the theatre property. The officer told Davis that the Messrs. Poole and Donnelly, the managers of the Opera House, did not admit colored persons. "Perhaps the managers do not," Davis retorted, "but the laws of the country [do]."

The following Monday, November 24, Davis filed a criminal complaint; on December 9, this time with witnesses in abundance, Singleton was indicted in what the press described as the first criminal proceeding under the 1875 act to go to trial in New York. When the case opened on January 14, 1880, Singleton's counsel argued that the 1875 law was unconstitutional. "It interferes," he said, "with the right of the State of New York to provide the means under which citizens of the State have the power to control and protect their rights in respect to their private property." The assistant United States attorney replied that such a conception of states' rights had been "exploded and superseded long ago." It was unthinkable, he declared, that "the United States could not extend to one citizen of New York a right which the State itself gave to others of its citizens—the right of admission to places of public amusement."

The presiding judge decided to take the constitutional challenge under advisement and referred it to the circuit court, for consideration at its February term. This left the decision up to Justice Samuel Blatchford of the Supreme Court, who was assigned to the circuit court for New York, and District Judge William Choate. The two judges reached opposite conclusions and certified the question to the United States Supreme Court.

Davis' case, under the title of *United States v. Singleton,* reached the Supreme Court in 1880. Already lodged on the Court's docket were four similar criminal prosecutions under the act of 1875. *U.S. v. Stanley* involved the refusal of Murray Stanley in 1875 to serve a meal at his hotel in Topeka, Kansas, to a Negro, Bird Gee. *U.S. v. Nichols* presented the refusal in 1876 of Samuel Nichols, owner of the Nichols House in Jefferson City, Missouri, to accept a Negro named W. H. R. Agee as a guest. *U.S. v. Ryan* involved the conduct of Michael Ryan, doorkeeper of Maguire's Theatre in San Francisco, in denying a Negro named George M. Tyler entry to the dress circle on January 4, 1876. In *U.S. v. Hamilton,* James Hamilton, a conductor on the Nashville, Chattanooga, and St. Louis Railroad, had on April 21, 1879, denied a Negro woman with a first-class ticket access to the ladies' car.

There was a fifth case, with a somewhat different setting. On the evening of May 22, 1879, Mrs. Sallie J. Robinson, a twenty-eight-year-old Negro, purchased two first-class tickets at Grand Junction, Tennessee, for a trip to Lynchburg, Virginia, on the Memphis and Charleston Railroad. Shortly after midnight she and her nephew, Joseph C. Robinson, described as a young Negro "of light complexion, light hair, and light blue eyes," boarded the train and started into the parlor car. The conductor, C. W. Reagin, held Mrs. Robinson back ("bruising her arm and jerking her roughly around," she alleged) and pushed her into the smoker.

A few minutes later, when Joseph informed the conductor that he was Mrs. Robinson's nephew and was a Negro, the conductor looked surprised. In that case, he said, they could go into the parlor car at the next stop. The Robinsons finished the ride in the parlor car but filed complaints with the railroad about their treatment and then sued for $500 under the 1875 act. At the trial, Reagin testified that he had thought Joseph to be a white man with a colored woman, and his experience was that such associations were "for illict purposes."

Counsel for the Robinsons objected to Reagin's testimony, on the ground that his actions were based on race and constituted no defense. Admitting the constitutionality of the 1875 law for purposes of the trial, the railroad contended that the action of its conductor did not fall within the statute. The district judge ruled that the motive for excluding persons was the decisive issue under the act: if the jury believed that the conductor had acted because he thought Mrs. Robinson "a prostitute traveling with her paramour," whether "well or ill-founded" in that assumption, the exclusion was not because of race and the railroad was not liable. The jury found for the railroad, and the Robinsons appealed.

These, with William Davis' suit against the doorkeeper of New York's Grand Opera House, were the six cases to which the Supreme Court finally turned in 1882. The Justices were presented with a learned and eloquent brief for the United States submitted by Solicitor General Samuel F. Phillips, who reviewed the leading cases, described the history of the Civil War amendments to the Constitution, and stressed the importance to the rights of citizens of equal access to public accommodation. Four times since 1865, Phillips noted, civil-rights legislation had been enacted by a Congress filled with men who had fought in the Civil War and had written the war amendments. These men understood that "every rootlet of slavery has an individual vitality, and, to its minutest hair, should be anxiously followed and plucked up. . . ." They also knew that if the federal government allowed Negroes to be denied accommodation "by persons who notably were sensitive registers of local public opinion," then "what upon yesterday was only 'fact' will become 'doctrine' tomorrow."

The Supreme Court Justices who considered Philips' brief and the six test cases were uncommonly talented, among them being Chief Justice Morrison R. Waite, a man underrated today; Joseph P. Bradley, that Court's most powerful intellect; and Stephen J. Field, a *laissez-faire* interpreter of American constitutional law. John Marshall Harlan, the youngest man on the Court, had already started on the course which was to mark him as the most frequent and passionate dissenter in the Gilded Age.

As a whole, the Court might have appeared to be one which would have looked favorably on the 1875 act. All were Republicans except Justice Field, and he was a Democrat appointed by Abraham Lincoln. All except Justice Harlan, who was the Court's only southerner, had made their careers primarily in the northern and western states. Without exception, all had supported the Northern cause in the war, and none had any hostility toward Negroes as a class.

Yet on the afternoon of October 15, 1883, Justice Bradley announced that the Court found Sections 1 and 2 of the Civil Rights Act of 1875 to be unconstitutional. (This disposed of five of the cases; the sixth, *U.S. v. Hamilton,* was denied review on a procedural point.) There was added irony in the fact that Bradley delivered the majority opinion for eight of the Justices. A one-time Whig, Bradley had struggled for a North-South compromise in the darkening months of 1860–61, then had swung to a strong Unionist position after the firing on Fort Sumter. He had run for Congress on the Lincoln ticket in 1862 and in 1868 headed the New Jersey electors for Grant. When the Thirteenth and Fourteenth Amendments were adopted, he had given them firm support, and his appointment to the Supreme Court by Grant in 1870 had drawn no criticism from friends of the Negro, as had the appointment of John Marshall Harlan seven years later.

Bradley's opinion had a tightly reasoned simplicity. The Thirteenth Amendment forbade slavery and involuntary servitude, he noted, but protection against the restoration of bondage could not be stretched to cover federal regulation of "social" discriminations such as those dealt with in the 1875 statute. As for the Fourteenth Amendment, that was addressed only to deprivations of rights by the *states;* it did not encompass *private* acts of discrimination. Thus there was no source of constitutional authority for "Sumner's law"; it had to be regarded as an unwarranted invasion of an area under state jurisdiction. Even as a matter of policy, Bradley argued, the intention of the war amendments to aid the newly freed Negro had to have some limits. At some point, the Negro must cease to be "the special favorite of the law" and take on "the rank of a mere citizen."

At the Atlanta Opera House on the evening of the Court's decision, the end man of Haverly's Minstrels interrupted the performance to announce the ruling. The entire orchestra and dress circle audience rose and cheered. Negroes sitting in the balcony kept their seats, "stunned," according to one newspaper account. A short time earlier, a Negro denied entrance to the dress circle had filed charges against the Opera House management under the 1875 act. Now his case—their case—was dead.

Of all the nine Justices, only John Marshall Harlan, a Kentuckian and a former slaveholder, announced that he dissented from the ruling. He promised to give a full opinion soon.

Justice Harlan's progress from a supporter of slavery to a civil-rights dissenter makes a fascinating chronicle. Like Bradley, he had entered politics as a Whig and had tried to find a middle road between secessionist Democrats and antislavery Republicans. Like Bradley, he became a Unionist after the firing on Fort Sumter. But there the parallels ended. Although Harlan entered the Union Army, he was totally opposed to freeing the slaves, and his distaste for Lincoln and the Radicals was complete. Between 1863 and 1868, he led the Conservative party in Kentucky, a third-party movement which supported the war but opposed pro-Negro and civil-rights measures as "flagrant invasions of property rights and local government."

Supreme Court Justice John Marshall Harlan who wrote
the dissenting opinion in *Plessy* v. *Ferguson*. (Library of
Congress)

By 1868, however, Harlan had become a Republican. The resounding defeat of the Conservatives in the 1867 state elections convinced him that a third
party had no future in Kentucky. His antimonopoly views and his general ideas
about economic progress conflicted directly with state Democratic policies,
and when the Republicans nominated his former field commander, Ulysses S.
Grant, for President, in 1868, Harlan was one of the substantial number of
Conservatives who joined the G.O.P.

His views on Negro rights also changed at this time. The wave of vigilante
activities against white Republicans and Negroes that swept Kentucky in
1868–70, with whippings and murders by the scores, convinced Harlan that
federal guarantees were essential. He watched Negroes in Kentucky moving
with dignity and skill toward useful citizenship, and his devout Presbyteri-
anism led him to adopt a "brotherhood-of-man" outlook in keeping with his
church's national position. Perhaps he may have been influenced by his wife,

Mallie, whose parents were New England abolitionists. As a realistic Republican politician, he was also aware that 60,000 Kentucky Negroes would become voters in 1870.

Thus a "new" John Harlan took the stump as Republican gubernatorial candidate in 1871, the year of the Louisville streetcar ride-ins. He opened his rallies by confessing that he had formerly been anti-Negro. But "I have lived long enough," he said, "to feel that the most perfect despotism that ever existed on this earth was the institution of African slavery." The war amendments were necessary "to place it beyond the power of any State to interfere with . . . the results of the war. . . ." The South should stop agitating the race issue, and should turn to rebuilding itself on progressive lines. When the Democrats laughed at "Harlan the Chameleon" and read quotations from his earlier anti-Negro speeches, Harlan replied: "Let it be said that I am right rather than consistent."

Harlan soon became an influential figure in the Republican party and, when President Rutherford B. Hayes decided to appoint a southern Republican to the Supreme Court in 1877, he was a logical choice. Even then, the Negro issue rose to shake Harlan's life again. His confirmation was held up because of doubts by some senators as to his "real" civil-rights views. Only after Harlan produced his speeches between 1871 and 1877 and party leaders supported his firmness on the question was he approved.

Once on the Supreme Court, Harlan could have swung back to a conservative position on civil rights. Instead, he became one of his generation's most intense and uncompromising defenders of the Negro. Perhaps his was the psychology of the convert who defends his new faith more passionately, even more combatively, than the born believer. Harlan liked to think that he had changed because he knew the South and realized that any relaxation of federal protection of the rights of Negroes would encourage the "white irreconcilables" first to acts of discrimination and then to violence, which would destroy all hope of accommodation between the races.

When Harlan sat down in October of 1883 to write his dissent in the *Civil Rights Cases,* he hoped to set off a cannon of protest. But he simply could not get his thoughts on paper. He worked late into the night, and even rose from half-sleep to write down ideas that he was afraid would elude him in the morning. "It was a trying time for him," his wife observed. "In point of years, he was much the youngest man on the Bench; and standing alone, as he did in regard to a decision which the whole nation was anxiously awaiting, he felt that . . . he must speak not only forcibly but wisely." After weeks of drafting and discarding, Harlan seemed to reach a dead end. The dissent would not "write." It was at this point that Mrs. Harlan contributed a dramatic touch to the history of the *Civil Rights Cases.*

When the Harlans had moved to Washington in 1877, the Justice had acquired from a collector the inkstand which Chief Justice Roger Taney had used in writing all his opinions. Harlan was fond of showing this to guests and remarking that "it was the very inkstand from which the infamous *Dred Scott* opinion was written." Early in the 1880's, however, a niece of Taney's, who was engaged in collecting her uncle's effects, visited the Harlans. When she saw the inkstand she asked Harlan for it, and the Justice agreed. The next morning Mrs. Harlan, noting her husband's reluctance to part with his most prized possession, quietly arranged to have the inkstand "lost." She hid it away, and Harlan was forced to make an embarrassed excuse to Taney's niece.

Now, on a Sunday morning, probably early in November of 1883, after Harlan had spent a sleepless night working on his dissent, Mallie Harlan remembered the inkstand. While the Justice was at church, she retrieved it from its hiding place, filled it with a fresh supply of ink and pen points, and placed it on the blotter of his desk. When her husband returned from church, she told him, with an air of mystery, that he would find something special in his study. Harlan was overjoyed to recover his symbolic antique. Mrs. Harlan's gesture was successful, for as she relates:

> The memory of the historic part that Taney's inkstand had played in the Dred Scott decision, in temporarily tightening the shackles of slavery upon the negro race in those ante-bellum days, seemed, that morning, to act like magic in clarifying my husband's thoughts in regard to the law . . . intended by Sumner to protect the recently emancipated slaves in the enjoyment of equal 'civil rights.' His pen fairly flew on that day and, with the running start he then got, he soon finished his dissent.

How directly the recollection of Dred Scott pervaded Harlan's dissent is apparent to anyone who reads the opinion. He began by noting that the pre-Civil War Supreme Court had upheld congressional laws forbidding individuals to interfere with recovery of fugitive slaves. To strike down the act of 1875 meant that "the rights of freedom and American citizenship cannot receive from the Nation that efficient protection which heretofore was unhesitatingly accorded to slavery and the rights of masters."

Harlan argued that the Civil Rights Act of 1875 was constitutional on any one of several grounds. The Thirteenth Amendment had already been held to guarantee "universal civil freedom"; Harlan stated that barring Negroes from facilities licensed by the state and under legal obligation to serve all persons without discrimination restored a major disability to slavery days and violated that civil freedom. As for the Fourteenth Amendment, its central purpose had been to extend national citizenship to the Negro, reversing the precedent upheld in the Dred Scott decision; its final section gave Congress power to pass appropriate legislation to enforce that affirmative grant as well as to enforce the section barring any state action which might deny liberty or equality. Now, the Supreme Court was deciding what legislation was appropriate and necessary for those purposes, although that decision properly belonged to Congress.

Even under the "State action" clause of the Fourteenth Amendment, Harlan continued, the 1875 act was constitutional; it was well established that

"railroad corporations, keepers of inns and managers of places of public accommodation are agents or instrumentalities of the State." Finally, Harlan
attacked the unwillingness of the Court's majority to uphold the public-carrier
section of the act under Congress' power to regulate interstate trips. That was
exactly what was involved in Mrs. Robinson's case against the Memphis and
Charleston Railroad, he reminded his colleagues; it had not been true before
that Congress had had to cite the section of the Constitution on which it relied.

In his peroration, Harlan replied to Bradley's comment that Negroes had
been made "a special favorite of the law." The war amendments had been
passed not to "favor" the Negro, he declared, but to include him as "part of
the people for whose welfare and happiness government is ordained."

> Today, it is the colored race which is denied, by corporations and individuals
> wielding public authority, rights fundamental in their freedom and citizenship.
> At some future time, it may be that some other race will fall under the ban of
> race discrimination. If the constitutional amendments be enforced, according to
> the intent with which, as I conceive, they were adopted, there cannot be in this
> republic, any class of human beings in practical subjection to another
> class. . . .

The *Civil Rights Cases* ruling did two things. First, it destroyed the delicate balance of federal guarantee, Negro protest, and private enlightenment
which was producing a steadily widening area of peacefully integrated public
facilities in the North and South during the 1870's and early 1880's. Second,
it had an immediate and profound effect on national and state politics as they
related to the Negro. By denying Congress power to protect the Negro's rights
to equal treatment, the Supreme Court wiped the issue of civil rights from the
Republican party's agenda of national responsibility. At the same time, those
southern political leaders who saw anti-Negro politics as the most promising
avenue to power could now rally the "poor whites" to the banner of segregation.

If the Supreme Court had stopped with the *Civil Rights Cases* of 1883,
the situation of Negroes would have been bad but not impossible. Even in the
South, there was no immediate imposition of segregation in public facilities.
During the late 1880's, Negroes could be found sharing places with whites in
many southern restaurants, streetcars, and theatres. But increasingly, Democratic and Populist politicians found the Negro an irresistible target. As Solicitor General Phillips had warned the Supreme Court, what had been tolerated
as the "fact" of discrimination was now being translated into "doctrine": between 1887 and 1891, eight southern states passed laws requiring railroads to
separate all whites and Negro passengers. The Supreme Court upheld these
laws in the 1896 case of *Plessy v. Ferguson*. Then in the Berea College case
of 1906, it upheld laws forbidding private schools to educate Negro and white
children together. Both decisions aroused Harlan's bitter dissent. In the next
fifteen or twenty years, the chalk line of Jim Crow was drawn across virtually
every area of public contact in the South.

Today, as this line is slowly and painfully being erased, we may do well to reflect on what might have been in the South if the Civil Rights Act of 1875 had been upheld, in whole or in part. Perhaps everything would have been the same. Perhaps forces at work between 1883 and 1940 were too powerful for a Supreme Court to hold in check. Perhaps "Sumner's law" was greatly premature. Yet it is difficult to believe that total, state-enforced segregation was inevitable in the South after the 1880's. If in these decades the Supreme Court had taken the same *laissez-faire* attitude toward race relations as it took toward economic affairs, voluntary integration would have survived as a countertradition to Jim Crow and might have made the transition of the 1950's less painful than it was. At the very least, one cannot help thinking that Harlan was a better sociologist than his colleagues and a better southerner than the "irreconcilables." American constitutional history has a richer ring to it because of the protest that John Marshall Harlan finally put down on paper from Roger Taney's inkwell in 1883.

20

The Week the World Watched Selma

by Stephen B. Oates

Even though the Supreme Court had declared state laws which required "separate but equal" facilities to be unconstitutional in 1954 in the historic *Brown v. Board of Education* decision, black Americans still faced blatant discrimination a decade later. One of the most fundamental results of that discrimination was the continued denial of the right to vote to blacks. In early 1965, national attention focused on Selma, Alabama, as civil rights marchers made ready to move against one of the strongest bastions of racism still existing in the United States.

Professor Stephen B. Oates of the University of Massachusetts, Amherst, recaptures the drama of that episode in the following essay. Professor Oates is uniquely qualified to provide this account, for he has written critically acclaimed biographies of Nat Turner, John Brown, Abraham Lincoln, and Martin Luther King. The Selma-to-Montgomery March had at least two significant results: it "trampled forever the old stereotype" of the compliant, submissive Southern Negro, and it led directly to the passage of the Voting Rights Act of 1965. Thus, it can truly be said that the road to Montgomery had led to a new era for black Americans.

From the frozen steps of Brown Chapel they could see the car moving toward them down Sylvan Street, past the clapboard homes and bleak, red-brick apartments that dotted the Negro section of Selma, Alabama. In a moment it pulled up at the chapel, a brick building with twin steeples, and the people on the steps sent word inside, where a mass meeting of local blacks was under way. *He was here. It was Dr. King.* They had waited for him much of the afternoon, singing freedom songs and clapping and swaying to the music. Now they rose in a burst of excitement, and local leaders rushed to greet King and his staff at the doorway. Dressed in an immaculate black suit and tie, he was a short, stocky man with a thin mustache and sad, Oriental eyes. As he mounted the speaker's platform, the crowd broke into such a tumultuous ovation that the entire church seemed to tremble.

It was January 2, 1965, a decade since the Montgomery bus boycott had launched the Negro protest movement in the South. Martin Luther King, Jr., leader of the boycott and founder and president of the Southern Christian Leadership Conference (SCLC), was here this day to help mount a concerted voting rights drive for Alabama's disenfranchised Negroes. And the cheering people in Brown Chapel were ready to follow him. Regardless of the danger, many of them believed, King would show them how to stand and walk with their backs straight, for he was the Moses of the movement and would lead them to the promised land. . . .

Civil Rights demonstrators marching from Selma to Montgomery, Alabama, in March 1965. (Library of Congress Photograph by James H. Karales. Look Collection.)

The movement had come to Selma two years before, when the Student Nonviolent Coordinating Committee (SNCC)—which King had helped establish—sent in several young workers as part of a campaign to organize Alabama blacks at the grass roots. But this proved a formidable task in Selma, an old black-belt town on the banks of the murky Alabama River, fifty-odd miles west of Montgomery. The lives of Selma's twenty-nine thousand people, more than half of them black, were regulated by a Jim Crow system that forced Negroes to live in an impoverished "colored" section and barred them from white schools, cafés, lunch counters, and theaters—and the polls.

White Selma recoiled from the boycotts and demonstrations and sit-ins and freedom rides that shook Dixie during the fifties and early sixties, recoiled from federal efforts to desegregate schools and public accommodations there. But worst of all was the arrival of the SNCC workers. A local judge, noting that they were racially mixed, wore blue overalls, and came mostly from outside Alabama, branded them "Communist agitators" in the employ of Moscow, Peking, and Havana. And agitate they did. They complained that of the fifteen thousand eligible Negro voters in Dallas County, just over three hundred were registered. Why? Because the county board of registrars met only two days a month and cheerfully rejected black applicants for reasons no more momentous than failing to cross a *t* on the registration form. The SNCC people also stirred up trouble by leading small, tentative protest marches to the courthouse in downtown Selma. At the same time, a dental hygienist named Marie Foster, a proud, forthright woman who served as secretary of a black organization called the Dallas County Voters League, conducted nighttime citizenship classes for her neighbors. These in turn led to weekly mass meetings at the Negro churches on Sylvan Street.

As the movement gained momentum in Selma, the white community sharply disagreed over what should be done. Wilson Baker, the hefty new director of the city police and a thoroughly professional lawman who had taught at the University of Alabama, was determined to avoid the kind of racial explosions that had rocked other Southern cities. With the support of Mayor Joe T. Smitherman and Selma's old and affluent families, Baker intended to meet nonviolent protest with nonviolent law enforcement, deal quietly with federal officials, and get around national civil rights laws with minimal compliance. But the die-hard segregationists—particularly the country people of Dallas County—vowed to protect the old ways, come what may.

Their spokesman was Sheriff Jim Clark, a burly fellow who hailed from rural Coffee County, where populism and Negrophobia both ran deep. Clark was out "to preserve our way of life," he told his wife, and "not let the niggers take over the whole state of Alabama." And nobody was going to get in his way.

In July, 1964, a segregationist state judge banned all marches and mass meetings in Selma, and Sheriff Clark enforced the injunction with a vengeance. By December the movement was paralyzed. In desperation local Negro leaders contacted SCLC headquarters in Atlanta and implored Dr. King to come and take charge.

So it was that King picked Selma as the next target for his civil rights crusade. Inspired by Gandhi, King had embraced nonviolent direct action as the most effective weapon to combat segregation in Dixie. While the Congress of Racial Equality had actually pioneered direct action in America, King and the SCLC had refined the technique in civil rights battlefields across the South, for the first time drawing the Negro masses there into the struggle for equality. King and his lieutenants would select some notoriously segregated city, mobilize the local blacks, and lead them on peaceful protest marches. They would escalate the marches, increase their demands, even fill up the jails, until they brought about a moment of "creative tension," when white authorities would either agree to negotiate or resort to violence, thereby laying bare the brutality inherent in segregation and appealing to the national conscience that would force the federal government to intervene. The technique failed in Albany, Georgia, where white authorities handled King's marchers with unruffled decorum ("We killed them with kindness," chuckled one city official). But it succeeded brilliantly in Birmingham, where Police Commissioner Eugene "Bull" Connor turned police dogs and firehoses on the marchers in full view of reporters and television cameras. Revolted by such scenes, Congress had produced the 1964 Civil Rights Act, which desegregated all public facilities.

And now, hurrying down to Selma in early January, 1965, King would employ nonviolent direct action again, this time against discrimination at the polls. He and his staff would defy Clark, challenge the court injunction, and start a movement that they hoped would force Congress to guarantee Southern blacks the right to vote. And Selma's embattled Negroes, thrilled that so celebrated a man would lead them personally, greeted King with the most incandescent mass meeting ever seen in Brown Chapel. They would start marching when the registrars next met, King promised them, and they would keep marching until victory was theirs. "Our cry to the state of Alabama is a simple one: *Give us the ballot!*" He had them shouting out. "We're not on our knees begging for the ballot. *We are demanding the ballot.*" They were on their feet cheering. Then they broke into the great hymn of the civil rights movement, "We Shall Overcome."

And so on January 18 the campaign began as King led four hundred people to the courthouse. Wilson Baker, however, broke them up into small groups. Otherwise, he said, he would have had to arrest them for parading without a permit, and Baker wanted no arrests.

At the courthouse, however, the marchers passed into Clark's jurisdiction. And the sheriff stood there now, in his uniform and braid-trimmed hat, gripping his billy club as King recited the grievances of local Negroes and in his most dignified manner asked that they be registered to vote. Going along with Baker for now, Clark simply ushered the demonstrators into a back alley and left them there.

But the next day wave after wave of Negroes besieged Clark's courthouse. With the campaign attracting blacks of all ages and occupations, civil rights workers told one another, "Brother, we got a *movement* goin' on in Selma."

On Monday, January 25, they were back at the courthouse again, demanding the right to vote and singing "Ain't Gonna Let Nobody Turn Me 'Round." Now they were protected by a federal court order, just handed down in Mobile over the weekend, that overruled Clark's injunction and barred city and county officials from impeding the "orderly process" of voter registration. Wearing a lapel button that read NEVER, Clark strode angrily down the line. When Mrs. Annie Lee Cooper, a huge woman, remarked that "there ain't nobody scared around here," Clark pushed her so hard that she lost her balance. She rose up, punched the sheriff to his knees, and then slugged him again. A deputy grabbed her from behind, but she stamped on his foot and elbowed him in the stomach and then knocked Clark down a second time. At last three deputies subdued Mrs. Cooper and held her fast as Clark beat her methodically with his billy club, ignoring the newsmen and their cameras.

Several black men started to interfere, but King stopped them. "Don't do it, men. I know how you feel 'cause I know how I feel. But hold your peace." He was determined to have his followers adhere to his philosophy of nonviolence, never hating or fighting their white oppressors but relying on the redemptive power of love and dignity. And it was the only way black men could protest in the South without getting killed. As the SCLC's James Bevel put

244

it later, any man who had the urge to hit white officers was a fool. "That is just what they want you to do. Then they can call you a mob and beat you to death." In any case, a photograph of the beating of Mrs. Cooper was soon circulating across the country.

That Monday night, with passions running high, local blacks crowded into Brown Chapel to hear Ralph Abernathy. A stout, earthy Baptist preacher who had marched and gone to jail with King since the early days of the movement, Abernathy soothed his people with a mixture of droll humor and defiance. He pointed to a radio antenna attached to the pulpit and said the police had installed that "doohickey" and had warned him to watch what he said. "But they forgot something when they said that," Abernathy exclaimed with his jowly face set in a frown. "They forgot that Ralph Abernathy isn't afraid of any white man, or any white man's doohickey either. In fact, I'm not afraid to talk to it, *man to man.*" He held the antenna up and cried, "Doohickey, hear me well!" and shouts and waves of laughter rolled over the sanctuary. "We don't have to spread out when we go down to that courthouse, doohickey. And the next time we go we're going to walk *together,* we're not going to go two together, twenty feet apart. We're not going to have a parade, we're just going to walk down to the courthouse. When we want to have a *parade,* doohickey, we'll get the R. B. Hudson High School Band and take over the town!"

His speech scared Mayor Smitherman. Convinced that mass demonstrations were afoot, he called in the Alabama state troopers under Colonel Al Lingo, an ally of Governor George C. Wallace and a small-town businessman with firm views about what should be done with "outside agitators." Lingo's troopers rumbled into Selma in their two-tone Fords, with the stars and bars of the Confederacy emblazoned on the front bumpers. Sensing that the moment of "creative tension" was fast approaching, King and his staff called for mass marches and mass arrests and decided that it was time for King himself to go to jail. Accordingly, on February 1, King led 250 people en masse down Selma's streets, forcing a disheartened Wilson Baker to arrest them for parading without a permit. By week's end, more than three thousand demonstrators—King and Abernathy included—were locked up in Dallas County jails, subsisting on a cup of black-eyed peas and a square of cornbread twice a day. King's incarceration, of course, made national headlines and brought reporters and television newsmen swarming into Selma.

Now that he had a national audience, King posted bond and held a news conference about his next step; he would personally ask President Lyndon Johnson to sponsor a voting rights bill for Negroes in Dixie. On February 9 King flew off to Washington for a round of talks with administration officials, including Johnson. Although the administration was actually planning some sort of voting legislation, Johnson and Vice President Hubert H. Humphrey doubted that Congress would pass an additional civil rights bill so soon after the 1964 measure. But Humphrey told King that Congress might do so "if the pressure were unrelenting."

In Selma, however, the number of marchers had begun to dwindle, and Baker's hopes were rising. If Clark could be restrained, maybe King's campaign could yet be derailed. But Clark could not be restrained. On February 10 he and his possemen attacked a column of young student marchers and drove them out of town at a run, hitting and shocking them with cattle prods. "You wanted to march, didn't you?" the possemen yelled. *"Now march!"* They chased the youngsters until they stumbled vomiting and crying into ditches.

Back from Washington, King led twenty-eight hundred furious Negroes on the biggest protest march of the campaign. At the courthouse a deputy smashed one of King's aides in the mouth with his billy club. As *Time* reported, Clark was the movement's energizing force: every time it faltered, the sheriff and his deputies revived it with some new outrage. *The Nation* proclaimed King himself "the finest tactician the South has produced since Robert E. Lee." And like Lee, *The Nation* observed, King got a lot of help from his opponents.

By now movement leaders had expanded the voting rights drive to contiguous Perry and Wilcox counties. In backwater Wilcox County racial oppression was so grim that blacks on one plantation had never even seen United States currency: they used octagonal tin coins parceled out by the white owners and shopped at a plantation commissary. Conditions were almost as bad in rural Perry County, where, aroused by King, a group of luckless Negroes attempted a night march in the county seat of Marion; Lingo's state troopers ambushed the blacks and clubbed them, sending them screaming through the streets. When Jimmie Lee Jackson, a young pulpwood cutter, tried to defend his mother and grandfather, a trooper shot him in the stomach with a revolver. An ambulance rushed him to the Negro hospital in Selma, and as he hovered near death, Colonel Lingo served Jackson for assault and battery with intent to kill a police officer. On February 26 Jackson died, and King and hundreds of blacks from the area buried him on a rainswept hillside.

After the funeral, King escalated the campaign once again. He announced a mass march to the Alabama capitol in Montgomery, to begin in Selma on Sunday, March 7, and to proceed down Highway 80—popularly known as the Jefferson Davis Highway. SCLC's James Bevel, a brooding young minister who wore denim overalls and a skullcap, had conceived the idea for the march. "I can't promise you that it won't get you beaten," King told his followers. "But we must stand up for what is right."

The announcement appalled Alabama officials: the image of hundreds of flag-waving Negroes descending on the state capitol was more than they could bear. Wallace banned the march and instructed Lingo to enforce his order "with whatever means are necessary." The governor's aides, though, assured Mayor Smitherman that there would be no violence, and Smitherman in turn promised the full cooperation of the city police. All of this infuriated Police Chief Baker. Smitherman and Wallace were both "crazy," he said, if they thought Lingo and Clark would not molest the marchers, and he threatened to resign before he would let his men participate in what was sure to become a blood bath. At last Smitherman relented and allowed the city police to stay out of the matter. Once the marchers crossed Edmund Pettus Bridge and left Selma, they would be in the hands of Lingo and Clark.

On Saturday, March 6, King was back in Atlanta, where he decided to postpone the march until the following Monday. On a conference phone call with his aides in Selma, he explained that for two straight Sabbaths he had neglected his congregation—he was co-pastor of Atlanta's Ebenezer Baptist Church—and that he really needed to preach there the next day. He would return to Selma on Monday to lead the march. All his staff agreed to the postponement except Hosea Williams, a rambunctious Army veteran with a flair for grass roots organizing. "Hosea," King warned, "you need to pray. You're not with me. You need to get with me."

On Sunday morning, though, King's aides reported that more than five hundred pilgrims were gathered at Brown Chapel and that Williams wanted permission to march that day. In his church office King thought it over and relayed word to Brown Chapel that his people could start without him. Since the march had been prohibited, he was certain that they would get arrested at the bridge. He would simply join them in jail. He expected no mayhem on Highway 80, since even the conservative Alabama press had excoriated Lingo's troopers for their savagery in Marion.

With King's blessings 525 people now left Brown Chapel in Selma and headed for Edmund Pettus Bridge toting bedrolls and blankets. Williams and John Lewis, a SNCC veteran who had been savagely beaten as a Freedom Rider several years earlier, were in the lead; an escort of borrowed ambulances took up the rear. It was gray and hazy, with a brisk March wind gusting up from the Alabama River as the column came over the crest of the bridge and saw a chilling sight. "Wallace's storm troopers," as civil rights workers called the state police, stood three deep across all four lanes of Highway 80, wearing gas masks beneath their sky-blue hard hats and armed with billy clubs. Williams turned to Lewis and asked, "John, can you swim?"

"No," Lewis replied.

"I can't either, and I'm sure we're gonna end up in that river."

As the blacks approached the wall of troopers, Major John Cloud raised a bullhorn and shouted, "You've got two minutes to disperse! Turn around and go back to your church! You will not be allowed to march any further!" Six seconds later Cloud ordered a charge, and the troopers waded in with clubs flailing. They shoved the front ranks back, fractured Lewis's skull, hammered women and men alike to the ground. Then they regrouped and attacked again, this time firing canisters. "Tear gas!" a marcher cried. Soon clouds of yellow and white smoke swirled across the highway, and the marchers fell back choking.

As white onlookers cheered, Clark's mounted posse now rode out from between two buildings, their leader bellowing, "Get those goddamn niggers!"

With a Rebel yell, the posseman charged into the Negroes, lashing out at them with bullwhips and rubber tubing wrapped in barbed wire. "Please, no!" a marcher cried. "My God, we're being killed." In chaos the blacks retreated to Brown Chapel, the road behind them littered with bedrolls, shoes, and purses. At the chapel some Negroes hurled bricks and bottles at the possemen, while Lewis—his head covered with blood—and Williams guided their stricken people inside. The air reeked of tear gas as they huddled in the sanctuary, some groaning and weeping, others in shock.

Outside, Wilson Baker tried to assume jurisdiction, but the sheriff pushed past him, shouting, "I've already waited a month too damned long about moving in!" At that, his possemen stormed through the Negro section, beating people, and shoving their way into the First Baptist Church, where they seized a black youth and flung him through a stained-glass window depicting Christ as the Good Shepherd. At last Baker ordered Clark to "get your cowboys the hell out of here," whereupon the possemen raged through downtown Selma, pounding on the hoods of Negroes' cars and yelling, "Get the hell out of town. We want all the niggers off the streets." By nightfall seventeen blacks had been hospitalized and seventy others treated for injuries.

That evening, ABC television interrupted its Sunday-night movie, *Judgment at Nuremberg,* to show a film clip of Selma's bloody Sunday. In Washington, President Johnson publicly deplored such brutality; thousands of people in cities all over the country marched in sympathy demonstrations over the next few days.

In Atlanta, Martin Luther King was horrified at the news and guilt-stricken that he had not been there with his people. But the events on Sunday also gave him an inspiration: he had long complained that clergymen "have too often been the taillight rather than the headlight" of the civil rights movement, and here was a tremendous opportunity to enlist them actively in the struggle. Accordingly he sent out a flurry of telegrams, summoning religious leaders across the nation to join him in Selma for "a ministers' march to Montgomery" on Tuesday, March 9.

The response was sensational. Overnight some four hundred ministers, rabbis, priests, nuns, students, and lay leaders—black and white alike—rushed to stand in Selma's streets with King. State authorities branded them all agitators. "Why not?" one retorted. "An agitator is the part of the washing machine that gets the dirt out."

On Monday morning King's attorneys filed into Judge Frank M. Johnson's U.S. District Court in Montgomery and asked that he enjoin Alabama officials from blocking Tuesday's march. King expected a favorable ruling since Johnson was thought to be the most sympathetic to civil rights of all the federal judges in the Deep South. But Judge Johnson refused to hand down an injunction that day. Instead he asked King to postpone the march until after a court hearing on Tuesday. At first King agreed. But when he reached Selma on Monday evening and found all those clergymen prepared to stand with him, he resolved to march as planned.

All that night civil rights leaders debated about what kind of march should be undertaken. Should they attempt to reach Montgomery or settle for a token demonstration here in Selma? Clearly the troopers and possemen would be massed out on Highway 80 tomorrow. Under considerable duress, King argued that it was not the nonviolent way to try to break through an armed wall, and he sold his colleagues on a compromise. They would march to the site of Sunday's beatings and confront the police line, making it clear to all the world that Alabama planned to stop them with violence. Then they would turn back.

Tuesday morning brought an unexpected blow: Judge Johnson officially banned the march that day. For the most part the federal judiciary had been a powerful ally of the movement; but now King would have to proceed in defiance of a federal court order, and some advisers pressed him to cancel the march lest he alienate the very Washington politicians on whom his hopes depended. But King would not cancel the march, he said; he could not cancel it. If he waited until after protracted court hearings, all the clergymen in Selma might leave, public interest evaporate, and a decisive moment in the struggle be irretrievably lost. And there was still another consideration: if he did nothing today, pent-up emotions might explode into "an uncontrollable situation." He had to march at least to the police barrier.

Attorney General Nicholas Katzenbach phoned and asked King not to march. "Mr. Attorney General," King said, "you have not been a black man in America for three hundred years."

At Brown Chapel that afternoon, some fifteen hundred marchers listened quietly as King spoke of his "painful and difficult decision" to defy the court injunction. "I do not know what lies ahead of us. There may be beatings, jailings, and tear gas. But I would rather die on the highways of Alabama than make a butchery of my conscience." He led them through town two abreast, stopping at the Pettus Bridge to hear a U.S. marshal read the court's restraining order. Then he walked them out to the Jefferson Davis Highway, where columns of state troopers, with billy clubs, again barred their way.

"You are ordered to stop and stand where you are," Major Cloud boomed through his bullhorn. "This march will not continue." King shot back, "We have a right to march. There is also a right to march on Montgomery."

When Cloud repeated his order, King asked him to let them pray. "You can have your prayer," Cloud replied, "and then you must return to your church." Behind him the troopers stood sullen and still. As hundreds of marchers knelt in the crisp sunlight, King motioned to Abernathy. "We come to present our bodies as a living sacrifice," Abernathy intoned. "We don't have much to offer, but we do have our bodies, and we lay them on the altar today." In another prayer, a Methodist bishop from Washington, D.C., compared this to the exodus out of Egypt and asked God to part the Red Sea and let them through. As he finished, Cloud turned to his men and shouted, "Clear the road completely—move out!" At that the troopers stood aside, leaving the way to Montgomery clear. The Methodist bishop was awe-struck, certain that God had answered his prayer.

King eyed the troopers suspiciously. He sensed a trap. "Let's return to the church," he said, "and complete our fight in the courts." And the marchers, some singing "Ain't Gonna Let Nobody Turn Me 'Round," headed unmolested back into town.

Back at Brown Chapel, King pronounced the march a victory and promised that he and his people would get to Montgomery one day. Most of his followers were content with the abbreviated march, but the Methodist bishop felt betrayed. And the SNCC people were furious. They wanted to storm on to Montgomery that day, even if it meant crashing through Lingo's line. Many of the students were already jealous of King, feeling that SNCC had begun the Selma movement but King and "SLICK" had received all the glory. Now they censured him bitterly for turning around at the police barrier, fumed about the white people he had brought into the movement, and denounced his admonitions to love those who oppressed them. "If we can't sit at the table of democracy," aged SNCC executive director James Forman, "we'll knock the ----ing legs off." Soon SNCC was in virtual rebellion against "de Lawd"— their name for King—and officially withdrew from his projected Montgomery trek, although members could still participate as individuals.

Harmony between King and SNCC was not the only casualty of Tuesday's demonstration. That night James Reeb, a Unitarian minister from Boston, and several other whites dined at a Negro café. Afterward, on their way to SCLC headquarters, four men emerged from the shadows and fell upon them with clubs, one smashing Reeb in the head. Reeb collapsed in a coma, and an ambulance sped him to a hospital.

In Selma, Reeb's beating touched off fresh waves of protest marches— one led by six smiling nuns from St. Louis. When Mayor Smitherman banned all demonstrations and Wilson Baker tied a rope across Sylvan Street, civil rights workers dubbed it the "Berlin wall" and started a round-the-clock, sit-down prayer vigil in front of Brown Chapel. Two days later, in a chill rain, an unshaven, red-eyed Baker brought them the news that Reverend Reeb had died.

Reeb's murder whipped up a storm of public indignation. Telephone calls and telegrams blazed into Washington with demands that federal troops be sent to Selma. President Johnson said that he was "concerned, perturbed, and frustrated," then came to a momentous decision: he announced that he intended to appear before Congress the following Monday night, March 15, and personally submit a strict new voting rights bill. The President even asked King to be his special guest in the Senate gallery.

But King was in Selma that Monday, conducting a memorial service for Reeb at the courthouse. That night he and his assistants settled down to watch Johnson's congressional appearance on television, the first time a President had personally given a special message on domestic legislation in nineteen years. "It is wrong—deadly wrong—to deny any of your fellow Americans the right to vote," Johnson said in his slow Texas drawl, and he reviewed all the obstacles to Negro voting in the South. His bill proposed to abolish these impediments through federal overseers who would supervise registration in segregated counties—exactly what King had been demanding. With Congress interrupting him repeatedly with applause, Johnson pointed out that "at times history and fate meet at a single time in a single place to shape a turning point in man's unending search for freedom. So it was at Lexington and Concord. So it was a century ago at Appomattox. So it was last week at Selma, Alabama." But "even if we pass this bill, the battle will not be over. What happened in Selma is part of a far larger movement . . . the effort of American Negroes to secure for themselves the full blessings of American life." In closing he spoke out of his south Texas past and his own brush with poverty and racism as a young school-teacher. "Their cause must be our cause too. Because it's not just Negroes, but really it's all of us who must overcome the crippling legacy of bigotry and injustice." He added slowly and deliberately, "And we *shall* overcome!"

Congress exploded in a standing ovation, the second of the night, indicating that the passage of Johnson's bill was certain. As television cameras swept the hall, King wept. "President Johnson," he said later, "made one of the most eloquent, unequivocal, and passionate pleas for human rights ever made by the President of the United States."

Nine days later, in Montgomery, Judge Frank Johnson handed the movement still another victory. After almost a week of hearings, during which contempt charges against King were dropped, Johnson ordered Alabama officials not to interfere with the Selma-to-Montgomery march. The plan Johnson endorsed, one worked out with military precision by civil rights leaders, called for the pilgrimage to commence on March 21 and culminate in Montgomery four days later. Only three hundred select people were to cover the entire distance, with a giant rally at the Alabama capitol to climax the journey. "The extent of the right to assemble, demonstrate, and march should be commensurate with the wrongs that are being protested and petitioned against," Judge Johnson ruled. "In this case, the wrongs are enormous."

King and his followers were ecstatic, but Wallace was furious. He telegraphed President Johnson that Alabama could not protect the marches because it would cost too much. Scolding Wallace for refusing to maintain law and order in his state ("I thought you felt strongly about this"), the President federalized 1,863 Alabama National Guardsmen and dispatched a large contingent of military police, U.S. marshals, and other federal officials to Selma.

And so on Sunday, March 21, some thirty-two hundred marchers left the sunlit chinaberry trees around Brown Chapel and set off for Montgomery. In the lead were King and Abernathy, flanked by Ralph Bunche of the United Nations, also a Nobel Prize winner, and Rabbi Abraham Heschel of the Jewish Theological Seminary of America, with his flowing white beard and wind-tossed hair. Behind them came maids and movie stars, housewives and clergymen, nuns and barefoot college students, civil rights workers and couples pushing baby carriages. In downtown Selma, Clark's deputies directed traffic, and the sheriff himself, still wearing his NEVER button, stood scarcely noticed on a street corner. As two state trooper cars escorted the marchers across the bridge, a record-store loudspeaker blared "Bye Bye Blackbird."

The procession headed out Highway 80 now, helicopters clattering overhead and armed troops standing at intervals along the route. Several hundred whites lined the roadside, too, and a car with "Cheap ammo here" and "Open season on niggers" painted on the sides, cruised by in the opposite lane. Confederate flags bristled among the bystanders, some of whom gestured obscenely and held up signs that read, "Nigger lover," "Martin Luther Kink," and "Nigger King go home!" A woman in her early thirties screeched, "You all got your birth-control pills? You all got your birth-control pills?" On the whole, though, the spectators looked on in silence as King and his fellow blacks, United States flags floating overhead, trampled forever the old stereotype of the obsequious Southern Negro.

At the first encampment, some seven miles out, most people headed back to Selma by car and bus. King and the rest bedded down for the night in well-guarded hospital tents, the men in one and the women in another. "Most of us were too tired to talk," recalled Harris Wofford, a friend of King and a former adviser to John F. Kennedy. But a group of Dallas county students sang on: "Many good men have lived and died,/So we could be marching side by side."

The next morning, wrote a *New York Times* reporter, "the encampment resembled a cross between a *Grapes of Wrath* migrant labor camp and the Continental Army bivouac at Valley Forge," as the marchers, bundled in blankets, huddled around their fires downing coffee and oatmeal. At eight they stepped off under a cloudless sky.

As they tramped through the rolling countryside, carloads of federal lawmen guarded their flanks, and a convoy of army vehicles, utility trucks, and ambulances followed in their wake. Far ahead Army patrols checked out every bridge and searched the fields and forests along the highway. Presently, a sputtering little plane circled over the marchers and showered them with racist leaflets. They were signed by White Citizens Action, Inc., which claimed the leaflets had been dropped by the "Confederate Air Force."

At the Lowndes County line, where the highway narrowed to two lanes, the column trimmed down to the three hundred chosen to march the distance. They called themselves the Alabama Freedom Marchers, most of them local blacks who were veterans of the movement, the rest assorted clerics and civil rights people from across the land. There was Sister Mary Leoline of Kansas City, a gentle, bespectacled nun whom roadside whites taunted mercilessly, suggesting what she really wanted from the Negro. There was one-legged James Letherer of Michigan, who hobbled along on crutches and complained that his real handicap was that "I cannot do more to help these people vote." There was eighty-two-year-old Cager Lee, grandfather of Jimmie Lee Jackson, who could march only a few miles a day, but would always come back the next, saying, "Just got to tramp some more." There was seventeen-year-old Joe Boone, a Negro who had been arrested seven times in the Selma demonstrations. "My mother and father never thought this day would come," he said. "But it's here and I want to do my part. "There was loquacious Andrew Young, King's gifted young executive director, who acted as field general of the march, running up and down the line tending the sick and the sunburned. And above all there was King himself, clad in a green cap and a blue shirt, strolling with his wife, Coretta, at the front of his potluck army.

They were deep inside Lowndes County now, a remote region of dense forests and snake-filled swamps. Winding past trees festooned with Spanish moss, the column came to a dusty little Negro community called Trickem Crossroads. Walking next to King, Andrew Young pointed at an old church and called back to the others: "Look at that church with the shingles off the roof and the broken windows! Look at that! That's why we're marching!" Across from it was a dilapidated Negro school propped up on red bricks, a three-room shanty with asphalt shingles covering the holes in its sides. A group of old people and children were standing under the oak trees in front of the school, squinting at King in the sunlight. When he halted the procession, an old woman ran from under the trees, kissed him breathlessly, and ran back crying, "I done kissed him! I done kissed him!" "Who?" another asked. "The Martin Luther King!" she exclaimed "I done kissed the Martin Luther King!"

On the third day out King left Alabama and flew off for an important speaking engagement in Cleveland; he would rejoin the marchers outside Montgomery. It rained most of the day, sometimes so hard that water splattered off the pavement. The marchers toiled seventeen endless miles through desolate, rain-swept country, some dropping out in tears from exhaustion and blistered feet. When they staggered into a muddy campsite that evening, incredible news awaited them from Montgomery. The Alabama legislature had charged by a unanimous vote that the marchers were conducting wild interracial sex orgies at their camps. "All these segregationists can think of is fornication," said one black marcher, "and that's why there are so many shades of Negroes." Said another, "Those white folks must think we're supermen, to be able to march all day in that weather, eat a little pork and beans, make whoopee all night, and then get up the next morning and march all day again."

On Wednesday, as the weary marchers neared the outskirts of Montgomery, the Kings, Abernathys, and hundreds of others joined them for a triumphal entry into the Alabama capital. "We have a new song to sing tomorrow," King told them. "We *have* overcome." James Letherer hobbled in the lead now, his underarms rubbed raw by his crutches and his face etched with pain. Flanking him were two flag bearers—one black and one white—and a young Negro man from New York who played "Yankee Doodle" on a fife. As the marchers swept past a service station, a crew-cut white man leaped from his car, raised his fist, and started to shout something, only to stand speechless as the procession of clapping, singing people seemed to go on forever.

253

And so they were in Montgomery at last. On Thursday the largest civil rights demonstration in Southern history made a climactic march through the city, first capital and "cradle" of the old Confederacy. Protected by eight hundred federal troops, twenty-five thousand people passed the Jefferson Davis Hotel, with a huge Rebel flag draped across its front, and Confederate Square, where Negroes had been auctioned in slavery days. There were the three hundred Freedom Marchers in front, now clad in orange vests to set them apart. There were hundreds of Negroes from the Montgomery area, one crying as she walked beside Harris Wofford, "This is the day! This is the day!" There was a plump, bespectacled white woman who carried a basket in one arm and a sign in the other: "Here is one native Selman for freedom and justice." There were celebrities such as Joan Baez and Harry Belafonte, the eminent American historians John Hope Franklin and C. Vann Woodward. Like a conquering army, they surged up Dexter Avenue to the capitol building, with Confederate and Alabama flags snapping over its dome. It was up Dexter Avenue that Jefferson Davis's first inaugural parade had moved, and it was in the portico of the capitol that Davis had taken his oath of office as President of the slave-based Confederacy. Now, more than a century later, Alabama Negroes—most of them descendants of slaves—stood massed at the same statehouse, singing "We Have Overcome" with state troopers and the statue of Davis himself looking on.

Wallace refused to come out of the capitol and receive the Negroes' petition. He peered out the blinds of his office, chuckling when an aide cracked, "An inauguration crowd may look like that in a few years if the voting rights bill passes." But a moment later Wallace said to nobody in particular, "That's quite a crowd out there."

Outside King mounted the flatbed of a trailer, television cameras focusing in on his round, intense face. "They told us we wouldn't get here," he cried over the loudspeaker. "And there were those who said that we would get here only over their dead bodies, but all the world today knows that we are here and that we are standing before the forces of power in the state of Alabama saying, 'We ain't gonna let nobody turn us around.' " For ten years now, he said, those forces had tried to nurture and defend evil, "but evil is choking to death in the dusty roads and streets of this state. So I stand before you today with the conviction that segregation is on its deathbed, and the only thing uncertain about it is how costly the segregationists and Wallace will make the funeral."

Not since his "I Have a Dream" speech at the Lincoln Memorial had an audience been so transfixed by his words rolling out over the loudspeaker in rhythmic, hypnotic cadences. "Let us march on to the realization of the American dream," he cried. "Let us march on the ballot boxes, march on poverty, march on segregated schools and segregated housing, march on until racism is annihilated and America can live at peace with its conscience. That will be a day not of the white man, not of the black man. That will be the day of man as man. How long will it take? I come to say to you this afternoon, however difficult the moment, however frustrating the hour, it will not be long, because truth pressed to earth will rise again. How long? Not long, because no lie can live forever. How long? Not long, because you will reap what you sow. How long? Not long, because the arm of the moral universe is long but it bends toward justice." Then King launched into "The Battle Hymn of the Republic," crying out, "Our God is marching on! Glory, glory hallelujah! Glory, glory hallelujah! Glory, glory hallelujah!"

In August, Congress enacted the voting rights bill, and Johnson signed it into law in the same room in which Lincoln had endorsed the first confiscation act, which seized all slaves employed in the Confederate war effort. And for those who had participated, the movement of 1965 became the central event in their lives. They were surprised at themselves, proud of the strength they had displayed in confronting the state of Alabama, happy indeed, as one of the marches put it, to be "a new Negro in a new South—a Negro who is no longer afraid."

During the summer of 1977 I visited Selma and interviewed some of the people who had been involved in the movement. Among them was Mrs. Richie Jean Jackson, an articulate, animated black teacher whose home had often served as King's Selma headquarters. On a brilliant June afternoon she took me to all the sites of the movement, to the marble courthouse, Sylvan Street, and Brown Chapel, wheeling her Gran Torino through Selma with uninhibited gusto. The city's police force and city council were both racially mixed now, she told me, the schools and public accommodations all integrated. She related how Wilson Baker had defeated Clark in a bitter election for sheriff in 1966, how Baker was dead now and Clark was gone (nobody knew where), and how she and her white team teacher could tease and talk to each other without worrying about a color barrier. "I would rather live here now than anywhere else," she said. "Though we still need a few more funerals."

Later that same day I called on Marie Foster, Mrs. Jackson's sister-in-law. As we sipped coffee in her neat, well-furnished home, she recounted those days in vivid detail, squinting her eyes and wrinkling her nose when she stressed a point. On the third day of the great march to Montgomery, she recalled, she became so tired that she could hardly lift her feet. "Andy Young saw how tired I was and walked a ways with me. 'Come on, Mrs. Foster,' he said, 'I'm gonna put you in one of the escort cars.' But I shook my head and kept on somehow, and Andy Young just smiled and shook his head and went on down the line. In camp that night I rubbed alcohol on my feet—there were all swollen and sore—and I prayed. I asked God to please help me, please give me the strength to go on tomorrow." She paused. "Well, He must've been working on me, because the next morning I was refreshed and ready. It was a wonderful experience—the march into Montgomery. We all felt so close to each other. I'll never forget it." She brought out a box and showed me a pair of shoes. Across the top of the box she had written: "Shoes that carried me through 50 mile trek from Selma to Montgomery, Ala. 1965. We walked for freedom, that we might have the right to vote."

21

The Great Fight: Mr. Jake vs. John L. Sullivan

by James A. Cox

As the United States was moving from a rural-agrarian society to an urban-industrialized nation in the late 19th century, more was changing than demographics and economics. America was experiencing soical change as well, including the emergence of spectator sports as a new found passion for city dwellers. Vicarious thrills were available by watching sporting events and from reading about them in the new sports pages of a few newspapers such as the *National Police Gazette*.

One of the most popular sports of the era was boxing. With its violence and rugged individual effort this brutal form of sporting encounter appealed to the hordes of Americans now trapped in the big cities and deprived of the adventure of the frontier. The great hero of these new boxing fans was the Boston Strong Boy, John L. Sullivan. Although Queensbury rules were coming into favor, in 1889 the Great John L. agreed to defend his championship title in a bare knuckles fight. In what would be the last major bare knuckles bout in America, Sullivan would fight Jake Kilrain. On a hot July day in Mississippi these two men would give the nation a last glimpse of a violent, bloody, hand-to-hand style struggle. America was changing, but on that day in July, sports fans would love the last of the frontier style fights.

James A. Cox, a free lance writer from New Jersey and the author of other sports related articles, gives us a vivid and entertaining look at this last great championship fight of its kind in the United States.

At a few minutes past 4 P.M. on July 7, 1889, a special three-car train chugs out of the Queen and Crescent Yards in New Orleans. In theory, the time of departure is known only to a privileged few, among them Bud Renaud, New Orleans sportsman and fight promoter, Col. Charles W. Rich, Mississippi gambler and sawmill operator, and, of course, the parties of the principals— John L. Sullivan, the celebrated "Boston Strong Boy" and heavyweight champion of the world, and challenger Jake Kilrain.

The train's destination is supposed to be secret, too. New Orleans has been seething with rumors for days, and the governors of Louisiana, Alabama, Mississippi and Texas in concert have vowed that no barbaric bare-knuckles contest—illegal in all 38 states—will take place within the borders of their fair constituencies. In fact, Governor Lowry of Mississippi has put out what almost amounts to a contract on Sullivan. He is still burning over indignities suffered seven years before when John L., a brash boozy youth, ignored his prohibitions and stripped the title from Paddy Ryan after nine brutal rounds in full view of the verandah of the gracious Barnes Hotel in Mississippi City. With vengeful spirit but no legal justification, he has offered a flat $1,500 reward for the arrest of the champion.

But now, somehow, the location of the fight site has leaked out: in Mississippi, somewhere in the 10,000-acre tract of pinelands surrounding Charlie Rich's place in Richburg, near Hattiesburg, about 100 miles north of New Orleans.

The telegraph chatters and Governor Lowry summons the militia to guard all the main roads and rail lines from Louisiana into Mississippi. In the Queen & Crescent rail yards, a mob scene takes place. Two cars of the special train are taken over by the fighters and their parties. A third car, the boxcar, separates them. A smiling Sullivan rides in the rear car with a handful of cronies, plus fighting gear—shoes, towels and sponges. In the front car with Kilrain are Richard K. Fox, publisher of the *National Police Gazette* of pink-sheet fame, Bat Masterson, former marshal of Dodge City, and various solemn-looking men who talk softly without moving their lips much. The crowd continues to gather, trying to clamber aboard. But before the militia catch them, the fighters' train pulls out, forcing its way through the crowds. Word spreads that the fight is scheduled now to start soon after dawn to avoid the heat. The operators of the Q & C, knowing a good thing when they see it, hastily assemble additional trains to accommodate the thousands left behind.

Two trains leave in the early morning, jammed so tight with gambling men, sports enthusiasts, pickpockets, armed thugs and opportunists—including Renaud, Charley Johnston, who was "a very important gentleman" from New York City, and Steve Brodie, still basking in the glory of his alleged leap off the Brooklyn Bridge—that a man can't reach for the pint flask in his own hip pocket without risk of starting a border war.

The ride, often through mist-shrouded swamps, is slow, with long delays, in sweltering boxes, over slippery tracks. There is some confusion as to what happens next. According to one version, when the trains reach the Mississippi state line, a company of Governor Lowry's militia is waiting, bayonets stacked in a barricade across the track. The fireman piles on the coal and the train barrels through, sending bayonets whizzing past the ears of the militiamen as they dive for the safety of trackside ditches. The other, more likely, version is that the railroad dispatcher reroutes the train along the ghost run through southwestern Mississippi—where gaunt cypress trees wade into dark grottoes, and frogs never hush—and then northeast to Hattiesburg.

Finally, at about 9 A.M., the engines wheeze to a stop at Charlie Rich's lumber camp. Carriages have been provided for the important people. Half of the rest scatter urgently into the underbrush, while the other half trail the carriages to a clearing in the woods where Charlie's crew has been working all night by the sputtering orange glare of pine-knot torches, erecting a ring, several tiers of wooden seats and spreading sawdust liberally on the ground.

While the fighters and their corner men are readying themselves for the upcoming fray (there'll be no steins of bourbon this time, John L., not with William Muldoon, a wrestling champion and physical-conditioning fanatic in charge of training), let's take a moment to look at the circumstances and personalities in the unfolding drama.

Richard Kyle Fox could have been a hero in the Horatio Alger stories. He arrived in New York City from Dublin in 1874, a penniless 29-year-old, got a job on a newspaper, saved his money and two years later purchased the *National Police Gazette,* a weekly heavy with scandal and sensation that had fallen on evil days. The first thing Fox did when he took over was to emblazon his name, "Richard K. Fox, Editor & Proprietor," on the masthead. The second thing was to add to the *Gazette's* pink pages a sports section, a feature unheard of in newspapers of the time. Baseball and football were just getting started and the first ball hadn't been tossed through a peach basket yet. But there were many races and prizefights, the latter growing in public interest despite—or because of—the proscriptions against them.

To add to the excitement and at the same time boost the *Gazette's* circulation, Fox promoted competitions of every kind imaginable, awarding "championship" belts, cups and trophies (which usually featured his mustachioed visage) with a lavish hand. There were contests for steeple climbing, oyster opening, hair cutting, one-legged dancing, sculling and female pugilism. There was a special trophy for one George A. Sampson, who supported a scale-model Ferris wheel on his chest; one for the bartender who could make a pousse-café with the most layers; and another one for poor Billy Wells, who balanced a block of iron on his head while somebody went at it with a sledge hammer.

The *Gazette,* avidly read by men and boys all over the country, soon became the sportsman's Bible. Its circulation zoomed and Richard K. Fox, now a dapper millionaire in his mid-30s, found himself the most influential figure in the sports world.

One evening in the spring of 1881, Fox was sitting at his usual table in Harry Hill's Dance Hall and Boxing Emporium, located on the edge of New York's Bowery. Harry Hill's was known as "the best of the worst places," and everybody who was anybody made it a point to be seen there—Diamond Jim Brady, Lillian Russell, P. T. Barnum, James Gordon Bennett Jr., Thomas A. Edison (ostensibly to see how his new light bulbs were working), even Oscar Wilde and the noted Brooklyn divine, Henry Ward Beecher.

The entertainment on this particular evening had been supplied by a muscular 22-year-old brawler from Boston named John Lawrence Sullivan. This was the same cocky young man who had been touring the vaudeville circuit, offering $50 to anyone who could last four rounds with him in "sparring exhibitions," so called in order to stay within the law. In fact, John L. would simply climb into the ring, glower at the audience and roar, "I can lick any sonovabitch in the house!"

The Boston Strong Boy knew little about ring science, but he carried 195 pounds of solid muscle on a 5-foot-10½-inch frame and packed a mighty wallop in either hand. "It was like being hit by a runaway horse," said Professor Mike Donovan, later to become famous as the sparring partner of Teddy Roosevelt. The professor was one of the few who managed to last for three rounds with Sullivan.

Now, at Harry Hill's place, John L. put away Steve Taylor, a good boxer with a local reputation, in the middle of the second round. Following his established pattern, he helped drag the fallen gladiator back to his corner, fussed over him until he came to and slipped him a couple of dollars for his trouble. Then, raising his arms for silence, he made a few remarks suitable to the occasion, ending up with the quaintly formal sign-off that was to become his trademark: "Always on the level, yours very truly, John L. Sullivan."

A short time later, back in his street clothes, he took over one of Harry Hill's tables and busied himself using the $50 he had kept from Steve Taylor to buy drinks for a crowd of friends and hangers-on.

"So that's Sullivan," said Richard K. Fox, seated a few tables away. He stroked his silky handlebar mustache with one beringed hand and raised a manicured finger on the other. "Tell Sullivan," he said to the waiter who materialized, "to come over here. I want to talk to him."

Surrounded by sycophants, pulling lustily on his stein of bourbon and very full of himself, John L. was in no mood to tug his forelock and play lackey to anyone. "You tell Fox," he bellowed, loud enough to be heard all over the room, "that if he wants to see me he can goddamn well come over to *my* table!"

No one had ever talked to the great Fox like that before. He never forgot it. And he never forgave it.

Time passed. The following February Sullivan took only ten minutes and 30 seconds to wrest the championship from Paddy Ryan, a husky immigrant bartender who enjoyed the support of Richard K. Fox. "When Sullivan struck me," Ryan confessed, "I thought a telegraph pole had been shoved against me endways." Game to the end, Paddy showed up at Sullivan's victory party at the St. James in New Orleans and, as John L. himself later put it, "partook of our festivities."

John L. Sullivan, champion of America, went on an eight-month tour across the country, now offering $1,000 to anyone who could stay four rounds with him, Marquis of Queensberry Rules. These rules, then coming into favor, were substantially the same as they are now: padded gloves, three-minute rounds with a one-minute recess, the count of ten for a knockout. In the old London Prize-Ring Rules, still in force when Sullivan began his career, the fighters fought bareknuckle or with skin-tight leather gloves. They wrestled, too, grabbing anywhere above the waist, which is why the old-time fighters shaved their heads. A round lasted until one fighter was knocked down by a punch, thrown by a wrestling hold or slipped. He then got a 30-second rest, after which "time" was called, giving him eight more seconds to come to the "scratch," a line marked in the middle of the ring. If he couldn't make it, he was declared "knocked out of time," which phrase was later shortened to "knocked out." There was no specified number of rounds—a bare-knuckle fight was a fight to the finish.

Sullivan much preferred the Queensberry Rules. But he took on anybody, any time, any rules. In exhibitions and official bouts his first two years as champ, he knocked out 34 men, failing to deck only Tug Wilson—an experienced pugilist backed by Fox—who managed to last the required four rounds by running, clinching, and slipping to the floor without being hit. In ensuing years hundreds more fell before the terrible power of Sullivan's fists, including a number of hopefuls handpicked by Fox in his vendetta to "get" Sullivan. By 1887, the Boston Strong Boy had grown into the Great John L., an international figure who shook the hands of princes and presidents and was lionized wherever he went.

Meantime, Fox had come up with a new pretender, a solid heavyweight born John Killion on Long Island, who fought under the name of Jake Kilrain. Jake had battled some of the best fighters around and had gone to a draw with Charlie Mitchell, the little Englishman who was growing into such a large thorn in John L.'s side. Somewhere along the line—the facts are unclear—Fox apparently goaded Sullivan into agreeing verbally to meet Kilrain for the championship. Later, John L. refused to acknowledge the agreement, if indeed there was one. Furious, Fox declared that Sullivan had forfeited the title. He announced that Jake Kilrain was champion of America, and awarded him a special diamond-studded silver *Police Gazette* championship belt, then matched Jake with the British champion Jem Smith for the world title.

Sullivan's loyal Boston admirers were not going to sit still for that. A committee was set up (by Pat Sheedy, John L.'s manager, some cynics claim) and contributions were solicited for a tribute that would make Fox look like a piker. From the proceeds came "The $10,000 Belt." It was reported to be the largest piece of flat gold ever seen in the country, 50 inches long and 12 inches wide. The center panel spelled out John L.'s name in tiny diamonds; eight other panels carried his portraits, the U.S. Seal and assorted American eagles and Irish harps. To top everything off, the entire bauble was studded with still more diamonds, 397 of them in all.

The presentation of the belt at the old Boston Theater on August 8, 1887, was attended by 3,500 fans, among them the mayor of the city and other local politicians. It was there that Sullivan probably uttered one of his most memorable statements: "I wouldn't put Fox's belt around the neck of a goddamn dog!" The crowd loved it. Somebody passed the hat. John L. took home $4,000.

A victorious six-month tour of England and the Continent followed. But returning home in April 1888, he embarked on another long toot. And this time the high living—night after night on the town, huge steaks, magnums of champagne, steins of bourbon and big black cigars without number—began to take its toll. From 195 pounds, his best fighting weight, he ballooned to 240, all flab. Worse, the booze accomplished what no man had been able to do—put him down for the count. For nine weeks Sullivan took to his bed, as he later noted in his autobiography, with "typhoid fever, gastric fever, inflammation of the bowels, heart trouble, and liver complaint all combined," which seemed to some cynics a rather elaborate way of describing the D.T.'s. Five physicians tapped and dosed him, and he thought he was going to die. Even when he got up he had incipient paralysis, whatever that is, and went on crutches for six weeks. There also were rumors of a "mysterious itch."

Never would there be a better time to "get" the bloated Boston boaster, Richard Kyle Fox reasoned. In barter shops, saloons, livery stables, firehouses and police stations all over the country, *Gazette* readers were told that Sullivan was near death's door and would probably never be able to fight again; and, conversely, that he was using his sickness as an excuse for evading a fight with the "real champion," Jake Kilrain.

Week after week the refrain grew, and at last John L., who still had his pride if not his health, rose to the bait. In January he agreed to meet Kilrain in New Orleans in July—London Prize-Ring Rules, no gloves, at Fox's insistence—for a purse of $20,000 winner take all, with a side bet of $1,000.

Sullivan's backers quickly called in icy-eyed Billy Muldoon, a trainer who, for a fee of $10,000, agreed to put John L. back into fighting shape (fee forfeited if Kilrain won). With one ironclad proviso: Muldoon was to be absolute boss. Sullivan would follow the regimen set up for every minute of every hour, 24 hours a day, without question or temperamental display. It was agreed, and one of the backers, the tough, pistol-packing gambler out of Brooklyn named Charley Johnston, vowed that he would answer for John L. But first they had to find him, because he was off on another bender. Inside his lavishly appointed offices, with their Turkish carpets, plush chairs and inlaid mother-of-pearl tables, Fox learned of all this and contentedly stroked his mustache. Muldoon had six months to whip Sullivan into shape, but what good came of flogging a dead horse? Sullivan was finished, washed up. Physical conditioning was Muldoon's stock-in-trade, not making miracles.

Six months passed and it is July 8, 1889. For weeks all across America, urchins and schoolboys, who are not the final arbiters in matters of sport, have been chanting a loyal battle cry: "Sull-i-van will KILLrain!"—and the *Gazette* be damned. But at ringside, where the sun is beating down mercilessly already, the smart-money men are worried. Can the Big Fellow still fight? And even if he can, how long can he possibly last? Kilrain isn't known as a slugger, but he's strong and he has great endurance. He's also a good wrestler, and in bareknuckle fighting a wrestling fall can be nearly as effective as a knockdown punch. "Sullivan is no wrestler," announces the New York *World* on the day of the fight, expressing the reservation that is in everybody's mind: "According to the history of all such drunkards as he, his legs ought to fail him after 20 minutes of fighting."

Ringside seats are snapped up at premium prices: 722 fans pay $15 each to perch on campstools, while 1,400 more part with a sawbuck for the privilege of standing behind them. There are grandstand seats ranging in price from 50 cents to $2, but the rowdy element in the crowd overruns them and the man who passes the hat doesn't get much. In all, more than 3,000 men and boys are in attendance. Ann Livingston, John L.'s beefy, bosomy, showgirl inamorata of many years, who sometimes went to his fights dressed in men's clothing, does not attend. But at least one woman does. She is a black lady named Aunt Mattie, who was elderly when she helped to raise Mississippi poet James H. Street in pre-Depression America, but is spry enough in 1889 to perch in the lower branches of an oak tree behind the grandstand.

It is Hades-hot. The sun is a burnished brass disk in the sky, the temperature at ringside 100 degrees F. And rising. It will be 110 degrees before the day is over. The crowd chews on rumors that the militia will show up at any moment. Newspapermen fume when they learn that most of their free seats have been sold by the managers, and that no special telegraphic facilities are furnished. The only wire, belonging to the railroad company, is taken up by railroad business. It is said that there is a rush for carrier pigeons, but none can be found. The reporters must go back to New Orleans to reach a telegraph station.

Shortly before 10 A.M., Jake Kilrain, his corner men Charlie Mitchell and Mike Donovan, and his timekeeper, Bat Masterson, push through the crowd to the ring. Jake tosses his hat over the ropes and follows it in, shouting in the prize ring's time-honored gesture of defiance, "Me hat's in the ring!" He looks New York pale but fit. His face, though, has a sour cast this morning, and the sweat that beads out over his body may not be entirely from the temperature and humidity.

Moments later, the champion strides down to the ring. He is wearing a long robe, and when he shrugs it off the ringsiders inhale appreciatively. Not for the emerald-green tights, flesh-colored stockings and glossy-black high-topped boots, as resplendent as they are, but for the miracle that William Muldoon has wrought. For there before them stands the Big Fellow of legend, down to 207 pounds and, except for a slight bulge that girdles his midriff, looking surprisingly fit.

In the ring, the fighters shake hands and each gives $1,000 in cash—the side bet—to the referee, John Fitzpatrick, who soon after will be elected mayor of New Orleans. Their boots are fitted with metal spikes to prevent them from slipping on the earthen floor of the ring. Then their seconds also shake hands, as is the custom, and return to their corners.

At 10:15, Fitzpatrick hollers "Time!" The two adversaries advance to the mark. They circle for an instant. Then Kilrain rushes in, grabs Sullivan by the shoulders and backheels him to the ground. The ringsiders cheer excitedly. First fall to Kilrain. Money changes hands. The round has lasted exactly five seconds.

The second round is Sullivan's. He lands a heavy blow on Jake's ribs and throws him. Thirty seconds. They clinch in the third round and Kilrain lands several foul blows. The crowd hisses. Sullivan pulls away and sends Kilrain tumbling with a right to the heart followed by a left to the head.

By the fourth round the strategy of the Kilrain corner becomes clear. Jake refuses to swap punches with Sullivan head on, instead jabbing and backing away until he sees an opportunity to clinch and throw his opponent to the ground. This is Charlie Mitchell's style—wear your opponent down. Charlie also maintains a steady stream of foul abuse from the corner, trying to goad John L. into blind anger. He seems to be succeeding. The round is approaching 15 minutes when the frustrated Sullivan lowers his fists and grasps, "Why don't you stand and fight like a man, you sonovabitch? Are you a fighter or a sprinter?"

Jake laughs, tauntingly.

In the seventh, Kilrain suddenly comes out of his shell and lands a vicious right on John L.'s ear, tearing it open. "First blood, Kilrain!" the referee cries out and a lot more money changes hands.

This is the last time Jake's supporters have much to cheer about. By the tenth round, Kilrain stumbles backward until Sullivan catches up with him, then falls to the ground without being hit to gain the automatic 38-second respite. Sullivan is enraged, the more so a round or two later when Jake steps on his foot, piercing it with one of his shoe spikes and drawing blood.

As the fight wears on, it becomes apparent that it is Kilrain, not Sullivan, who is wilting under the terrible heat. The steep wooden grandstands cut off any movement of air; the ring becomes a sun-scorched inferno. Men keel over like ninepins. The fighters continue their grotesque dance, one backpedaling, the other advancing and swinging ponderous blows. Their backs and shoulders are blistered crimson by the sun; blood, most of it Kilrain's, streaks their bodies. Sullivan's fists are beginning to swell.

Kilrain's seconds have a quart of whiskey and he takes sips and nips to keep his strength up. Sullivan is drinking tea. He refuses even to sit during the 38-second breaks. "What the hell is the use?" he asks his anxious seconds. "I just have to get back up again, don't I?" Muldoon asks him how long he thinks he can stay. "Till tomorrow morning, if it's necessary," Sullivan snarls.

In the 44th round, somebody—possibly even Muldoon—spikes the champion's tea with whiskey. John L. takes a huge gulp, goes out to toe the mark and gets sick. Instead of lacing into him, Jake asks if he want to call it a draw. John L., still vomiting, responds by knocking him down. A wag at ringside starts a witticism that whirlwinds throughout the crowd: John L.'s stomach is getting rid of the tea but hanging on for dear life to the whiskey.

Kilrain's seconds carry him to his corner after every round now, and as he comes back out to the mark his head rolls loosely on his shoulders as if his neck has been broken. Charley Johnston offers $500 to $50 at ringside, with no takers. After the 75th round a physician from the New York Athletic Club pulls Mike Donovan aside and says, "Your fighter will die if you keep sending him out there. Think of the heat, man!"

At the same time, Mitchell sends a message to Sullivan's corner: if Kilrain retires, will Big John give him $2,000? His object apparently is to show that Sullivan is as eager to stop the fight as Kilrain. But before a deal can be struck, Donovan, who has seen two men die in the ring, throws in the sponge. Mitchell raves and Kilrain blubbers like a babe. Without waiting for congratulations, Sullivan bounds across the ring and challenges Charlie Mitchell to climb in and have it out to a finish right then and there. Charlie is more than willing, and it takes a half-dozen stout men to keep them apart.

So, after two hours, 16 minutes and 25 seconds, the last bareknuckle championship bout in history goes into the record books. A wad of $100 bills is counted out into John L.'s hands, swollen to three times their normal size, and somebody remembers to pass him the *Police Gazette* belt. The story goes around that he tossed it to Charley Johnston "for his bulldog." If so, he may have lived to regret the gesture, for in later, leaner days he will pawn his own belt for $175—after the diamonds have been pried out.

The country's newspapers carried the story the next day. The headline writers for the *New York Times* waxed smugly righteous: "The Bigger Brute Won." Literally accurate, but not in fact very significant. Jake weighed 190 pounds to John L.'s 207. Years later, poet James Street preferred Aunt Mattie's version of the fight, recited to him when he was a boy on her knee, calling it the best piece of sports reporting he had ever heard. "They knocked each other down so many times I quit countin' them," she said. "Mr. John started a sweatin' about the second round. He grunted and snorted a heap. Mr. Jake danced like a bridegroom at his weddin' dinner. Finally Mr. John hit Mr. Jake so hard Mr. Jake just didn't get up and that's all it was to it."

Well, not quite. Mr. John was tried by the State of Mississippi, convicted and sentenced to a year in jail. His lawyers appealed and at the retrial agreed to plead guilty in return for a $500 fine. Sullivan paid the fine and hotfooted it back to New York and a monumental celebratory binge. Jake Kilrain, cast aside by Richard K. Fox and broke, was paroled under a quaint old Mississippi law to work off his fine to a respectable private citizen of the state—in this case Charlie Rich, who kept him busy shooting pool in a place he owned in Hattiesburg. Jake, incidentally, so near death's door after the fight, managed to live long enough to serve as a pallbearer at John L.'s funeral in 1918. He didn't get counted out himself until 1937, when he was 78.

22

Jane Addams: Urban Crusader

by Anne Firor Scott

American political history during the past century reveals alternating periods of political activism and relative calm if not reaction. The quietude of national politics had been disturbed by William Jennings Bryan's energetic campaign in 1896, but his defeat by William McKinley seemed to assure that few changes would take place. However, the issues that Bryan had spoken to would not be suppressed. Furthermore, McKinley's assassination in 1901 elevated Theodore Roosevelt to the presidency, and national politics took on a different outlook.

The Progressive Movement is often dated from Roosevelt's presidency to the U.S. entrance into World War I in 1917. Like the Populists, the Progressives sought to restore opportunity in American society through a more democratic government. But the Progressives were much more broadly based than the Populists. Most Progressive leaders were urban middle-class professionals who sought to use the national, state, and local governments as instruments for political reform.

Jane Addams personifies progressivism at work on the local level. Her remarkable career is sketched in the following essay by Anne Firor Scott of Duke University. Professor Scott, author of *The Southern Lady: From Pedestal to Politics* and *The American Woman: Who Was She?*, shows how Addams had to do battle with the boss system in Chicago (see "The Age of the Bosses" in this volume). Addams' crusade for honest and efficient government service to society's less fortunate citizens can serve as a timeless example to later generations.

If Alderman Johnny Powers of Chicago's teeming nineteenth ward had only been prescient, he might have foreseen trouble when two young ladies not very long out of a female seminary in Rockford, Illinois, moved into a dilapidated old house on Halsted Street in September, 1889, and announced themselves "at home" to the neighbors. The ladies, however, were not very noisy about it, and it is doubtful if Powers was aware of their existence. The nineteenth ward was well supplied with people already—growing numbers of Italians, Poles, Russians, Irish, and other immigrants—and two more would hardly be noticed.

Johnny Powers was the prototype of the ward boss who was coming to be an increasingly decisive figure on the American political scene. In the first place, he was Irish. In the second, he was, in the parlance of the time, a "boodler": his vote and influence in the Chicago Common Council were far from being beyond price. As chairman of the council's finance committee and boss of the Cook County Democratic party he occupied a strategic position. Those who understood the inner workings of Chicago politics thought that Powers had some hand in nearly every corrupt ordinance passed by the council during his years in office. In a single year, 1895, he was to help to sell six important city franchises. When the mayor vetoed Powers' measures, a silent but significant two-thirds vote appeared to override the veto.

Ray Stannard Baker, who chanced to observe Powers in the late nineties, recorded that he was shrewd and silent, letting other men make the speeches and bring upon their heads the abuse of the public. Powers was a short, stocky man, Baker said, "with a flaring gray pompadour, a smooth-shaven face [*sic*], rather heavy features, and a restless eye." One observer remarked that "the shadow of sympathetic gloom is always about him. He never jokes; he has forgotten how to smile. . . ." Starting life as a grocery clerk, Powers had run for the city council in 1888 and joined the boodle ring headed by Alderman Billy Whalen. When Whalen died in an accident two years later, Powers moved swiftly to establish himself as a successor. A few weeks before his death Whalen had collected some thirty thousand dollars—derived from the sale of a city franchise—to be divided among the party faithful. Powers alone knew that the money was in a safe in Whalen's saloon, so he promptly offered a high price for the furnishings of the saloon, retrieved the money, and divided it among the gang—at one stroke establishing himself as a shrewd operator and as one who would play the racket fairly.

From this point on he was the acknowledged head of the gang. Charles Yerkes, the Chicago traction tycoon, found in Powers an ideal tool for the purchase of city franchises. On his aldermanic salary of three dollars a week, Powers managed to acquire two large saloons of his own, a gambling establishment, a fine house, and a conspicuous collection of diamonds. When he was indicted along with two other corrupt aldermen for running a slot machine and keeping a "common gambling house," Powers was unperturbed. The three appeared before a police judge, paid each other's bonds, and that was the end of that. Proof of their guilt was positive, but convictions were never obtained.

On the same day the Municipal Voters League published a report for the voters on the records of the members of the city council. John Powers was described as "recognized leader of the worst element in the council . . . [who] has voted uniformly for bad ordinances." The League report went on to say that he had always opposed securing any return to the city for valuable franchises, and proceeded to document the charge in detail.

To his constituents in the nineteenth ward, most of whom were getting the first initiation into American politics. Powers turned a different face. To them, he was first and last a friend. When there were celebrations, he always showed up: if the celebration happened to be a bazaar, he bought freely, murmuring piously that it would all go to the poor. In times of tragedy he was literally Johnny on the spot. If the family was too poor to provide the necessary carriage for a respectable funeral, it appeared at the doorstep—courtesy of Johnny Powers and charged to his standing account with the local undertaker.

If the need was not so drastic, Powers made his presence felt with an imposing bouquet or wreath. "He has," said the Chicago *Times-Herald*, "bowed with aldermanic grief at thousands of biers."

Christmas meant literally tons of turkeys, geese, and ducks—each one handed out personally by a member of the Powers family, with good wishes and no questions asked. Johnny provided more fundamental aid, too, when a breadwinner was out of work. At one time he is said to have boasted that 2,600 men from his ward (about one third of the registered voters) were working in one way or another for the city of Chicago. This did not take into account those for whom the grateful holders of traction franchises had found a place. When election day rolled around, the returns reflected the appreciation of job-holders and their relatives.

The two young ladies on Halsted Street, Jane Addams and Ellen Starr, were prototypes too, but of a very different kind of figure: they were the pioneers of the social settlement, the original "social workers." They opposed everything Johnny Powers stood for.

Jane Addams' own background could hardly have been more different from that of John Powers. The treasured daughter of a well-to-do small-town businessman from Illinois, she had been raised in an atmosphere of sturdy Christian principles.

From an early age she had been an introspective child concerned with justifying her existence. Once in a childhood nightmare she had dreamed of being the only remaining person in a world desolated by some disaster, facing the responsibility for rediscovering the principle of the wheel! At Rockford she shared with some of her classmates a determination to live to "high purpose," and decided that she would become a doctor in order to "help the poor."

After graduation she went to the Woman's Medical College of Philadelphia, but her health failed and she embarked on the grand tour of Europe customary among the wealthy. During a subsequent trip to Europe in 1888, in the unlikely setting of a Spanish bull ring, an idea that had long been growing in her mind suddenly crystallized: she would rent a house "in a part of the city where many primitive and actual needs are found, in which young women who had been given over too exclusively to study, might restore a balance of activity along traditional lines and learn something of life from life itself. . . ." So the American settlement-house idea was born. She and Ellen Starr, a former classmate at the Rockford seminary who had been with her in Europe, went back to Chicago to find a house among the victims of the nineteenth century's fast-growing industrial society.

The young women—Jane was twenty-nine and Ellen thirty in 1889—had no blueprint to guide them when they decided to take up residence in Mr. Hull's decayed mansion and begin helping "the neighbors" to help themselves. No school of social work had trained them for this enterprise: Latin and Greek, art, music, and "moral philosophy" at the seminary constituted their academic preparation. Toynbee Hall in England—the world's first settlement house, founded in 1884 by Samuel A. Barnett—had inspired them. Having found the Hull house at the corner of Polk and Halsted—in what was by common consent one of Chicago's worst wards—they leased it, moved in, and began doing what came naturally.

Miss Starr, who had taught in an exclusive girls' preparatory school, inaugurated a reading party for young Italian women with George Eliot's *Romola* as the first book. Miss Addams, becoming aware of the desperate problem of working mothers, began at once to organize a kindergarten. They tried Russian parties for the Russian neighbors, organized boys' clubs for the gangs on the street, and offered to bathe all babies. The neighbors were baffled, but impressed. Very soon children and grownups of all sorts and conditions were finding their way to Hull-House—to read Shakespeare or to ask for a volunteer midwife; to learn sewing or discuss socialism; to study art or to fill an empty stomach. There were few formalities and no red tape, and the young ladies found themselves every day called upon to deal with some of the multitude of personal tragedies against which the conditions of life in the nineteenth ward offered so thin a cushion.

Before long, other young people feeling twinges of social conscience and seeking a tangible way to make their convictions count in the world of the 1890's came to live at Hull-House. These "residents," as they were called, became increasingly interested in the personal histories of the endless stream of neighbors who came to the House each week. They began to find out about the little children sewing all day long in the "sweated" garment trade, and about others who worked long hours in a candy factory. They began to ask why there were three thousand more children in the ward than there were seats in its schoolrooms, and why the death rate was higher there than in almost any other part of Chicago. They worried about youngsters whose only playground was a garbage-spattered alley that threatened the whole population with disease. (Once they traced a typhoid epidemic to its source and found the sewer line merging with the water line.) In the early days Hull-House offered bathtubs and showers, which proved so popular a form of hospitality that the residents became relentless lobbyists for municipal baths.

Hull-House was not the only American settlement house—indeed, Jane Addams liked to emphasize the validity of the idea by pointing out that it had developed simultaneously in several different places. But Hull-House set the pace, and in an astonishingly short time its founder began to acquire a national reputation. As early as 1893 Jane Addams wrote to a friend: "I find I am considered the grandmother of social settlements." She was being asked to speak to gatherings of learned gentlemen, sociologists and philosophers, on such subjects as "The Subjective Necessity for Social Settlements." When the Columbian Exposition attracted thousands of visitors to Chicago in 1893, Hull-House became—along with the lake front and the stockyards—one of the things a guest was advised not to miss. By the mid-nineties, distinguished Europeans were turning up regularly to visit the House and examine its workings.

W. T. Stead, editor of the English *Review of Reviews,* spent much time there while he gathered material for his sensational book, *If Christ Came to Chicago.* By that time two thousand people a week were coming to Hull-House to participate in some of its multifarious activities, which ranged from philosophy classes to the Nineteenth Ward Improvement Association.

Neither her growing reputation nor the increasing demand for speeches and articles, however, distracted Jane Addams from what was to be for forty years the main focus of a many-sided life: Hull-House and the nineteenth ward. Much of her early writing was an attempt to portray the real inner lives of America's proliferating immigrants, and much of her early activity, an effort to give them a voice to speak out against injustice.

The Hull-House residents were becoming pioneers in many ways, not least in the techniques of social research. In the *Hull-House Maps and Papers,* published in 1895, they prepared some of the first careful studies of life in an urban slum, examining the details of the "homework" system of garment making and describing tumble-down houses, overtaxed schools, rising crime rates, and other sociological problems. The book remains today an indispensable source for the social historian of Chicago in the nineties.

Jane Addams' own interest in these matters was far from academic. Her concern for the uncollected garbage led her to apply for—and receive—an appointment as garbage inspector. She rose at six every morning and in a horse-drawn buggy followed the infuriated garbage contractor on his appointed rounds, making sure that every receptacle was emptied. Such badgering incensed Alderman Powers, in whose hierarchy of values cleanliness, though next to godliness, was a good bit below patronage—and he looked upon garbage inspection as a job for one of his henchmen. By now John Powers was becoming aware of his new neighbors; they were increasingly inquisitive about things close to Johnny Powers' source of power. By implication they were raising a troublesome question: Was Johnny Powers really "taking" care of the poor"?

For a while, as one resident noted, the inhabitants of the House were "passive though interested observers of their representative, declining his offers of help and co-operation, refusing politely to distribute his Christmas turkeys, but feeling too keenly the smallness of their numbers to work against him." They were learning, though, and the time for passivity would end.

In company with many other American cities, Chicago after 1895 was taking a critical look at its political life and at the close connections that had grown up between politics and big business during the explosive era of industrial expansion following the Civil War. "The sovereign people may govern Chicago in theory," Stead wrote; "as a matter of fact King Boodle is monarch of all he surveys. His domination is practically undisputed."

The Municipal Voters League, a reform organization that included many of Jane Addams' close friends, was founded in 1896 in an effort to clean up the Common Council, of whose sixty-eight aldermen fifty-eight were estimated to be corrupt. The League aimed to replace as many of the fifty-eight as possible with honest men. But it was not easy: in 1896, as part of this campaign, a member of the Hull-House Men's Club ran for the second aldermanic position in the ward and against all expectations was elected. Too late, his idealistic backers found that their hero had his price: Johnny Powers promptly bought him out.

Jane Addams was chagrined but undiscouraged. By the time Powers came up for re-election in 1898, she had had time to observe him more closely and plan her attack. Her opening gun was a speech—delivered, improbably enough, to the Society for Ethical Culture—with the ponderous and apparently harmless title, "Some Ethical Survivals in Municipal Corruption." But appearances were deceptive: once under way, she took the hide off Powers and was scarcely easier on his opponents among the so-called "better elements."

She began by pointing out that for the immigrants, who were getting their first initiation in self-government, ethics was largely a matter of example: the officeholder was apt to set the standard and exercise a permanent influence upon their views. An engaging politician whose standards were low and "impressed by the cynical stamp of the corporations" could debauch the political ideals of ignorant men and women, with consequences that might, she felt, take years to erase.

Ethical issues were further complicated, she said, by habits of thought brought to the New World from the Old. Many Italians and Germans had left their respective fatherlands to escape military service; the Polish and Russian Jews, to escape government persecution. In all these cases, the government had been cast in the role of oppressor. The Irish, in particular, had been conditioned by years of resentment over English rule to regard any successful effort to feed at the public crib as entirely legitimate, because it represented getting the better of their bitterest enemies.

On the other hand, Miss Addams continued, there was nothing the immigrants admired more than simple goodness. They were accustomed to helping each other out in times of trouble, sharing from their own meager store with neighbors who were even more destitute. When Alderman Powers performed on a large scale the same good deeds which they themselves were able to do only on a small scale, was it any wonder that they admired him?

Given this admiration, and their Old World resentments toward government, the immigrants' developing standards of political morality suffered when Powers made it clear that he could "fix" courts or find jobs for his friends on the city payroll. It cheapened their image of American politics when they began to suspect that the source of their benefactor's largess might be a corrupt bargain with a traction tycoon, or with others who wanted something from the city of Chicago and were willing to pay for it.

Hull-House residents, Miss Addams said, very early found evidence of the influence of the boss's standards. When the news spread around the neighborhood that the House was a source of help in time of trouble, more and more neighbors came to appeal for aid when a boy was sent to jail or reform school, and it was impossible to explain to them why Hull-House, so ready to help in other ways, was not willing to get around the law as the Alderman did.

Removing Alderman Powers from office, Jane Addams told the sober gentlemen of the Society for Ethical Culture, would be no simple task. It would require a fundamental change in the ethical standards of the community, as well as the development of a deeper insight on the part of the reformers. These latter, she pointed out, with all their zeal for well-ordered, honest politics, were not eager to undertake the responsibilities of self-government 365 days a year. They were quite willing to come into the nineteenth ward at election time to exhort the citizenry, but were they willing to make a real effort to achieve personal relationships of the kind that stood Johnny Powers in such good stead?

On this last point, Hull-House itself had some experience. As Florence Kelley—a Hull-House resident who was to become a pioneer in the Illinois social reform movement—subsequently wrote:

> The question is often asked whether all that the House undertakes could not be accomplished without the wear and tear of living on the spot. The answer, that it could not, grows more assured as time goes on. You must suffer from the dirty streets, the universal ugliness, the lack of oxygen in the air you daily breathe, the endless struggle with soot and dust and insufficient water supply, the hanging from a strap of the overcrowded street car at the end of your day's work; you must send your children to the nearest wretchedly crowded school, and see them suffer the consequences, if you are to speak as one having authority and not as the scribes. . . .

By 1898, after nine years of working with their neighbors, the Hull-House residents were ready to pit their influence against that of Powers. Jane Addams' philosophical address to the Ethical Culture society was followed by others in which she explained more concretely the relationships between Yerkes, Chicago's traction czar, and the city council, relationships in which Johnny Powers played a key role. With several important deals in the making, 1898 would be a bad year for Yerkes to lose his key man in the seats of power.

The election was scheduled for April. The reformers—led by Hull-House and supported by independent Democrats, the Cook County Republicans, and the Municipal Voters League—put up a candidate of their own, Simeon Armstrong, to oppose Powers, and undertook to organize and underwrite Armstrong's campaign. By the end of January, the usually imperturbable Powers suddenly began paying attention to his political fences. The newspapers noted with some surprise that it was the first time he had felt it necessary to lift a finger more than two weeks in advance of election day.

His first move was an attack on Amanda Johnson, a Hull-House resident who had succeeded Miss Addams as garbage inspector. A graduate of the University of Wisconsin and described by the papers as blond, blue-eyed, and beautiful, she had taken the civil service examination and duly qualified for the position. Alderman Powers announced to the world that Miss Johnson, shielded by her civil service status, was telling his constituents not to vote for him. The Chicago *Record* dropped a crocodile tear at the sad picture of the martyred alderman:

> General sympathy should go out to Mr. Powers in this, his latest affliction. Heretofore he has been persecuted often by people opposed to bad franchise ordinances. He has been hounded by the upholders of civil service reform. He has suffered the shafts of criticism directed at his career by disinterested citizens. A grand jury has been cruel to him. Invidious comments have been made in his hearing as to the ethical impropriety of gambling institutions. . . . It is even believed that Miss Johnson in her relentless cruelty may go so far as to insinuate that Mr. Powers' electioneering methods are no better than those attributed to her—that, indeed, when he has votes to win, the distinctions of the civil service law do not deter him from going after those votes in many ways.

Powers' next move was to attempt a redistricting that would cut off the eastern, or Italian, end of his ward, which he took to be most seriously under Hull-House influence. It was reported that he also felt this area had been a "large source of expense to him through the necessity of assisting the poor that are crowded into that district." "These people," the Chicago *Record* reported, "formerly tied to him by his charities are said to be turning toward Hull-House and will vote solidly against him next spring.

Neither of Powers' first efforts was notably successful. A few days after his attack on Miss Johnson the *Tribune* reported:

> Trouble sizzled and boiled for Alderman John Powers in his own bailiwick last night. The Nineteenth Ward Independent club raked over the Alderman's sins . . . and . . . much indignation was occasioned by Alderman Powers' opposition to Miss Amanda Johnson. One Irish speaker says Johnny is a disgrace to the Irish race now that he has descended to fighting "poor working girls."

Meantime, Powers' colleagues on the council redistricting committee had no intention of saving his skin at the expense of their own, and stood solidly against his gerrymandering effort. Now the shaken boss began to show signs of losing his temper. He told reporters that if Miss Addams didn't like the nineteenth ward she should move out. Later, still more infuriated, he announced that Hull-House should be driven out. "A year from now there will be no such institution," he said flatly, adding that the women at Hull-House were obviously jealous of his charities. The *Record* published a cartoon showing Powers pushing vainly against the wall of a very substantial house.

The news of the campaign soon spread beyond the bounds of Chicago. The New York *Tribune* commented that Powers

> wouldn't mind Miss Addams saying all those things about him if he didn't begin to fear that she may succeed in making some of his well-meaning but misled constituents believe them. She is a very practical person, and has behind her a large volunteer staff of other practical persons who do not confine their efforts to "gassin' in the parlors," but are going about to prove to the plain people of the nineteenth ward that a corrupt and dishonest man does not necessarily become a saint by giving a moiety of his ill-gotten gains to the poor.

By March the campaign was waxing warm, and Powers resorted to an attempt to stir up the Catholic clergy against Miss Addams and the reform candidate. One of the Hull-House residents, a deputy factory inspector and a Catholic herself, went directly to the priests to find out why they were supporting Powers. When she reported, Jane Addams wrote to a friend:

> As nearly as I can make out, the opposition comes from the Jesuits, headed by Father Lambert, and the parish priests are not in it, and do not like it. Mary talked for a long time to Father Lambert and is sure it is jealousy of Hull-House and money obligations to Powers, that he does not believe the charges himself. She cried when she came back.

In another letter written about the same time, Miss Addams said that Powers had given a thousand dollars to the Jesuit "temperance cadets," who had returned the favor with a fine procession supporting Powers' candidacy. "There was a picture of your humble servant on a transparency and others such as 'No petticoat government for us. . . .' We all went out on the corner to see it, Mr. Hinsdale carefully shielding me from the public view."

By now the battle between Hull-House and Johnny Powers was sharing headlines in Chicago newspapers with the blowing up of the *Maine* in Havana's harbor and the approach of the war from Spain. "Throughout the nineteenth ward," said the *Tribune,* "the one absorbing topic of conversation wherever men are gathered is the fight being made against Alderman Powers." It was rumored that Powers had offered a year's free rent to one of the opposition leaders if he would move out of the ward before election day, and the Hull-House group let it be known that the Alderman was spending money freely in the ward, giving his lieutenants far more cash to spread around than was his custom. "Where does the money come from?" Jane Addams asked, and answered her own question: "From Mr. Yerkes." Powers was stung, and challenged her to prove that he had ever received one dollar from any corporation.

"Driven to desperation," said the *Tribune,* "Ald. Powers has at last called to his aid the wives and daughters of his political allies." Determined to fight fire with fire, he dropped his opposition to "petticoat politicians" and gave his blessing to a Ladies Auxiliary which was instructed to counteract the work of the women of Hull-House. An enterprising reporter discovered that few of the ladies had ever seen Miss Addams or been to Hull-House, but all were obediently repeating the charge that she had "blackened and maligned the whole ward" by saying that its people were ignorant, criminal, and poor.

As the campaign became more intense, Jane Addams received numbers of violent letters, nearly all of them anonymous, from Powers' partisans, as well as various communications from lodginghouse keepers quoting prices for votes they were ready to deliver! When the Hull-House residents discovered evidence of ties between banking, ecclesiastical, and journalistic interests, with Powers at the center, they proceeded to publicize all they knew. This brought upon their heads a violent attack by the Chicago *Chronicle,* the organ of the Democratic ring.

Suddenly a number of nineteenth-ward businessmen who had signed petitions for the reform candidate came out for Powers. They were poor and in debt; Powers gave the word to a landlord here, a coal dealer there, and they were beaten. The small peddlers and fruit dealers were subjected to similar pressure, for each needed a license to ply his trade, and the mere hint of a revocation was enough to create another Powers man.

When Alderman John M. Harlan, one of the stalwarts of the Municipal Voters League, came into the ward to speak, Powers supplied a few toughs to stir up a riot. Fortunately Harlan was a sturdy character, and offered so forcefully to take on all comers in fisticuffs that no volunteers appeared. Allowed to proceed, he posed some embarrassing questions: Why did nineteenth-ward residents have to pay ten-cent trolley fares when most of the city paid five? Why, when Powers was head of the city council's free-spending committee on street paving, were the streets of the ward in execrable condition? Why were the public schools so crowded, and why had Powers suppressed a petition, circulated by Hull-House, to build more of them?

Freely admitting Powers' reputation for charity, Harlan made the interesting suggestion that the councilman's motives be put to the test: Would he be so generous as a private citizen? "Let us retire him to private life and see."

Powers was pictured by the papers as being nearly apoplectic at this attack from Miss Addams' friend. He announced that he would not be responsible for Harlan's safety if he returned to the nineteenth ward. (Since no one had asked him to assume any such responsibility, this was presumed to be an open threat.) Harlan returned at once, telling a crowd well-laced with Powers supporters that he would "rather die in my tracks than acknowledge the right of John Powers to say who should and who should not talk in this ward." Summoning up the memory of Garibaldi, he urged the Italians to live up to their tradition of freedom and not allow their votes to be "delivered."

In a quieter vein, Miss Addams too spoke at a public meeting of Italians, where, it was reported, she received profound and respectful attention. "Show that you do not intend to be governed by a boss," she told them. "It is important not only for yourselves but for your children. These things must be made plain to them."

As the campaign progressed, the reformers began to feel they had a real chance of defeating Powers. Jane Addams was persuaded to go in search of funds with which to carry out the grand finale. "I sallied forth today and got $100," she wrote, and "will have to keep it up all week; charming prospect, isn't it?" But on about the twentieth of March she began to have serious hopes, too, and redoubled her efforts.

As election day, April 6, approached, the Chicago *Tribune* and the Chicago *Record* covered the campaign daily, freely predicting a victory for the reformers. Alas for all predictions. When election day came, Powers' assets, which Jane Addams had so cogently analyzed in that faraway speech to the Society of Ethical Culture, paid off handsomely. It was a rough day in the nineteenth ward, with ten saloons open, one man arrested for drawing a gun, and everything, as Miss Addams wrote despondently when the count began to come in, "as bad as bad can be." Too many election judges were under Powers' thumb. The reform candidate was roundly defeated. Hull-House went to court to challenge the conduct of the election, but in the halls of justice Powers also had friends. It was no use.

Even in victory, Powers was a bit shaken. Hull-House had forced him, for the first time, to put out a great effort for re-election. It was obviously *not* going to move out of the nineteenth ward; indeed, if the past was any portent, its influence with his constituents would increase.

Powers decided to follow an ancient maxim, "If you can't lick 'em, join 'em." Early in the 1900 aldermanic campaign, several Chicago papers carried a straight news story to the effect that Hull-House and Johnny Powers had signed a truce, and quoted various paternally benevolent statements on the Alderman's part. In the *Chronicle,* for example, he was reported to have said: "I am not an Indian when it comes to hate . . . let bygones be bygones." A day or two later another rash of stories detailed a number of favors the Alderman was supposed to have done for Hull-House.

Jane Addams was furious, and after considerable deliberation she decided to reply. It was one of the few times in her long public career when she bothered to answer anything the newspapers said about her. She knew that with his eye on the campaign, the master politician was trying to give the appearance of having taken his most vigorous enemy into camp. She had been observing him too long not to realize what he was up to, and she could not possibly let him get away with it.

On February 20, 1900, a vigorous letter from Miss Addams appeared in nearly all the Chicago papers, reaffirming the attitude of Hull-House toward Mr. Powers. "It is needless to state," she concluded, "that the protest of Hull-House against a man who continually disregards the most fundamental rights of his constituents must be permanent."

Permanent protest, yes, but as a practical matter there was no use waging another opposition campaign. Powers held too many of the cards. When all was said and done, he had proved too tough a nut to crack, though Hull-House could—and did—continue to harass him. An observer of the Municipal Voters League, celebrating its success in the *Outlook* in June, 1902, described the vast improvement in the Common Council, but was forced to admit that a few wards were "well-nigh hopeless." He cited three: those of "Blind Billy" Kent, "Bathhouse John" Coughlin and Johnny Powers.

From a larger standpoint, however, the battle between "Saint Jane" (as the neighbors called Jane Addams when she was not around) and the Ward Boss was not without significance. It was one of numerous similar battles that would characterize the progressive era the country over, and many of them the reformers would win. Because of her firsthand experience, because she lived *with* the immigrants instead of coming into their neighborhood occasionally to tell them what to do, Jane Addams was perhaps the first of the urban reformers to grasp the real pattern of bossism, its logic, the functions it performed, and the reason it was so hard to dislodge. Years later political scientists, beginning to analyze the pattern, would add almost nothing to her speech of 1898. If copies of *The Last Hurrah* have reached the Elysian fields, Jane Addams has spent an amused evening seeing her ideas developed so well in fictional form.

The campaign of 1898 throws considerable light on Jane Addams' intensely practical approach to politics, and upon a little-known aspect of the settlement-house movement. If anyone had told her and Ellen Starr in 1889 that the logic of what they were trying to do would inevitably force them into politics, they would have hooted. But in due time politics, in many forms, became central to Hull-House activity. For Jane Addams herself, the campaign against Powers was the first in a long series of political forays, all essentially based on the same desire—to see that government met the needs of the "other half."

The regulation of child labor, for example, was one political issue in which Hull-House residents became involved because of their knowledge of the lives of the neighbors. The first juvenile court in Chicago was set up as a result of their efforts; it was a direct response to the anxious mothers who could not understand why Hull-House would not help get their boys out of jail. The first factory inspection law in Illinois was also credited to Hull-House, and Florence Kelley became the first inspector. Another Hull-House resident—Dr. Alice Hamilton—pioneered in the field of industrial medicine. Because of their intimate acquaintance with the human cost of industrialization, settlement workers became vigorous advocates of promoting social justice through law.

It was a long jump but not an illogical one from the campaign against Powers to the stage of the Chicago Coliseum in August, 1912, when Jane Addams arose to second the nomination of Teddy Roosevelt by the Progressive party on a platform of social welfare. More remarkable than the ovation—larger than that given to any other seconder—was the fact that the huge audience seemed to listen carefully to what she had to say.

Some newspapers grandly estimated her value to T. R. at a million votes. "Like the report of Mark Twain's death," she commented, "the report is greatly exaggerated." But she campaigned vigorously, in the face of criticism that this was not a proper role for a woman, and when the Bull Moose cause failed, she did not believe it had been a waste of time. It had brought about, she wrote Roosevelt, more discussion of social reform than she had dared to hope for in her lifetime. Alderman Powers was still in office—as were many like him—but the sources of his power were being attacked at the roots.

When the 1916 campaign came around, Democrats and Republicans alike made bids for Jane Addams' support. The outbreak of war in Europe had turned her attention, however, in a different direction. As early as 1907, in a book called *Newer Ideals of Peace,* she had begun to elaborate William James's notion of a "moral equivalent of war," and had suggested that the experience

Chicago's State Street. (Library of Congress)

of polyglot immigrant populations in learning to live together might be laying the foundations for a true international order. Like her ideals of social justice, those that she conceived on international peace had their beginning in the nineteenth ward.

To her, as to so many idealistic progressives, world war came as a profound shock. Her response was a vigorous effort to bring together American women and women from all the European countries to urge upon their governments a negotiated peace. In Europe, where she went in 1915 for a meeting of the Women's International Peace Conference, she visited prime ministers; at the end of that year she planned to sail on Henry Ford's peace ship, but illness forced her to withdraw at the last moment. At home she appealed to President Wilson. Unshaken in her pacifism, she stood firmly against the war, even after the United States entered it.

Her popularity seemed to melt overnight. Many women's clubs and social workers, who owed so much to her vision, deserted her. An Illinois judge who thought it dangerous for her to speak in wartime was widely supported in the press. For most of 1917 and 1918 she was isolated as never before or again. But she did not waver.

When the war ended she began at once to work for means to prevent another. Through the twenties she was constantly active in searching for ways in which women could cut across national lines in their work for peace. In 1931, in her seventy-first year, she received the Nobel Peace Price—the second American to be so recognized. She died, full of honors, in 1935.

As for Johnny Powers, he had lived to a ripe old age and died in 1930, remaining alderman almost to the end, still fighting reform mayors, still protesting that he and Miss Addams were really friends, after all. From whichever department of the hereafter he ended up in, he must have looked down—or up—in amazement at the final achievements of his old enemy, who had been so little troubled by his insistence that there should be "no petticoats in politics."

23

Full Speed Ahead and Damn the Tomorrows: Our Frontier Heritage of Waste

by Ray Allen Billington

One of the most difficult adjustments being made by Americans living in the late twentieth century concerns the relationship of the people with the environment. Many Americans refuse to accept seriously the fact that natural resources are limited and that the environment is really threatened by the barrage of pollutants which assault it.

As the late Ray Allen Billington demonstrates in the following essay, American attitudes toward the environment are deeply rooted in our historical experience. Our frontier heritage helped develop many national characteristics, including wastefulness. In this instance, the extent to which we can break away from old beliefs and practices and adapt to a new set of environmental conditions will greatly affect our future.

Historians of the future, looking back on the twilight years of the twentieth century, may designate the mid-1970's as worthy of that supreme accolade accorded only the most significant dates in history: to serve as a dividing point between chapters in their textbooks. If they do, their judgment will be based not on the Watergate scandals (they would know that Grant and Harding had occupied the White House in the past and that human frailty could occasionally tarnish even a President), or even on the bitter conflict over the "Imperial Presidency" (they would be aware that Congress and the President traditionally had vied for power and that authority had fluctuated between the two in unpredictable cycles).

Instead, those historians might recognize the mid-1970's as a turning point in national development because suddenly, almost without warning, the American people were advised by their leaders that they must abandon a way of life to which they had been accustomed for three centuries. They were told that they could no longer squander the natural resources with which their continent was so richly endowed. Those resources, seemingly inexhaustible, were in increasingly short supply; food, energy, and raw materials were diminishing at a rate that could mean disaster for today's generation, let alone those of the future. The "land of plenty," Americans were told, could within a few years become a "land of want" unless they changed their life patterns drastically.

This rude awakening began with the Arab oil boycott that followed the Yom Kippur War of 1973; the United States, its people learned, was dependent on foreign producers for an ingredient essential to the economy. This was bad enough, but worse were the continuing alarms that sounded over the next months—from the President, from the United Nations, from commissions, from experts, from anyone who could speak with real or pretended authority. Shortages of oil, gasoline, and natural gas would continue and worsen unless the nation practiced voluntary belt-tightening. The nation's farms could no longer keep pace with the world's needs; mass starvation was possible within a decade without population controls. Dozens of items essential to the economy were so scarce that the industrial machine might lumber to a halt at any moment; we were underproducing plastics, paper, steel, cotton, copper, propane, nylon, acetate yarns, penicillin, cement, aluminum, vinyl, paints, electrical items, and on and on and on.

The people of the United States were shocked by these unpleasant facts, but the experts who voiced the warnings were just as shocked by the popular reaction. For the great mass of the people simply refused to listen. Savants and politicians and newspaper editorialists might paint the future black, but most Americans refused to remove their rose-tinted glasses. The fifty-five-mile-an-hour speed limit might grace the statutes, but, within months of the fuel crisis, highway speeds were creeping back into the sixty-mile range; Los Angelenos bound for Las Vegas were so eager to lose their money that special police patrols were necessary on weekends to convoy reluctant motorists at legal limits. Administrative efforts to curb the use of gasoline by drastic price increases were rigidly resisted by congressmen more closely tuned to the public's wishes than the President. President Carter used a week of press conferences and television appearances to try to convince the nation that some form of energy saving was "the moral equivalent of war" in meeting "the greatest challenge that our country will face during our lifetime," fully anticipating that such a plea would reduce his popularity by fifteen per cent. Even then only forty-five per cent of the public tested in opinion polls thought the energy situation was worse than "fairly serious." Americans were too accustomed to squandering their heritage to change their ways; full speed ahead and damn the tomorrows.

Why does this heedless attitude persist? Why do Americans blindly mortgage the future rather than curb their enjoyment of the present? That is a question of enormous complexity, answerable only by an analysis of the national character. My purpose is to isolate one strand of our history that seems to me particularly important in understanding our current dilemma. This is the fact that our culture originated and solidified during the three centuries that the nation was expanding westward.

Expansion began with the first settlements at Jamestown and Plymouth and Massachusetts Bay, at Philadelphia and Charleston. From these outposts the population spread slowly over the interior, reaching the crest of the Appalachians before the end of the eighteenth century, moving across the Mississippi Valley during the first half of the nineteenth, engulfing the Pacific Provinces and the Great Plains in the second half. From the beginning to the end of the nation's formative period, expansion was a dominant force in the lives of its people. Not until 1890 could the director of the census announce that an unbroken frontier line could no longer be drawn across a map of the United States separating the settled and unsettled portions of the continent.

The frontier did not "close" in 1890, of course; population continued to shift westward during the twentieth century, and still shifts today. But the census announcement foretold the future; the era of the conquest of untapped virgin resources was drawing to a close. Today, with the cries of the conservationists ringing in our ears, we are experiencing the first shock waves of that closing, and more are inevitable.

During those three centuries of westering, the American people enjoyed a degree of opportunity for individual self-advancement unknown elsewhere in the world. Basic in frontiering was the altered ratio of man to land; in Europe and the settled East, land was scarce and men were many; in the advancing West, land was plentiful and men were few. Each move forward opened fresh resources to exploitation: fur-bearing animals to be trapped, mineral riches to be mined, lush pasture lands to be grazed, virgin soils to be cultivated, timber to be stripped from the hills. Here was opportunity unlimited for the ambitious and the energetic.

Moreover, these virgin resources served as an avenue of escape from poverty and subservience. Those with the skills and wherewithal for pioneering were offered a recurring opportunity to better themselves economically and socially. That few found the pot of gold at the end of their rainbows made little difference; all were certain that their luck would be better. This was the American dream during the nineteenth century, and that dream helped shape the habits, attitudes, and ambitions of generations of Americans. Those attitudes persist in the frontierless land of today and underlie the problem of the nation's leaders who would reshape the nation's temperament to the realities of the modern world.

What are those frontier-engendered habits and attitudes that distinguish the American character? One national trait, traceable in part to our frontier heritage, is that most criticized today: our heedless wastefulness of our resources. Throughout our history, visitors from overseas have been shocked by our reckless spending of nature's riches; travelers today find but slight improvement. The United States is known as the land of the paper towel, of disposable tissue, of no-deposit-no-return bottles, of throwaway beer cans, of the bag within the bag within the bag at the supermarkets. American machines are viewed by visitors as cunningly contrived for premature obsolescence within a disgracefully short time; American homes have been compared to reverse assembly lines deliberately designed to reduce the gadgets with which they are stocked to rubble so that replacements will be required. . . .

Our wastefulness is a habit taught us by our pioneering ancestors. As the frontiersmen moved westward, they were confronted with such an abundance of natural riches that their exhaustion was inconceivable. Why bother to conserve amidst such plenty? If asked about posterity, they were likely to answer: "What has posterity done for me?" So they exterminated, or nearly exterminated, every animal species of value, the beaver and buffalo being the most notable examples. They grubbed out mineral wealth by destroying the countryside; strip mining and sluice mining were commonplace even though they left the countryside an unsightly shambles. They slashed away the timber, and moved on. They mined the soils of their fertility, leaving behind unsightly fields, gullied and worn. There was no need to conserve; the resources were inexhaustible. There was no compulsion to protect the landscape; moving on to an unspoiled countryside was easier and more profitable.

So destruction became a virtual obsession among frontiersmen. To those in forested areas, the tree was an enemy—a symbol of the savagery of nature—that must be removed. Pioneers cut every tree in sight, even those needed for shade, shelter, windbreaks, even maple groves useful for sweets. The true Westerner's ideal was a flat field, beautified perhaps by a smoking factory. Once the land was cleared, the destruction continued. Farmers in that day knew about fertilizers and crop rotation, but they preferred to butcher the soil, then press ahead to virgin fields. "Why, son," boasted one Nebraska farmer, "by the time I was your age, I had wore out three farms."

So it was that moving became a habit of the pioneers, and of their descendants. This was noted by nineteenth-century travelers; it is noted by visitors from overseas today. Americans, they say, are perpetually on the move. We live in automobiles. In 1973, of the 210 million people in the United States, 121,383,381 were licensed drivers, operating 125,156,876 automobiles and trucks over nearly 4,000,000 miles of surfaced roads, burning 105,944,521,000 gallons of gasoline, and killing 55,800 persons yearly.

The compulsion to move about is carried into our living habits. We are always shifting residences—from farm to city, from city to suburb, from one city to another. The Bureau of the Census reported after its last nose count that during the past year 36,000,000 persons had moved within the county where they lived, and another 13,000,000 had shifted from one county to another. Americans shift about so regularly that bank statements, dividend checks, and magazines are delivered with a change-of-address slip automatically enclosed. To live in the same house where we were born, or where our parents were born, is almost unheard of; a few years ago the *New York Times* considered newsworthy the fact that a California family had lived in the same house for fifty years, a journalistic judgment that the London *Times* would have considered incomprehensible.

We learned our habit of musical chairs from our pioneering ancestors. The frontiersmen *must* move, for ahead lay riches and opportunity: untrapped beaver streams, veins of gold, rich pasturage, virgin fields, rising land values— all the ingredients of the better life that was the American dream. So they pushed on—toward opportunity. The outer fringe of pioneers—the restless "squatters" who made the first clearings—usually shifted from five to seven times during their lifetimes, slashing away a few trees, building a rough lean-to or cabin, planting a few crops—then succumbing to the migratory fever and moving on to begin the process anew. Travelers in the Ohio Valley during the early nineteenth century reported abandoned farms, even though uncleared lands were still available. Their owners had been lured onward by hoped-for better lands in Indiana; they would soon leave Indiana for Illinois, Illinois for Missouri or Iowa.

The restless mobility bred into the frontiersmen by three centuries of migration westward has remained a heritage of the American people. Nor has the habit been totally discarded with industrialization and stabilization of society. An American child moved frequently from place to place by his parents develops less of an attachment to a community than does a European youngster reared in the home of his parents and grandparents. He will be more inclined to move himself, and in turn to infect his children with "movingitis." We Americans remain unusually mobile because of our frontier background.

People moved to better their lot socially as well as economically. Horace Greeley, it should be remembered, did not urge his fellow New Yorkers simply to "Go west, young man"; what he said was "Go west, young man, and grow up with the country." That was the magic phrase: "Grow up with the country." The dream of every ambitious young man was to step aboard the escalator of cheap lands and ride upward to a higher place in the social order. This could best be accomplished in frontier communities where unexploited resources, rising land values, and a plastic society allowed a higher rate of vertical social mobility than anywhere in the world. The unshakable belief that the next move westward would open the gates to a fortune and a spot in the elitist upper crust was the hope of all, and a primary triggering impulse that underlay the western movement.

The endurance of that dream helps explain the basic differences in the social attitudes of Americans and Europeans today. The British taxi driver who calls you "sir" is mirroring his social background in a class-oriented society; the American driver who calls you "Mac" is doing the reverse. One is the product of the highly stratified society observed by Karl Marx in nineteenth-century England, the other of a social order where frontier opportunity had blurred class lines. British travelers in mid-nineteenth century America never realized that the term "gentleman" was properly applied to all men because all were prospective "gentlemen"; instead they took delight in reporting such usages of the term as "He and another gentleman had been shoveling mud," or "Two gentlemen were convicted and sentenced to six months' imprisonment for horse stealing." Frontier opportunity was an alchemist's stone that profoundly altered the social structure.

This is not to suggest that a classless society thrived in the successive Wests. Social organisms instinctively divide themselves according to the status and ability of their component parts; pioneer communities had their elitist groups and their lower classes almost from the beginning—the "better element" and "common folk" in the language of the day. A visitor in pioneer Indiana was not far wrong when he sniffed that two classes were discernible there, "the superior and the inferior—the former *shaved* once a week, the latter once in *two* weeks." Distinctions did exist, even though the basis for division might seem strange to Europeans.

These class distinctions differed, however, from those in established societies in the relative ease of access to the upper strata. Society on the frontier was atomized, with no established group in control. Instead, a power vacuum existed at the top, beckoning the able and the ambitious. The relative ease of economic self-advancement for the fortunate few was determined by no set guidelines. Class distinctions were difficult to maintain where a servant girl might marry the community's leading citizen (by no means unusual along the frontiers, where women were few), where the town ne'er-do-well could be sky-rocketed to riches with a turn of his shovel in a placer mine, where the poorest farmer could reap a fortune with a lucky land speculation. The class structure was more "open ended" in such regions than in the settled East or Europe.

Equally fatal to traditional distinctions were two popular attitudes universal along the frontiers. One was belief that monetary wealth, not distinguished ancestry, was the measure of social eminence. What a man was, not what his family had been, determined his place in society. "Out west," a British visitor noted, "the one question is 'what can you do,' not 'who was your father?' "

Just as important was a universal refusal to recognize that class lines did exist, even when they were apparent. The lowest figure on the social totem pole saw his lot as only temporary, soon to be replaced by affluence and prestige, and acted accordingly. When a stranger in a pioneer town spoke of "servants," he was rudely reminded: "There are no servants here; all are hired hands." When a worker was asked who his "master" was he answered: "I have no master. My employer is Mr. So-and-so." Servant girls expected to be treated as equals and made part of the family. If, wrote a housewife from the Michigan frontier, a servant "was not invited to sit at first table with company, not included in invitations, . . . not called Miss Jane or Miss Eliza, she was off in a moment." An Ohioan lost a crew of hard-to-get workers when he neglected to invite them to breakfast with the family; a honeymooning couple was abandoned by their driver when they tried to have one meal by themselves.

Nor was this insistence on equality confined to the "common folk"; the "better sort" were just as eager to prove that they were no better than their neighbors and hence entitled to the same treatment. One pioneer housewife, dismayed at seeing a guest dip her fork into the serving dishes, offered to serve her. "I'll help myself, thank ye," she snapped back. "I never want no waitin' on." Those with more possessions than others apologized rather than boasted, saying that carpets were "*one* way to hide the dirt," a fancy table "dreadful plaguy to scour," and that kitchen conveniences were "lumberin' up the house for nothin'." "In the West," wrote a French traveler, ". . . every man with a coat to his back is a gentleman, quite as good as his neighbors." This was the frontier creed, whatever the realities of the social structure.

These attitudes, bred into generations of Americans during their three centuries of westering, persist even today. Our distinctive social democracy encourages Americans to believe that the upper levels of society are not automatically closed to them, places a higher value on merit than on ancestry, and minimizes hereditary prestige as a factor in the escalation process. That view was captured by a cartoon published some years ago showing an Englishman saying disdainfully to an American hostess: "It is a defect of your country that you have no leisure class." "But we have them," she answers, "only we call them tramps."

By opening the gates to all the aspiring and worthy, frontiering contributed to the emergence of another unique facet of the American character. This was the compulsion to work hard. As early as 1633 the Massachusetts General Court decreed that "No person, householder or other, shall spend his time idly or unprofitably, under pain of such punishment as the court shall think fit to inflict." Here was voiced the frontier creed. For in the early West endless labor was essential not only to the individual's personal success but to the welfare of society. Forests must be cleared away, stumps grubbed from the ground, trees burned, cabins built, crops planted, the necessities of life fashioned from nature's materials. Each individual's efforts were a measure not only of his own success but of the success of the community in its struggle for survival. Those who failed to contribute their share were shirking their duty to society no less than to themselves. They were branded as social outcasts, and were driven out or "hated out" of the community. Work thus became a habit as well as a necessity, not simply in regions swayed by the Puritan ethic, but on all frontiers. Even the games played by pioneers were insidiously contrived to masquerade work as play; barn-raisings, and log-rollings, and husking bees, and quilting parties might be pleasureful for the frontiersmen, but they served a practical end that was even more essential.

This habit of work has become, after three centuries of pioneering, a compulsion of the American people. We labor endlessly, not simply to achieve success, but because society decrees continuing hard labor even for the affluent. Social pressures no less than individual ambition drive Americans into ulcers, heart attacks, and premature death. There is no time in the United States for the noontime siesta that eases pressure in Latin lands, the leisurely tea hour that is one of Britain's most sacred traditions, the lingering over a glass of wine at a sidewalk café that is a treasured practice in Paris or Rome. Instead, the typical American gulps his meal at his desk or at a quick-service restaurant, flirts with speeding tickets as he rushes to business appointments, and glories in boasting that he works harder than his neighbor. Even the cocktail hour, the one socially acceptable leisure period allowed by the nation's mores, is devoted to the consumption of beverages of such lethal intensity that the maximum degree of rejuvenation is achieved in the minimum space of time.

**The Kingston Steam Plant of the TVA on Watts Bar Lake
near Kingston, Tenn.** (Library of Congress)

Today, as I have suggested, the national mores are changing as the United Staes adjusts to the same closed-space world that has shaped European civilizations for generations. The gospel of hard work is losing its appeal as machines increasingly assume the burdens of production; the coffee break, the two-martini luncheon, the popularity of tennis and skiing and golf and other time-consuming sports, and the mounting demand for a shorter work week all testify to the fact that endless labor is no longer a social necessity. Mobility, both spatial and social, is gradually slowing in the United States, at the same time that it is increasing in the developed countries of the Old World where industrial opportunity assumes the role of frontier opportunity in America's past. And certainly today, if we may believe our political leaders and headline writers wastefulness is a luxury that vanished with the free lands of the West.

What does the future hold for a frontierless United States? Historians should stick to the past; those who do speculate about the future are notorious for their inaccuracies. But I am foolhardy enough to venture that during the mid-1970's the nation experienced its first hint of basic changes that lie ahead. Unless I am mistaken, our children and grandchildren will be forced—by decree and public pressures—to substitute conservation for their traditional wasting of natural resources. They will be required to adjust to a society in which physical mobility is slowing as individual opportunity lessens with the expansion of the corporate business structure. They will rearrange their ambitions as they realize that the upward social mobility which has gone hand-

286

in-hand with physical mobility is increasingly difficult in a society that is gradually stratifying. And they will witness a restriction on individual freedom as governmental controls are extended to assure an equitable allotment of the dwindling natural resources. The years that lie ahead, in other words, may produce what the great historian of the frontier, Frederick Jackson Turner, once called the "Europeanization" of the United States. If that transformation does take place, the mid-1970's will have truly served as a watershed in our history.

Epilogue

What Is Past Is Prologue:
An Interview with Professor
Henry Steele Commager

by Henry Steele Commager

Throughout this book of readings, we have emphasized the importance of studying the past in order to gain an understanding of the present. In many ways, the future of our nation depends upon how well our citizens develop a sense of critical thinking, an ability to sort out the facts and to make reasonable judgments. Furthermore, in our times there is little doubt that any major decision made in the United States will have world-wide effects.

Henry Steele Commager, one of America's foremost historians, has carefully considered how the past has shaped the present and could affect the future. Professor Commager originally made these remarks in 1979 in an interview conducted by Kenneth G. Alfers and other members of the staff of the Center For Telecommunications, the Dallas County Community College District. Although students and viewers of the telecourse, *America: The Second Century,* have heard Dr. Commager's remarks before, this is the first time they have been published. As you will realize, Professor Commager's observations are extremely relevant and provocative of critical thinking by all students of American and World History.

The difficulties we have had ever since the end of the great world war [World War II] are, I think, all rooted in the same thing. We adopted a whole series of assumptions about the relations of the great powers to each other, about the proper role of the United States in world affairs.

We have tried to deal with world problems on the basis of assumptions that, if they were ever tenable, are no longer tenable. I suppose the most elementary of those assumptions is that the nation is the only conceivable organization, that national sovereignty is sacred. We forget that nationalism is a very recent phenomenon in the history of mankind. Nationalism as we know it is a matter of the last two hundred years or so. It is one of the shorter periods of history. It is not part of the cosmic system. It is now the most powerful single force in international relations and in many other areas.

To my mind it is as impossible to solve the problems confronting us through a series of national organizations as it was to solve the problems that confronted the United States in the nineteenth century on the principle of states' rights. The most elementary fact of our time is one that most everyone gives lip service to, but no one seems to act on. It is that every major problem that confronts us is a global problem. There is no single problem of any major dimensions that one nation can solve by itself. You can go up and down the list of these problems: the problem of the exhaustion of natural resources, the problem of environmental control, the problem of energy, the problem of population which would reach seven or eight billion by the year two-thousand and two hundred, 2020 perhaps even. The problems of control of nuclear power, the problems of saving the ocean—you can go on and on. All of these are international, all of them are global.

What is needed, therefore, is a reconsideration of very fundamental things like the viability of nationalism in our own day. And what is needed is a resourcefulness which we lack in a spectacular manner, a resourcefulness on our part and the part of other leaders of other nations to assign the nation to those tasks which it can best do, as we have assigned certain tasks to the states and local governments, and to leave the great global problems to international organizations of one kind or another, particularly the specialized agencies which now, on the whole, perform a first-rate job.

Basically, the notion which caught our imagination and seduced our thinking during and after the great war is that the world is divided between the world of slavery and the world of freedom, the world of Communism and the world of democracy and so forth and so forth.

You will remember that when Communism triumphed in China we added Communist China to the other world with which we could never have peace and that we conjured up a danger from Communist China, comparable to the danger we conjure up from the Communist Soviet world.

That mentality persisted down to just the other day, and we suddenly discovered that it was all nonsense, it was all paranoia. We got along perfectly well with China, and we wonder what all of the fussing was about, what all of the fear was about, what the paranoia was about.

This is part of, again, as is almost everything that I speak of, a much larger assumption of a double standard in the world: One standard for Americans who are a virtuous and peace-loving people and could never do wrong or mean to do wrong, and other standards for imperialist countries and Communist countries and wicked countries who have designs on everyone else in the great world.

Almost every show we see on television, every editorial we read in newspapers, speeches made in the halls of Congress, demands made by the Pentagon and others are based on the assumption that the conflict between the Communist and the free world is inevitable, chiefly a conflict between the Soviets and the United States. That is followed by a whole series of wildly misguided assumptions—first, that the Soviet Union has some designs on the United States and that it actually threatens the United States.

That the Soviets would have any, any advantage whatever in destroying the United States is, of course, utmost folly. It has no basis whatever in our long historical experience, and it has no foundation and logic whatever. It might not be wholly inappropriate to say as far as our experience is concerned that on the whole our relations with Russia had been those of friendship through the years. Russia was our ally in both the First and Second World Wars, not our enemy. Nevertheless, we seem to regard her as our inveterate enemy.

Another of the assumptions linked to this whole paranoia about Communism is that we must be the military equal or superior to Russia. We seem to think that Russia glares upon the United States with ceaseless hostility and we glare upon the Soviets with ceaseless hostility. Russia is, of course, a great military power and will be a greater power. The Russian situation has no analogy in our own history. We would have to imagine Russia where Canada now is and China where Mexico now is to imagine an analogous situation, a situation which would indeed, or might indeed go far to justify arming to the teeth. Russia is threatened over a three thousand mile border from the largest nation in the world [China], but it is actually the most powerful nation in the world, and one which has been a hereditary enemy for some centuries. She is threatened, or thinks she is, from the NATO powers on the East and by dissident groups and all the satellite countries all the way from the Baltic to the Mediterranean. She feels herself beleaguered. She has been invaded again and again in the last two or three centuries from the West. She has never herself invaded the West beyond the Elbe.

An associated misguided assumption here is that any country could survive an atomic war. That is so grave, so fundamental an assumption that it is just superfluous, I think, to enlarge upon. We can, of course, destroy each other. One of the odd subordinate features of this assumption is that there is an allowable degree of destruction that we could somehow survive if only a hundred and thirty or forty million Americans were killed and only half of our cities destroyed. It is a notion so deeply immoral that the imagination boggles.

Related to this is the curious notion that God and nature have always meant that the United States must be number one. This whole notion of being number one is one of the most vulgar notions ever conjured up by man. It really means number one militarily, but it has come to mean number one in everything else.

I suppose the historian looking back over the past might indulge himself from time to time in saying not who is number one but which nation has contributed most. It would rarely be a powerful nation. It would be Judea. It would be Athens. It would be Republican Rome, not Imperial Rome. It would be the city states of Florence and Venice. It would be the Low Countries. It would be Elizabethan England or perhaps later England or Denmark in the early nineteenth century or France in the middle of the century. It would be the days of glory of the United States before it was the United States, when Virginia and Massachusetts—with populations not much larger than Columbus, Ohio, or Rochester—produced the greatest leaders we have ever known. And when an unsophisticated people created all the great political institutions that we now have, for every major political institution we now have was invented before the year 1800 and not one since the year 1800. This is a kind of aside to validate, as I think it does, my observation that being number one should not mean being number one militarily. It might mean being number one in the welfare of the people, in education, in science, in the reduction of infant mortality, in the elimination of poverty, in this fight on disease, in saving of the environment and a whole host of things which may go to make up civilization. And that is why this particular assumption is one of the most pernicious of all of the assumptions that now bemuse the American mind. I have already spoken of the assumption that we are an Asian power as well as an American and European—that should, I think, be expanded.

No man is an island unto himself but part of a continent. No nation is an island unto itself but part of the globe. But if the word power means what we generally take it to mean, we can no more exercise power in Asia or in Africa than any African or Asian country can exercise power in North America. The day may come when this will be possible, but possible as it is possible for California and New York to exercise power in the whole of the United States through their authority in the legislative branches of the Government. The day may come when the great nations such as China, Russia, and the United States along with the smaller ones can indeed have far reaching power in global organization. That day has not, alas, come yet. When it does come it will not be military power that is exercised, but power of other forms.

This complex of assumptions to which I have referred—that we are a world power which means that we are a power everywhere, that everything is dependent on us, that we can find military solutions for our major problems—has led us down labyrinthine paths in our relations with the rest of the world. It has meant that we have associated ourselves with reactionary and dictatorial and tyrranical regimes throughout the world. We seem to accept as a bedfellow any nation or any party which proclaims its hostility to Communism. And we seem to exclude from the society of acceptable nations any country which is favorable to or associated with Communism.

We are the major power defending the *status quo* everywhere. We set our face like flint against revolution everywhere in the world. We, who were the first country to justify and vindicate revolution; we, who were the first nation to be created new, created through revolution; we, who in the eyes of all of Europe, were as despicable, as wicked, as dangerous, as pernicious as we now think Russia is pernicious and dangerous.

We had a great opportunity to go back to an American tradition of accepting revolution, of welcoming new nations, of presiding over the greatest revolution in the whole of history: the emergence of two-thirds of the people of the globe out of the long night of slavery and exploitation and despotism and tyranny and poverty and misery into a new day, when they might be independent and might solve their problems. And, instead of rallying to the support of this movement in China, of this movement in India, of this movement in Africa and Latin America, we opposed it. This was all dictated by this paranoia about Communism and about the delusion or illusion that God in his wisdom has somehow appointed the United States to order the affairs of the globe.

All of this, I think, comes back in a sense to the notion of security, a notion which I believe I said earlier has taken on almost purely military connotations. National security is not only a legitimate but, in the present situation, an ultimate objective of nations. It is to be found in the health, the morals, prosperity, the virtue of the people. It is to be found in a sound economy. Inflation threatens our national security far more than Soviet Russia does. It is to be found in an environment which we hand down to our posterity. Once again the destruction, the systematic and reckless destruction of the environment in America does far more to threaten national security than any military threat on the globe. It is to be found in the integrity of the political system, an integrity which is all but corrupted and disintegrated both on the local and on the national scene. I refer not to particular members of Government but to the whole method of conducting Government: the special interest groups, the degree of corruption in politics, corruption in elections, corruption through lobbies, all of these things which are in such flagrant contrast to the ideas and the principles and standards set up by the founding fathers. These things threaten national security. Racial hostility, poverty, misery threaten national security. The antagonisms of black to white and white to black and of both apparently to the peoples of Asia, the inability to conquer poverty, all of these threaten national security. These problems, unlike the problems of world power, can be solved to some degree at home.

We have all the talent. We have far more resources than other countries and, because we are not prepared to put our minds and our talents to these tasks, because we prefer private enterprise to public enterprise, we seem incapable of dealing with these fundamental problems.

Unlike the generation of the founding fathers, unlike Washington, Jefferson, and John Adams, and Hamilton, and John Jay, and others who gave their whole life to public service and beggared themselves in public service, we are not prepared to put public enterprise ahead of private enterprise. We are not prepared, for example, to say with Hamilton, that great arch-conservative, that "all the resources under the earth belong, of course, to the Nation and are to be disposed of by the Congress as benefits the national interest." For we think not of posterity's need for oil and other resources but of the need of the great oil corporations or of our own immediate need. This failure to put public enterprise ahead of private enterprise is the most glaring contrast between our generation and the generation that created the United States.

How do we get back to the standards that dominated the 18th and much of the 19th century? How do we re-vitalize the sense of public enterprise, that sense of virtue which was always in the minds of the founding fathers and usually on their tongues as well?

Have you ever heard anyone speak of the thousandth generation or the hundredth generation or the tenth generation today? We scarcely think of the next generation. We are prepared to destroy the natural resources of the country just so we can drive 70 miles an hour across the continent or use up whatever resources there are. I think the fundamental problem is, almost always in politics, a moral problem. I don't mean moral in the simplistic sense of the term. I mean moral probably with the sense that Plato used the term or that Aristotle used the term or that founding fathers used the term—the problem of ethics, or morality, of enlightened interest and self interest. It is somehow to recover that sense of indebtedness to the nation, to the history of the past of the nation, to posterity in the future of the nation so that the problems can be solved. They cannot be solved if we always put private enterprise ahead of public. They cannot be solved if we take for granted that all the natural resources of the country belong of course to corporations rather than to posterity. They cannot be solved if we assume that we can pile up endless debts, we can pile up endless obligations for our children and their children to pay rather than meeting these obligations ourselves. Jefferson had a very remarkable idea. He proposed not only that there should be a new constitution every twenty years—twenty years being statistically the length of time from one generation to the next—but that all public debt should be wiped out every twenty years on the ground that no one generation had the right to impose its debts on the next generation. That's going pretty far, but there is a great deal of truth in this notion.

I think we can find in our history and in our traditions the resources for the restoration of virtue, the restoration of devotion to the public welfare, the recreation of that great word—that word which we use without thinking here, the Commonwealth of Massachusetts, the Commonwealth of Virginia. That great word, the commonwealth—one of the great words of our language. Remember that's all the wealth, and wealth is not just property. Wealth is history, wealth is culture, wealth is morals, wealth is the whole of it. That great wealth which is common and must be common if the nation is to survive and indeed if mankind is to survive. For it cannot be supposed that any one great nation would go under without drawing the whole of mankind down with it.

Index

Rayburn, Sam, 206
Reagan, Ronald, 96, 113ff
Reuther, Roy, 46
Reuther, Victor, 51
Reuther, Walter, 46ff
Ripley, William Z., 30
Roosevelt, Franklin D., 39–40, 46, 120, 126, 150ff, 190
Roosevelt, Theodore, 36, 62, 73, 83, 119, 135ff, 141, 259, 276ff
Roskob, John J., 32

Sanborn, James, 104
San Martin, Dr. Grau, 190
"Saturday Night Massacre", 109
Schwab, Charles, 11–13
Selma, Alabama, 242
Sheridan, Gen. Philip, 220–221
Sherman, Gen. William T., 220–221
Shirtwaist Makers Union, 18
Short, Gen. Walter C., 150ff
Silver Purchase Act of 1890, 66
Sinclair, Harry, 107
Sinclair, Upton, 83
Sioux Indians, 222
Sloan, Alfred E., 22
Southern Christian Leadership Conference, 242ff
Spencer, Herbert, 6
Stalin, Joseph, 176ff
Stark, Adm. Harold R., 150ff

Starr, Ellen, 267ff
Stimson, Henry, 183
Sullivan, John L., 256ff
Sumner, Charles, 231

Taft, William H., 94
Teapot Dome, 106–107
Texas *Observer,* 212
Travis, Robert C., 42ff
Treasury Scandal of 1873, 104
Treaty of Versailles, 144
Triangle Shirtwaist Co., 16ff
Truman, Harry, 93, 116, 175ff

United Automobile Workers, 42ff
United States Steel, 24
U.S. v. Singleton, 233
U.S.S. Maine, 134

Vance, Cyrus, 118, 124

Wagner, Robert F., 22, 44
Wallace, George, 117, 245
Welles, Sumner, 190
Weyler, Gen. Don Valeriano, 131
Wiley, Dr. Harvey W., 78ff
Wilson, Woodrow, 74, 140ff
Wood, Charles Erskine, 225–226
Woodruff, T. T., 8–9
Works Progress Administration, 39–40